Bonds and Bondholders

Bonds and Bondholders

*British Investors and Mexico's
Foreign Debt, 1824–1888*

MICHAEL P. COSTELOE

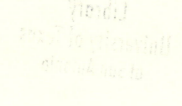

PRAEGER

Westport, Connecticut
London

Library of Congress Cataloging-in-Publication Data

Costeloe, Michael P.
    Bonds and bondholders : British investors and Mexico's foreign debt, 1824–1888 /
Michael P. Costeloe.
      p. cm.
    Includes bibliographical references and index.
    ISBN 0–275–97939–3 (alk. paper)
    1. Government securities—Mexico—History—19th century. 2. Investments,
British—Mexico—History—19th century. 3. Debts, External—Mexico—History—19th
century. 4. Bondholders—Great Britain—History—19th century. 5. Committee of
Mexican Bondholders—History. 6. Debt relief—Mexico—History—19th century.
I. Title.
HG5165.C68   2003
332.63'232'097209034—dc21   2002029868

British Library Cataloguing in Publication Data is available.

Library of Congress Catalog Card Number: 2002029868
ISBN: 0–275–97939–3

First published in 2003

Praeger Publishers, 88 Post Road West, Westport, CT 06881
An imprint of Greenwood Publishing Group, Inc.
www.praeger.com

Printed in the United States of America

The paper used in this book complies with the
Permanent Paper Standard issued by the National
Information Standards Organization (Z39.48–1984).

10 9 8 7 6 5 4 3 2 1

Contents

Illustrations   vii

Tables (Bond Prices)   ix

Acknowledgments   xi

Introduction   xiii

I.   **Mexican Bonds, Certificates, Debentures**   1

1.   A Guide   3

Introduction   3

1824 Five per Cents and 1825 Six per Cents   11

1831 Deferred Five per Cents: Deferred Six per Cents   27

1837 Active and Deferred Five per Cents   32

Customs Certificates and Debentures   44

Clandestine 1837 Bonds   51

1843 Five per Cents   54

1846 Five per Cents   58

1837 Five per Cent Deferred: Excess Bonds   65

1851 Three per Cents   71

1864 Three per Cents   81

1886 Three per Cents   90

1888 Six per Cents   95

English Convention Bonds   99

2. Dividends, Coupons, and Certificates   115

3. A Brief Postscript: The Fate of the Bonds   145

II. The Bondholders   149

4. The Committee(s) of Mexican Bondholders, 1830–1887   151

   Some Preliminary Observations   151

   Origins, 1827–1830   161

   The First Committee of Mexican Bondholders, 1830–1836   165

   *The Committee of Spanish American Bondholders,
1836–1850*   175

   The Committee of Mexican Bondholders, 1850–1862   183

      The W.P. Robertson Committee, 1850   183

      The Goldsmid Committee, 1850–1853   187

      The Capel Committee, 1853–1854   194

      The McGarel Committee, 1854–1856   198

      The D. Robertson Committee, 1856–1862   203

   *Barings; The Committee of Deferred Bondholders; The
Dutch Committee, 1862–1867*   214

   *The Provisional Committee of Mexican Bondholders,
1867–1868*   217

   The Committee of Mexican Bondholders, 1868–1876   220

   The Sheridan Committee, 1876–1886   231

   Finance   247

5. The Investors   263

6. The Bondholders and the British Government, 1824–1886   301

Epilogue   325

Appendix   331

Sources and Works Cited   337

Index   349

Illustrations

1. 1824 Buenos Aires Six per Cent Loan Scrip Certificate   7
2. 1864 Mexican Empire Six per Cent Loan Scrip Certificate   9
3. 1824 Buenos Aires Six per Cent Loan Bond   17
4. 1837 Five per Cent Deferred Bond   41
5. Motif from 1837 Five per Cent Deferred Bond   42
6. 1837 Fractional Certificate/Land Warrant   43
7. 1842 Debenture   48
8. 1842 Debenture (reverse)   49
9. 1843 Five per Cent Bond   55
10. 1846 Five per Cent Bond   64
11. 1851 Three per Cent Bond   77
12. 1864 Imperial Three per Cent Bond   86
13. 1864 Barings Fractional Certificate   88
14. 1886 Three per Cent Bond   92
15. 1888 Six per Cent Scrip Certificate   98
16. Spanish Convention Bond   101
17. Bill of Lading (1840)   124
18. Dividend Coupons: 1837 Five per Cents; 1851 Three per Cents   129
19. Dividend Coupons: 1864 Three per Cents; 1886 Three per Cents   130

20.	1843 Dividend Certificate	133
21.	1867 Barings Certificate	134
22.	1851 Certificate	137
23.	Portrait of John Marshall	170
24.	Portrait of Sir Robert Wilson	172
25.	Portrait of Sir Isaac Lyon Goldsmid	190
26.	Portrait of James Capel	195
27.	Portrait of Charles McGarel	199
28.	Portrait of David Robertson	204
29.	Portrait of Henry Brinsley Sheridan	218

Tables (Bond Prices)

1.	1824 Five per Cents	25
2.	1825 Six per Cents	26
3.	1831 Deferred Five per Cents	32
4.	1831 Deferred Six per Cents	33
5.	1837 Active Five per Cents	44
6.	1837 Deferred Five per Cents	45
7.	1842 Debentures	50
8.	1846 Five per Cents	65
9.	1851 Three per Cents Stamped	80
10.	1851 Three per Cents	82
11.	1864 Three per Cents	89
12.	1886 Three per Cents	95
13.	1888 Six per Cents	99

Acknowledgments

Grateful acknowledgment is made to the many scholars and to the staffs of archives, libraries, Record Offices, banks, and companies in Great Britain, Holland, Mexico, and the United States, without whose assistance and cooperation the research for this book would not have been possible. I am particularly indebted to John Orbell, Jane Waller, Stephen Freeth, Sarah Millard, Hazel Anderson, Henry van Glabbeek, Michael Hironymous, and Roberto Marín Maldonado for help in using their archives. Henry Askew allowed me to examine his family papers at Ladykirk and helped in gaining access to private archives. Sir Thomas Ingilby, R.J. Marjoribanks, Henry MacKenzie Johnston, Juan Caamano, Roger Guedalla, Bill Rubinstein, Brian Mills, Ian Wei, Anne Staples, and Josefina Vázquez were among many who helped with books, photocopies, microfilm, documents, and essential information. For the most part, the bonds illustrated in this work are from my own collection, but copies of some were generously given to me by Joachim Block. Others were kindly provided by the archivists of ING Barings; the Guildhall Library, London; the Archivo Genaro Estrada, Mexico City; and the National Archives of Canada, Ottawa. Portraits and photographs are reproduced here with the permission of those acknowledged in the respective illustrations. The British Academy and the University of Bristol (especially its Department of Hispanic, Portuguese and Latin American Studies), in the persons of David Brookshaw, Sally-Ann Kitts, and David Hook, provided essential financial and administrative support. Finally, my wife Eleanor, as ever, provided indispensable help with the research on many occasions.

Introduction

Mexican Treasury bonds were offered for sale in London for the first time in 1824. The total face or par value was £3,200,000 and the annual rate of interest or dividend promised was 5%, payable in sterling. A year later, a second bond issue was placed in the market with the same par value of £3,200,000 but with an annual interest of 6%, also payable in sterling. The exchange rate with sterling at the time, and throughout much of the nineteenth century, was approximately five Mexican pesos, or dollars as they were more commonly known, to the pound. The loans, therefore, were for a total of £6,400,000 or 32,000,000 dollars. Mexico defaulted on the dividend payments in October 1827 and the country's first foreign or external debt, often referred to in the nineteeth century as the London debt, was thus incurred. It was not until 1888 that the accumulated debt of principal and interest arrears was finally liquidated. During that span of sixty-four years between 1824 and 1888, the debt was converted or rescheduled several times but successive Mexican governments failed to fulfill their contractual agreements with their creditors. As a result, Mexico was excluded from Europe's capital markets for much of the nineteenth century as Stock Exchanges in London, Amsterdam, and elsewhere refused to allow the flotation of any new loans as long as the debt remained unpaid.

Mexico, of course, was not the only, or the first, country to default on its loans. Following the end of the Napoleonic era at Waterloo in 1815, European reconstruction was funded by borrowed money, and with the success of the post-war French reparations loan (arranged by Barings in 1815), numerous other foreign issues were released in the London market. Russia, Austria, Spain, Portugal, Denmark, Greece, and Naples were among the nations whose securities were offered for sale. After the emancipation of Spain's colonial empire in Spanish America in the early 1820s, the Europeans were joined in their search for capital by six of the new American nations, as well as Mexico. Between 1822 and 1825, they contracted debts in the London market in excess of £21,000,000. Within two years, Chile, Colombia, Peru, and Guatemala had already failed to pay dividends on time and when Buenos Aires did the same in January 1828, all of the six Spanish American debtor republics were in default. They were in good company. By the end of that year (1828), of the twenty foreign loans still traded on the London Stock Exchange, only seven were being serviced and repaid. Portugal and Spain were among the defaulters, and only Brazil from the Hispanic world remained, for the time being, able to pay its debts.

This book, therefore, is about Mexico's nineteenth-century foreign debt. But it must be emphasized that it is not a general history or survey of the topic. Such works already exist in abundance. Contemporary politicians and diplomats personally involved in the negotiations with creditors, for example, Lucas Alamán, Manuel Payno, and Tomás Murphy, published their own accounts.[1] Even more comprehensive volumes, some of several hundred pages in length, were produced by the next generation of Mexican economists and accountants. Most notable among these were those of Joaquín Casasús, published in 1885 and Mariano Ortíz de Montellano, published in 1886. Renewed interest appeared in the twentieth century when, after some years of financial stability and regular debt servicing, Mexico again fell into default, largely as a result of the 1910 Revolution and its aftermath of economic recession. U.S. accountants, such as Thomas Lill, examined the history and present status of the debt in a study published in 1919. This was followed in 1921 by W.F. McCaleb's book *The Public Finances of Mexico* and a decade later by what was certainly the best and most comprehensive history to that time, the 449-page work by Edgar Turlington, published in 1930 as *Mexico and Her Foreign Creditors*. Since then there have been many other works, notably in 1968, Jan Bazant's succinct and generally accurate *Historia de la deuda exterior de México (1823–1946)*. Another recent work is José Zaragoza's *Historia de la deuda externa de Mexico, 1823–1861*, published in 1996. In addition to these and other monographs, there are also several volumes of essays in which specific aspects are examined, one of the most recent (1998) being the collection edited by Leonor Ludlow and Carlos Marichal under the title *Un Siglo de Deuda Pública en México*. Finally, many other studies of Mexico's debt may be found in more general works concerned with the whole of Latin America's foreign debt. Two of the better ones in this category are certainly those by Dawson, *The First Latin American Debt Crisis* (1990) and by Marichal, *A Century of Debt Crises in Latin America* (1989).

This historiography compiled over a century and a half has provided us with a substantial amount of information about the debt, especially its financial aspects. There are numerous calculations of the financial statistics, the value of dividends paid or not paid, the total amount paid or owed, and literally page after page of figures (see, for example, Casasús and Lill, in which the accounts are dissected, analyzed, and recalculated). No two authors, it may be added, seem to agree on the exact amount of the accumulated debt.

It has not been my intention, however, to add to this already voluminous literature on the balance sheet of the debt and I have made no attempt to add to the financial statistics. Instead, where numbers are required, and naturally they cannot be avoided in a basically financial topic, I have tended to follow Bazant, whose calculations always appear accurate. My interest has been in two other aspects of the subject which, considering the volume of work already done, perhaps surprisingly have not been investigated to any extent by previous scholars. In short, these are the bonds and the bondholders. The debts incurred by borrowing nations consisted of money received from investors in exchange for bonds. Among various other promises, the bonds committed the borrower to pay dividends to their owner, maintain a Sinking Fund, and eventually to buy back or redeem them at their par value. On each occasion when the debt was rescheduled, the existing bonds were converted or cancelled and exchanged for new ones. A whole range of bonds, certificates, debentures, receipts, or acknowledgments was issued in recognition of unpaid principal and dividend arrears. These securities, or obligations as they were sometimes called, constituted the contract between borrower and lender and as such they were the essential documents of Mexico's foreign debt. But what form did the bonds take? What was written on them? What was their design, size, and color? How many were printed, and by whom? How many were sold and at what price? What happened to them, and above all, are there surviving examples which would answer these questions?

In none of the works so far published on Mexico's foreign debt is there any illustration or reproduction of a bond or dividend coupon. There may be good reasons for their absence. Several hundred thousand such "obligations" were printed and circulated in the market throughout the course of the nineteenth century, but with each conversion of the debt the existing bonds were cancelled and withdrawn. It was normal procedure until quite recently for stockbrokers, banks, and other agencies involved to shred or otherwise destroy what to them was waste paper of no commercial value. Hence, there was no obvious source or location for scholars to find examples of the cancelled stocks.

Fortunately for the present generation of historians, however, in recent years stocks and shares, bonds, and certificates of all types have become collectors' items and in the expanding world of what is now called "scripophily," there are flourishing markets for them in many countries.[2] This has meant that original examples, some from very early times, have been discovered and preserved. There are several sources. First, in the case of Mexico, and probably most others, the cancellation and withdrawal of a bond issue was never 100% complete. For whatever reason, there were always some bondholders who failed to present their bonds for cancellation or to cash their dividend coupons. Some of these have survived and, with the renewed interest by collectors and others, as well as their increasing monetary value, examples have found their way onto the commercial market. Second, merchant banks and other financial institutions have become more aware of the historical value of their archives. Hence, rather than destroying "waste paper," some has been preserved or entrusted to a public archive for conservation. The Guildhall Library in London, for example, now houses an outstanding collection of such business archives. Among these are the records of merchant banks and stockbrokers who were directly involved in or even responsible for many of the later nineteenth-century bond issues. They contain specimen bonds supplied by printers, including some of the Mexican stocks. The Guildhall Library also contains the archive of the London Stock Exchange which has Mexican certificates submitted by stockbrokers and others but never returned. Similarly, the Amsterdam Stock Exchange archive (Mexico's stocks were quoted on most European Bourses) has an impressive collection, including original examples of several bonds. Another important source is the archive of Barings Bank (now ING Barings). Barings acted as Mexico's European Financial Agent in the 1820s, 1830s, and again in the 1860s, and it was always closely involved in the foreign debt arrangements. It also has retained bonds which presumably at one stage belonged to clients. Finally, Mexican diplomats and Financial Agents in London sent sample or specimen bonds back to their government in Mexico City for information or approval and some of these have survived in archives such as the Archivo General de la Nación and the archive of the Ministry of Foreign Affairs.

It has proved possible, therefore, to find original examples of most of the bonds and diverse other certificates which formed the contracts entered into by Mexico with its creditors. These have been illustrated in Part I of this book. Chapter 1 provides a short description and analysis of each of the various reschedulings of the debt. Following the default in 1827, there were negotiations with the creditors more or less continuously for the next sixty years and these brought about new agreements in 1831, 1837, 1846, 1851, 1864, 1886, and 1888. All of these so-called conversions generated new bonds or certificates. In addition, a variety of other stocks such as debentures, dividend certificates, and land warrants were issued to meet specific needs or claims. All of these stocks are explained and illustrated. Details are given of their number and value, the procedures and negotiations involved, the financial agencies, marketing, and sale. Also, the eventual cancellation and withdrawal of the bonds from the market are indicated. Tables have been compiled of the monthly high and low prices of all of Mexico's stocks quoted on the London Stock Exchange. Finally, I have included in Part I some fairly detailed calculations of the number of bonds and certificates of each issue which may have survived. I appreciate that this kind of information may not interest the more general historian, who will perhaps prefer to peruse it only lightly, but I have retained it largely for the benefit of bond collectors and scripophilists, without whose help this part of the work could not have been completed.

Apart from their intrinsic interest and importance in the history of the debt, there is another reason for closely examining these various reschedulings and the securities that accompanied them. Admirable though many of the existing works on the subject are, they contain a surprising number of factual errors and misunderstandings of the details. To give just a few examples: Dawson (p. 196) states that the new bonds agreed on in the 1830–1831 conversion "were never issued," when, in fact, almost 12,000 were distributed.[3] In discussing the 1850–1851 conversion, Liehr, in an otherwise outstanding article, incorrectly states that the money assigned to the bondholders in payment of dividend arrears did not involve the shipment of cash when again, in fact, 2,500,000 silver pesos were shipped from Mexico City to London in the summer of 1852.[4] In his summary of the terms of the 1830–1831 conversion, Marichal wrongly asserts that interest payments were to be suspended between 1832 and 1836. He also appears unaware of the details of the 1837 conversion which leads him, again incorrectly, to conclude that "the Mexican government was able to avoid having to pay interest on its external debt during almost a decade."[5]

Chapter 2 deals with the payment of dividends and in short, seeks to show how silver pesos mined and minted in northern Mexico ended up as pounds, shillings, and pence in the pockets of country vicars, solicitors, and other bondholders thoughout the British Isles. Again, various dividend coupons and certificates have been found and are used as illustrations. The transport and shipping of silver from Mexico for the dividend fund, exchange rates, dividend payments, confiscations, arrears, and various related topics are discussed. Finally, in a brief postscript, the fate of Mexico's nineteenth-century bonds is revealed. Evidence has been found in the Bank of England that almost all the many thousands of cancelled bonds issued between 1824 and 1886 were destroyed.

Part II is about the bondholders. They form the second major gap in the existing literature. Given that much of the writing on Mexico's debt has been done by Mexicans, it is no surprise that their focus and emphasis have been largely on the debtor rather than the creditor. Much attention, for example, has been given to the fact that Mexico received only a relatively small proportion of the 32,000,000 dollars it borrowed, after commission payments and other costs had been deducted. The effect of the debt on the country's foreign relations, its economic and political development, the efforts of governments to service it, and the general consequences of being unable to attract significant foreign investment have all been examined. For some writers, the burden of the debt was a main cause of Mexico's problems of political instability, lack of economic progress, and general decline throughout the first half century of its independence until the dictatorial era of Porfirio Díaz imposed stability and, it must be noted, paid off the debt. Students of economic imperialism, informal or formal empires, the influence of capitalism and, in general terms, what is now termed Third World debt, have all been interested in the first external debts of Mexico and the other Latin American nations. While most of these works have been properly objective, some have been highly critical, especially of Britain's role in the debt. To cite just one example, Dr. True concluded that British participation in the debt revealed "a most wanton and destructive type of nineteenth century imperialism."[6] Professor Platt, while certainly not sharing this view, noted that "the bondholders have served as scapegoats in interpretations of economic imperialism."[7]

Such interpretations reflect misunderstandings of the debt in at least two respects. The first is the common misconception that the money provided for the loans came from banks or, in other words, from institutions rather than individuals. In fact, the lenders, or loan contractors as they were known, were not banks or large financial institutions with substantial surplus capital that they were anxious to invest. Nor were they large companies with some Machiavellian imperial ambition to gain domination of the borrower by manipulation of the debt. Of the twelve loans offered by Latin American governments between 1822 and 1825, only two were managed by what might be properly described as established merchant banks. These were Barings, which organized the 1824 Buenos Aires loan, and Rothschilds, which won the contract for the 1825 Brazilian loan. Both were certainly experienced in the loan market, especially for European countries, but they showed little enthusiasm for the Latin American issues and neither was interested in those of Mexico. Instead, the field was left to the loan contractors. Some of these were recognized mercantile businesses of sound standing and reputation, such as Goldsmidt & Co., which obtained the contract for Mexico's first loan; but the majority were relative newcomers. For the most part, they were newly formed partnerships of individual merchants who had some experience in overseas trade and contacts in foreign markets. With the consolidation of the independence of the Spanish American republics after around 1820, they quickly sent agents to seek business opportunities in the new markets. Then, with the contract for the first national government loan (for Colombia) being awarded to Charles Herring, William Graham, and John Diston Powles, a merchant partnership trading with the Caribbean, their interests and attention turned to finance as well as trade. Several more partnerships were formed, and in the boom times of the early 1820s when many foreign governments were seeking capital in the London market, there was fierce competition to get the profitable loan contracts. Among the successful contractors for the Spanish American loans were Hullett Brothers & Co. with the Chilean loan; Thomas Kinder & Co. for Peru; Barclay, Herring, Richardson & Co. for Mexico and Guatemala.

None of these merchant partnerships were especially well known, even at the time, and none were of long duration, most having been formed to seize the commercial opportunities of the moment. Those who were fortunate enough to get the loan contracts certainly made very substantial profits from commission (agreed, of course, in advance with the borrower) and speculation in the market, but risks were high and it is noticeable that both the contractors for Mexico's loans were bankrupt less than two years afterwards. Also, there is nothing to support the kind of claim made by Sr. Zaragoza that the contractors "took advantage of the loans to open up large markets both in Mexico and in Latin America."[8] Equally, the impression given by some writers on the subject that naive Spanish Americans were duped by corrupt capitalists into agreeing to onerous and unfair contracts cannot be justified by the evidence. In the Mexican case, its representatives who negotiated the loans in the 1820s were successful merchants with long experience of European financial markets. The conversions agreed upon in the 1830s and 1840s were similarly in the control of experienced merchants, both Mexican and English. Subsequent agreements, without exception, strongly favored Mexican interests with bondholders agreeing to major reductions in the debt in response to Mexican promises of future regular dividend payments, none of which, incidentally, were fulfilled.

Another misconception relates to the role of the British government. Here I do not propose to enter into the controversies surrounding British imperial policy and its commercial practices. My concern is only with those who invested their money in Mexican bonds. As far as they were concerned, and this is the subject of a separate chapter in Part II, the British government persistently failed to help them recover their money. Its response to literally decades of pressure and appeals for help was to deny any responsibility. In sum, the Foreign Office attitude was that those who bought foreign stocks did so for personal profit and must accept the consequences of their speculations, whatever they might be. While unofficially, British diplomats and others might give moral and verbal support, they would never adopt the Spanish American debts as matters of official concern. Of course, in the Mexican case, there was what appeared to be an exception to this general policy, which was the British participation in the Tripartite Intervention in Mexico in 1861–1862. That episode has also caused some confusion. British participation was intended to force Mexico to adhere to the terms of Diplomatic Conventions signed by both countries. Those agreements were certainly to do with debts Mexico owed, as it happens, mostly to foreign nationals, some of whom were naturalized British. These were known as the English Convention Debt but that was separate from Mexico's debt to the bondholders. They and their representatives had long pressed British foreign secretaries for similar Conventions regarding the money owed to them, but without success. Although they had achieved a brief mention in some of the Conventions, specifically with reference to their dividends but not their capital debt, in terms of the Tripartite Intervention, they were not the main factor. Foreign Office policy, and hostility toward them did not change. The bondholders' influence and significance in this episode are discussed in the aforementioned chapter and I have included a short account of the English Convention Debt in Part I.

In sum, it was not powerful banks, influential financial institutions, or the British government to which Mexico owed money. The loan contractors and other financial agents were no more than intermediaries between the borrower and lender. Who, then, were the creditors? The answer is that they were the so-called "Mexican bondholders," a term used to describe the largely, but not exclusively, British investors who for myriad reasons invested their money in Mexico's stocks in the decades from 1824 to 1888. It is with them that Part II of this book is entirely concerned. Although they are mentioned in general rather than individual terms, en passant, as it were, in some of the studies cited above (notably, those of Turlington and Bazant), nothing of substance has been written about them, and in most books on Mexico's debt they are ignored completely. They were, however, and there were probably several thousand of them, Mexico's nineteenth-century creditors. It was their interests which were at stake in all the negotiations which took place over the debt. It was with them, not the British government or banks, that the Mexican authorities had to talk and they were the ones directly affected by the non-payment of dividends and Mexico's failure to honor its agreements.

Who, then, were the bondholders and who represented them? It is with the latter question that the main section of Part II of this study is concerned. Most of those people who put their money into the bonds of the various foreign loans offered in the London market in the 1820s, and were rapidly faced with defaults on their dividends, formed committees to represent their interests. There were such committees, for example, of the bondholders of all the Latin American debtor nations and of Spain, Portugal, and many other countries. From 1836 until 1850, the various, separate committees of the Latin American national bondholders joined together and formed the Committee of Spanish American Bondholders, believing that collective action would be more effective. In the 1870s, the creditors of all the foreign countries, not just the Latin American, formed the Corporation of Foreign Bondholders which quickly became a very wealthy and influential body. Notwithstanding the fact that these organizations were the only recognized representatives of the creditors and as such were directly involved in every debt-conversion agreement, almost nothing is known about them. This is certainly the case in respect of the Committee of Mexican Bondholders. To my knowledge, apart from one article and again, passing reference, no study of the Committee has been made.[9]

Part II of this book, therefore, is mainly devoted to the Committee of Mexican Bondholders. It comprises a brief synopsis of the Committee's work on behalf of the bondholders from 1830 to 1887. Its formation and development, organization, activities, and financing are all described, as well as the many public and private campaigns which it waged in its efforts to persuade Mexico to pay its debts by redeeming its bonds. Above all, however, I have been interested in identifying the men—there were no women—who served on the Committee. With only a handful of exceptions, it has proved possible to find some biographical information about all of them, including their professional occupations and, in some cases (especially the chairmen), details of their investments in Mexican stocks.

The information about the Committee and its members is used in Chapter 5. This deals with the bondholders at large and seeks to complete the picture of Mexico's creditors by analyzing who bought Mexico's bonds and why. Several hundred bondholders have been identified. Information, discovered for the most part in local Record Offices all over Britain, about their socioeconomic background, places of residence, value of investments, and other details, has enabled a reasonably broad gallery to be formed. Among them there were certainly rich investors, including manufacturers, merchants, stockbrokers, and millionaire financiers. The broader picture, however, is more of middle- to lower-income groups, of country clergy, doctors, solicitors, widows, and spinsters who were tempted by the glamour of the newly independent nation of Mexico and its promise of high dividends guaranteed by its legendary and inexhaustible deposits of silver to risk all or part of their savings. They were not capitalists bent on imperial domination but ordinary people the length and breadth of Britain who hoped, in vain, to increase their incomes by buying Mexico's bonds.

· These, then, are the subjects and themes of this book. It is my hope, and claim, that by concentrating here for the first time on its creditors, a new and more accurate understanding and perspective can now be added to the much studied topic of Mexico's first foreign debt. It is to the bonds and the bondholders that we now turn.

NOTES

1. Full bibliographical details of the works mentioned below are given in the Sources and Works Cited.

2. The International Bond and Share Society and especially its journal *Scripophily* have been very helpful to me in the preparation of this work.

3. There is also an uncorrected printing error on the same page where the sum "£625" should read £62.5.

4. R. Liehr, "La deuda exterior de México y los 'merchant bankers' británicos, 1821–1860," *Ibero-Amerikanisches Archiv.* 9 (1983), p. 432.

5. C. Marichal, *A Century of Debt Crises in Latin America* (Princeton, N.J., 1989), pp. 62–63.

6. C.A. True, "British Loans to the Mexican Government, 1822–1832 (A Decade of Nineteenth Century Financial Imperialism)," *The Southwestern Social Science Quarterly* 17(4), (1967), p. 362.

7. D.C.M. Platt, *Finance, Trade and Politics in British Foreign Policy, 1815–1914* (Oxford, 1968), p. 50.

8. J. Zaragoza, *Historia de la deuda externa de México, 1823–1861* (Mexico, 1996), p. 13.

9. P.J. Sheridan, "The Committee of Mexican Bondholders and European Intervention in 1861," *Mid-America* 42 (1960), pp. 18–29.

Part I

Mexican Bonds, Certificates, Debentures

Chapter 1

A Guide

INTRODUCTION

The first part of this study is intended as a guide to the Mexican bonds and other stocks sold in the London market between 1824 and 1888, together with an explanation of how each was produced, marketed, converted, and eventually redeemed. Before examining each of the specific bond issues, however, some general characteristics of the procedure for floating a loan and of the type of stocks offered for sale may be usefully noted.[1] There were several stages for a foreign government which sought to raise money in the London market. The process usually began with the government establishing a legal basis or authority to seek the loan and to mortgage assets as security for the payment of dividends and eventual redemption of the sum borrowed. The basis of Mexico's first loan, for example, was a congressional decree of 1 May 1823. This gave the Executive branch of the Mexican government permission to negotiate a loan of 8,000,000 dollars as soon as possible and to mortgage all the revenues of the State as security.

With this congressional support, the next stage was for the government to appoint agents overseas to investigate possible sources and terms of a loan. The agents were either members of the country's diplomatic corps or specially appointed financial representatives. They approached financiers and potential lenders to see what sort of terms might be negotiated. As noted in the Introduction, contrary to what is sometimes stated, the lenders, or loan contractors as they were known, were normally not banks or large financial institutions. Nor were they incorporated companies with limited liability, which were rare at the time.[2] They were usually merchants who formed temporary alliances or partnerships to bid for the loan contracts.

Once the agent had selected a contractor and the basic terms had been agreed, a prospectus was prepared and published in the daily press. It gave details of the amount of the loan to be floated, its division into certificates or bonds of a given value, and the price at which the stock would be offered for sale in the market. The price of the bonds was always quoted as a percentage of £100. Hence, a bond of £100 nominal or par value might be quoted at £58 which was in fact the price of the first Mexican bond offered for sale in 1824. Higher nominal value bonds, for example, of £150 or upwards, cost proportionately more. Details of interest rates or dividends, and of the Sinking Fund always promised for the redemption of the loan, as well as of the security offered, were also to be found in the prospectus.

Confident that he could sell foreign securities to the British public, the contractor usually in effect bought the loan and the stock into which it was divided for an agreed price. His main profits came from the difference between the price he guaranteed to pay the foreign government for each bond and the price at which he was able to sell them in the market. Again, the first Mexican loan provides a clear example. The contractor bought the bonds at £50 per cent and sold them at £58, taking an immediate profit of 8%. Partly to spread the risk in case the sale price to investors was pitched too high, the prospectus was sometimes circulated privately in advance to the contractor's friends or clients who were offered participation or a proportion of the bonds at a price lower than that at which they were to be offered to the public. There is some evidence, albeit rather circumstantial, that Mexico's first Financial Agent and his friends also profited in this way.[3] It also seems that some contractors at times held back portions of stock in order to create artificial shortages and inflate the market price. Commission payments for management and administration of the loan also provided handsome fees. Repeat commissions of 1% or 1½% were payable, for example, if the contractor was given the contract for the management of future dividend payments.[4]

It was clearly in the interest of both borrower and contractor for the bonds to fetch at least the base price when they were offered for public sale and various devices were used to "make the market."[5] Publicity was important, and both before and after the prospectus was advertised, reports and articles extolling the wealth and untapped resources of the borrowing country appeared. The young Benjamin Disraeli, for example, was the author of three pamphlets used to extoll the economic potential and especially mining resources of the new Spanish American republics.[6] All manner of other techniques were used to inflate the price, or in the Stock Exchange jargon of the 1870s, to puff it up.[7] In the 1820s syndicates of speculators seeking to make quick profits in what was a rising market were common, and they were even more prominent in later decades when rumors of re-schedulings or possible redemptions were often circulated.

Finally, the bonds were sold on the Foreign Exchange in London. This was set up in 1822 in premises adjacent to the main Stock Exchange to cater to the increasing business being transacted in foreign securities. It was managed by a committee of Stock Exchange members and representatives of foreign fund brokers. Regulations were quickly devised and the first eighty-nine members were admitted early in 1823. The loan contractors, who were not necessarily members of the Exchange, always sought to have the bond prices quoted on it. After the initial flotation, prices were set by brokers and jobbers (there was as yet little distinction between the two) who chose to trade in the particular bonds on offer. In 1835, the separate Foreign Exchange was abolished and all stocks were traded on the main Exchange. Some were also traded on continental Bourses, notably Amsterdam, and there was always a significant amount of buying and selling by European and to a lesser extent, North American investors.

The total nominal value of each loan was divided into several classes or series of bonds with par values of varying amounts. These values were usually £100, £150, £250, £500. Each bond was given a letter and a number. Most of the early bonds seem to have been printed in black ink on white paper, but in later issues each of the series was printed in a different color ink—usually black, red, blue, and green. In 1886, there was an exceptionally large issue with a total value of £30,000,000. This was divided into nine series, letters A-I, each of a different color, and values from £5 to £1,000, giving a total of 446,931 separate bonds. Printed on not always good quality paper, the overall dimensions were approximately 16" × 11" with text printed on both sides and set out in a way that was convenient for folding. The artistic design was always ornate and, with one exception—the Maximilian Imperial 1864 Three per Cents—the Mexican national emblem of an eagle and serpent over a cactus plant was prominently displayed. As may be seen in the illustrations given in following sections, the designers of the early bonds and certificates of the 1830s, 1840s, and 1850s seem to have based their work on the official design set out in the congressional decree of 14 April 1823. This ordered that the eagle should be perched on its left foot on a cactus plant growing out of a rock situated in a lake. In its right claw, there was to be a serpent which the eagle was about to tear apart with its beak. Finally, the whole image should be bordered by entwined branches of laurel and oak. Although there were many variations of this design in the nineteenth century, for example, the use of the left or right foot or wings open or closed, the basic outline remained more or less intact. This can be clearly seen in the 1886 Three per Cent bond (see Illustration 14). This uses the design of Tomás de la Peña which was adopted as a result of the law of 30 December 1880, which required a uniform design for the national emblem.

The written text varies both in content and language (more details will be given in later sections). The main issues of which original examples have been located—those of 1837, 1846, 1851, 1864—have the front page exclusively in English, but the one of 1886 is in Spanish. A smaller issue of 1843 has the relevant decree authorizing the loan in both Spanish and English. Often on the reverse side, the text of relevant laws and other documents is in both languages. The place of printing and the printer also varies. We do not know who produced Mexico's first bonds of 1824 and 1825, but it seems that the talents of London's best-known engraver, Rudolph Ackermann, were not used. He had been responsible for the 1822 Colombian bond, which in engraving and design is said to have been unsurpassed throughout the nineteenth century. Ackermann did, however, invest £800 in Mexican bonds.[8] Later Mexican bonds, certificates, and debentures issued in the 1830s and 1840s were the work of the printers known as Whiting. The firm of Whiting and Branston of Beaufort House in the Strand, London, were specialists in security printing. They developed color printing processes for the production of lottery bills and tickets until the abolition of the lottery in 1826.[9] Soon afterwards the partnership ended, but James and later Charles Whiting continued the business and the firm's commissions certainly included the Mexican 1837 bonds and land warrants, 1842 debentures, 1846 bonds, and various dividend certificates. Subsequent Mexican securities were produced by other printers. The 1851 bonds were by Letts, Son, and Steer, of London; the 1864 bonds by Chait et Cie., of Paris; the 1886 bonds by the American Bank Note Company, New York.

Each of the bonds had to be signed by two or more officials. These included Mexican Treasury officials, London-based diplomatic representatives, financial agents, and loan contractors organizing the loans. Given that in some issues there were more than 50,000 bonds to be signed, and no mechanical process seems to have been used, that must have been a long and tedious process even if some form of signature stamp were available. On occasion, for example, in 1851, the bonds were printed in London but then shipped to Mexico for signature by Treasury officials and returned to London for distribution and sale. Again, that added considerably to the time scale involved in the launch of a new issue and invariably bonds were advertised for sale long before they were available. Purchasers were given instead provisional certificates on payment of a deposit which guaranteed eventual delivery of the bonds once full payment had been made. These documents were known as Scrip and until the actual bonds were ready, they were traded in the market, often at a premium or discount. Early examples of Scrip are now very rare and none have been found for the first Mexican loans of 1824 or 1825. Fortunately, however, a Scrip issued for a Buenos Aires loan in July 1824 has been discovered.[10] This is reproduced in Illustration 1 and the bond to which it refers is also reproduced in Il-

£1000

Loan TO THE GOVERNMENT OF BUENOS AYRES,

FOR £1,000,000 STERLING.

Nᵒ

RECEIVED *One Hundred Pounds*, being the first Instalment on ONE THOUSAND POUNDS STOCK of the Loan to the Government of Buenos Ayres, as negociated by the Agents of the said Government, Don FELIX DE CASTRO and JOHN PARISH ROBERTSON, whose special Power of Attorney for that purpose is now in our possession; and we engage to furnish to the Bearer, upon delivery of this Receipt, Obligations issued by the said Don FELIX DE CASTRO and JOHN PARISH ROBERTSON, on Account of the said Government, bearing interest from the 12th day of July 1824, at Six per Cent. per Annum; but if Default be made in the Payment of any of the Sums hereafter expressed, at the Dates on which they respectively become due, then the Payments before made will be forfeited, and the Engagement to deliver Obligations will be void.

THE PAYMENTS are to be made to us as follows:

First Instalment, 10 per Cent. on Monday, the 12th July 1824	£ 100
Second Instalment, 20 per Cent. on Thursday, the 12th Aug 1824	£ 200
Third Instalment, 10 per Cent. on Wednesday, the 15th Sept. 1824	£ 100
Fourth Instalment, 20 per Cent. on Thursday, the 14th Oct. 1824	£ 200
Fifth Instalment, 15 per Cent. on Thursday, the 15th Nov. 1824	£ 150
Sixth Instalment, 10 per Cent. on Wednesday, the 15th Dec. 1824	£ 100
£1000 Stock, at 85 per Cent. is sterling	£ 850

DISCOUNT, at the Rate of 3 per Cent. per Annum, will be allowed for Payment in full, from the Date of the respective Instalments.

London, 12th July 1824.

1824.
12th August.—Received Two Hundred Pounds, for Second Instalment.

Entered

1824.
15th September.—Received One Hundred Pounds, for Third Instalment.

Entered

1824.
14th October.—Received Two Hundred Pounds, for Fourth Instalment.

Entered

1824.
15th November.—Received One Hundred and Fifty Pounds, for Fifth Instalment.

Entered

1824.
15th December.—Received One Hundred Pounds, for Sixth Instalment.

Entered

1. 1824 Buenos Aires Six per Cent Loan Scrip Certificate.

lustration 3. It seems reasonable to assume that the first Mexican Scrip, which was circulated just a few weeks earlier in 1824, would have been similar in design and content. Later Scrip certificates were much more ornate, as can be seen in the 1864 Six per Cent Mexican Empire issue shown in Illustration 2.[11]

The signatures, alphabetical and numerical identifications, together with the complex and colorful designs, were essential for several reasons. These securities were Bearer bonds, payable to the unnamed holder rather than to a named owner. Identification by means of color, denomination, and number enabled both buyer and seller to prove authenticity or ownership. The complexity of design, apart from a degree of national pride, also reduced the risk of forgery. The use of elaborate borders, controlled by geometric lathes with sophisticated sets of gear-wheels and discs, and impossible to reproduce without similar equipment, was a very effective deterrent to would-be forgers.[12] The financial agents responsible for administering the sales also went to great lengths to ensure that records were kept of each and every bond issued or cancelled. The relevant archival records are filled with pages of numbers of bonds redeemed or exchanged each time a conversion was carried out.

These precautions against forgery were by and large very successful. The only known instance of clear fraud occurred in 1838 when a clerk employed by Mexico's Financial Agent, Lizardi & Co., forged signatures on blank certificates which he then used as security to borrow money.[13] There was another case of alleged fraud in 1842, also involving Lizardi. In a particularly acrimonious dispute between the company and the bondholders, it was alleged that Lizardi had put into circulation £100,000 worth of bonds over and above the authorized number. The Stock Exchange Committee ruled that any bonds bearing numbers higher than the agreed maximum would not be recognized. For example, the £100 bonds of the time were numbered from 1 to 10,300. Any with numbers higher than that were declared non-negotiable. Subsequently, the Mexican government recognized the extra issue.

Bonds were cancelled by perforating or cutting a half-inch-diameter hole in the center. Together with unissued bonds, they were usually stored in deposit boxes in the Bank of England where they were placed in a formal ceremony witnessed by public notaries. There were two keys to each box, one kept by a senior Mexican diplomat and the other by the Financial Agent. Problems were caused, perhaps inevitably, by keys being lost. In 1844, for example, the Mexican Chargé d'Affaires, Tomás Murphy, asked Baring Brothers, formerly Financial Agent for the Mexican government, if it knew the whereabouts of the keys for certain boxes. The ones he wanted to open had been used to store the cancelled bonds of the 1824 and 1825 issues. He had been told by the notary, who had witnessed the deposit at the time, that there had been two keys, both of which had been given to

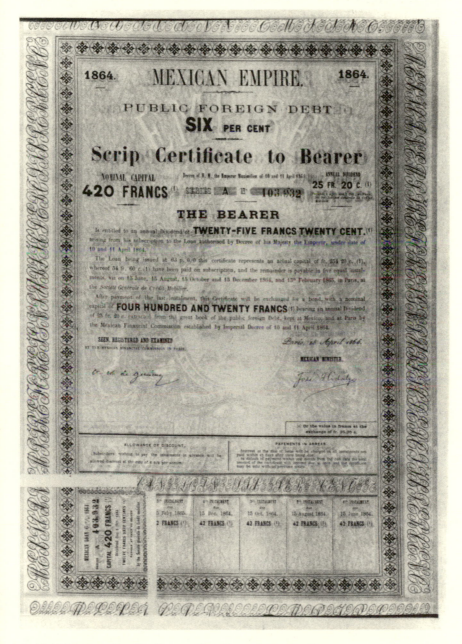

2. 1864 Mexican Empire Six per Cent Loan Scrip Certificate.

persons no longer (in 1844) resident in England. It is not known if Murphy found the original keys but Barings made various suggestions, also assuring him that the Bank would allow him to open the boxes. Certainly, shortly afterwards, the boxes were opened.[14]

The various means of identification also, of course, enabled buyers to prove their ownership and the careful owner kept a list of the letters and numbers of all of his bonds in case of loss or theft. The importance of this can be shown in a case which arose in the 1840s. John Tebbutt, a London solicitor, bought Mexican bonds on various dates in 1834 and 1835. His main purchase was seventy-five bonds, with all the dividend coupons, of the £150 series of the 1825 Six per Cents. These had a face value of £11,250 for which he paid in cash £4,841. In a later purchase, he obtained another fourteen bonds of the same series with a face value of £2,100 at a cost of £892. His broker, who acquired the bonds on his behalf, was Messrs. Boughton and Grinstead. As no dividends were being paid on Mexican securities at the time, Tebbutt was presumably speculating in the market in the hope of some capital appreciation.

In 1837, according to Tebbutt's legal deposition, one of his relatives stole the Mexican bonds, and also some of his Chilean stock, and to avoid detection burned or destroyed them. Tebbutt had taken the precaution, however, of keeping a note of the numbers of his bonds, or rather of the seventy-five he initially bought, but not of the other fourteen. His stockbroker also had failed to keep a record of the numbers of the fourteen. In the same year of the theft, 1837, the Mexican government agreed to reschedule the debt. Events intervened—notably a French attack on Veracruz in 1838—and the conversion was not finally settled until 1839. More details of the conversion will be given elsewhere. At this point, it is sufficient to note that bondholders were allowed one year to present their bonds to the Financial Agent, Lizardi & Co., who exchanged them for new ones. Tebbutt informed Lizardi of his lost bonds and their numbers and value before the deadline for conversion expired. Lizardi told him that nothing could be done until the deadline date in case the missing bonds were presented.

None of the bonds were presented, at least in the early stages of the conversion, and Tebbutt began what became a protracted attempt to have them replaced with those of the 1837 issue. He composed a memorial, witnessed and notarized, in which he set out the circumstances of his case. He claimed that he was entitled to have his missing bonds and dividend coupons replaced with new bonds to the value of £16,621, which was his valuation of the principal and interest. Lizardi made promises but did nothing. An agent Tebbutt appointed in Mexico City to put his case had no success. The British Foreign Office, to which Tebbutt turned for help in 1843, was more responsive. Lord Aberdeen, Foreign Secretary, agreed to send instructions to the British Legation in Mexico City to do what it could to help, although it was not a matter for "the authoritative interference of H.M. Government." Tebbutt also persuaded the Mexican Chargé d'Affaires in London to add his support. After much delay, the Mexican Finance Minister, in December 1843, accepted the claim for the seventy-five bonds for which Tebbutt had been able to provide the numbers, but not for the remaining unnumbered fourteen. Eventually, after more delays by Lizardi and more letters to Lord Aberdeen, Tebbutt was given his new bonds. Apparently, some time later, three of those which had disappeared from his house were presented to Lizardi for conversion but Murphy, who mentions this in a report to the Mexican Foreign Office, gives no further details.[15]

1824 FIVE PER CENTS AND 1825 SIX PER CENTS

There is an immediate problem with the 1824 and 1825 bonds because despite searches in many British and Mexican public and private archives, including those of banks and stockbrokers operating at the time, no example of either bond has been found. Unfortunately, therefore, it is not possible to illustrate a bond or indicate any definite description of color or design. Similarly, the dividend coupons which were attached to each bond have disappeared and cannot be illustrated. Fortunately, on the other hand, a handwritten copy of the text of an 1824 bond has been discovered, but before turning to it, a brief explanation of the background to its issue and sale is necessary. After several unsuccessful attempts by Mexico's first independent governments to raise loans on the international markets, the national congress approved a law on 1 May 1823 which authorized the Executive to borrow 8,000,000 dollars or £1,600,000. Shortly afterwards, a Mexican merchant, Francisco de Borja Migoni, who had resided in Europe for several years, was appointed as Mexico's Financial Agent and Consul-General in London with authority to raise the loan. He promptly began negotiations with various parties and although rival offers were simultaneously made to the Mexican government both in Mexico City and in London, Migoni soon concluded an agreement with B.A. Goldsmidt & Co.[16]

Little is known about the Goldsmidt firm and none of its records appear to have survived. It was one of many partnerships operating in London at the time. Its business activities included financial operations as well as trade. It had contracts for Portuguese and Colombian loans, as well as the Mexican, and it acted as agent for the payment of dividends on others, for example, that of Denmark, for which it received commission. Its mercantile interests involved Spain and Spanish America, Holland, Germany, and Russia. Described sarcastically by one contemporary as the banker of the Holy Alliance,[17] it was, as the city editor of *The Times* (16 February 1826) put it, "an eminent house." At its head was the senior partner, I.A. Goldsmidt, and its office was at 5 Great St. Helen's passage, Bishopsgate Street.

The Goldsmidt Company, like many others, failed early in 1826 but, just two years earlier, there had been no sign of difficulties and on 2 January 1824, Migoni entered into a verbal contract with the company for the first loan. A prospectus was quickly prepared and published in the daily press on 24 January. This announced the flotation of a loan for £3,200,000 to be divided into the following bonds:

12,000 of £100 each
4,000 of £250 each
2,000 of £500 each

This stock was to be issued at £58 per cent or per £100 bond with proportionately higher prices for the larger value bonds. Interest was to be at 5% per annum with dividends paid twice yearly in London. Payments for the stock were to be by installments, as follows:

10% on 29 January
10% on 28 February
10% on 9 April
14% on 19 April
14% on 21 June

Interest at 4% would be charged on the final two installments from 9 April but a discount of 4% would be allowed on all advance payments. The Mexican government undertook not to seek any other loan within twelve months and that one-quarter of any future loan thereafter would be used to redeem bonds of the present one. All of Mexico's revenues were pledged as security. The loan was to have a thirty-year term and there was to be a Sinking Fund to redeem it with £64,000 in the first year and £32,000 in succeeding years plus interest saved on cancelled stock. Finally, a special General Mortgage Bond to guarantee the whole loan was to be deposited in the Bank of England.

A week before publication of this prospectus, the Foreign Exchange Committee had agreed that the loan stock could be quoted on the Exchange. A few days later, a settling day for payment of the Scrip was fixed for 29 January and within a couple of days it was selling at a premium of just under 5%. This was certainly in part owing to the favorable reception accorded to the loan in the city columns of the daily press. *The Morning Chronicle* (27 January 1824), for example, reported that "the terms of this contract are considered favourable and a great deal of business has been done in it." Most of the proceeds, it added, would be spent on British manufactures and arms needed to protect "this populous and rich republic."

The next stage came on 7 February when two documents were signed. The first of these was the formal contract for the loan. This was signed by Migoni on behalf of the Mexican government; by Goldsmidt & Co.; and by a Public Notary, John Newton. One copy of this "Transaction," as it is entitled, with the signatures and seals of the three parties concerned, is in Mexico's National Archive.[18] It has two columns on each page, the left containing the text in English and the right a translation into Spanish. Only a summary of the main clauses is given here. Goldsmidt agreed to pay to the Mexican government the sum of £1,600,000 within fifteen months. To raise this amount, the government agreed to issue 18,000 bonds with a total face value of £3,200,000 redeemable within thirty years from 1 October 1823, paying interest until maturity of 5% per annum. These bonds, and the sixty dividend coupons attached to each one, were sold to Goldsmidt at £55 per cent inclusive of £5 taken by the company as commission. The right to manage payment of dividends for a period of ten years for a commission of 1% was also granted to the company. Funds to pay the first four dividends and to amortize stock in the first two years were to be retained by the company from the loan proceeds. To secure all payments of principal and interest, there was a general pledge of all of Mexico's revenues and a special pledge of one-third of the duties collected by customs houses at ports on the Gulf of Mexico—effectively Veracruz and Tampico—after 1 April 1825.

Also in the National Archive is the second document signed by Migoni on 7 February 1824, which was a General Mortgage Bond. Written in English, the opening paragraph states the origins of the loan and of Migoni's authority to contract it. This is followed by six articles which restate the main commitments of the loan prospectus. Article 1 stipulates that there shall be 18,000 "special bonds" amounting in total nominal value to £3,200,000. Annual interest was to be 5%, payable half-yearly in London without deductions. Article 2 concerns the security. It pledges all the revenues of the State for payment of both principal and interest. This general mortgage was additional and independent of the specially assigned tax which the law of 1 May 1823 had stated would be introduced for the exclusive service of the debt. Article 3 promises that the Treasurer-General of Mexico shall be bound by law to give absolute priority to repayment of the loan and to ensure that none of the money raised for that purpose was diverted to other State expenses. Details of the Sinking Fund follow in Article 4 with purchases from it to start on 1 April 1824. All redeemed stock was to be cancelled and deposited in the Bank of England. Any stock unredeemed at the expiry of the thirty-year term from 1 October 1823 was to be paid off at par. The remittance of all funds to London was to be at the expense and risk of the Mexican government. Finally, two articles, 5 and 6, refer to the deposit in the Bank of England of the General Bond and the special authority given to Migoni to raise the loan. Neither was to be removed from the Bank until the whole of the loan was repaid. All payments would be made in time of peace or war "without distinction whether the holder of any of the special bonds belongs to a friendly or hostile nation."

Important amendments were subsequently made to this General Bond. It was deposited on 7 February 1824 by Migoni and Goldsmidt in what the Bank of England's registry of deposits describes as "A Tin Box marked Mexican Loan 1824."[19] Shortly afterwards, however, questions were raised—we do not know by whom—regarding possible tax liabilities. English law, under a statute issued in the reign of George III, required the payment of Stamp Duty ad valorem on bonds and interest coupons above a certain value which were signed and sold within England. One way of avoiding the tax, which had already been adopted for a Colombian loan, was to have the bonds signed in Paris. Migoni did not favor that solution because, as he told his Finance Minister, it was too dangerous given the close alliance at that time between France and Spain.[20] Ferdinand VII of Spain had only recently regained his absolute monarchist powers with the help of the French army and he had made no secret of his determination to reconquer his lost colony of Mexico.

Migoni and Goldsmidt decided to seek counsel's opinion on the taxation issue. The lawyer they turned to was Samuel Marryat. He was sent copies of the contract signed with Goldsmidt; the text of the General Bond; and the text of the special bonds to be sold to the public. On 18 February 1824, he advised that "the special Bonds, in the form which has been printed and which accompanies this case, would require the ad valorem Stamp duty on each, according to amount." The main reason for this liability was that "although the special Bond in its printed form has something of the language of Certificate, it has too much the language of Security to be exempt from Stamps." The half-yearly dividend warrants had the same characteristic and would also be liable to Stamp Duty.

Another lawyer, Fred Pollock, of York, was then consulted. He advised on 1 March that the solution was first, to increase the number of bonds, eliminating those of the higher values; and second, to make the dividend payments quarterly rather than half-yearly. Each dividend warrant would thus be of lower value.[21] The texts of both the General Mortgage Bond and the special bonds were quickly rewritten. Apart from various stylistic changes, three main alterations were made. First, the word "bond" was removed from all references to the "Special Bonds" and replaced with the word "Certificate." Second, the loan was now to be divided into 24,000 Certificates rather than, as before, 18,000 bonds. These Certificates were to be numbered as follows:

Series A   8,000 certificates numbered 1–8,000, each of £100

Series B   16,000 certificates numbered 1–16,000, each of £150

Third, interest payments were to be made quarterly on 1 January, 1 April, 1 July, and 1 October.

The new texts were referred back to Marryat. He replied that with the changes made, in particular, the use of the word "certificate" and the reduced dividend warrants, there was now no liability for Stamp Duty because the amounts were below the sums on which tax was payable. Following receipt of this opinion, on 20 March 1824, Migoni and Abraham Goldsmidt, accompanied by the notary John Newton, went to the Bank of England. There they retrieved the box containing the General Mortgage Bond which they had deposited on 7 February and formally cancelled it by tearing off the seal. Then, the new General Bond was signed by Migoni and Goldsmidt. It was replaced in the "Tin Box marked Mexican Loan 1824," together with a copy of the contract with Goldsmidt which had also been amended to take into account the changes.[22] Finally, the three seals of Migoni, Goldsmidt, and the notary were applied to the box which was locked with two keys. One key was taken by Migoni and the other by Goldsmidt. Two other notaries witnessed the proceedings.

From these events, it seems that at least some of the individual bonds, or certificates, to be sold to the public had already been printed when the doubts over the taxation issue were raised. As indicated above, Marryat referred to "the special Bond in its printed form." We can only assume that these bonds were destroyed and new orders were given to the printer to produce the revised version for the 24,000 that were eventually released into the market. No example of these printed 1824 bonds (henceforth I will refer to them as bonds rather than certificates) has been found. Fortunately, however, a handwritten copy has been discovered. This was sent to the British Foreign Office in June 1857 by David Robertson, then chairman of the Committee of Mexican Bondholders. Robertson was engaged in a vigorous campaign to persuade the British government to intervene on behalf of the bondholders. As part of his campaign, and to demonstrate that the security originally offered to guarantee the loans remained in force, he sent what he described as "authoritative" and "literal" copies of the main bonds issued to that time. These copies included the bonds of 1837, 1846, and 1851, as well as that of 1824. The accuracy of the transcription of the later bonds has been verified by comparison with originals in the possession of the author. They are exact copies and, therefore, it may be safely assumed that the 1824 copy is also accurate.[23]

As the Robertson copy is the only known reproduction of an 1824 bond, it is reproduced in full in the Appendix to this book. The original was of the Letter A series, value £100. The text reproduces the amended version of the General Mortgage Bond, including the changes in the number of bonds to 24,000, the quarterly dividend payments, and the use of the word "certificate" throughout. The design and color, as well as the printer, are unknown. The entire text is in English and there is no indication that it is a translation. Hence, it appears that the printed bonds were in English. On the other hand, some Spanish American bonds of similar date, and several of the later Mexican, suggest that the text might have also been printed in Spanish. This can be illustrated with a Buenos Aires bond, dated London, 1 July 1824, which is reproduced in Illustration 3. It is distinctly possible that the Mexican bond was likewise set out in double columns. Clearly, there would have been no point, in the Robertson transcription, for the copyist to have reproduced the Spanish text as well as the English.

With the publication of the prospectus, agreements with loan contractors signed, acceptance of the loan by the Stock Exchange, and the sale of the Scrip at a healthy premium, all that remained was for the bonds to be distributed to buyers. It is not clear exactly when they became available. Final payment on the Scrip, due on 21 June, was postponed until 14 July. A few days later, confirmation that the contract signed with Goldsmidt had been ratified in Mexico arrived at Plymouth on the cutter *Lion*, after a forty-one day voyage from Veracruz. The post was said to contain all the relevant documentation and securities.[24] At any rate, when they were finally put into circulation, the flotation was a definite success. Strong demand for the Scrip meant that the bond price first quoted on the Foreign Exchange was 69, an 11% premium on the issue price of 58. Even more substantial profits were probably made by Goldsmidt, and Migoni and his friends, who had taken the stock at 58.[25] Although events, notably the fortunes of former Mexican Emperor Agustín de Iturbide, caused the price to fluctuate considerably to a low of 48 over the remaining months of 1824, by the end of the year, the bonds were at 72. Final confirmation, after months of rumors that Britain was certain to recognize Mexican independence, gave a further boost, and by February 1825, the price was at 83.

The first dividends were paid in April and quarterly thereafter—1 July, 1 October, 1 January. Redemptions of the stock also began in April. Bonds were bought in the market and the series and numbers of each one published in the daily press. The bonds were cancelled and, in the presence of representatives of the Mexican government, Goldsmidt, and a public notary, they were deposited in the Bank of England. The first of these redemptions was confirmed on 10 April when it was announced that 500 of the A series, each of £100 nominal value, had been bought and cancelled. These bonds had been placed in the Bank on 6 April in a box marked "Mexican Certificates cancelled, April 1824." In October, 53 of the £100 and 334 of the B series, each of £150—a total nominal value of £55,400— were likewise redeemed and deposited at the Bank on 5 October. Over following months to May 1826, another fifteen redemptions took place

3. 1824 Buenos Aires Six per Cent Loan Bond.

with all the cancelled bonds left at the Bank in the customary wooden or tin boxes.[26] In total, 2,283 of the £100 bonds and 5,608 of the £150 were amortized.

Here it may be noted that neither these bonds nor any of the later Mexican issues were of the category known as "lottery loans," which Dawson states were widely used.[27] The lottery loans were certainly very popular in later years, especially with foreign issues. As an incentive to the market, a small amount of bonds were regularly drawn by lot to be redeemed at par regardless of the prevailing market price. The holders of the lucky numbers were paid the full nominal value and thus made handsome profits, as *The Times* (18 May 1875) put it, "of 20, 40, or 50 per cent." The Mexican bonds, however, usually included a clause which states that the government retained the right to redeem them at par if they reached par or above in the market and that the numbers to be bought in would be drawn by lot. The third article of the 1843 bond, for example, makes this clear. Interest on the bonds was to be paid from an allocation of customs revenues, but in the event that any surplus was accumulated from such revenues,

it is agreed that the Surplus shall be appropriated to the redemption of the Principal at the market value of the Bonds, if under par—but, should the market value exceed par, then the Agents shall cause to be detemined, by lot, as many numbers of the bonds, constituting this Loan, as shall in their aggregate amount be equivalent to the amount of the Surplus Funds remitted from Mexico; and the numbers of all Bonds thus paid off or redeemed in any one year, shall be published in the LONDON GAZETTE, and, after cancelling, be deposited in the BANK OF ENGLAND, in the presence of a Notary Public, some time in the month of January following.

Hence, the 1824 bonds that were redeemed were bought at the market price which Turlington calculated to be an average of 63.[28] Of the original 24,000 bonds placed in the market, 16,109 remained.

The money used to amortize the 1824 bonds, and to pay the dividends, came from two sources. The first of these was the Sinking Fund retained by Goldsmidt out of the proceeds of the loan. The other source was a second loan, the so-called Barclay loan of 1825. A Mexican congressional decree of 27 August 1823 had authorized the Executive to seek a loan of 20,000,000 pesos. Protracted negotiations with interested financiers were held in Mexico City and London and the final contract was not signed until 25 August 1824. The signing took place in Mexico City by the Mexican authorities and Robert Manning and William S. Marshall, who were agents for the London-based partnership of Barclay, Herring, Richardson & Co. Little is known about this partnership. The three senior partners— David Barclay, Charles Herring, and Christopher Richardson—were all prominent figures in the London mercantile community of the time. Although it is not entirely clear, given that there were several "Davids" in the Barclay family, it is likely that this David Barclay was the son of Robert Barclay, a leading brewer. One history of the family states that by 1830, he was a partner in a firm of merchants known as Barclay Brothers.[29] Herring was an experienced loan contractor who also had trading interests in the Caribbean and investments in the Mexican mining industry.[30] Other partners included Herring's son, also Charles; Richard Jaffrey; and John Potter.[31]

The contractual negotiations in London were conducted by Barclay's solicitor, E.H. Plumptre. He had several meetings with Mexico's recently appointed Minister Plenipotenciary, José Mariano Michelena, in January 1825 to go over the details.[32] The full text of the contract is readily available elsewhere and only a brief summary is given here.[33] The loan was for £3,200,000 or 16,000,000 pesos for a thirty-year term at 6% interest, payable quarterly in London. This sum was divided into separate bonds as follows:

Series C   16,000 bonds numbered 1–16,000 each of £150
Series D   8,000 bonds numbered 1–8,000 each of £100

These Bearer bonds were to be printed in London and signed by Michelena and Barclay & Co. All 24,000 were to be ready for sale no later than 7 February 1825 and they were to be sold "at the best possible price." This date corrresponded to the clause in the Goldsmidt contract, signed on 7 February 1824, that no new loan would be introduced within one year. £50,000 per month of the money raised was to be used to redeem up to 25% of the 1824 stock—hence the redemptions noted earlier. A further £32,000, together with interest accruing from cancelled bonds, was to be put into a Sinking Fund and used to buy stock at six monthly intervals "at current prices." For payment of dividends, "the third part of the produce of all the maritime customs of the Mexican federation" was assigned. This assignment was without prejudice to the general mortgage of all national revenues. Also, it was additional to the one-third of the customs dues in the Gulf ports already allocated to the first loan. The customs were calculated to yield 4,000,000 pesos a year which, with the anticipated regular stock redemptions lowering the principal debt, were reckoned to be easily enough to service both loans. Funds for the first six quarterly dividends and the first three half-yearly redemptions were to be deducted from the loan proceeds to ensure their punctual payment. Finally, the General Mortgage Bond, congressional decree, and Executive authorization, were all to be deposited in the Bank of England.

The second loan, therefore, was contracted on much the same basis as the first, the main difference being the interest rate offered at 6% rather than 5%. Barclay's commission was set at 6% of the sale price and 1½% on redemption and dividend payments. Although it seems to have been originally intended that Barclay would underwrite the issue at 70, no minimum price was inserted in the contract. This was partly because the 1824 Five per Cents had reached 70 soon after issue and it was reasonable to expect that the higher yielding 6% bonds would rate a market price of over 80.

Barclay began to advertise the loan in London on 31 January 1825.[34] It did not, however, offer the bonds directly to investors. Instead, it invited sealed bids for the whole of the "special obligations" or bonds on offer. Bidders were asked to submit their tenders between 12:00 and 1:00 P.M. on 7 February at the London Tavern in Bishopsgate Street. Application forms were available from Barclay's office at Winchester House, Broad Street.

At 1:05 P.M. on 7 February, David Barclay entered the designated room in the London Tavern to open the bids. Contrary to expectations, there were only two, several others having arrived too late to be considered. One of the bids was by Mr. W. Morgan and the other by Mr. Stokes, acting on behalf of Goldsmidt & Co. After a few minutes, Mr. Barclay announced that the Goldsmidt bid was the higher and had been accepted. Its bid was £86 15s. per cent against that of Mr. Morgan of £86 9s.4d.[35]

The Goldsmidt company, already selling the 1824 issue, thus won the right to market the new bonds. On the same day (7 February in the afternoon), a notice was posted in the Stock Exchange inviting applications to buy them. No applications, the notice said, would be received after 4:00 P.M. that day, and applicants were obliged to express "their willingness to receive them at the price at which they (Goldsmidt) may issue them to the public."[36]

Goldsmidt was able to require buyers to apply for the stock immediately and without knowing the final price because it knew that demand exceeded supply. The loan had been welcomed by city editors as a potentially lucrative investment. It was no surprise when it was reported a couple of days later (*The Times*, 11 February 1825) that the issue had been very much oversubscribed with applications totalling £40,000,000 for the £3,200,000 of stock on offer. Goldsmidt had paid 86¾% and now set the issue price at 89¾%, inclusive of a quarterly dividend due on 1 January 1825. Buyers had to pay for their bonds with a 15% deposit, followed by the usual installments, starting on 14 March with 5%, then six monthly payments of 10%, until the final one of 9¾% on 26 November.

No original example of an 1825 Six per Cent bond has been found and we cannot know for certain its printer, design, or contents. The contract with Barclay required that the bonds "shall be drawn up and printed in the usual form," and signed by Michelena and the Barclay partnership. It seems reasonable to assume that the format and design were similar, if not the same, as those used in the 1824 Five per Cents. The main parts of the General Mortgage Bond would have been included in the text together with some of the relevant Mexican legislation. According to the Bank of England's deposit book, David Barclay himself left what was probably the General Bond and a copy of the contract for the loan on 14 June 1825. The entry for that date refers to the customary tin box marked "Documents relative to the Mexican Loan of 1825."[37]

There is some evidence to suggest that like the 1824 bond, the text was also in English. Years later, in 1839, a firm of merchants, Rougement Brothers, protested about the non-payment of dividends. They held, they said, a large number of the 1825 bonds on their own account and "for numerous of our friends." They went on to quote the fifth clause of the bonds as being the following:

In order to carry into due and compleat [*sic*] effect, as well the Redemption of the loan as the Payment of the interest in manner above-mentioned, the Supreme Executive Power by virtue of the aforesaid Authority from the Constitutional Sovereign Congress doth appropriate and especially mortgage by these presents one third part of the Revenues arising from Maritime Customs of the Mexican Federation which produce upwards of Four millions of dollars yearly, or so much thereof, as shall be requisite and sufficient for covering the respective dividends and the said redemption independently of the General Mortgage of the other revenues of the nation as well as the ways and means of other resources needed.

In addition to the above, Rougement stated, each bond had a certificate by Michelena to the effect that

the said United States and all the public authorities which now exist, or may hereafter exist, are bound to perform faithfully and truly all the foregone Engagements and Conditions; and for no reason and for no pretence whatever are they at any time or under any circumstance to refuse, evade, or delay the full and ample performance of all and every Engagement contained in the said Instrument.

These conditions, they concluded bitterly, "were violated before the ink with which they were written was hardly dry."[38]

In the next few months to 26 November when the final installment was due from buyers, the Scrip fluctuated from an initial premium of around 4% to a discount of 19%. For those who had already paid in full, their bonds also fluctuated from an opening price of 86 in June to a low of 56 in December. Such big price movements were not unusual in what was always a volatile market. In December, for example, *The Times* (14, 16 December) reported "a dreadful panic" in the stock market: "The difficulty of raising money on stocks, bills, or any species of security, whether private or public, is entirely without example in the city of London."

Both the 1824 Five per Cents and the 1825 Six per Cents remained available in the market until September 1840, after which they were re-placed by new bonds of the 1837 conversion. Very few of the Six per Cents had been redeemed. In the first two redemptions, 284 of the C Series, each of £150, and 59 of the D Series, each of £100, were bought, and eventually the total redeemed only reached £49,100.[39] This lack of redemptions was caused by the insolvency of both the Goldsmidt and Barclay companies in 1826. The former collapsed in February with estimated liabilities of £300,000. Among the trustees appointed to sort out its affairs were David Barclay and Thomas Richardson. The senior partner, I.A. Goldsmidt, died a few days later, having "sunk under the pressure of mental anxiety" caused by the failure.[40] A few years later, however, the company continued to exist. In 1830, B. Goldsmidt & Co. claimed commission on any payment of dividends on the grounds that its original contract with the Mexican government in 1824 had given it the right to manage dividend payments on commission for a period of ten years.[41]

In August 1826, the Barclay partnership also collapsed and the Mexican government thereby lost well over £300,000 of the proceeds of the second loan still in the possession of the failed company.[42] For a time, the bond prices fell to their lowest point—Five per Cents to 31 and Six per Cents to 39. Another major stock market panic and collapse in the autumn of 1826—there were 636 insolvency petitions betweeen 13 October and 7 November—also affected Mexican securities.[43] They recovered quickly, however, and by early 1827, the minutes of the Foreign Exchange Com-mittee refer to a severe scarcity of the £100 bonds in particular. The minutes also reveal that speculators continued to invest in both issues al-though several dealers miscalculated and were obliged to default.

Dividends on both stocks were paid until the quarterly payment due on 1 October 1827. Several remittances of money amounting to about £280,000 had been received from Mexico for the dividend account. By July 1827, however, there were insufficient funds available to cover the dividend due on the first of that month and it was only paid by means of a loan advanced by Barings. Following the insolvency of the loan contractors, Barings had agreed in September 1826 to become the Mexican govern-ment's Financial Agent for Europe. The July 1827 dividend was the last to be paid until 1831. In that year, half a quarterly dividend was paid after an agreement with bondholders to capitalize interest arrears. Only two further payments were made in 1832 before the bonds were exchanged in accordance with the 1837 conversion.

The two issues had comprised a total of 48,000 separate bonds. Of these, we know that 7,891 of the Five per Cents and 347 of the Six per Cents were amortized and placed in the Bank of England. A further eighty-nine bonds were lost by Mr. Tebbutt. No less than 39,673 bonds, therefore, remained in the market until the 1837 conversion was implemented. It was carried out by Lizardi & Co., then Mexico's Financial Agent in London.

They were responsible for collecting the old stock and issuing the new. They began to deposit the old bonds in the Bank of England on 2 December 1837 and thereafter made further regular deposits, until eventually there were fourteen boxes.[44] Then, starting in April 1844, the boxes were taken out and each of the bonds in them was cancelled, presumably following the established practice of cutting or punching holes in each one. By the beginning of June, three of the boxes had been completed and Murphy estimated that it would take another eight to ten weeks to finish the process. On 1 September, he informed his Minister of Foreign Affairs that the cancellation exercise had been completed.[45] A few weeks later, Murphy and Raymond Pelly, acting for Lizardi, took the fourteen boxes back to the Bank of England. The entry in the deposit book for 22 October 1844 reads as follows:

We Don Thos. Murphy, Envoy Extraordinary and Minister Plenipotenciary of the Mexican Republic near H.B.M and Messrs. F. de Lizardi & Co as Financial Agents for the said Government of Mexico *desire leave to deposit in the Bank, at our own risk and peril agreeably to the conditions prefixed to this Book.* fourteen Wooden Boxes, marked F. de Lizardi & Co MB and No. 1 to 14 containing documents relating to the Mexican Loans, to be delivered and or inspected by the abovenamed parties or their representative or representatives in their Official capacity, or by an order from the one consenting to the other having access thereto.

The signatures of Murphy and Pelly follow the entry.[46]

Murphy had kept a detailed record of the series and numbers of all the cancelled bonds and he sent it to the Ministry of Foreign Affairs on 1 December 1844.[47] According to his figures, of the 48,000 bonds issued, all were cancelled except seventy-five of the 1824 Five per Cents and ninety-nine of the 1825 Six per Cents which were not presented for conversion; 174 bonds were, therefore, outstanding. A few can be explained. On 10 September 1850, Samuel Herbert, of Durham House, near Chelsea College in London, wrote to the Mexican Minister: "I am the owner of two of the original Mexican bonds which have been in my family, I believe, from the very time they were first issued. One is a 5 per Cent and the other a 6 per Cent Bond." He went on to say that all the coupons in arrears from October 1827 were still attached and neither bond had been presented for any of the conversions. The Five per Cent matured on 1 October 1853 and the Six per Cent on 1 January 1855 "at which time," he said, "both bonds will be redeemable." In the meantime, he expected the Mexican government to pay him the interest he was due.[48]

Almost half a century after the bonds were withdrawn from the market, F.H. & A. Collier, merchants of 42 New Broad Street, London, wrote to the Stock Exchange Committee on 12 July 1886. They protested against a proposal to allow a new issue of Mexican stocks to be given an official quotation. They were holders, they said, of original bonds including both 1824 Five per Cents and 1825 Six per Cents which had never been presented for conversion in any of the several conversions of the past half century. The Mexican Financial Agency had now refused to accept their bonds in the new 1886 conversion. They insisted that this was unjust discrimination against holders such as themselves "who have never converted their bonds."

The Colliers did not specify how many of the original bonds were in their possession. Nor did they indicate whether they had had them, which seems unlikely, for more than sixty years since they were issued or why they had not been previously presented for conversion. Two years later in 1888, at the time of another Mexican bond issue, they renewed their protest to the Stock Exchange, repeating that theirs had still not been accepted. Whether they were eventually is not known and no trace of them has been found.[49]

Tables 1 and 2 give the prices of the 1824 and 1825 bonds. Several features need to be noted of these and all subsequent tables of bond prices. They show the approximate monthly high and low prices for each year that the stocks were quoted on the London Stock Exchange. The figures have been compiled from a weekly sample of the daily prices given in the press— mostly *The Times*—and in an official Stock Exchange price list. Several publications of the time claimed to give "official" prices but the one I have used was the *Course of the Exchange*. This was a biweekly publication by James Wetenhall from March 1825 onwards and by his successors throughout the nineteenth century. As the figures given are weekly samples, it is possible that on one or two days the prices were marginally higher or lower than indicated here. This will be rare, however, because in all instances where there were price movements of more than a couple of points from week to week, daily price checks were made. The condition of both sources—*The Times* and *Course of the Exchange*—dictated another feature of the lists. As most scholars will be aware, original copies of *The Times* are now rarely available in libraries. The historian has to rely instead on microfilm, and even allowing for the sometimes poor condition of the original, microfilm reproduction does not always make for easy reading. In this case, bond prices were quoted in fractions down to 1/16 but it is often impossible to make out the fractions from a microfilm copy. Even when the original issues of *The Times* were available, the print is so small and frequently in such poor condition that the fractions could not be read. Hence, I decided it was safer to omit them.

The prices are per £100 bond and such features as "ex-dividend" have not been shown. Also, at times, two prices were quoted, one for purchases on account and the other for cash. Again, the very marginal differences in the two have not been included. Occasionally, in the early years and quite often in later times, no prices are quoted either in the newspapers or in the

Table 1
1824 Five per Cents

		J	F	M	A	M	J	J	A	S	O	N	D
1824	H	-	-	-	69	65	61	56	52	58	61	70	72
	L	-	-	-	68	65	58	49	48	49	59	65	71
1825	H	83	83	81	79	77	77	77	75	78	71	67	60
	L	75	80	81	79	73	75	75	74	66	69	60	50
1826	H	64	60	60	58	54	53	42	46	53	54	58	59
	L	59	49	55	53	50	42	31	37	41	50	54	50
1827	H	54	57	58	59	57	58	58	58	54	44	42	39
	L	48	54	56	57	55	56	55	54	35	33	41	35
1828	H	36	29	24	26	32	30	30	28	30	28	27	25
	L	30	25	24	24	25	26	29	27	30	26	25	25
1829	H	26	23	19	17	17	18	18	16	15	17	19	21
	L	25	20	18	16	16	18	16	16	15	15	17	18
1830	H	23	23	29	30	33	32	31	31	30	29	25	29
	L	21	21	23	28	31	29	30	30	27	27	22	21
1831	H	26	28	28	28	30	31	30	30	28	/	26	29
	L	25	27	27	27	27	30	29	29	28	/	26	28
1832	H	27	28	25	26	27	26	25	22	22	21	/	/
	L	27	25	25	26	26	26	24	21	22	21	/	/
1833	H	22	27	32	31	28	30	34	34	29	/	29	29
	L	20	25	28	25	28	29	30	31	29	/	28	29
1834	H	30	31	/	33	35	36	35	29	31	30	31	30
	L	29	31	/	29	33	34	32	29	29	30	31	30
1835	H	31	31	33	40	37	27	26	25	27	28	26	28
	L	31	31	30	33	30	26	24	24	24	28	26	26
1836	H	27	/	24	25	23	25	23	21	/	16	/	15
	L	27	/	23	20	22	22	22	20	/	16	/	15
1837	H	17	17	19	18	15	15	19	18	24	24	24	24
	L	17	17	17	18	15	15	17	18	19	22	22	21
1838	H	23	25	25	22	23	22	20	18	18	15	/	17
	L	21	24	25	22	23	19	19	18	16	15	/	17
1839	H	18	18	17	17	19	19	24	23	23	27	25	23
	L	17	18	17	16	18	19	23	22	20	25	23	22
1840	H	24	24	24	/	27	27	27	/	24			
	L	24	24	24	/	24	27	26	/	19			

Table 2
1825 Six per Cents

		J	F	M	A	M	J	J	A	S	O	N	D
1825	H	-	-	-	-	-	86	85	84	79	77	76	65
	L	-	-	-	-	-	86	85	80	75	75	67	56
1826	H	70	66	70	68	63	61	50	54	65	65	68	71
	L	66	59	62	60	61	50	39	48	49	61	64	60
1827	H	66	69	70	71	69	70	70	70	67	56	54	52
	L	59	63	69	70	67	68	68	67	47	43	53	44
1828	H	47	44	34	35	44	42	42	39	40	38	34	33
	L	44	33	31	31	35	36	39	38	39	34	32	32
1829	H	33	32	24	21	20	21	21	18	18	20	24	26
	L	32	23	21	19	20	21	19	17	17	18	21	24
1830	H	27	26	32	35	40	38	38	39	38	38	37	37
	L	25	24	27	31	37	35	36	36	36	36	30	35
1831	H	36	37	37	37	39	40	39	38	36	36	36	36
	L	33	35	35	36	36	39	36	36	35	32	32	34
1832	H	35	35	32	33	32	33	31	28	28	26	27	26
	L	34	30	30	30	33	29	29	26	26	26	26	24
1833	H	28	34	37	37	35	36	44	43	39	35	36	38
	L	25	27	33	32	31	34	37	37	34	33	34	36
1834	H	38	43	40	42	46	46	46	42	40	41	42	42
	L	37	38	38	38	42	44	41	39	39	40	41	41
1835	H	43	43	45	51	49	39	37	36	39	39	38	39
	L	41	42	41	45	36	33	36	34	35	37	36	35
1836	H	38	37	36	36	35	35	34	32	28	23	22	22
	L	37	36	33	35	32	32	33	27	22	21	22	21
1837	H	27	25	25	24	24	21	25	25	30	30	29	28
	L	23	25	24	23	24	20	22	24	25	26	27	25
1838	H	27	30	30	28	28	26	25	25	23	23	23	23
	L	26	27	27	27	26	24	24	24	22	21	22	22
1839	H	25	24	24	25	26	27	29	29	30	32	31	29
	L	22	23	23	23	24	25	26	27	28	31	29	27
1840	H	30	29	29	28	32	32	31	29	26	25	-	-
	L	28	28	28	28	28	31	28	28	24	25	-	-

Stock Exchange lists. This was because no deals in the stocks had been made on the day or month in question. As the city editor of *The Times* (9 December 1831) pointed out to a correspondent who had queried the absence of some stock prices, brokers would not quote a price in the abstract. In the tables, the gaps are where no prices were published.

1831 DEFERRED FIVE PER CENTS: DEFERRED SIX PER CENTS

Mexico defaulted on the dividend payments due on its 1824 and 1825 bonds on 1 October 1827. For the next three years, its Finance Ministers made promises, initiated legislation, and generally reassured the bondholders that dividends would soon be resumed. In particular, congressional decrees and Executive circulars were promulgated in 1828 to the effect that one-eighth of customs revenues on imports together with taxes on gold and silver exports were specifically allocated to the payment of dividends. On 28 October of that same year, another law was approved which stated that overdue dividends would be capitalized and new bonds given to the bondholders for their arrears. None of these promises of cash remittances to Barings for the dividend account nor of new bonds for arrears were kept. Political circumstances, including internal riot and rebellion, and an invasion by Spain in 1829 in a futile attempt to reconquer its lost colony, meant that all available funds were diverted to domestic needs. As Britain's Chargé d'Affaires in Mexico City reported on 29 November 1829, the Mexican authorities were well disposed toward the bondholders but no money was available.

One of the consequences of the internal unrest was the rise to power of General Anastasio Bustamante, who took control of the federal government in January 1830. He instituted a strongly conservative regime in which the leading political figure was Lucas Alamán, who was made Minister of Internal and External Affairs. Alamán had wide experience and many personal contacts in Europe and one of his main priorities was to attract capital investment into his country. He had already been involved in securing largely British investment in several mining companies. Also, he was well aware, perhaps more so than many of his contemporaries, of the need to restore Mexico's credit in foreign capital markets, especially in Britain. Hence, after only a few weeks in office, he began to try to sort out the problem of the foreign debt. On 5 March 1830, he made a series of proposals designed to assure the bondholders that their dividends would be paid. He promised that the one-eighth of import dues would in future definitely be set aside for the dividend fund. To ensure this, he suggested that the bondholders should appoint an agent in Mexico City and agents in Mexican ports. The former would maintain direct and rapid contact with the federal authorities while the latter in the ports would be able to take immediate possession of the import taxes as the ships arrived. Mexico would pay freight, insurance, and commission charges on dividend remittances sent to London. As Barings was already Mexico's Financial Agent in London, it would be advantageous if the bondholders were also to appoint the company to represent them. Finally, hitherto banned cotton goods were to be allowed into Mexico for a limited period. Customs revenues would certainly increase as a result, yielding "on a moderate calculation," as Alamán put it, 7,000,000 to 8,000,000 dollars annually. The one-eighth alone allocated to the bondholders would be almost enough to meet the annual dividend. Finally, the Mexican Minister in London to whom Alamán sent his proposals, Manuel Eduardo de Gorostiza, was instructed to start talks with leading bondholders.[50]

Gorostiza received this letter on the postal packet which arrived on 1 May. He consulted leading bondholders and on 13 May it was announced in the press that a public meeting was to be held at the London Tavern on 26 May to consider Alamán's proposals. At the meeting, the bondholders decided to set up a committee to represent their interests. Thus, the first Committee of Mexican Bondholders was formed.[51] Following discussions, and misunderstandings, with the British Foreign Office, the bondholders' chairman began to confer with Gorostiza.[52] He suggested several amendments to Alamán's proposals, but in general he welcomed the idea of agents in the Mexican ports of Tampico and Veracruz. He also put forward a scheme for the capitalization of the interest arrears. According to his calculations, allowing for the bonds already redeemed, the total debt was £5,281,400. The amount of annual dividends on the Five and Six per Cents was respectively £106,525 and £189,054 or a total of £295,579. Since the last dividend payment in July 1827, accumulated arrears to 1 April 1830 totalled £812,842. Allowing one more year for negotiations, by 1 April 1831, the arrears would amount to £1,108,421 5s.

Second, it was proposed that for a period of five years from 1 April 1831, "the Mexican government be relieved from the payment of one half of the interest on its bonds." The sum of that half dividend over the five years amounted to £738,947.10s. Adding that to the arrears gave a final total of interest arrears of £1,847,368.15s by 1 April 1836. New bonds to that amount, it was urged, should be given to bondholders. No interest would be payable on them until the expiry of the five years' period of grace on 1 April 1836.

In sum, the bondholders' proposal was that all interest arrears plus half of future interest for five years should be capitalized with an issue of new, non-interest bearing bonds. The original Five and Six per Cents would attract half the dividends due for the next five years. Thereafter, both the original and the new bonds would receive the full interest.

As the bondholders explained, the reasoning behind their idea was that it would enable Mexico "to provide regularly and punctually for the annual charge without any inconvenient immediate pressure." Second, postponing payment of the arrears through the issue of new bonds allowed Mexico time to develop its resources, so that by 1836 there would be no difficulty in meeting the "entire charge of its foreign debt."[53]

Gorostiza welcomed these proposals and agreed to forward them to Mexico with his support. Several more months elapsed, however, before a final agreement was reached. In October 1830, the Mexican Congress accepted all the terms suggested by the bondholders except the immediate issue of new stock. Reluctant to add to the country's capital debt with more bonds and wanting to retain the freedom to pay off arrears if funds became available, the Congress resolved that no new stock should be issued until 1 April 1836. It also accepted that the general one-eighth of import dues through all ports assigned to the dividend fund should be replaced by one-sixth of those collected at Veracruz and Tampico.

The bondholders were unwilling to accept any delay in the issue of the new bonds. After more discussions with Gorostiza, he referred the matter back to Mexico and on 20 May 1831, the Congress reversed its decision and decided to allow the issue of the new stock.[54] Eventually, again after much discussion between Gorostiza, Barings, and the bondholders' representatives, Gorostiza published on 28 September 1831 the final terms of the capitalization.[55] These were as follows.

In exchange for fifty of the quarterly dividend coupons of the Five per Cent £100 bonds, a new bond of £100 face value would be given. Each coupon was worth £1 5s. and the exchange, therefore, was £62 10s. of coupons for each new £100 bond. Similarly, fifty coupons of the £150 series, each worth £1 17s.6d., would be exchanged for a new £150 bond.

The same arrangement applied to the Six per Cents: fifty coupons of £1 10s. each or £75 worth for a new £100 bond; fifty of £2 5s. or £112 10s. for a new £150 bond. None of the new bonds would pay interest before 1 April 1836.

Bondholders were asked to obtain from Barings the necessary forms on which to list their claims.[56] They were to enter on these forms the numbers of at least fifty dividend coupons falling due between 1 October 1827 and 1 April 1831. Completed lists and coupons had to be handed in to Barings on any Wednesday after 12 October between the hours of 10:00 A.M. and 2:00 P.M. New bonds could be claimed four weeks after the date of delivery of the coupons.

With regard to the half dividends to be deferred until 1836, new bonds were not issued. Instead, the following procedure was set out. Coupons falling due from 1 July 1831—a half dividend had been paid on that date with the coupon cut in half—until 1 April 1836 had to be delivered to Barings on or after 1 January 1832, when the next dividend was due. In return for handing over their coupons, bondholders would be paid the half dividend and given an acknowledgment or receipt. They were promised that these receipts would be exchanged for new bonds in April 1836. The coupons were now expressed as half-yearly dividends because the bondholders had agreed with Gorostiza that future payments should be every six months rather than quarterly "to diminish the risk of contingencies and delays."[57]

In sum, the 1831 arrangement provided for the issue of new bonds of £100 and £150 face value but not paying interest until 1836 in exchange for the interest arrears from 1 October 1827 to 1 April 1831; and the issue of receipts for the half dividends which were to be deferred for five years until April 1836. At that time, the receipts would be exchanged for new bonds on which interest would be paid. No example of these receipts has been found and it is probable that very few were issued. Bondholders were reluctant to hand over their coupons, which could be sold in the market, in return for a piece of paper on which no cash could be immediately realized. New bonds for the dividend arrears, however, were produced and distributed according to the following procedure.

There were fifteen unpaid quarterly dividend coupons from 1 October 1827 to 1 April 1831 but to receive the new bonds for these arrears, bondholders were required to present "the numbers of Fifty Coupons, or any number of Coupons divided by fifty." There were bondholders with no more than one or two bonds who would not have the required fifty coupons. As there was a market in coupons detached from the bonds, such small bondholders were presumably expected to buy in those they needed to make up the total to fifty. It seems unlikely that many would have done so because it meant investing more capital in the non-interest-bearing securities of a nation already in default. Future conversions allowed for smaller sums by the issue of various kinds of certificates.

The effect of the capitalization of arrears was the issue of so-called Deferred Five per Cents to a value of £639,255, and of Deferred Six per Cents for £945,270, for a total of £1,584,525. These new bonds replaced interest arrears on the 1824 Five per Cents of £399,534 and on the 1825 Six per Cents of £708,952. As those of 1824 and 1825 had used the letters A through D for the four series, the new ones carried letters E, F, G, and H. The following were printed and signed by Gorostiza:

Five per Cents:
    Series E   1,745 bonds numbered 1–1745 each of £100
    Series F   3,098 bonds numbered 1–3098 each of £150
Six per Cents:
    Series G   4,642 bonds numbered 1–4642 each of £150
    Series H <u>2,438</u> bonds numbered 1–2438 each of £100
          11,923

The total value of these bonds was £1,579,300 or £5,225 less than needed to capitalize the whole debt at £1,584,525. According to Murphy's account (pp. 7–9), Barings eventually distributed bonds to a total value of £1,575,800, leaving just £3,305 of Five per Cents and £5,420 of Six per Cents to complete the capitalization.[58] He goes on to say that Barings exhausted its supply of bonds and instead gave out certificates for £1,126 worth of the Five per Cents and £2,746 of the Six per Cents. Finally, he asserts that except for 32 damaged bonds which Barings retained (25 of the E Series; 5 of F; 1 each of G and H), all but £2,719 of the Five per Cents and £2,674 of the Six per Cents were issued.

Again, as no original example of these deferred bonds has been found, we cannot know for certain the design or contents. There are good indications, however, of what the text contained. Gorostiza told Alamán, for example, that the text would include in both Spanish and English the laws of 2 October 1830 and 20 May 1831. A statement would also be added to confirm that no interest was payable before 1836 and that Mexico reserved the right to amortize the bonds before then, if funds became available.

Regarding the design, there is a printer's estimate in Barings Archive.[59] This is from Perkins and Bacon and it gives an itemized estimate for the production and printing of 2,000 bonds of two kinds, "one of 5 and the other of 6 per cent substitutes." The design on both sets of bonds was to be similar. The basic copper plate cost £2 2s. and the engraving of the Mexican arms, eagle, and serpent £8 8s. Various other items such as typesetting, retouching, and five reams of paper at £5 5s. each brought the total estimate up to £165. The estimator added that producing a larger run of more than 2,000 would not significantly add to the cost. We do not know if this estimate was accepted by Barings. It is dated 4 October 1831 and as Gorostiza had promised bondholders that they would start to receive their new bonds by 12 November, it seems possible that it was accepted. Certainly, Barings sent the first 450 bonds to Gorostiza for his signature on 5 November and he signed them on the next day.[60] Thereafter, they were released in batches by Barings as bondholders brought in their arrear coupons. They were still being issued as late as October 1840.[61] For his part, Gorostiza kept a record of the series and numbers of those he signed and he sent regular reports of them to his Ministry of Foreign Affairs.[62]

Thus, 11,891 new Mexican bonds were put into circulation and although no interest was payable on them, they were still a negotiable security in the market until 1840 when they were withdrawn as part of the next rescheduling of the debt.[63] Using Murphy's figures again, only 40 bonds of the whole issue were not presented for conversion. At least some of these were possessed by the Colliers who, as indicated previously, tried in 1886 and again in 1888 to cash or convert their holdings of unconverted 1824 and 1825 bonds. They also held, they said, 1831 Five and Six per Cents. Those

Table 3
1831 Deferred Five per Cents

		J	F	M	A	M	J	J	A	S	O	N	D
1831	H	-	-	-	-	-	-	-	-	-	-	14	16
	L	-	-	-	-	-	-	-	-	-	-	13	14
1832	H	15	14	14	/	15	15	/	13	/	/	12	/
	L	14	13	13	/	14	15	/	13	/	/	12	/
1833	H	/	12	/	/	/	/	22	20	/	/	/	16
	L	/	12	/	/	/	/	19	20	/	/	/	15
1834	H	18	22	22	/	24	24	22	20	/	/	20	21
	L	17	22	22	/	24	23	22	20	/	/	20	20
1835	H	22	22	23	27	26	/	/	/	20	21	/	23
	L	21	22	21	25	25	/	/	/	20	21	/	23
1836	H	22	21	/	/	20	/	/	/	/	/	/	11
	L	21	21	/	/	20	/	/	/	/	/	/	11
1837	H	/	14	/	/	/	/	/	/	17	17	20	21
	L	/	14	/	/	/	/	/	/	17	17	19	21
1838	H	17	/	20	/	/	/	15	/	/	15	/	/
	L	17	/	19	/	/	/	15	/	/	14	/	/
1839	H	/	/	/	12	/	/	13	16	/	18	19	19
	L	/	/	/	12	/	/	13	16	/	18	19	19
1840	H	/	20	20	20	23	-	-	-	-	-	-	-
	L	/	20	20	20	23	-	-	-	-	-	-	-

that were converted—11,851—were cancelled in 1844 at the same time as the earlier issues of 1824 and 1825. They were placed in the fourteen boxes deposited in the Bank of England by Murphy on 22 October 1844. The 32 damaged ones that were not issued have disappeared from Barings' archive.

Tables 3 and 4 give the Stock Exchange prices from 1831 to 1840. The occasionally notable price fluctuations reflect the interest of speculators. For example, significant rises occurred in 1835 as investors speculated that the Mexican government would keep its promise to pay dividends from 1 April 1836. Not for the first nor the last time, the bondholders were to be disappointed.

1837 ACTIVE AND DEFERRED FIVE PER CENTS

In the 1831 agreement, Mexico had promised that on 1 April 1836, full interest payments on its bonds would be resumed. The promise was not

Table 4
1831 Deferred Six per Cents

		J	F	M	A	M	J	J	A	S	O	N	D
1831	H	-	-	-	-	-	-	-	-	-	-	19	20
	L	-	-	-	-	-	-	-	-	-	-	16	20
1832	H	18	18	16	17	19	18	17	/	17	/	/	13
	L	17	16	16	16	17	17	17	/	17	/	/	13
1833	H	/	18	24	23	/	23	26	25	23	/	20	22
		/	18	19	18	/	22	23	24	23	/	20	22
1834	H	23	28	25	26	/	30	27	26	25	25	26	25
	L	22	23	25	26	/	28	27	26	24	25	26	25
1835	H	27	28	29	32	32	24	/	24	24	26	25	28
	L	25	28	26	30	31	23	/	22	23	25	24	24
1836	H	/	24	25	/	/	25	/	/	/	16	/	/
	L	/	24	23	/	/	25	/	/	/	16	/	/
1837	H	/	17	/	/	/	/	/	/	27	21	22	22
	L	/	17	/	/	/	/	/	/	20	20	21	22
1838	H	20	23	24	21	/	/	18	/	/	/	/	/
	L	20	21	22	21	/	/	18	/	/	/	/	/
1839	H	/	/	/	/	18	/	/	/	/	24	22	22
	L	/	/	/	/	18	/	/	/	/	22	20	20
1840	H	22	/	/	23	/	25	/	/	25	-	-	-
	L	22	/	/	23	/	24	/	/	22	-	-	-

kept and nor were the other commitments. Some money for dividends arrived from time to time in the monthly packets but only in small amounts, and after 1832 there was never enough to pay even the half dividend that had been promised. The situation was made worse in February 1833 when the Mexican government decided that it could not afford the one-sixth of import taxes assigned to the dividend fund. Orders were given that in future only 6% was to be set aside to service the foreign debt. The bondholders protested with irate letters to Gorostiza and with deputations and appeals for help to the British Foreign Office. British diplomats in Mexico were instructed to press the bondholders' case and their pressure had some effect inasmuch as the one-sixth proportion was reinstated in 1834. In practical terms, however, there was little result because dividend remittances continued to be few and far between.

The political situation in Mexico remained unstable. Military conflicts, often in the Gulf area, which seriously affected imports through Veracruz and Tampico, were frequent. A major constitutional change from federal to centralized republic in 1835 brought further turmoil, in particular, the revolt and separation of Texas. The only positive development for the bondholders was the news that Spain was to recognize the independence of Mexico. The reactionary Spanish king, Ferdinand VII, died in September 1833. Within a few months, talks about recognition were being planned and in March 1835, Mexico's recently appointed Minister Plenipotentiary in London, Miguel Santa María, was instructed to proceed to Madrid to start the formal negotiations. All Spanish American bond prices rose, albeit temporarily, in anticipation of increased trade once normal relations had been resumed between Spain and the new republics.

As the external debt deadline of 1 April 1836 approached, however, it was clear that Mexico was not in a position to meet its obligations. On 1 March, Barings, still the Financial Agent, asked for instructions. It pointed out that on 1 April next, the receipts which had been issued in lieu of the deferred half dividends were to be exchanged for bonds. A dividend was also due to be paid "to the so long neglected bondholders," and there was also the matter of interest arrears since 1833. The Chargé d'Affaires, now Agustín de Iturbide, referred these points to his government. On 21 April, it instructed Barings to proceed with the issue of the supplementary bonds in accordance with the 1831 agreement. As for the dividends, proposals designed to ensure regular, future payments were said to be under consideration.[64]

Barings was not reassured by this reply and resigned as Mexico's Financial Agent. The bondholders themselves were also angry. One wrote to *The Times* (4 March 1836) to denounce Mexico's "suicidal contempt of good faith," and the chairman of the bondholders' committee resigned in despair. Then, early in June 1836, bondholders of the six Spanish American nations which had floated loans in London decided to form a single association to represent their collective interests in a "combined effort." The first chairman of this Committee of Spanish American Bondholders was George Richard Robinson (more information on the formation of the Committee and its membership appears in Part II). These developments and more hostile articles in the press, with growing demands for British government intervention, alarmed Mexican diplomats. Although in Madrid, Santa María was kept informed and, writing to his Foreign Minister, he urged that a solution be found as soon as possible. He himself, he said, had pledged his word of honor to bondholders that dividend payments would be resumed. Emphasizing the bad publicity Mexico was attracting in Europe over the debt issue, he urged that it was time for "a big idea" to resolve the matter. During his stay in London, a scheme for refunding the debt had been put to him by the firm of Francisco de Lizardi & Co. He had had dealings with Lizardi in the past; they were patriotic Mexicans, and he recommended that the company now be given the financial agency in place of Barings.

The Lizardi company was appointed to the agency a few months later. Although it was to have a controversial role in the history of Mexico's external debt, very little information about it is available. It was founded by Francisco de Paula de Lizardi. He was born at Veracruz in 1800 into a merchant family, and as his mother's maiden name was Migoni, he may have been related to the Borja Migoni who had arranged the first loans in the 1820s. At any rate, Lizardi and his brother, Manuel Julián, came to Europe to set up the business. It was successful and there were soon branches in London, Liverpool, Paris, and New Orleans. Its mercantile activities included trade with Europe and North America and eventually it became "the oldest and for many years the most substantial house in London in connexion with the Mexican trade."[65] It was also involved in financial operations and was recognized as one of London's leading acceptance houses and merchant bankers.[66] The founder, Francisco, died unexpectedly on a visit to Paris in March 1842, leaving a widow, Helena de Cubas, and six young children. He bequeathed control of the company to his brother, Manuel Julián, who had managed the Paris branch. The only other senior partner, Alexander Gordon, who owned 20% of the company, retired about the same time, enabling Manuel to assume sole control. His relationship with both the Mexican government and the bondholders was turbulent, involving allegations of fraud, financial mismanagement, if not corruption, and several court cases. After a few years, probably in the early 1850s, he returned to Mexico where he became a prominent figure in the capital's social and commercial elite. The company continued its financial and trading activities until 1873. In February of that year, it was forced into bankruptcy with liabilities estimated at the enormous sum (for the time) of £1,200,000. The only surviving family member in England, and son of the founder, was John Javier de Lizardi. He persuaded the firm of Glyn, Mills, Currie & Co. to lend him £12,000 just a few days before the bankruptcy. It instigated fraud charges against him and he was arrested and jailed. Soon released on bail on his "own recognizance in the sum of 50001, and the bail of two substantial securities each in the sum of 60001," he promptly disappeared, probably to Mexico or the United States.[67] When the Bankruptcy Court met on 3 May to consider the situation, it was advised that Extradition Treaties were not applicable. The Registrar concluded that all that could be done was to record Lizardi's non-appearance. No further mention of the firm in Britain has been found.[68]

Shortly after Santa María recommended Lizardi for the financial agency, one of the firm's partners, Pedro de la Quintana, went to Mexico to discuss its proposals for the external debt. Quintana had previously worked in London for Borja Migoni, who appointed him as one of his executors because of his familiarity with his mercantile affairs, "having for a long time had the management of them."[69] The result of his discussions was two laws of 4 and 12 April 1837. In the first, Congress instructed the Executive to proceed with the colonization of lands belonging to the nation "by means of sales, long leases or mortgages." Money raised in this way was to be used, in part, for "the redemption of the national debt contracted or to be contracted."[70]

On 12 April, interim President José Justo Corro published a decree which indicated the means whereby the colonization was to be achieved, allied to a rescheduling of the external debt. A national consolidated fund, paying interest at 5%, was to be established "with the sole and determinate object of converting thereinto the entire foreign debt." To carry out this operation, Lizardi & Co. was appointed as the Financial Agent. It was to issue new bonds of the consolidated fund "in pounds sterling, payable in London on 1 October 1866, with interest coupons in the margin for each half year until said date."[71]

Holders of the existing Five and Six per Cents were to be given the opportunity to exchange them for new consolidated bonds under these terms. The Five per Cents were to be received at par and the Six per Cents at a 12½% premium to compensate for the lower interest rate now offered—in other words, an 1825 Six per Cent bond with a face value of £100 would be exchanged for £112 10s. worth of the new stock. Unpaid interest coupons would also be accepted at par. In exchange for their bonds and coupons, holders would receive half of the value in the new Five per Cent consolidated bonds, and half in land warrants valid for vacant lands in the departments of Texas, Chihuahua, New Mexico, Sonora, and California. The amount of land to which each warrant gave title varied from 400 to 10,000 acres, valued at five shillings an acre. The warrants carried interest at 5% from the date of issue to the date when the holder took possession of the land. The interest was not to be paid in cash but in added value to the warrant.

Interest payments on the new stock were payable in London half-yearly on 1 April and 1 October, commencing on 1 October 1837. Until regular dividend remittances could be arranged, unpaid coupons could be exchanged for special certificates obtainable from Lizardi. These certificates, soon known as customs certificates, would be received as the equivalent of cash in payment of customs taxes at Veracruz and Tampico. When presented at the customs houses, the value of each certificate would be enhanced by 6% and accepted at an exchange rate of five pesos to the pound sterling.

As additional security of the principal and interest of the consolidated debt, Mexico was to hypothecate especially 100 million acres of the vacant lands in the five departments already mentioned. If any of the said lands were sold, the money received would be sent to Lizardi who was to use it to redeem consolidated bonds. Holders of the new bonds could also exchange them for land warrants. Foreigners who established themselves on their properties under this scheme would be known as colonists. No individual would be allowed to hold more than "one square league of 5000 yards of land capable of irrigation, four square leagues of land fit for cultivation, and six leagues of pasture land." Mining rights and other privileges would be in conformity with relevant laws. Finally, the conversion was to be completed within one year of the date of publication in London of the 12 April decree.[72]

Lizardi announced its receipt of these proposals in *The Times* on 22 July 1837, followed two days later by an English translation of the 12 April decree. The city editor (24 July) gave a guarded welcome but added that "the real difficulty is that of reposing entire faith on the declarations of a Government which has so frequently failed in its engagements." Bondholders shared these doubts and they had the chance to express them at a public meeting on 9 August, held, as usual, at the London Tavern.[73] The meeting was chaired by George Robinson, Chairman of the Committee of Spanish American Bondholders. He began by explaining that detailed discussions had been held with Lizardi and he then read a statement from the company which sought to explain the proposals. According to this, the owner of an 1825 Six per Cent £100 bond with 23½ unpaid dividend coupons would receive £147 15s.:

One Six per Cent £100 bond	=	£112 10s.
23½ coupons of 30s. each	=	35 5s.
		£147 15s.

One-half to be paid in new Consolidated Bonds	=	£73 17s.6d.
One-half in land warrants	=	£73 17s.6d.

Five percent interest on £73 17s.6d. was £3 13s.10d. "or nearly 15% on the entire present value of the £100 bond" (the 1825 Six per Cents were around 25 at this time).

The annual interest charge on the debt was now at approximately £500,000. Mexico could not meet that yearly obligation; hence the idea of converting half the capital into land which, if accepted, would leave an interest burden of £250,000 which could be met from the one-sixth allocation of customs duties. In addition, there were the customs certificates to be given if dividends were not paid and which could easily be sold to merchants and exporters.

The remainder of Lizardi's memorandum concentrated on the excellent prospects for Mexico's economy once the dispute with Texas had been settled. Finally, the government was willing to assign millions of acres of land to the bondholders. If political and military circumstances meant that the land could not be in Texas, "there is a tract of country between Rio del Norte and Rio Nueces fronting one hundred miles on the Mexican Gulf and extending back to the mountains, containing about 30,000,000 acres and being still vacant, could be appropriated to the bondholders."[74] The area had rich, fertile soil suited to the production of cotton, rice, tobacco, timber, and all kinds of livestock.

It seemed a tempting prospect that was being put to the bondholders, but few at the meeting were impressed. Some urged total rejection while others thought that parts of the offer were acceptable. All appreciated, of course, that by offering land in the northern departments, Mexico hoped to attract British settlers and, therefore, British protection against the expansionist ambitions of the United States. In particular, the Mexicans hoped to win support for their efforts to regain control of Texas. The offer of land in Texas was criticized by British supporters of its independence, and the Texan representative in London, General J. Pinkney Henderson, warned in letters to the Foreign Office and to Lizardi that no land transactions with the bondholders would be recognized.[75]

After more debate, the bondholders decided to refer the offer to a subcommittee for further examination and discussion with Lizardi and Iturbide. Their negotiations produced several agreed-upon changes which were incorporated into the subcommittee's report. It was presented to another general meeting of bondholders on 5 September.[76] The main changes were that in place of land warrants for half the debt, bondholders would be given Deferred bonds which would pay no interest for ten years until 1 October 1847 when they would become "Active" and pay 5%. These Deferred bonds, however, could also be used to buy lands at the rate indicated in the 12 April decree, that is, at 5 shillings an acre. If used for land purchase, the value of the bonds would be increased at the rate of 5% per annum as from 1 October 1837. Second, 25 million acres in departments nearest to the Atlantic were to be "specially and exclusively held open for the location of deferred bonds, when lands are applied for in exchange." Third, the customs certificates were to be enhanced by 10% rather than 6%, as previously offered. Finally, the allocation of one-sixth of customs duties at Veracruz and Tampico for the dividend fund was restated, as was the mortgage of "the whole revenues of the state, as provided in the original bonds."

After long debate, and much opposition, the bondholders voted to accept these amended terms for the conversion. A week later, on 14 September 1837, a formal agreement was signed by Iturbide and Lizardi on behalf of the Mexican government, and by seven of the principal bondholders, led by Robinson.[77]

Ratification in Mexico was seriously delayed by the so-called Pastry War of 1838. In February of that year, the French government demanded that

Mexico should pay compensation for losses suffered by its citizens in civil and military disturbances since independence. One of the demands was for the obviously excessive amount of 60,000 pesos claimed by a French pastry chef—hence the name given to the conflict. Mexico refused and a French fleet blockaded the Gulf ports for several months. After unsuccessful talks in November, the French ships opened fire and quickly captured Veracruz. War was declared by Mexico in early December but the arrival of a British fleet enabled and encouraged both sides to resume talks. A settlement was reached in March 1839.

The French blockade and hostilities delayed ratification of the agreement with the bondholders but after pressure from the British government, the Mexican Executive recommended approval to Congress in December 1838. Six months later, on 1 June 1839, Congress gave its assent and regulations for the conversion were finally published on 29 July.[78] These contain many relatively minor adjustments. For example, an English acre was defined as "4840 English yards," and much attention is given to the management and recording of the customs certificates. No total sum was included for the external debt but Article 19 stipulates that "the issue of new bonds shall be limited to the precise sum required to satisfy the amount of the old bonds, with arrears."

The bondholders calculated the total debt to be £9,247,378 8s.6d. This included the nominal value of all the remaining 1824 Five per Cents; 1825 Six per Cents; 1831 Deferred Five and Six per Cents; and dividend coupons in arrears. All of these securities were to be exchanged for new bonds of the Five per Cent Consolidated Fund. Bondholders received half the value of their old stock in the new Active bonds paying 5% interest from 1 October 1837, and half in Deferred stock, paying no interest until 1 October 1847. The exchange or conversion was completed by the deadline of October 1840, after which the old stock was no longer quoted on the Stock Exchange. As explained earlier, the actual cancellation of the original bonds and coupons took place at the Bank of England in 1844.

Lizardi had begun to release the new bonds in October 1837. The following numbers were printed:

Active Series A	10,400 bonds numbered 1–10,400 each of £100	
Active Series B	4,900 bonds numbered 1–4,900 each of £150	
Active Series C	5,000 bonds numbered 1–5,000 each of £250	
Active Series D	4,950 bonds numbered 1–4,950 each of £500	
	25,250 bonds with a total value of £5,500,000.	

Deferred bonds of the same series, numbers, and values were also printed but not all were put into circulation.

No example of an Active bond has been found but several of the Deferred have survived. Some have been sold in London in recent years and others remain in the Barings Archive. They were printed in London in black ink on white paper. Illustration 4 reproduces the main page of an A Series bond for £100 which also served as a land warrant entitling the owner to 400 acres at the agreed price of 5 shillings an acre. As stated in the final paragraph, the owner had exchanged £200 worth of securities for this bond and one of the Active series of £100.

The bond illustrated is dated 30 September 1837 and bears the signatures of Iturbide and Lizardi. All 50,500 bonds that were produced had the same date and signatures. They were delivered to Lizardi by the printer in batches and the signing process presumably took place over several months between October 1837 and April 1838 when Iturbide resigned. As the General Purposes Committee of the Stock Exchange noted in 1842, the bonds were unusual in that they "neither specify the quantity, nor the numbers of the respective series, as has been used in similar cases."[79]

The reverse side of all the bonds has the text of the 12 April 1837 decree in both Spanish and English and also, but only in English, the text of the agreement signed on 14 September 1837. There are various elaborate designs, one of which from a £500 bond of the D series is shown in Illustration 5. Finally, the bonds have attached to them a sheet of interest coupons. Examples of these, again from a D Series, are illustrated in Chapter 2.

One difficulty which often occurred with the debt conversions was that the value placed on the old stock and coupons did not correspond to the face value of the new bonds. For example, in this conversion the owner of an 1825 Six per Cent with 23½ coupons was offered £147 15s., half in Active bonds worth £73 17s.6d. and the other half in Deferred worth the same amount. The new stocks were priced in values of £100 upwards and hence the £73 17s.6d. was insufficient for a new bond. Two solutions were possible. Dividend coupons were traded in the market separately from the bonds and a bondholder could buy more coupons to increase his £73 17s.6d. to the £100 necessary for a new bond. Alternatively, anticipating the problem, the Financial Agent provided what were usually known as fractional certificates which were given in exchange for securities whose value did not reach £100. The next Illustration (6) is a fractional certificate and land warrant issued by Lizardi on 8 September 1840. It is Number 52, List 615, value £35 or 140 acres. It was printed by Whiting in black ink on white paper.

Finally, the 1837 Active and Deferred bonds were quoted on the Stock Exchange from November 1839 until July 1846 when the next conversion began. Almost all were withdrawn from the market and exchanged for the new 1846 Five per Cents. The whole process took several years to complete. The Financial Agent, managing the conversion, sent monthly reports to Mexico detailing the bonds received and cancelled. By October 1849, for example, £10,496,990 worth had been "brought in and cancelled" and

4. 1837 Five per Cent Deferred Bond.

5. Motif from 1837 Five per Cent Deferred Bond.

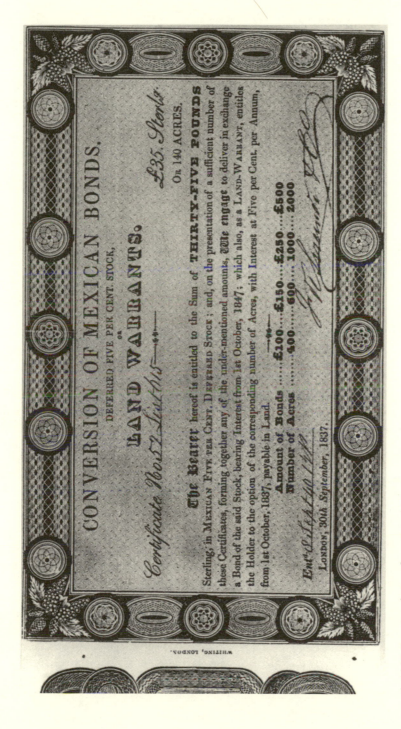

6. 1837 Fractional Certificate/Land Warrant.

Table 5
1837 Active Five per Cents

		J	F	M	A	M	J	J	A	S	O	N	D
1839	H	-	-	-	-	-	-	-	-	-	-	29	28
	L	-	-	-	-	-	-	-	-	-	-	28	27
1840	H	30	29	30	29	34	34	33	31	28	27	30	30
	L	28	28	29	28	29	32	31	30	25	25	27	27
1841	H	29	28	30	31	29	28	27	26	26	25	25	27
	L	28	27	27	29	28	26	25	25	25	23	24	25
1842	H	30	36	42	42	38	37	36	36	36	33	33	32
	L	28	30	36	35	33	36	36	34	34	32	30	30
1843	H	32	32	31	30	30	29	32	37	37	34	32	31
	L	31	30	29	29	28	28	28	32	33	29	29	30
1844	H	34	35	36	36	35	35	36	36	37	35	36	37
	L	32	34	34	35	35	34	35	35	35	34	34	35
1845	H	36	36	37	38	38	38	37	36	34	32	31	31
	L	34	34	36	35	36	37	36	34	32	30	28	29
1846	H	32	31	31	32	33	30	27	-	-	-	-	-
	L	30	30	30	31	29	27	26	-	-	-	-	-

£7,920,000 of the new stock issued in exchange. The conversion continued into 1851 and on 14 April of that year, the Chargé d'Affaires, José María Mendoza, left the cancelled bonds at the Bank of England in "Fifteen Tin Boxes lettered in front 'Mexican Stock' and sealed with the seal of the Legation of Mexico."[80] Two years later, tardy bondholders were still presenting their bonds and on 26 April 1853 a "Paper Parcel" marked "£18,600 Mexican Old Stock of 1837" was also deposited at the Bank.[81] (Tables 5 and 6 give the prices.)

CUSTOMS CERTIFICATES AND DEBENTURES

The third article of the September 1837 agreement stipulated that if future half-yearly dividends were not paid within ten days of the due date, bondholders had the right to exchange their dividend coupons for customs certificates, obtainable from Lizardi. These certificates were to have the same cash value as the coupons plus a 10% premium to cover exchange costs and any other expenses. They could be used at the ports of Veracruz and Tampico as the equivalent of cash in payment of one-sixth of import taxes.

As previously explained, the Pastry War and related factors both delayed

Table 6
1837 Deferred Five per Cents

		J	F	M	A	M	J	J	A	S	O	N	D
1839	H	-	-	-	-	-	-	-	-	-	-	9	8
	L	-	-	-	-	-	-	-	-	-	-	9	7
1840	H	9	9	9	9	10	9	9	9	8	9	10	10
	L	8	8	8	9	8	9	8	8	6	6	8	9
1841	H	9	9	10	10	9	9	8	8	8	8	7	9
	L	9	9	9	9	9	8	8	8	8	7	7	7
1842	H	9	10	12	12	11	10	9	9	9	9	9	9
	L	8	9	10	10	9	10	9	9	9	9	8	8
1843	H	9	9	9	8	8	8	9	10	10	9	10	9
	L	8	8	8	8	8	8	8	9	9	9	9	9
1844	H	10	12	16	17	15	15	16	16	15	15	16	17
	L	9	10	12	15	15	14	15	15	15	15	15	15
1845	H	16	17	17	19	18	21	21	20	18	17	17	18
	L	15	15	16	16	17	17	20	19	16	16	15	15
1846	H	18	17	16	17	17	17	16	-	-	-	-	-
	L	16	16	16	16	15	15	15	-	-	-	-	-

ratification of the 1837 agreement until 1839 and seriously interrupted maritime trade through the Gulf ports. Import duties were not collected and the proportion of them assigned to servicing the external debt could not be remitted to England. Hence, by the time the agreement was ratified in 1839 and the news had reached London, four interest payments had been missed. Bondholders promptly demanded the customs certificates from Lizardi. Clearly, having anticipated this demand, Lizardi had had them printed in advance. It began to release them almost at once in exchange for the four coupons for April and October 1838 and the same for 1839. Batches were regularly sent to Murphy for his signature and by December 1839, certificates worth £95,310 had already been presented at Veracruz.[82] By the end of 1841, those presented amounted to £272,666.[83]

No examples of these certificates have been found but the Mexican government's instructions indicate their format. Each included details of the dividend coupons for which they were exchanged and the cash value. They were signed by Lizardi and Murphy and each was numbered "in strict numerical order." They were payable to the Bearer, who was to meet any insurance or other costs, and they had "such marks and checks considered necessary to prevent errors or fraud."[84] When they were presented at Veracruz, the holder was given a receipt indicating the taxes for which they were being accepted in payment.

There are a large number of these receipts in the Veracruz customs archive, now in the Archivo General, Galería 6, Aduanas, vol.1051 (1840), but, unfortunately, the certificates have disappeared. From Alamán's account which is dated 19 April 1842, we know that numbers 1–343 were issued. Two years later, an irate bondholder complained in a letter to *The Morning Herald* (11 July 1844) that another £25,000 worth had just been released. He wrote that "The unfairness of this mode of payment has been made manifest over and over again, independent of the confusion which grows out of it." His complaint of unfairness referred to a problem to which *The Times* (11 June 1840) had already drawn attention. This was that those bondholders who lived in London or had the right connections or contacts were able to sell their certificates to merchants trading with Mexico. Many bondholders, however, as *The Times* pointed out, neither lived in London nor had contacts with the mercantile community. They, "the country holders of Mexican securities," were very aggrieved because they lacked the opportunity to acquire the certificates, and even those fortunate enough to get some found that they were only offered about half their face value in London. The result was discrimination in that some bondholders were receiving their dividends in cash via the certificates while others received nothing. There was, as R.C. Wyllie, a bondholder and member of the Committee of Spanish American Bondholders, put it, "a certain confusion . . . , placing different bondholders on an unequal footing."[85]

By March 1840, it was clear to Lizardi and the bondholders that a solution to the problems arising from the customs certificates had to be found. The bondholders' committee met several times to discuss the situation and on 14 April 1840, the chairman, still G.R. Robinson, submitted a list of proposals to Murphy.[86] In brief, he suggested another capitalization of the dividend arrears with new Five per Cent bonds which would be exchanged for the four unpaid coupons since April 1838. The use of these additional bonds would increase the size of the principal debt and therefore the interest on it. To meet this extra interest, the proportion of customs duties assigned to the dividend fund should be raised from one-sixth to one-fifth.

Murphy had been sending letters to the press under the pseudonym "Un Mexicano" to defend his country against bondholders' accusations of dishonesty and bad faith in not fulfilling the 1837 agreement.[87] He now welcomed the new proposals and urged his government to accept them. He, and Lizardi, also agreed with Robinson that the customs certificates should be restricted and only given in exchange for the coupon due in April 1838, rather than on all the coupons in arrears.[88]

The Mexican government considered the proposals and put to Congress in January 1841 its own ideas for the capitalization of the arrears. Several months later, on 3 August 1841, Congress approved a decree by which the proportion of customs duties assigned to the external debt was increased to one-fifth or 20%. This decree, however, was not published because the government hoped, and instructed Lizardi accordingly, that it could be used to extract concessions from the bondholders. Lizardi was told to argue that as Mexico was reducing its own revenues by giving more taxes to dividends, it was expected that the bondholders would respond by agreeing to a reduction of the debt. In fact, the decree did not remain secret for very long because the bondholders' agents in Mexico City, the firm of Manning and Marshall, reported its contents to London early in September 1841.

Over following months Lizardi negotiated with the bondholders' committee and on 10 February 1842, an agreement was reached. This was considered and approved the next day at a general meeting. All the main newspapers of the time carried the full text of the agreement and generally welcomed it.[89] Murphy was so pleased that he sent several newspaper cuttings back to Mexico.[90] One of those he sent was *The Morning Chronicle*, 12 February 1842, which in addition to the full text, contained the following succinct summary:

The claim for one-half the overdue dividends is to be abandoned, and debentures to be issued against the Coupons for the other half. No special fund is set apart from [*sic*] these debentures, but they are to be liquidated out of such surplus as may accumulate occasionally from that proportion of the custom-house revenue of Mexico set apart for the payment of regular dividends, such surplus to be divisible whenever its amount shall be equal to a payment of five per cent among the holders. In consideration of this surrender of one-half of the dividends in arrear and acceptance of debentures so to be discharged for the remainder, Mexico covenants to make over one-fifth instead of one-sixth of the customs revenue for securing the more punctual payment of future accruing dividends in regular order. Messrs Lizardi engage to use their best offices with the Mexican Government for procuring a larger allocation out of the customs revenue than one-fifth for the purpose of paying off the debentures but, should these not be paid off by the 1st of April, 1845, they are to bear interest from that date; and should the next four regular dividends fail to be paid in course, then the debentures are to be considered as representing the whole amount of dividends in arrear, instead of the one-half as now agreed upon.

In sum, this meant that the bondholders gave up their entitlement to four of the eight half-yearly dividends in arrears since April 1838. In exchange for the remaining four coupons, they were to accept non-interest-bearing Debentures. Bondholders who had already taken customs certificates for their coupons had to present those not yet due from 1842 and 1843 to make up the minimum of eight required. In this way, as the agreement stated, "the concession be made equally by all."

Illustrations 7 and 8 reproduce Debenture number 299 for £25, dated 1 April 1842. It is signed by Manuel Lizardi and as stated, it was exchanged for dividend warrants worth £50. The reverse (Illustration 8) was intended to record the staged liquidation of the Debenture with occasional payments

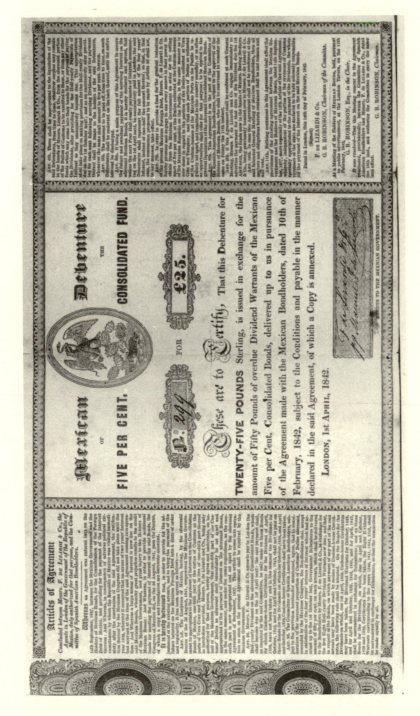

7. 1842 Debenture.

MEXICAN DEBENTURE FOR £25.

N°.

1	Paid on the within Debenture, Five per Cent.	. . . .	£
	London,		
2	Paid on the within Debenture, Five per Cent.	. . . .	£
	London,		
3	Paid on the within Debenture, Five per Cent.	. . . .	£
	London,		
4	Paid on the within Debenture, Five per Cent.	. . . .	£
	London,		
5	Paid on the within Debenture, Five per Cent.	. . . .	£
	London,		
6	Paid on the within Debenture, Five per Cent.	. . . .	£
	London,		
7	Paid on the within Debenture, Five per Cent.	. . . .	£
	London,		
8	Paid on the within Debenture, Five per Cent.	. . . .	£
	London,		
9	Paid on the within Debenture, Five per Cent.	. . . .	£
	London,		
10	Paid on the within Debenture, Five per Cent.	. . . .	£
	London,		
11	Paid on the within Debenture, Five per Cent.	. . . .	£
	London,		
12	Paid on the within Debenture, Five per Cent.	. . . .	£
	London,		
13	Paid on the within Debenture, Five per Cent.	. . . .	£
	London,		
14	Paid on the within Debenture, Five per Cent.	. . . .	£
	London,		
15	Paid on the within Debenture, Five per Cent.	. . . .	£
	London,		
16	Paid on the within Debenture, Five per Cent.	. . . .	£
	London,		
17	Paid on the within Debenture, Five per Cent.	. . . .	£
	London,		
18	Paid on the within Debenture, Five per Cent.	. . . .	£
	London,		
19	Paid on the within Debenture, Five per Cent.	. . . .	£
	London,		
20	Paid on the within Debenture, Five per Cent.	. . . .	£
	London,		

£25.

£25.

£

8. 1842 Debenture (reverse).

Table 7
1842 Debentures

		J	F	M	A	M	J	J	A	S	O	N	D
1842	H	-	-	-	25	20	19	19	18	/	14	12	/
	L	-	-	-	18	17	16	16	18	/	13	12	/
1843	H	9	9	9	8	8	8	9	10	10	9	10	9
	L	8	8	8	8	8	8	8	9	9	9	9	9
1844	H	10	12	16	17	15	15	16	16	15	15	16	17
	L	9	10	12	15	15	14	15	15	15	15	15	15
1845	H	/	/	/	/	11	14	/	/	9	/	/	/
	L	/	/	/	/	11	12	/	/	8	/	/	/
1846	H	/	/	/	16	14	15	-	-	-	-	-	-
	L	/	/	/	16	8	15	-	-	-	-	-	-

of 5% of its value whenever "sufficient surplus had accrued in the dividend fund"—hence the twenty sections shown in the illustration.

The number of Debentures distributed to the bondholders is not known (the author also has a copy of number 699) but their total value amounted to £499,096 which equalled half the dividend arrears of £998,192. Their face values varied from £10 to £100. William Smythe, for example, who lived at 22 John Street, Bedford Row, received, in exchange for interest coupons, 514 Debentures with a total face value of £40,000, as follows:

351 of £100
42 of £50
35 of £30
25 of £25
47 of £20
9 of £15
5 of £10

Given the large amount involved, Smythe was probably acting on behalf of clients rather than solely on his own account.[91]

The Debentures remained in circulation until the next conversion in 1846 when they were withdrawn and cancelled. They were kept in the "Fifteen Tin Boxes" deposited by Mendoza in the Bank of England in 1851. Recognized as legitimate securities by the Stock Exchange, they were traded in the market, although demand was small and prices always low. (Table 7 gives the prices.)

CLANDESTINE 1837 BONDS

One unusual feature of the 1837 bonds is that they do not contain the customary details of the series, letters, numbers, and value of the whole issue. According to the 1837 agreement, the debt was £9,247,937. The issue, therefore, should have consisted of Active bonds for half that amount or £4,623,968, and of Deferred bonds for the same sum. The final paragraph of the text of the bond specifically states that "this Bond is issued by us in consideration of having received, for the purpose of Conversion, Bonds of the Mexican Government proceeding from the loans effected in London." This clause reflected Article 19 of the Mexican law of 29 July 1839, which had ratified the terms of the conversion:

The issue of new Bonds shall be limited to the precise sum required to satisfy the amount of old Bonds with arrears etc. which shall be presented for Conversion, so that there shall never be issued one new Bond, except to replace an old one.

In short, new bonds were only to be released in exchange for old and the total of both Active and Deferred should not exceed the recognized debt of £9,247,937.

In November 1842, however, rumors began to circulate in London that Lizardi had placed in the market more bonds than were needed to redeem the debt. An unnamed member of the Stock Exchange brought these rumors to the attention of the General Purposes Committee on 22 November. Over the next ten days, an extraordinary exchange of letters—at times two or three a day—took place between the Committee's secretary, James Van Sommer, George Robinson for the Committee of Spanish American Bondholders, and Lizardi.[92] Robinson and the Stock Exchange demanded that Lizardi should publish the series, numbers, and values of all the bonds both Active and Deferred which had been placed in the market. At first, Lizardi refused but then replied that Iturbide had given it £5,500,000 worth of bonds of each type or £11,000,000 in total. All were dated 30 September and had been signed by Iturbide. Of the Actives, Lizardi stated that "the following numbers of each series are all which can be issued":

No. 1 to 10,300 of £100 each	£1,030,000
No. 1 to 4,800 of 150 each	720,000
No. 1 to 4,800 of 250 each	1,200,000
No. 1 to 4,900 of 500 each	2,450,000
Total	£5,400,000

The amount in circulation at present, Lizardi added, was £5,254,500.

There was no reference to the Deferred stock but further insistent requests from the Stock Exchange persuaded Lizardi to affirm that "the amount of Bonds of the Deferred Debt, deposited with us, is £5,400,000, bearing the same numbers as those of the Active Debt . . . the amount issued by us of the Deferred Stock is £4,615,600." Lizardi refused all further requests to provide details of the exact numbers and series of the bonds and Debentures in circulation.

The situation was, therefore, that Lizardi had sold several hundred thousand pounds worth of Active bonds more than was needed to convert the debt. Its explanation for this was that its commission had to be added to the debt total of £9,247,937 and that "the amount of our commission is provided for in the aforesaid creation of Bonds for £5,400,000."

The Stock Exchange Committee decided to take no action in the matter other than to publish all the correspondence for the information of the public at large and the bondholders in particular. The press was very critical of Lizardi's conduct. *The Times* (2 December 1842), for example, noted the company's "bad faith" and "deceit" and attacked the brokers who had acted for the sale of the stock: "they no doubt invented, day after day, excuses, all lies of course, for such a constant supply of the article." The bondholders' Committee sent a protest to Mexico to which they received no reply and at a public meeting on 9 May 1843, at the London Tavern, Lizardi's conduct was bitterly condemned. Robinson explained to the large number of bondholders present that the excess issue of "surreptitious bonds" had caused a severe decline in the market price from around 40 in April to less than 30 in November 1842. Furthermore, the addition to the principal of the debt represented by the excess bonds meant that the amount needed to pay the annual dividend had risen by £31,527.[93]

The May meeting had been called to consider a proposal which Lizardi had recently made to pay the April 1843 dividend with one-third in cash and two-thirds in Deferred bonds. The offer was rejected by the meeting, but subsequently, many bondholders took advantage of it with the result that a further £91,650 worth of Deferred stock entered the market. Then another dispute with the company arose over the dividend fund accounts when Lizardi insisted that it only had sufficient funds to pay half the October dividend. Murphy sided with the bondholders and joined in their and the press's criticism of the company. Finally, in a letter of 14 September, Lizardi revealed that the total of Active stock in circulation had risen to £5,500,000 or £100,000 more than a few months earlier.[94] The Actives were now as follows:

1 to	10,400 of £100	£1,040,000
1 to	4,900 of £150	735,000
1 to	5,000 of £250	1,250,000
1 to	4,950 of £500	2,475,000
	25,250	£5,500,000

This new revelation incensed the bondholders and the city editors even more. At another public meeting on 6 October 1843, Lizardi's actions were condemned by every speaker. According to James Capel, its conduct was "atrocious"; for Albert Levy, it was "robbery"; and for David Salomons, it was "criminal."[95] The bondholders appealed to the Foreign Office for help and Lord Aberdeen ordered the British Chargé d'Affaires in Mexico City, Percy Doyle, "to use his good offices, as far as may be proper, on behalf of the Mexican bondholders."[96] *The Standard* (7 October 1843) referred to Lizardi's "dirty work" and urged the Stock Exchange Committee to ascertain "if the statute of frauds will not reach the original delinquents." In the face of this widespread protest, the Stock Exchange intervened to order that dealings in the £100,000 excess bonds would not be recognized and no buyer was obliged to accept them.

Murphy shared the bondholders' anger at Lizardi, whom he accused of defrauding the Mexican government, and he sent press cuttings and the Stock Exchange resolutions to his Foreign Ministry.[97] The Mexican government responded with the law of 15 December 1843, which was intended to draw the various strands of the external debt together into a coherent and concise account. The debt now recognized by Mexico was stated to be as follows:

Active Bonds

Series:

A	10,400 bonds numbered 1–10,400, each of £100 =	£1,040,000
B	4,900 bonds numbered 1–4,900, each of £150 =	735,000
C	5,000 bonds numbered 1–5,000, each of £250 =	1,250,000
D	4,950 bonds numbered 1–4,950, each of £500 =	2,475,000
	25,250 bonds	£5,500,000

Deferred bonds converted to Active	£ 91,650
Deferred bonds, same letters etc. as Actives	4,624,000
	£10,215,650

Debentures issued at 50% for eight coupons worth £998,192	£499,096
1843 bonds	£200,000

The next rescheduling of the debt took place in 1846, and the sums recognized in the December 1843 decree given above formed the basis of that conversion. The total of Deferred bonds recognized, however, was £4,624,000 which was half the debt of £9,248,000 accepted in the 1837 agreement. Lizardi had already disclosed that the number of Deferred printed and signed amounted to £5,500,000. Hence, there was an excess of £876,000 of which £91,650 had been used to pay the April 1843 dividend. In short, there was an outstanding surplus of Deferred bonds with a face value of £784,350. Their fate is discussed in a later section.

1843 FIVE PER CENTS

The commission paid to bankers or financial agents for arranging a conversion or managing a dividend fund was usually 1–1½%. Lizardi, however, successfully argued for a much higher rate for its work with both the 1837 conversion and the 1842 Debentures. Both commissions proved to be controversial with consequences for bondholders that were to last for almost fifty years. The controversy over the 1837 conversion and Lizardi's method of ensuring its commission has been indicated in the previous section on the clandestine bonds. Here, our concern is with the Debentures. On 10 October 1842, Lizardi was awarded a commission of 5%, amounting to approximately £50,000, for having arranged the February 1842 agreement whereby interest arrears of almost £1,000,000 were converted into Debentures. The money for this commission was to be obtained either by additional assignments on the customs revenues or by the issue of more Active Five per Cent bonds. Having allegedly paid generous bribes in Mexico to President Santa Anna and others, Lizardi was allowed to choose which payment method it preferred.[98] Subsequent Mexican decrees confirmed the commission and on 28 July 1843, the amount of any new bonds to be issued was restricted to a par value of £200,000. This total was based on the assumption that the bonds would be sold at about 25 (compared to the 30 which the 1837 Active Five per Cents were fetching at the time) and thus the £50,000 commission would be met. Finally, the general decree on the external debt of 15 December 1843 confirmed the £200,000 figure.

Lizardi opted for the bond issue and early in 1844, 1,500 were printed by C. Whiting as follows:

Series A   1,000 bonds numbered 1–1,000 each of £100

Series B   500 bonds numbered 1–500 each of £200

The next Illustration (9) reproduces the main page of a bond of the B series for £200. It is printed in blue ink on a white background.

As can be seen, the bond has the text of the 28 July 1843 decree in both English and Spanish, together with a notarial "attestation" by A. de Pinna confirming the authenticity of the original Spanish and the translation. The main text asserts that the payment of principal and interest was by means

9. 1843 Five per Cent Bond.

of a charge of 5% on the import taxes paid at ports in both the Gulf of Mexico and on the Pacific coast, namely, Veracruz, Tampico, Guaymas, Mazatlán, and San Blas. Although the bond is dated 1 October 1843, the 5% annual interest is backdated to start on 1 October 1842. The interest warrants also reflect this date. There is a sheet of fifty half-yearly coupons, the final one being due on 1 October 1867. Hence, the bond was for a twenty-five-year term, maturing at the same time as the thirty-year bonds issued in the 1837 agreement. Finally, the bond does not have the required signatures and that of Lizardi on the main page has been crossed out. There are two reasons for this omission. First, this particular bond was probably sent to Mexico as an example of the issue rather than being sold in the market. It is now in the archive of the Mexican Foreign Office.[99] The second reason, however, is possibly more significant. Lizardi had the bonds printed early in 1844 and asked Murphy to sign them in his capacity as Minister Plenipotentiary. Murphy refused to comply with this request on the grounds that the firm had already been paid sufficient commission for work on the conversions. Then, in February and March 1844, a broker, Stephen Cannon, tried to persuade the Stock Exchange General Purposes Committee to grant the bonds an official quotation. At first, he said he had acquired a "£500 Mexican 5 pc Stock of 1842." He failed to produce the bond (none of that value had been printed), but he did subsequently present Bond number 201 for £200. The Committee required him to disclose the name of his Principal or the person on whose behalf he had acquired the bond. When he refused to reveal the name, his request was refused, probably because the Committee suspected collusion with Lizardi.[100] Finally, Lizardi referred the matter to Mexico and the government ratified the loan issue and the commission on 29 June 1844. Murphy, however, persisted in his opposition, still refusing to sign the bonds. According to his own very detailed explanation of the dispute, he heard no more from Lizardi about the unsigned bonds.[101]

Three years later, in 1847, Murphy was replaced as Minister by the prominent Mexican liberal, José María Luis Mora. He took up his post in March and was immediately confronted with a demand to sign the bonds. The London stockbrokers, Sheppard & Son, had written to the Legation a few weeks earlier to explain that on 30 November 1843, they had entered into a contract with Lizardi to buy for one of their clients the whole of the £200,000 bond issue. They enclosed copies of the various decrees and ministerial orders relating to the bonds and insisted that there was no reason not to sign them.[102] Mora sought instructions from Mexico and after receiving approval to proceed, he reported in September that he had signed the £200,000 bonds of the 1843 issue.

What happened to the now signed and therefore negotiable bonds immediately thereafter is not clear, but it seems that Sheppard & Son had acquired them on behalf of a New Orleans–based partnership by the name of D.G. Masson and Company. In 1848, Masson asked the Mexican government to redeem £500,000 worth of bonds; £300,000 of these were 1837 Deferred but the other £200,000 comprised the entire 1843 issue.[103] Like many others at that time, including the British bondholders, Masson tried to take advantage of the fact that Mexico was to receive an indemnity of 15,000,000 dollars from the United States following the end of the United States–Mexican war of 1846–1848. His claim was based on the argument that as Mexico had ceded about half of its national territory to the United States, including Texas, California, and other areas north of the Rio Bravo, the security or mortgage for its loans was invalidated. Hence, Mexico was bound to pay off its creditors. Mora and others submitted long reports on the claim advising rejection on several grounds and, in December 1848, a congressional committee on Public Credit reached the same conclusion. Although Masson himself apparently died at Veracruz on the way to Mexico City to press his claim, the U.S. Legation in the capital both in 1850 and 1852 continued to argue his case, but with no success.[104]

The 1843 bonds then disappeared. They were not included in subsequent conversions and they were not quoted on the Stock Exchange. In fact, no more was heard of them until 1884. In that year, a provisional agreement was reached between bondholders and Mexican representatives for another rescheduling of the debt. The agreement was not ratified for various reasons including protests against it from several interested parties. One such protest came in the form of a letter to the Stock Exchange Committee from the London firm of solicitors, Foss and Ledsam, whose office was at 3 Abchurch Lane. It revealed that the firm represented holders of unredeemed 1837 Deferred stock and of 1843 bonds "which latter are not even mentioned in the agreement." There had been no consultation with these bondholders and they would not accept the proposed agreement.[105]

Again, nothing more was heard of the 1843 bonds until two years later. On 23 June 1886, an agreement was signed between representatives of the bondholders and General Francisco Mena on behalf of the Mexican government for the final redemption of all outstanding bonds, coupons, and certificates which had arisen from the original loans of 1824 and 1825. This settlement, soon known as the Dublán conversion, will be examined in a later section. Surprisingly, the 1843 bonds were still not mentioned. Foss and Ledsam had written to Mena on 20 May 1886 to argue the case for their inclusion. They did not reveal the identity of their clients who held them except to say that the current holders were not connected to those persons who had acquired the bonds when they were first issued. They suggested that they should be treated in the same way as other holders of Mexican stocks.[106] Their case was not at first accepted by Mena and in a letter to *The Times* (25 June 1886), Foss and Ledsam argued that the terms offered in the agreement signed on the twenty-third were inadequate. They invited all dissatisfied bondholders to contact them "with a view to concerted action" to achieve a better deal. Three days later, the firm summoned a public meeting of bondholders to be held at the Cannon Street hotel on 30 June.[107] At the meeting, Mr. Foss announced that in addition to representing owners of 1837 stock, his firm was also acting on behalf of the holders of £199,500 worth of the 1843 bonds. They had not received, he said, a penny in interest in almost fifty years and they had now been unfairly omitted from the recent settlement. Legal opinion had been sought from Sir Richard Webster whose advice was that the bonds remained valid.[108]

Reporting the meeting a few days later, *The Bullionist* (3 July 1886) noted that the 1843 bonds "are held exclusively by American citizens." Unfortunately, no details of the identity of these American holders were revealed and we cannot know if there was any link with Masson and his associates of New Orleans and their claim of 1848.

Foss and Ledsam began negotiations with the Mexican government representatives in London. On 16 November 1886, they summoned a meeting of the holders of the 1843 bonds at their office to consider an offer to settle the issue received from the Mexicans.[109] Foss chaired the meeting and since, as he repeated, he represented holders of £199,500 worth of the stock, it is unlikely that more than a couple of other holders were present. At any rate, the arrangement he had reached with the Mexican Financial Agency was accepted. Under its terms, holders of the 1843 bonds received 20% of their face or par value in the recently issued 1886 Three per Cent Consolidated Bonds. In addition, the overdue interest coupons were exchanged for the same new bonds at the rate of 9% of their nominal value. There were fifty coupons each worth £2 10s. or £125 in total, which at 9% gave £11 5s. Hence, the holder of an 1843 £100 bond, with all the coupons, received £31 5s. worth of 1886 Three per Cents. Eventually, £199,700 worth of the bonds were redeemed, leaving only £300 outstanding.[110] Those found in Mexico's Foreign Ministry Archive may include the missing bonds.[111]

1846 FIVE PER CENTS

The third rescheduling of Mexico's external debt was agreed upon in June 1846. During the previous two years, several plans for refunding the debt had been discussed in both London and Mexico City. These had concentrated on the 1837 Deferred stock on which interest was due to be paid from October 1847, that is, ten years after the 1837 agreement. The 1842 Debentures were also included in the discussions for two reasons. First, nothing had been paid on them and their market price was low. Second, they had been accepted by the bondholders in place of half the interest arrears. The other half of the arrears was written off but only on condition that future dividends were paid on time. If they were not, then the 50%

of arrears written off were reinstated. In other words, a £50 Debenture issued for £100 of arrears would double in value, at least nominally. Some dividends on the Active stock had been paid but by October 1844 arrears had again begun to accumulate.

As noted in an earlier section, the failure to pay dividends, together with more disputes over their commission and the surreptitious issue of extra bonds, had brought Lizardi into bitter wrangles with Murphy and the bondholders. Hence, it was no surprise that on 5 April 1845, the company's contract as Mexico's Financial Agent was terminated. Lizardi was replaced by John Schneider & Co., whose office was at New Broad Street Mews, London. Not much is known about the company. Although it was registered as company number 101705, it was subsequently dissolved and its records destroyed some time after 1857.[112] The two main partners were John Henry Powell Schneider and his son, Henry William Schneider. Both were active and prominent members of the London business community. John, for example, was chairman of the Anglo-Mexican Mint Company and of the Mexican and South American Company which was involved in copper smelting in Chile. Henry was also later chairman of the English and Australian Copper Company. Under the terms of their contract they became Mexico's Financial Agent in Europe, receiving 2½% commission on funds advanced to the country's European Legations. They were to receive all money shipped from Mexico, and act as agents in debt negotiations, as well as paying dividends.

Schneider's involvement with the Mexican debt seems to have originated in 1844. At that time, the Mexico City–based British firm, Manning and Mackintosh (formerly Manning and Marshall) appointed Schneider to be its agent in London. Robert Manning and Ewen Mackintosh were among Mexico's leading financiers and entrepreneurs with investments in many industrial and commercial activities, notably in the tobacco industry. They were also agents for the bondholders and Mackintosh had been appointed British Consul in Mexico City. Early in 1844, they began to put to the Mexican government various ideas for the flotation of a new loan designed to convert the 1837 Deferred stock and the 1842 Debentures.[113] They sent Mexico's best-known businessman and speculator, Manuel Escandón, to London to investigate the possibilities. He was soon in discussions with Schneider but the first proposals put forward all failed to make progress.

The failure of the first schemes did not obviate the need to sort out the question of the Deferred bonds and the Debentures. Consequently, on 28 April 1845, Congress authorized the Mexican Executive "to liquidate and definitively arrange the external debt." The decree imposed these restrictions: there was to be no capitalization of interest; no interest rate higher than 5%; no increase in the current legal size of the debt; no alienation of any national assets nor mortgage of all or part of national territory.

Murphy received his copy of this decree, with appropriate instructions from the Mexican Treasury, in the middle of June 1845. These told him that the aim was to refund the Deferred stock and the Debentures and that a commissioner would soon arrive in London to help him. This turned out to be William O'Brien. He had worked in the Mexican Legation in London in the 1820s when he had advised on the Goldsmidt loan.[114] Nothing is known about him thereafter except for the fact that he lived in Paris, and that he was handsomely rewarded with a fee of £2,132 for his help with the 1846 conversion.

Much of Murphy's time for the remainder of 1845 was taken up in consideration, and rejection, of the Manning and Mackintosh proposals, some of which had reached the stage of being signed as contracts between the company and the Mexican government.[115] Eventually, in January 1846, he was given broad powers to negotiate a settlement with the bondholders. He started discussions in London, but simultaneously more talks were going on in Mexico City with Manning and Mackintosh. These resulted in another contract, the main parts of which were incorporated in a decree on 5 March 1846. This stipulated the creation of a new consolidated fund of £4,650,000 for which bonds paying 5% annual interest were to be offered for sale in London. As security for the principal, amortization, and interest payments, there was to be a general mortgage of all of Mexico's revenues and a specific mortgage of those of the tobacco monopoly. Potential investors were promised that a monthly sum of £23,541 from the tobacco revenues would be remitted to Schneider for the dividend and Sinking Funds. The money raised by the sale of the new bonds was to be used to redeem the Deferred stock and the Debentures at the rate of 40%, that is, £40 worth of new bonds for £100 worth of Deferred and Debentures. Also, some of the money would be used to pay interest arrears on the 1837 Actives. The tax on silver exports out of Pacific coast ports was assigned to pay future dividends. This was additional to the 20% of import taxes at Veracruz and Tampico already allocated to the dividend fund.

Murphy received this new scheme on the packet steamer which arrived early in May 1846. He began discussions at once with Schneider and the bondholders' Committee. These led to a decision to summon a general meeting of bondholders for Monday, 18 May, at the London Tavern. In the days preceding the meeting, details of the proposals became known and as *The Times* put it on 15 May, "For some time past, there has not been a question discussed with so much interest in the city circles as that of the acceptance or rejection of the Mexican propositions." By the day of the meeting, it was clear that the bondholders were divided. The Tavern was "filled to overflowing" and the proceedings were "more stormy than any assembly of the kind that has taken place for years."[116] The main division of opinion was between Deferred and Active holders. The latter were in favor of the proposal but the former were very strongly opposed, largely on the grounds that their Deferred bonds were due to become Active and interest bearing in a year's time. They would then have the same nominal value as the Actives. To treat them differently, therefore, was unfair. Several other technical objections were raised concerning the allocation of dividend revenues between the two stocks. After some hours of noisy debate, the "share and share alike" principle which had been put by several speakers was accepted. A large majority voted to adjourn sine die, which meant in effect the rejection of the proposal.

After the meeting, leading bondholders "connected with the Stock Exchange" met and agreed on a revised scheme which they suggested to Murphy.[117] Their idea was to capitalize the whole debt, including Actives, Deferred, and Debentures. Murphy made an amended counteroffer and a new agreement was quickly reached. Another general meeting of bondholders was held on 4 June and it approved the new proposal.

The 1846 conversion, therefore, was agreed. Its terms were briefly the following. A new national consolidated debt to the amount of £10,241,650 was to be established with the issue of a corresponding amount of bonds in London. All existing Active and Deferred bonds and Debentures were to be exchanged for the new bonds. The Actives were to be converted at 90% of their face value and the Deferred and Debentures at 60%. These conversion rates included all interest arrears on the Actives, except for £2 10s. per cent which was to be paid in cash. As guarantees for the redemption of the principal and payment of interest at 5% per annum from 1 January 1847, there was a general pledge of all Mexico's revenues; a special assignment on the tobacco revenue; export duties on silver shipped from Pacific ports; one-fifth of import and export duties at Veracruz and Tampico. For the Sinking Fund, £100,000 per annum would be sent to London to be used to buy in bonds "at the market value." If the bonds were above par, those to be redeemed at par would be drawn by lot. Agents for the conversion were Schneider & Co., whose commission was fixed at 1%–1½%. Finally, Mexico agreed to pay all expenses, including exchange rate and other costs incurred in remitting payments to the dividend fund.

Two effects in particular of this conversion caused one Mexican to describe it as "one of the most advantageous and brilliant financial operations" ever achieved by Mexico.[118] The first was that the external debt was reduced. The existing debt recognized by all parties was that specified in the decree of 15 December 1843, with the exception of the £200,000 of 1843 bonds which Lizardi had been authorized to sell for its commission. These bonds had not been signed by Murphy and were not in circulation. The debt, therefore, was £11,204,015, inclusive of Active bonds (£5,500,000 plus £91,650 Deferred made Active); Deferred (£4,624,000); Debentures (£499,096); interest arrears (£489,269). The new debt was fixed at £10,241,650, a reduction of £962,365.[119]

The second cause for Mexican satisfaction was that because the existing stocks were to be converted at less than par, that is, at 90% and 60%, the value of the new bonds needed in exchange was only £8,106,295, leaving more than £2,000,000 worth of the new issue at the disposal of the Mexican government. It chose to sell them to Manning and Mackintosh in exchange for various internal credits, including tobacco bonds, and a small amount in cash. For their part, Manning and Mackintosh used the bonds in their own commercial and financial operations in London. In March 1849, for example, Schneider accepted bonds with a face value of £70,000 as security for drafts it held against the company. In December of the same year, Barings sold £70,000 worth in the market at prices ranging from 25 to 27, raising £18,662. Shortly afterwards, it sold another £4,032 worth "which completes the sales of this stock on your behalf." A few months later, Barings credited the company with a dividend payment on the bonds.[120]

Any additional funds available to the Mexican government at that time were especially important because of the outbreak of war with the United States, news of which had arrived in London at the end of May. Some bondholders had been skeptical that in the circumstances Mexico was hardly likely to be able to meet its obligations under the new conversion. Few bondholders, however, could have anticipated the bizarre reception which the June agreement had in Mexico City. Partly but not entirely caused by the war, there were frequent changes of administration in 1846. In August, following one such change, the federal form of government was reintroduced in place of centralism. That, allied to chronic internal party political strife, brought, if not chaos in government circles, then certainly a large degree of instability. In particular, ministerial changes were frequent, most notably in the Treasury. In 1846, there were no less than sixteen Finance Ministers and a further eight took the office between January and September 1847 when the U.S. army effectively ended the war by occupying Mexico City. The June agreement had reached Mexico City in August 1846, shortly after the new federal government had taken control. It rejected the agreement but two months later in October, a new Finance Minister gave it his approval. In November, his successor again rejected it, referring the whole external debt question to Congress. It was not until 19 July 1847 that the contract was finally ratified.

This chronic instability in Mexico City brought turmoil to London. Valentín Gómez Farías, the Minister who had rejected the contract on 28 August, accused both Murphy and Schneider of failing to safeguard Mexico's interests. He dismissed both from their posts. In place of Murphy, General José María Mendoza, recently named consul in London, was appointed interim Chargé d'Affaires until the arrival of the new incumbent. This was José María Luis Mora, who arrived from Paris in March 1847. Gómez Farías also sent his son, Benito, to London to supervise the removal of Schneider and to arrange new negotiations with the bondholders. Benito

and Mendoza were soon in league with Manuel Lizardi who was reap-
pointed as the Financial Agent.

Murphy refused to hand over the Legation to Mendoza; Schneider refused to give up the agency to Lizardi or to deliver to it any records. Mendoza started court proceedings against them. For their part, the
bondholders appealed to the British government for help and sought counsel's opinion as to the validity of the June contract. Queen's Advocates Dr.
Robert Phillimore and John Dodson concluded, "We are of the opinion
that by the law of nations neither of the contracting parties, without the
consent of the other, can recede from this engagement."[121]

Eventually, the situation settled down to some extent when Mora arrived
to take charge of the Legation. Both Schneider and Lizardi continued to
claim to be the Financial Agent but it was Schneider who carried out the
conversion. Murphy retired to Paris to write his account of the debt and
his role in all the negotiations since his arrival in London in 1837.

Unaware, of course, that all these complications were to ensue, Schneider
had started the exchange of new bonds for old soon after the agreement
of 4 June. As early as 6 July, the company announced in press notices that
the conversion would start on 15 July.[122] The half dividend of £2 10s. in
cash would also be paid at the same time.

The new bonds were printed by Whiting in the following series:

A　25,993 bonds numbered 1–25,993 each of £100

B　　8,949 bonds numbered 1–8,949 each of £150

C　　8,400 bonds numbered 1–8,400 each of £250

D　　8,400 bonds numbered 1–8,400 each of £500

51,742 bonds entered the market with a combined face value of
£10,241,650 which was now recognized as the total of the external debt.
Illustration 10 reproduces a bond of the A Series for £100.

This particular bond was found in the Mexican Foreign Office records
and there is another example of the A Series in Shropshire Records Office
and of the D Series for £500 in the Public Record Office.[123] All are printed
in black ink on white paper and it may be assumed that the other Series
were similar in this respect. None of the examples are signed either by
Murphy or the special commissioner, William O'Brien, because these were
specimen bonds rather than those sold in the market. The reverse has the
text of the decree of 28 April 1845 in Spanish and English in which the
Mexican government ordered the rescheduling of the debt. It also has, in
English only, the full text of the proposals accepted by the bondholders at
their meeting on 4 June 1846. As usual, there are elaborate designs on the
reverse.

The 1846 Five per Cents were first quoted on the Stock Exchange in July

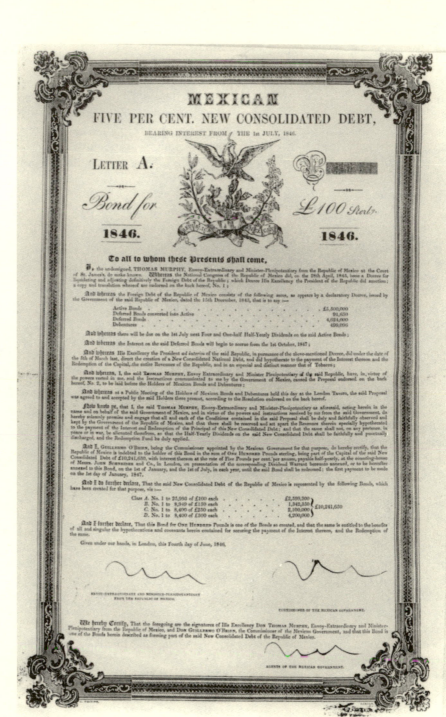

10. 1846 Five per Cent Bond.

Table 8
1846 Five per Cents

		J	F	M	A	M	J	J	A	S	O	N	D
1846	H	-	-	-	-	-	-	27	26	27	25	22	24
	L	-	-	-	-	-	-	25	22	24	21	21	22
1847	H	25	23	22	21	21	20	19	19	20	19	16	18
	L	21	21	21	20	19	19	18	17	18	15	15	16
1848	H	18	19	16	15	16	16	17	18	17	21	22	25
	L	17	17	14	13	15	14	16	16	16	18	21	22
1849	H	27	26	33	32	32	30	30	28	28	27	27	30
	L	24	25	26	29	29	29	27	27	27	26	25	27
1850	H	29	29	29	29	31	32	30	30	31	31	32	37
	L	29	29	29	28	28	29	29	29	29	31	30	32
1851	H	35	33	34	35	35	34	34	31	28	27	25	28
	L	32	33	33	33	34	34	30	28	25	25	23	23
1852	H	30	33	33	34	34	33	33	32	-	-	-	-
	L	27	30	30	32	31	30	32	32	-	-	-	-

1846. They remained in the official price list until August 1852 when they began to be withdrawn and exchanged for new Three per Cents under the terms of the next rescheduling of the debt. As usual, the cancelled bonds were placed in the Bank of England. On 12 January 1853, twenty-one "Deal Boxes" were deposited.[124] These contained 51,025 bonds which had been cancelled "by having a hole punched through."[125] Eventually, by 1857 (according to figures provided by Payno), of the 51,742 bonds originally printed, all but 249 with a face value of £30,600 had been cancelled. A few more trickled in in later years until by 1862 only £7,000 worth were thought to be outstanding.[126] This was a slight underestimation because almost forty years after they were first issued, another £10,750 worth of bonds and £10,742 of interest coupons were presented for redemption under the terms of the 1886 Dublán conversion.[127] (Table 8 gives the prices.)

1837 FIVE PER CENT DEFERRED: EXCESS BONDS

One not entirely unexpected consequence of the 1846 conversion was a prolonged controversy over the unauthorized sale of a number of 1837 Deferred bonds. The identity of those unlucky investors, who had acquired or bought the bonds in good faith, and their efforts to obtain redress from the Mexican authorities, will be described in another part of this study. It is convenient at this point, however, to outline the course of the dispute until its final resolution in the 1886 Dublán conversion.

Under the terms of the 1837 conversion, Lizardi had been authorized to issue Active and Deferred stock in equal amounts of £4,624,000. As noted earlier, the company had been given signed bonds of both types to a value of £5,500,000. It had sold the extra Active stock in the market and after this became known in 1842, the Mexican government chose to recognize the Active debt at £5,500,000 in its decree of December 1843. In the same decree, however, the amount of Deferred stock was recognized at £4,624,000. In short, with £5,500,000 of Deferred printed and £4,624,000 accepted as in circulation, that left £876,000. Of these, £91,650 had been used, that is, made active or interest bearing, toward payment of the 1843 dividend. Hence, £784,350 remained with Lizardi. The company had revealed to the Stock Exchange Committee in 1842 the numbers of each of the series of bonds it had received to £5,500,000, but as the bonds were not sold in any particular numerical order, there was no way of knowing if more than the authorized amount had been placed in the market. Lizardi told the Stock Exchange Committee that "although higher numbers are in circulation than would appear to represent the above amount of £4,615,600, still, as inferior numbers are in our possession, the actual amount issued is as above stated."[128] In other words, only Lizardi knew which and how many of each series of Deferred had been sold. Various court cases pursued by the bondholders and by the Mexican government all failed to persuade the company either to hand over the excess bonds or to release details of which had been placed in the market.

Under the terms of the 1846 conversion, £4,624,000 worth of Deferred were to be exchanged at 60% of their nominal value for the new 1846 Five per Cents. Schneider was given exactly enough of the new bonds to effect this exchange, which it carried out on a first-come, first-served basis. It was quickly evident to Schneider, however, and there had been rumors in the market for some time, that Lizardi had in fact sold more than the authorized maximum of Deferred. Hence, Schneider did not have enough of the new bonds to give in exchange for the old. Two options were open. The first was legal proceedings against Lizardi to obtain an injunction preventing the sale of any more Deferred. Such an injunction was granted in May 1846. As noted above, further legal attempts to force Lizardi to hand over any remaining bonds failed.

The second option involved what were known as E Bonds. In May 1846, Schneider pointed out to the Mexican government that there was no way of telling which of the Deferred were valid as within the authorized maximum, and which were invalid as part of the unauthorized excess. Lizardi continued to refuse to give any details of the series and numbers it had put into circulation. It followed, therefore, that once the authorized maximum of Deferred had been reached, there would still be bondholders with stocks which could not be converted because there were no 1846 bonds left. The solution, Schneider suggested, was to have printed a special bond issue to be used when required for the conversion of the excess Deferred. The assumption had to be that all the excess Deferred to a face value of £784,350 would eventually be presented for conversion. As the agreement with the bondholders was that the Deferred were to be converted at 60%, it would be necessary to have these special bonds printed to a nominal value of £470,610 or 60% of £784,350. The 1846 bonds already printed were in letters A through D. These additional would have the letter E.

Murphy accepted this idea and E Bonds numbered 1–4705, each of £100, and one numbered 4706 of £110, totalling £470,610, were printed. They were placed in two tin boxes in the Bank of England by Murphy and Schneider on 20 August 1846. The boxes were marked "Messrs. John Schneider & Company, to be delivered to our joint order only."[129] Of the two keys to each box, one was given to Schneider and the other to the Mexican Legation. It was agreed that the contents would only be removed for the sole purpose of converting any Deferred bonds presented in excess of the authorized maximum of £4,624,000.

The exchange of the 1837 bonds and 1842 Debentures for the new 1846 Five per Cents began in July 1846. Knowing or suspecting that Lizardi had already sold at least some of the excess Deferred, Schneider decided to try to identify which they were. It promised the Mexican Minister of Finance that "we shall thoroughly investigate the claims which may henceforth be presented by Holders of Deferred Bonds, and reject those of every party who cannot prove satisfactorily that they became possessed of such Bonds either in exchange for old stock, or by purchase, or by some other legitimate mode of acquisition."[130]

Applying this test to those bondholders who presented their bonds for conversion, Schneider soon concluded that some of those brought in were part of the excess. On 23 December 1846, for example, the company placed an announcement in *The Times* stating that it had rejected £27,500 worth of Deferred as part of the excess "and which consequently ought not to have been issued." A few months later, it refused to receive 95 bonds of the £500 series which were submitted for conversion by Sheppard & Son.[131] That company requested the Mexican Minister's support and Mora ordered Schneider to accept the bonds. Again, it refused to do so on the grounds that they were part of the excess. Mora then released an order that he had from Mexico that all the E Bonds in the Bank of England should be handed over to Messrs. Aguirre, Bengoa & Sons. Again, Schneider refused to cooperate or to hand over the key to the deposit box.

Early in 1849, the Mexican government told Schneider of the Masson claim in respect of £300,000 of Deferred bonds. It may be recalled that the Masson partnership of New Orleans, where, incidentally, Lizardi had an office, had demanded full redemption of the 1843 Five per Cents and at the same time of £300,000 worth of Deferred. Schneider responded on 1 May 1849 that we have great reason to apprehend that the Deferred Bonds held by Messrs. Masson & Co. may be found to form part of the £784,350 which Messrs. Lizardi & Co. ought to have given up on withdrawing from the Agency and we shall certainly not admit the said Bonds to the conversion without any satisfactory proof that they are not what we apprehend them to be.[132]

The Masson claim was rejected and at the end of June 1849, Schneider reported that the full amount of Deferred bonds, "namely, £4,624,000 has now been converted into the new Consolidated Stock of 1846."[133] The only Deferred still in circulation, therefore, had to correspond to the unauthorized excess. As had been predicted, it was now clear that some were in the hands of "innocent holders"; £94,500 worth had already been presented but there was no 1846 stock left to exchange. There was no doubt that "bona fide holders" were being penalized because they had not presented their stocks for exchange much earlier in the process. To illustrate the problem, Schneider listed the claimants it had been obliged to turn away. At the head of the list was Barings who, acting on behalf of the trustees of E.H. Adams, had presented for conversion Deferred bonds to a value of £60,600. Why Barings had waited so long to come forward with these bonds is not clear. It had affirmed in writing that it had received the bonds from Lizardi "in exchange for Original Bonds converted in 1837" and that they had been in its possession on behalf of the owner ever since. "This claim, therefore," wrote Schneider, "is unquestionable." The other claims had also been investigated and proved to be fully substantiated.

Over the next few months, more bondholders came forward, only to be turned away. By October, the total value of the rejected bonds amounted to £110,500, including many small-scale holders of only one or two of the £100 or £150 series. Eventually, the total presented to Schneider rose to £252,600. More than sixty bondholders were left holding legitimately acquired 1837 Deferred stock which could not be converted or sold in the market.

Schneider's solution was to utilize the E Bonds created and deposited in the Bank of England for the very contingency which had arisen. In its letters to the Mexican Finance Ministry throughout 1849, it pleaded for permission to use the E Bonds to meet the claims of the Deferred bondholders, but the Mexican authorities refused. They preferred to seek a negotiated settlement with Lizardi and in June 1849, Schneider was ordered to suspend all judicial proceedings against that company. For the time being, no progress was made in the talks.

The next full rescheduling of the debt took place in 1850–1852 when the 1846 Five per Cents were exchanged for new Three per Cents. Much to the anger of the Deferred bondholders, they were also excluded from this conversion. In vain they appealed for help to the Mexican, British, and Dutch governments (some of the holders were Dutch), but they were offered no compensation for their now worthless bonds. Even the Committee of Mexican Bondholders was reluctant to help on the grounds that its duty was confined to representing those who held recognized bonds.

It was the Committee of Mexican Bondholders which blocked the first attempted solution to the problem. In September 1854, the Mexican government, headed again by Lizardi's patron, Santa Anna, ordered a new issue of Three per Cent bonds to the value of £470,610. The bonds were printed, signed by the General Treasurer of Mexico, and sent to London. They were to be used to convert the £784,350 excess Deferred at 60%. The E Bonds, created for the same purpose and still in the Bank of England, were to be destroyed.

The Committee of Mexican Bondholders refused to accept this procedure. It argued that the Deferred bonds still in circulation and unconverted in either the 1846 or 1851 conversions amounted to £252,600, which was the sum total of the bonds presented to and rejected by Schneider.[134] If exchanged at 60%, only £151,560 of new stock was required. Hence, what Mexico was in fact attempting was to add an additional £319,050 to its foreign debt. As it was already in default on interest payments, the bondholders could not agree to any such addition.

This opposition, and the fall of Santa Anna from power in August 1855, were enough to block the proposal and the September 1854 decree was revoked. The bonds were sent back to Mexico. More talks followed in Mexico City with Manuel Lizardi and these brought an agreement with the Mexican government which was signed on 21 February 1856. One result of this agreement (it involved various matters) was that in 1857, Lizardi delivered to the Mexican Financial Agency in London £350,000 worth of the 1837 Deferred stock. Included were the following bonds:

Series A	395 each of £100	=	£ 39,500
Series B	295 each of £150	=	44,250
Series C	395 each of £250	=	98,750
Series D	335 each of £500	=	167,500
			£350,000[135]

Lizardi had at last produced 1,420 of the excess bonds. Further talks with the company were held in Mexico over the next few years which brought unfulfilled promises that it would hand over more of the bonds, and eventually its account with the Mexican government was liquidated in 1866. Those investors who still held the unredeemed bonds were left to fight their cause as best they could. An agreement recognizing their claim was reached with the Maximilian government which ruled Mexico from 1864 to 1867, but it was not implemented. After the fall of the imperial regime, the triumphant liberal administration led by Benito Juárez suspended diplomatic relations with Britain. The bondholders continued to put their case in letters to the press, to the Foreign Office, and to the Mexican authorities, but in reality there was little they could do.

The resolution of the claim, in fact, came within the terms of the 1886 Dublán conversion. In the years preceding this and especially after the restoration of diplomatic relations with Britain in 1884, there was a long series of negotiations between the bondholders' representatives and several Mexican agents. The publicity these talks generated in the press attracted the attention of those who now held the excess Deferred. In 1883, for example, in a letter to *The Bullionist* (2 June), "Another Mexican Bondholder" complained of discrimination against the Deferred holders who had received not a penny of interest on their stocks for over forty years. In the next year, 1884, again during talks on the debt, the proposed settlement included an offer to convert the 1837 Deferred into new bonds at the rate of 24%. The firm of Foss and Ledsam, which we have already encountered as representing the 1843 bondholders, immediately protested to the Stock Exchange. It was also acting, it said, on behalf of the Deferred holders who had not been consulted about the proposed agreement, and it would not accept it. Two years later, the Dublán conversion included provision for the 1837 Deferred holders to be offered new 1886 Three per Cent bonds at the rate of 20% of the nominal value of their bonds. They were offered nothing for the unpaid coupons.

Again, Foss and Ledsam protested. It was acting, it said, on behalf of holders of £128,350 of the Deferred stock.[136] The protests failed to achieve a better offer and the bondholders finally decided to accept. By September 1887, 1,538 bonds with a nominal value of £332,060 had been delivered to the Mexican Financial Agency.[137] More were handed in during following weeks and by the end of the conversion in August 1888, the total had reached £366,601. Hence, of the original £784,350 excess bonds, a total of £716,601 were accounted for: Lizardi's £350,000 handed over in 1857 and £366,601 in 1886–1888; £67,749, therefore, remained uncancelled. Of these, it is likely that some were presented before and after the Dublán conversion. Five years later, in May 1895, the Financial Agency in London placed a notice in the press inviting those who still held 1837 Deferred to present them for conversion on terms "to be agreed upon."[138] Forty-nine of the £500 series had been stolen by a Lizardi clerk.[139] Others may have been destroyed when Manuel Lizardi's house in Mexico City was ransacked in 1855. Finally, a number remain extant. Several have been sold in London auctions in recent years and there are still two in Barings' archive.

As for the E Bonds specially created in 1846, they had been placed in the Bank of England where they remained untouched for twenty years. In 1865, during the discussions with the Maximilian regime regarding a settlement with the holders of the Deferred stock, it was suggested that the E Bonds were no longer required and could be destroyed. Hence, on 29

March 1866, the Mexican Minister in London at the time, José María Durán, accompanied by one of the Bank of England's directors, Daniel Kerkman Haydson, went to the Bank to find the boxes in which the bonds were stored. The two boxes were located but it was found that before they could be opened, the consent of Schneider was necessary because, as indicated earlier, each box carried the words "to be delivered up to our joint order only." Schneider, it will be recalled, had been Mexico's Financial Agent in 1846 when the bonds were printed and placed in the Bank and the company had retained one of the keys to the boxes. One of the Schneiders was approached—it is not clear if it was the father or son—but he refused to allow the boxes to be opened. He insisted that the E Bonds were security for the Deferred holders and until their claims had been definitively settled, he could not agree to the destruction of the bonds.[140] Nothing came of the negotiations with the Deferred bondholders and the E Bonds remained locked away in the Bank of England.

1851 THREE PER CENTS

From the bondholders' viewpoint, the 1846 conversion was not a success. The Mexican prevarication over its ratification had brought confusion and concern into what was already a volatile situation. With events in revolutionary Europe taking a dramatic turn, especially after the abdication of Louis Phillipe in February 1848, the stock market was very unstable. There were large fluctuations in many stocks, even, for example, in the usually solid British Consols which varied by as much as 15% in 1847. As the *The Times* put it on 1 January 1849, the previous two years of 1847 and 1848 had been "momentous years in the financial market." Mexican stocks could not escape the general instability and the prices of the 1846 bonds were poor, rarely reaching the average of the 1837 Actives which they had replaced. Except for a partial payment of one coupon, dividends went unpaid. More expensive legal cases were brought by the bondholders in a vain attempt to extract money from the Financial Agent. The disputes between Schneider and Lizardi over who had the agency continued and relations between Mora at the head of the Mexican Legation and the bondholders' representatives were never harmonious.

Sustained pressure by the bondholders of many defaulting nations, including those of Mexico, finally brought a response from the British government. Disraeli had continued his support of their case and on 6 July 1847, in a Commons debate introduced by the Tory leader Lord George Bentinck, Foreign Secretary Palmerston was obliged to adopt a more aggressive stance than he had hitherto sustained. He warned debtor nations that public opinion in Britain could oblige the government "to insist upon the payment of those debts."[141] A few months later, the Foreign Office released a circular which had gone to British diplomats overseas in which Palmerston repeated his warning.[142]

Above all, the Mexican bondholders were alarmed by the outbreak of war between Mexico and the United States. The invasion of Mexico by American armies, including the occupation of the Gulf ports, brought disruption of trade and especially of the import taxes assigned to the dividend fund. The tobacco industry, which was supposed to provide cash for the dividends under the 1846 agreement, was also destroyed. In the circumstances, there was clearly no possibility of interest payments being made on the new bonds and that fact was reflected in the market prices. Peace was restored with the Treaty of Guadalupe Hidalgo, signed on 2 February 1848.

Two aspects of the peace treaty were of special interest to the bondholders. The first was the cession of territory to the victorious United States. About half of Mexico's territory including Texas, California, New Mexico, and other areas north of the Rio Bravo were ceded. This concerned the bondholders because according to their interpretation of the terms of the original loan contracts of 1824 and 1825, repeated in subsequent conversions, their money was guaranteed by a mortgage on all of Mexican territory and "the whole of the revenues of the State." Half of their security had disappeared. In addition, such a large territorial loss was bound to affect Mexico's economic development, especially its trade. Hence, the customs revenues, one-fifth of which were assigned to the dividend fund, would diminish. Similarly, the possibility of land grants in payment of interest arrears was also correspondingly reduced.

The bondholders wanted compensation. In this respect, they looked to a second part of the peace treaty concerning an indemnity payment. The United States agreed to pay Mexico an indemnity of 15,000,000 dollars at the rate of 3,000,000 dollars per annum, starting in May 1849. Major European bankers, including Rothschilds and Barings, intrigued to get the lucrative contract to manage the transfer of the annual tranches. Also, as Tenenbaum puts it, "Everyone who held Mexican debt paper, native or foreign, inside or outside the country, wanted his or her share."[143] The Committee of Spanish American Bondholders was no exception and at once began a campaign of public and private lobbying to persuade the Mexican government that the bondholders should have priority. Letters were dispatched to Manning and Mackintosh, still the bondholders' agents in Mexico City, urging them to press the claim. The arguments were put in some detail but the essence was neatly expressed in a letter of 1 May 1848: "Any portion of that territory (Mexico) surrendered to a third party for a valuable consideration, carries with it necessarily the obligation to compensate the mortgagee, i.e. (in this case), the British creditor."[144]

More letters and personal delegations went to the Foreign Office to plead for help. Palmerston responded by again instructing his diplomats in Mexico to give what help they could. The vice-chairman of the bondholders' committee made the perhaps surprising point that despite the war, Mexico was by no means poor because, in addition to the indemnity, more money had been produced by Mexican mints in 1847 than for many years past. He also asked Palmerston to have a private word with Mora on their behalf.[145]

Mora's position was soon made very clear. In a letter published in *The Times* on 7 August 1848, he emphatically rejected the bondholders' demands. "There is no right to demand," he wrote, "nor is it convenient to grant" any of the indemnity money. Furthermore, under the terms of the 1846 agreement, "it was a clause and special condition agreed to by the bondholders, to renounce the mortgaged territory which previously existed for the payment of its creditors." Finally, there was no mention in the means of payment stipulated on the bonds "of an indemnification which did not and was not likely to exist."

The bondholders reacted angrily to Mora's peremptory dismissal of their claim. They insisted that according to the terms of the bonds, Mexico's entire revenues, from whatever source, were mortgaged to them. Additional to the general mortgage, specific revenues such as customs and tobacco were assigned and it was undeniable that "in the event of their proving insufficient, all the other sources of the revenue of the State are made responsible for the deficiency." To reinforce their case, counsels' opinion was sought. The two lawyers, T. Dodson and Robert Phillimore, were unequivocal in their support:

We cannot, therefore, doubt that the Mexican Republic will, as the letter and spirit of her engagement appear to us to require, allot an equitable portion of the sum received for the hypothecated territory as a partial liquidation of the principal and interest of her debt to the foreign creditor.[146]

Mora refused to give way and the bondholders' committee decided to send a special commissioner to Mexico to put their case. At a general meeting on 6 September 1848, the idea of a commissioner was approved, as was the committee's nomination for the job. This was William Parish Robertson. His mission was to be of fundamental importance in the development of the Committee of Mexican Bondholders and it is dealt with in some detail in Part II of this work. All that we need to note at this point is that he left for Mexico in December 1848.

A few weeks before his departure, Mora was sent a highly confidential note from the Mexican Foreign Ministry.[147] To this point, the Mexican official response to the bondholders' claim to the indemnity had been negative. Now, in the letter to Mora, dated 13 October 1848, a change of policy was revealed. In the first place, Mora was reprimanded for participating in the polemic in the London newspapers over the indemnity issue.

He was told that, in future, such publicity, which was bad for Mexico's image in Europe, had to be avoided. Second, no part of the indemnity money would be allocated to the foreign debt unless the "imprudent agreement" of 1846 could be renegotiated. In particular, what was now wanted was a new settlement in which the interest rate on the debt was reduced from 5% to 3%.

In short, Mexico had decided to use the promise of giving the bondholders some of the indemnity money in return for another rescheduling of the debt and a lower rate of interest. When Robertson arrived in Mexico City early in 1849, he found a willingness to negotiate and by 6 July, he had concluded an agreement with the Finance Minister, Francisco Arrangoiz. This provided for the bondholders to receive 4,000,000 dollars from the indemnity money in settlement of unpaid dividends. In exchange, they were to accept a reduction in the interest rate on the capital debt from 5% to 3½%.

Robertson also arranged for the appointment of a new Financial Agent. Schneider, who had been in dispute with Mora and with the bondholders over the payment of dividends, was dismissed. In its place, Colonel Francisco Facio was appointed. He had come to Europe in October 1826 as a member of a delegation sent to negotiate a trade treaty with Britain.[148] Thereafter, he held various diplomatic posts and in 1849, he was Mexico's Consul at Hamburg. The terms of his new appointment were set out in an agreement made between Arrangoiz and Robertson on 8 July 1849.[149] He was to maintain the records of the debt transactions; to receive and deposit in the Bank of England all dividend remittances; and to publish in the press the amount received on each monthly packet. On 11 September, Facio announced that he had opened an office at 32 Great Winchester Street where his hours of business were 11:00 A.M. to 3:00 P.M. His secretary was Benito Gómez Farías, son of the liberal leader, Valentín. Facio was to remain Mexico's Financial Agent until at least 1864, despite many attempts by the bondholders to have him removed.

With his deal on the debt in his pocket, Robertson returned to London in October 1849. The Mexican Congress, however, rejected the proposals and referred the matter to a congressional committee on public credit. It put forward various proposals which formed the basis of the law issued on 14 October 1850.[150] The terms offered were briefly as follows:

1. If the bondholders agreed to the following conditions, a draft for 2,500,000 dollars of the United States indemnity payment would be given to them.
2. The conditions were:
    a. Acceptance of a total capital debt of £10,241,650 on which henceforth an annual interest rate of 3 per cent would be paid.
    b. The 2,500,000 dollars plus all dividend monies in hand to be accepted as full settlement of all unpaid interest.

    c. To pay the 3 per cent interest on the capital debt, the following revenues to be specifically assigned: 25 per cent of import dues at maritime and frontier customs; 75 per cent of export dues collected at Pacific coast ports; 5 per cent of export dues collected at Gulf ports; any deficit in the interest due after the aforesaid collections to be made up from general government revenues.

    d. After a period of six years, 250,000 pesos a year to be sent to London to amortize the capital debt.

3. The 1846 bonds to be exchanged for new ones to be issued in London.

4. The bondholders to appoint agents in Mexican ports but from the moment they received any dividend monies, all responsibility on the Mexican government for those monies ended; the Mexican government would pay the usual costs of embarcation, disembarcation, insurance and freight of such monies.

The bondholders calculated that these proposals meant that the sum of £868,111 was on offer.[151] This included the 2,500,000 dollars, equivalent to £500,000 of the indemnity, plus further sums due from the tobacco and other revenues previously allocated to the dividend fund. That meant a loss of about £1,200,000 of the interest arrears in addition to "sacrifices" of £3,400,000 already suffered in previous conversions. When the bondholders met at the London Tavern on 23 December to hear the details, their committee's recommendation to accept the offer was approved with only three dissenters.

We can only speculate on the reasoning of the bondholders in accepting an offer which Mexican negotiators considered their best ever deal on the British debt. Bazant gives all the figures and there is no need to repeat them here except perhaps to note that the interest reduction to 3% alone saved the Mexicans over 1 million dollars a year.[152] The bondholders may have had several thoughts in mind. The old adage of a bird in the hand was probably one. Another was that the money was from the United States and could be presumed secure. A third was the assumption that the note for the 2,500,000 dollars could be negotiated either in London or New York. In other words, it could be sold to a bank, obviously at a discount, but at least the cash could be realized fairly quickly. In fact, attempts to negotiate the note with bankers proved difficult but eventually Barings agreed to advance a large sum on account. It was estimated that the 2,500,000 dollars would produce about £510,000, which was enough for a payment of approximately £5 per £100 bond. Barings agreed to advance £4 10s. to any bondholder or holder of the certificates which Facio had recently offered in exchange for the arrear coupons from the 1846 bonds. When the dollars were sold, there was enough for a further payment of 13 shillings.

The bondholders' acceptance of the 14 October decree reached Mexico in February 1851 via the January packet. On 16 February, the Mexican Treasury accordingly issued in triplicate the certificate for the 2,500,000 dollars. Then, on 8 May, the Royal Mail Company's steamship *Great*

Western arrived at Southampton. It brought 40,000 dollars in cash for the dividend fund and among its 120 passengers, Manuel Payno, the former Finance Minister who had been instrumental in drawing up the October agreement and steering it through Congress. He had now been sent as Chargé d'Affaires in place of Mora, who had recently died in Paris. Payno brought with him the original of the Treasury certificate for the 2,500,000 dollars and part of his instructions was to ensure that the terms of the October agreement were carried out. In particular, he had to arrange for the printing of the new Three per Cent bonds and their exchange for the 1846 Five per Cents. From Southampton, he sent the certificate to the bondholders' chairman, assuring him that proper steps had been taken in Mexico to collect the revenues assigned for future interest payments. There was no doubt, he said, that the anticipated revenues would be enough to meet the dividends in full. Finally, he conveyed a vote of thanks from the Mexican Congress to the bondholders for their patience and generosity. His country, he added, considered it "a point of honour to pay this debt."[153]

The new Three per Cent bonds were printed in London in September 1851. Some delay had been caused by bondholders' attempts to get certain clauses relating to dividend expenses inserted on the bonds. Payno and Facio had resisted these attempts and the printing proceeded without them. The bonds were produced, and presumably designed, by the London firm of Letts, Son, and Steer. (Illustration 11 reproduces bond number 3187 of the letter A Series, of £100.)

The original of the bond illustrated is in the author's collection. It is in black ink on white paper. Examples of the other series have not been found but it is possible that they were in different colors, which was certainly the normal practice in later issues. The reverse has the text in Spanish and English of the 14 October 1850 decree. Also, but in English only, there is the text of a resolution taken by bondholders at their meeting on 23 December 1850 to accept the terms of the decree. There are the customary ornate motifs and a sheet of forty-eight dividend coupons was attached, the first payable on 1 July 1851 and the last on 1 January 1875.

As can be seen in the illustration, the bond contains details of the number and value of the four series which comprised the whole issue. A total of 51,742 were printed at a cost of £1,000.[154] They were shipped to Mexico for signature and the example illustrated is dated 1 December 1851. They were returned to London where Facio added his signature. All this, of course, took time. Facio asked bondholders in February 1852 to start handing in their 1846 bonds for which they were given receipts. A month later, on 23 March, he announced that the first of the new bonds were available for collection by holders of receipts numbered 1–238. After another two weeks, he announced that all the bonds of the B, C, and D series were

MEXICAN
THREE PER CENT. NEW CONSOLIDATED STOCK,

BEARING INTEREST FROM THE 1st JANUARY, 1851;

DIVIDENDS PAYABLE EVERY 1st JANUARY AND 1st JULY.

LETTER **A.**

3187

Bond for

1851.

£100 *July*

1851.

To all to whom these Presents shall come,

We, the undersigned, Ministers of the General Treasury of the Mexican Republic, do make known: **Whereas** the National Congress of the Republic of Mexico, did on the 14th October, 1850, issue a Decree for liquidating and adjusting definitively the Foreign Debt of the Republic; which Decree His Excellency the President of the Republic did sanction; a copy and translation whereof are inserted on the back hereof, No. 1;

And Whereas, at a Public General Meeting of the Holders of Mexican Bonds, held at the London Tavern on the 23rd December, 1850, the said Decree was agreed to and accepted by the said Holders there present, according to the Resolution inserted on the back hereof, No. 2;

Now know ye, that We, the said Ministers of the General Treasury of the Mexican Republic, acting in the name and on behalf of the Government of Mexico, do hereby solemnly promise and engage that all and each of the Conditions contained in the said Decree shall be duly and faithfully observed and kept by the Government of the Republic of Mexico, and that as guarantee for the payment of the Interest and also for the redemption of the Principal of the said New Consolidated Debt, the Mexican Republic hereby solemnly hypothecates its whole and entire Revenues from whatever source derived, but in a more especial and distinct manner, one fourth part of the Import Duties of Customs wherever levied, 75 per cent. of the Export Duties from the Ports of the Pacific, and 5 per cent. of the same Duties in the Ports of the Atlantic, and that the same shall not, on any pretence, be alienated therefrom, so that the Half Yearly Dividends on the said New Consolidated Debt shall be faithfully and punctually discharged.

And We declare, that the said New Consolidated Debt of the Republic of Mexico, amounting to £10,241,650, is represented by the following Bonds, which have been created for this purpose, viz:—

Class A. No. 1 to 25,993 of £100 each	. . . .	£2,599,300	
B. No. 1 to 8,949 of £150 each	. . . .	1,342,350	
C. No. 1 to 8,400 of £250 each	. . . .	2,100,000	£10,241,650
D. No. 1 to 8,400 of £500 each	. . . .	4,200,000	

And We further declare, That this Bond for ONE HUNDRED POUNDS is one of the Bonds so created, and that the same is entitled to the benefits of all and singular the hypothecations and covenants herein contained for securing the payment of the Interest thereon, and the Redemption of the same.

Given under our hand, in Mexico, this *1st* day of December, 1851.

MINISTER OF THE GENERAL TREASURY.

MINISTER OF THE GENERAL TREASURY.

I hereby Certify, That the foregoing are the Signatures of the Ministers of the General Treasury, and that this Bond is one of the Bonds herein described as forming part of the said New Consolidated Debt of the Republic of Mexico.

MEXICAN FINANCIAL AGENT.

11. 1851 Three per Cent Bond.

ready but that only 8,949, or about one third of the A series of £100 had been returned from Mexico.[155]

Eventually, all the bonds arrived but the exchange procedure continued over several years. By 1856, however, Facio was able to report that only 244 of the 51,742 remained to be issued. Outstanding were 218 of the A series (£100); 11 of the B series (£150); 6 of the C series (£250); 9 of the D series (£500).[156]

Once again, the bondholders' hopes of a regular income from their new bonds were frustrated. The first few dividends were paid and the indemnity money provided a perhaps unexpected contribution toward arrears. Nevertheless, after 1854, with just three exceptions, no further interest was paid on the 1851 Three per Cents. There were many reasons why Mexico failed to pay, several of which will be explained in other parts of this study. Here, all that is necessary is an outline of the main events which stopped dividend remittances. First, there was the major civil war in Mexico of the so-called Reform period from 1857 to 1860. This was followed by the Tripartite Intervention in which British, French, and Spanish armies occupied Veracruz in a futile attempt to force Mexico to pay its debts. The prompt withdrawal of the British and Spanish left the way open for the French invasion which brought about the Maximilian Empire of 1864–1867. As far as the bondholders were concerned, that episode brought one benefit which was the capitalization of interest arrears for which they were given more bonds (these will be explained in the next section). Unfortunately, however, from the bondholders' viewpoint, British recognition of Maximilian also had long-term negative consequences. After the departure of the French armies and the defeat of Maximilian's regime, the victorious Mexican government, led by the liberal Benito Juárez, suspended or refused to renew diplomatic relations with those nations, including Britain, which had recognized Maximilian. The bondholders were left, at least on an official level, without any diplomatic support for their case.

Notwithstanding the lack of formal relations between the two countries, bondholders' representatives, both in London and Mexico City, conducted numerous negotiations with Mexican commissioners throughout the late 1860s and the 1870s. None of these produced any money and it was not until after the renewal of relations with Britain in 1884 that the government of Porfirio Díaz decided to sort out the foreign debt once and for all. As with the earlier bonds of 1837, 1843, and 1846, those of 1851 were finally redeemed through the procedures set out in the Dublán conversion of 1886.

There were several stages in the redemption of the 1851 bonds. The first was the Mexican law of 22 June 1885 which established the Consolidated Debt of the United States of Mexico.[157] The purpose of this consolidation was in effect to gather in all of the debts which the government recognized, both internal and external, within one account. Various securities were immediately accepted as forming part of the debt while other liabilities such as interest arrears or Deferred stocks were left for separate negotiation with individual creditors. All the recognized stocks or credits were to be exchanged for new Three per Cent Bonds of the Consolidated Debt or were to be converted into the equivalent of the new bonds. The 1851 bonds were declared to be convertible at par, cent per cent, into the new bonds. In other words, the 1851 bonds were not withdrawn from the market but were to be "converted" and allowed to remain in circulation alongside the new bonds, attracting the same dividends. The rate of interest, payable half-yearly, was set out in the 1885 decree as follows:

1% in 1886

1½% in 1887

2% in 1888

2½% in 1889

3% thereafter

The recently established National Bank of Mexico was charged with servicing the Consolidated Debt, in particular, the provision of funds for interest payments. Money for these was to be drawn from the Veracruz customs, and in London dividends were to be paid by the Bank's agents, Glyn, Mills, Currie & Co.

Months of negotiation with the bondholders' representatives followed the promulgation of the 1885 decree. These resulted in the agreement signed on 23 June 1886 with the Mexican representative, General Mena.[158] Several clauses concerned the 1851 bonds. The unpaid interest on them from 1854 to 1863 had already been capitalized into bonds in 1864 and these will be explained in the next section. At the insistence of Mexico, interest due in the Maximilian years was waived. The twenty dividends from 1 July 1866 to 1 July 1886, amounting in total to £6,144,000, were recognized as legitimate debts. It was agreed that those outstanding coupons would be exchanged at 15% of their value; in short, for the twenty 3% coupons with a nominal value of £60 attached to a £100 bond, holders would receive £9 in bonds of the new issue.

Finally, Mexico reserved the right to set a date for the exchange of all the 1851 bonds for the new Three per Cents before 31 December 1890. Until that date, it was entitled to buy in at market prices any number of the 1851 bonds. Similarly, to the same final date, it could redeem the bonds at 40% of their nominal value by drawings of those to be redeemed.

In sum, therefore, under the Dublán conversion and Mena agreement, holders of 1851 Three per Cents retained their bonds and were given new ones in exchange for their unpaid dividend coupons. They were promised that interest payments would resume on 1 July 1886. Although there was a slight delay, Glyn, Mills, Currrie & Co. advertised on 2 September that

Table 9
1851 Three per Cents Stamped

		J	F	M	A	M	J	J	A	S	O	N	D
1886	H	-	-	-	-	-	-	-	-	-	23	28	29
	L	-	-	-	-	-	-	-	-	-	23	23	27
1887	H	28	26	28	29	32	32	32	30	33	38	37	38
	L	27	25	26	28	29	31	30	30	31	34	35	33
1888	H	38	40	/	/	/	/	-	-	-	-	-	-
	L	38	40	/	/	/	/	-	-	-	-	-	-

they were ready to pay the ½% dividend due on 1 July. Bondholders were invited to deposit their bonds at the company for verification and each one on which a dividend was paid was stamped with these words: "Dividend of one half of one per cent paid 1st July 1886 in pursuance of the Agreement dated June 23rd 1886 between the Mexican government and the holder of this bond."[159] Within just one week, £2,330,800 of 1851 bonds had been presented for stamping.[160] Now known as the 1851 Three per Cents Stamped, they were granted an official quotation by the Stock Exchange Committee to date from 30 September.[161] For the time being, therefore, they were traded separately from the non-stamped bonds. (Table 9 gives the prices.)

Not all the bondholders were happy with the Mena agreement and some were reluctant to have their bonds stamped in return for such a small dividend. They preferred to wait until the conversion procedure was implemented. To carry this out, a new Financial Agency was opened in London at Blomfield House, London Wall. The first director was the same Benito Gómez Farías who had been Facio's secretary in 1849 when the agreement leading to the issue of the 1851 bonds was being negotiated. Now, almost forty years later, he returned to arrange the conversion and eventual redemption of the bonds. The procedure had been set out in the 1885 law and in the Mena agreement. Bondholders were required to present their bonds at the Agency where all the details of series, value, and number were recorded. Once accepted and registered, a "note of registration" was affixed on the bond to indicate that it had been "converted." Valid coupons were detached and new Three per Cent bonds were given in exchange at the agreed rate of 15% of nominal value. A new sheet of eight coupons was attached to each bond. These were for the eight half-yearly dividends payable from 1 January 1887 through to 31 December 1890, which was the final date by which Mexico was to exchange or redeem the bonds.

The conversion began in December 1886 and the Financial Agency published regular progress reports. By June 1887, for example, 30,862 of the 1851 bonds had been converted and by September, the number had risen to 41,051 with a nominal value of £8,207,000.[162] By the end of the conversion in August 1888, only £96,750 of the original issue of £10,241,650 remained outstanding. Of the arrear coupons, with a total face value of £6,144,000, converted at 15%, £60,773 remained in the market.[163]

The 1851 bond prices in the market had steadily increased because it was expected that Mexico would exercise its right under the terms of the Mena agreement to redeem them at 40% of their nominal value before the end of 1890. The success of the whole Dublán conversion had restored Mexico's credit in Europe and that encouraged the government to proceed to the final stage of buying in all the so-called "old" debts. This was done by floating an entirely new loan in 1888. Details of this are given in another section and all that needs to be noted here is that some of the funds raised by it were used to redeem the 1851 Three per Cents at 40%. The exact number of bonds which were bought in and cancelled is not known, but by 1894, of the original total issue of £10,241,650, bonds worth just £45,100 were still outstanding.[164] Four years later, the Mexican Financial Agency offered to convert "old titles" including any remaining 1851 Three per Cents at a price to be negotiated.[165] How many bondholders took advantage of this offer was not disclosed but it is unlikely that many of the 51,742 bonds originally produced were left in the market. (Table 10 gives the prices.)

1864 THREE PER CENTS

Details of the Allied intervention in Mexico following the Tripartite Alliance signed by Britain, France, and Spain on 31 October 1861 are readily available elsewhere and are, therefore, omitted here. Provoked directly by Mexico's decision of 17 July 1861 to suspend all payments on its debts for two years, the Intervention failed in its objective of enforcing the resumption of payments. The prompt withdrawal from Veracruz of the British and Spanish forces allowed the French to pursue their greater ambitions and especially Napoleon III's Grand Design of founding monarchies in the New World. Mexicans resisted as best they could the power of the invading French armies, but with the United States preoccupied with its own civil war, there were no allies to help them.

The military defeat of Mexico, therefore, was probably inevitable, but resistance by the liberal leader Benito Juárez and his guerrilla units was enough to delay the French advance. It was not until June 1863 that the French commander-in-chief, General Forey, was able to take control of Mexico City. A month later, on 10 July, an assembly of 215 so-called "notables" voted to offer the throne of Mexico to the Archduke Maximilian of Austria.

Maximilian, although anxious to accept the offer and thus escape the hostility of his elder brother Franz Joseph, Emperor of Austria, took his

Table 10
1851 Three per Cents

		J	F	M	A	M	J	J	A	S	O	N	D
1852	H	-	-	26	29	28	27	27	25	26	26	25	25
	L	-	-	26	26	24	23	25	24	25	24	24	23
1853	H	23	24	26	28	27	28	27	27	26	25	26	25
	L	23	22	24	26	26	25	26	26	22	23	24	23
1854	H	24	26	24	24	24	24	24	24	25	25	22	21
	L	22	24	22	23	23	23	24	24	24	23	21	29
1855	H	21	21	21	21	22	22	22	21	21	21	19	20
	L	21	20	20	20	20	21	21	21	21	19	19	19
1856	H	21	20	20	23	23	23	23	23	23	22	22	22
	L	19	20	19	20	22	22	22	22	21	21	21	21
1857	H	21	22	24	23	23	22	22	22	22	21	19	20
	L	21	21	22	23	22	22	22	22	20	18	17	18
1858	H	21	20	20	20	21	20	20	21	21	21	20	20
	L	20	20	19	19	20	20	19	21	21	20	20	20
1859	H	20	20	21	21	17	18	19	20	24	23	23	22
	L	19	20	19	16	16	17	18	19	20	21	22	22
1860	H	22	21	22	22	22	21	21	21	22	22	22	22
	L	21	20	21	21	21	21	20	21	21	21	21	21
1861	H	23	24	24	24	23	22	22	22	27	26	28	28
	L	21	23	23	23	22	22	22	21	21	25	25	27
1862	H	33	35	34	35	32	31	29	29	35	34	33	33
	L	27	33	34	31	31	27	28	28	29	33	33	31
1863	H	32	33	33	35	37	38	38	39	47	47	41	37
	L	31	32	31	33	35	33	34	36	39	41	37	31
1864	H	36	45	46	48	45	45	44	29	28	27	29	29
	L	34	34	41	45	42	43	28	28	27	25	27	29
1865	H	28	28	26	27	26	26	24	23	27	27	26	25
	L	27	26	26	26	24	25	23	22	24	25	25	24
1866	H	24	23	22	21	19	18	17	17	17	16	18	19
	L	20	20	21	20	15	14	14	15	15	15	16	18
1867	H	18	18	18	16	17	17	16	15	15	15	16	16
	L	17	17	16	14	15	16	15	14	15	14	14	15
1868	H	16	16	16	16	16	16	16	15	15	16	16	16
	L	15	15	15	15	15	15	15	14	14	15	15	14
1869	H	15	16	15	15	14	13	13	12	12	13	13	14
	L	14	15	14	14	12	12	12	11	11	12	13	13
1870	H	15	14	14	15	15	17	16	14	15	15	15	14
	L	13	13	14	14	14	15	11	12	14	14	13	13

Table 10 (continued)

		J	F	M	A	M	J	J	A	S	O	N	D
1871	H	15	14	14	15	15	15	14	14	14	14	14	14
	L	13	13	13	14	14	14	14	14	13	13	13	13
1872	H	15	15	16	16	16	15	15	16	16	16	17	19
	L	14	14	14	15	15	14	14	14	14	15	16	17
1873	H	19	18	18	17	16	16	15	16	16	15	16	17
	L	17	17	17	16	15	15	15	15	15	14	14	16
1874	H	16	16	16	17	17	16	16	16	16	16	16	16
	L	15	15	15	15	16	15	15	16	15	15	16	16
1875	H	16	17	17	17	17	16	15	15	15	15	14	13
	L	15	16	16	16	16	15	14	15	15	14	12	12
1876	H	13	11	10	9	7	7	8	8	8	8	8	8
	L	9	10	8	6	4	5	6	7	7	7	7	6
1877	H	7	7	7	7	7	7	7	8	8	8	8	8
	L	6	7	7	6	6	6	6	7	8	7	7	7
1878	H	7	7	7	7	8	8	8	7	7	7	8	8
	L	7	7	7	7	7	7	7	7	7	6	6	7
1879	H	8	8	8	8	9	12	11	10	10	11	12	11
	L	7	7	7	7	8	9	10	10	9	10	11	10
1880	H	14	14	14	14	11	10	11	12	12	14	16	17
	L	11	13	13	11	10	10	10	11	11	12	14	15
1881	H	28	26	25	27	26	25	23	26	26	26	25	26
	L	18	24	25	24	24	21	21	23	24	23	24	24
1882	H	26	21	23	24	24	23	22	24	27	27	26	24
	L	20	19	21	23	22	20	21	20	24	26	23	23
1883	H	24	25	26	27	31	32	31	29	26	25	23	20
	L	23	24	25	26	27	31	29	27	25	23	19	20
1884	H	22	21	22	22	22	22	23	24	24	23	23	21
	L	20	21	20	21	20	21	21	22	23	23	21	19
1885	H	20	20	20	19	18	19	18	18	18	19	21	20
	L												
1886	H	19	20	20	20	20	22	22	22	24	24	28	29
	L	18	19	20	20	20	21	22	21	21	23	24	27
1887	H	28	27	28	30	32	32	32	31	34	37	38	38
	L	25	25	26	28	29	32	31	30	30	34	36	36
1888	H	38	40	43	43	43	44	-	-	-	-	-	-
	L	35	38	40	41	42	43	-	-	-	-	-	-

time with preparations and consultations around the courts of Europe. By early 1864, there were strong rumors of financial negotiations with European bankers and when Maximilian went to Paris to discuss arrangements with his patron, Napoleon III, *The Times* (8 March 1864) reported that he was surrounded by "a swarm of speculators." Aware of all the speculation, Barings wrote to the British Foreign Secretary, Earl Russell. It would be helpful, Barings suggested, if the British government, "in a friendly spirit," were to ensure that both Maximilian and the French government were fully informed of the debt owed to British bondholders. To facilitate this, a copy of a brief history of the debt prepared by Barings' agent, George White, who had recently returned from Mexico, was enclosed.[166]

Barings' involvement in the Mexican debt had been renewed in 1862. In January of that year, with the Allied forces occupying Veracruz, the Committee of Mexican Bondholders had resolved to wind up its affairs and hand over the responsibility for representing the bondholders' interests to the company. It had agreed (after years of persuasion, it should be added) to accept the task, and it lost no time in pressing the British government for assistance.

Maximilian and his entourage, including his wife Carlotta and the Count and Countess of Zichy, travelled to London on 14 March 1864 for more talks with bankers and others. They left after two days at the Clarendon Hotel but Count Zichy stayed behind.[167] On 20 March, he signed a contract with Glyn, Mills, Currie & Co. for the flotation of a new loan for £8,000,000. Interest was to be at 6% and the issue price at £63 per cent.[168]

The bondholders welcomed the new loan because included in its terms was a commitment to allocate some of the proceeds to meet two years' interest payments on the 1851 Three per Cents as from 1 January 1864. Dividends on the 1851 bonds, however, were ten years in arrears. The bondholders pressed for an offer on these arrears. Negotiations were held and after several postponements, the bondholders were summoned to a public meeting on 11 April 1864 to hear the result.[169] It seems that the discussions continued to the last minute because just prior to the meeting, Maximilian's representatives—Glyn, Mills, Currie & Co. and R.A. Heath, Chairman of the International Financial Society—sent the final terms to James Capel who was to chair the meeting. Their letter, they said, confirmed "our verbal communications" and "we now have officially to submit for the consideration of the Mexican Bondholders, over whose meeting you are about the preside, the terms proposed to them."[170] In brief, the offer was as follows. Dividends on the 1851 Three per Cents were ten years in arrears. There were twenty unpaid half-yearly coupons from 1 July 1854 to 1 January 1864, worth in total £30. The most recent coupon of 1 January 1864 was to be paid in cash from the proceeds of the Six per Cent loan. The remaining nineteen coupons for £28 10s. were to be capitalized into new Three per Cent bonds at the rate of £60 of coupons for one new

£100 bond or an enhancement of 40%. Hence, the holder of a single 1851 bond with a par value of £100 was entitled to £47 10s. in new bonds in exchange for his arrear coupons of £28 10s. Additional money from the proceeds of the Six per Cent loan was promised to meet the first dividend payments on the new bonds. All the rights and securities appertaining to existing stocks under the settlement of October 1850 remained intact. Finally, proposals to be submitted by Barings and Glyn, Mills, Currie & Co. on behalf of the 1837 Deferred bondholders "will be favourably considered by His Majesty."

The overall effect of these proposals was that new bonds with a total nominal value of £4,864,800 were to be issued. The basis of that sum was that the principal of the debt, accepted by all parties to the 1850–1851 settlement, was £10,241,650. Annual interest at 3% was £307,249. Ten years' interest owed was £3,072,495. One half-yearly coupon or £153,624 was paid in cash, leaving interest to be capitalized at £2,918,870.[171]

James Capel presented these terms to the bondholders at the London Tavern on the day he received them, 11 April. They were accepted with little opposition. On the same day, Maximilian formally approved the Six per Cent loan and the agreement with the bondholders. The day before, he had established a Mexican Financial Commission in Paris under the chairmanship of the former French Finance Minister, Count de Germiny. It began to implement these several decisions. First, the prospectus for the Six per Cent loan was published. Its bonds were offered for sale in London, where sales were below expectation, and in France where the majority were placed. About £1,000,000 worth were unsold.[172]

Second, the Commission arranged for the design and printing of the new Three per Cents to be offered to the bondholders. Known henceforth as the 1864 Three per Cents, Illustration 12 reproduces bond number 32,971 of the F series, value £200.[173]

As indicated on the bond, the issue was in three series—E for £500; F for £200, and G for £100—with the total number of bonds being 35,648. The letters used followed on alphabetically from those of the 1851 Three per Cents which remained in the market. The printer, shown at the bottom of the bond, was the Imprimerie Centrale des Chemins de Fer de Napoleon Chaix et Cie., Paris. The identity of the designer is unknown. The words "Empire du Mexique" are just visible as is the imperial crown which is symbolically placed above the Mexican eagle and serpent emblem. Unusually, the text which is superimposed on the design is entirely in English. Forty dividend coupons were attached, payable half-yearly from 1 July 1864 to 1 January 1884.[174]

The bond is dated 15 June 1864. Two weeks later, on 28 June, Barings announced that it was ready to start the exchange of the new bonds for the overdue coupons. It also announced payment of two dividends—1 January and 1 July 1864—on the 1851 Three per Cents, and the first dividend

12. 1864 Imperial Three per Cent Bond.

on the new Three per Cents due on 1 July. Bondholders were reminded that the conversion of their coupons had to be completed by the end of the year.

The conversion required some arithmetical calculations. The bond illustrated shows that the coupons from a £100, 1851 Three per Cent were to be exchanged for new bonds to the value of £47 10s. The nominal value of the new stocks, however, started at £100. In other words, there was no new bond worth £47 10s. and therefore, a straight exchange was not possible. The same situation applied to the coupons from the higher value 1851 bonds which as shown were entitled to £71 5s. (£150 bond); £118 15s.(£250 bond); or £237 10s. (£500). Fractional certificates were obviously required. Fortunately, Barings' archive has retained several specimens of these and one is reproduced in Illustration 13. Bondholders were thus obliged to buy additional 1851 bonds to accumulate the required number of coupons to exchange for a new bond. Alternatively, they could buy the fractional certificates which were promptly sold in the market. As the text of the certificate shows, even then the values might not match exactly, in which case they would be given "a new Provisional Certificate for any balance that may remain over and above the amount of such Bond."

We do not know how many of the coupons were converted into the 1864 Three per Cents. At first, there was some resistance to the agreement and dissatisfied bondholders summoned a protest meeting for 13 April but no reports of its proceedings seem to have survived. The new Three per Cents were distributed and given an official quotation by the Stock Exchange Committee. As may be seen in Table 11, which gives the prices, at first the market valued them as more or less comparable with the 1851 Three per Cents. The collapse of Maximilian's empire and his execution in June 1867 brought a severe fall and for several months there were no trades reported in the Stock Exchange. Even more damaging was the news that Mexico had repudiated the bonds. Bondholders' agents had tried to ascertain the new republican government's attitude toward the English debt. In response to their enquiries, the Finance Minister, Matías Romero, gave his government's reply on 28 December 1868. He was blunt. As far as his government was concerned, the bondholders had helped Maximilian and thereby contributed to the "prostration and annihilation" of Mexico. By entering into agreements with the imperial regime, they had "rescinded by that act of their own will all the arrangements they had made with the Government of the Republic." All contracts between Mexico and the bondholders had been rendered invalid. Mexico would not recognize any agreement made with Maximilian nor would it pay any interest due during the imperial occupation.[175]

The market price fell to around £7 for a £100 nominal bond. Although negotiations with Mexican representatives in the early 1870s brought occasional, temporary hopes to the holders, by 1876 the price was down to

MEXICAN EMPIRE.

NEW 3 PER CENT. STOCK OF 1864, FOR CONSOLIDATIO
OF ARREARS OF INTEREST ON THE MEXICA
3 PER CENT. BONDS OF 1851.

N°2056

The Bearer hereof is entitled to

£

Sterling in the New Mexican 3 per Cent. Stock of 1864, and o
presentation, *within Six Months from the date hereof,* of a sufficien
number of similar Certificates forming together One Hundre
Pounds, or more, we engage to deliver in exchange a Mexican 3 pe
Cent. Bond of the said Stock, bearing Interest from 1st Januar
1864, and a new Provisional Certificate for any balance that ma
remain over and above the amount of such Bond.

London, July 1, 1864.

MEXICAN EMPIRE.

NEW 3 PER CENT. STOCK OF 1864, FOR CONSOLIDATION
OF ARREARS OF INTEREST ON THE MEXICAN
3 PER CENT. BONDS OF 1851.

N°2055

The Bearer hereof is entitled to

£

Sterling in the New Mexican 3 per Cent. Stock of 1864, and on
presentation, *within Six Months from the date hereof,* of a sufficient
number of similar Certificates forming together One Hundred
Pounds, or more, we engage to deliver in exchange a Mexican 3 per
Cent. Bond of the said Stock, bearing Interest from 1st January
1864, and a new Provisional Certificate for any balance that may
remain over and above the amount of such Bond.

London, July 7, 1864.

13. 1864 Barings Fractional Certificate.

Table 11
1864 Three per Cents

		J	F	M	A	M	J	J	A	S	O	N	D
1864	H	-	-	-	-	-	-	29	26	25	25	27	27
	L	-	-	-	-	-	-	26	26	25	24	26	27
1865	H	26	26	25	26	25	25	23	22	26	26	24	24
	L	26	25	25	25	23	23	22	22	23	24	24	21
1866	H	22	20	20	19	16	16	16	15	12	12	14	13
	L	18	17	19	18	13	11	11	11	10	11	13	12
1867	H	13	11	11	10	11	11	10	/	/	/	/	/
	L	11	11	11	9	9	10	7	/	/	/	/	/
1868	H	/	/	/	11	10	10	9	9	9	9	9	9
	L	/	/	/	9	9	9	8	8	7	8	7	7
1869	H	9	8	8	8	7	7	7	7	6	7	7	7
	L	7	7	7	6	5	5	5	4	4	5	5	6
1870	H	8	7	7	7	7	8	8	/	8	8	8	7
	L	6	5	5	6	6	6	7	/	7	7	6	6
1871	H	8	8	8	8	8	8	8	8	8	8	8	8
	L	6	7	7	7	7	7	6	7	7	7	6	6
1872	H	8	8	8	8	8	8	8	9	9	9	9	10
	L	7	6	6	7	7	7	7	7	7	7	8	8
1873	H	10	9	9	9	9	9	7	8	8	8	8	9
	L	9	8	8	8	7	7	7	7	7	7	7	8
1874	H	9	8	8	8	8	8	8	8	8	8	8	8
	L	8	8	7	7	7	7	6	7	7	7	7	6
1875	H	7	8	8	8	8	7	7	7	7	7	6	6
	L	6	6	7	7	6	6	5	6	6	6	5	5
1876	H	5	5	6	5	5	4	4	5	5	5	5	4
	L	3	3	4	3	2	2	2	3	3	4	4	3
1877	H	/	3	3	/	3	3	3	4	4	3	3	/
	L	/	3	3	/	3	3	3	3	3	3	3	/
1878	H	3	3	3	/	4	4	3	3	/	3	4	4
	L	3	3	3	/	4	3	3	3	/	3	3	3
1879	H	4	4	/	4	/	5	5	5	5	5	5	5
	L	3	3	/	3	/	3	4	4	4	4	5	5
1880	H	8	9	8	8	6	6	6	7	7	7	8	8
	L	4	7	7	6	5	5	5	6	6	6	7	8

Table 11 (continued)

		J	F	M	A	M	J	J	A	S	O	N	D
1881	H	18	15	14	17	16	16	15	17	17	16	16	16
	L	9	14	13	13	16	14	14	15	16	14	14	15
1882	H	15	14	13	13	13	13	11	12	14	14	14	12
	L	12	12	11	12	12	10	10	10	12	13	11	11
1883	H	12	12	12	13	18	19	18	17	15	15	13	12
	L	11	11	12	12	13	17	17	14	14	12	10	11
1884	H	12	11	11	12	11	11	12	12	11	11	10	9
	L	10	10	11	11	9	9	9	10	10	10	9	8
1885	H	9	9	9	9	8	9	8	8	8	8	9	8
	L	8	8	8	7	7	8	6	6	7	7	8	7
1886	H	8	10	10	10	10	10	10	10	10	10	12	13
	L	7	8	9	9	9	9	9	9	9	10	10	12
1887	H	13	12	13	13	14	15	15	14	15	16	17	17
	L	12	11	11	12	14	14	14	14	13	15	16	16
1888	H	18	18	18	18	19	20						
	L	17	17	17	17	17	19						

£3. In the 1880s, talks brought more false hopes, reflected in the price increases shown in Table 11. As with all the other bonds and certificates which had their origins in the 1824 and 1825 loans, it was not until the Dublán conversion of 1886 that the 1864 bonds were finally recognized.

Under the terms of the Mena agreement of 23 June 1886, the 1864 bonds were converted into the new 1886 Three per Cents at the rate of 50% of par. In other words, two £100 1864 Three per Cents were exchanged for one new 1886 Three per Cent. It seems that most of the 1864 bondholders responded quickly to the offer for their stocks. By September 1887, 28,133 bonds with a total nominal value of £3,817,000 had been exchanged. By the end of the conversion in August 1888, the amount had reached £4,791,943 10s., leaving £72,856 10s. of the original total of £4,864,800 outstanding.[176] Exact figures are not available but it is probable that eventually most of the 35,648 bonds printed in Paris in 1864 were handed in and cancelled. Fortunately, from our point of view, a few were retained by their holders and have survived. As indicated, Barings' archive has several and, in recent years, at least one has been offered for sale in London.

1886 THREE PER CENTS

The law of 22 June 1885 affirmed that Mexico's recognized legitimate debts, both internal and external, were to be consolidated into new bonds paying interest from 30 June 1886 at a rate of 1% per annum rising in stages to 3% in 1890. The wording, design, and numeration of the bonds and the forty half-yearly dividend coupons attached were to be the subject of a separate regulation. This was published on 29 January 1886.[177] It stipulated that bonds to a nominal value of 150 million pesos were to be issued in the following colors, series, letters, numbers, and values:

Color	Series	Numbers	Values (£)
Scarlet	A	1–140,000	5
Green	B	1–110,015	10
Chestnut	C	1–90,000	20
Orange	D	1–48,000	100
Blue	E	1–8,930	150
Red	F	1–24,046	200
Olive	G	1–8,393	250
Crimson	H	1–8,390	500
Light Brown	I	1–9,157	1,000

The bonds were to be authorized by the signatures of the Treasurer-General and the Director of the Public Debt and bear on the obverse the series, number, and value corresponding to each one. The following text was to be put on each bond:

The Mexican Federal Treasury will pay to the bearer in (space for place where payment is to be made) the sum expressed in this bond in the national money of said country, and in conformity to the provisions of the law of the 22nd of June inserted on the reverse. This bond is admissible for the whole its value in payment for waste lands, and nationalized capitals and estates, belonging to the federation.
    Their matured but unsettled coupons are admissible in payment, to the amount of five per cent, of all federal taxes which originate in the fiscal year following that in which they are due. The settlement and service of interest are regulated by the provisions of the appropriate law of the 22nd of June, 1885.

Articles 2–13, 15, and 20 of the 1885 law were to be printed on the reverse. As noted above, a space was left in the text for the insertion of the place. Both bonds and coupons were to be printed on special paper "with such marks and counter-marks as the Ministry of Finance may designate."
    Illustration 14 reproduces bond number 05741 of the D series, value £100. This bond, and others of the issue seen by the author, are dated 31 December 1885, thus predating the regulatory law which was not sanctioned until 29 January 1886. There is no obvious explanation for this discrepancy. Otherwise, the text is exactly as stipulated in the regulation.
    The bonds were produced by the American Bank Note Company of New

14. 1886 Three per Cent Bond.

York. The general designer is unknown but the borders and images are clearly more elaborate than those used on earlier issues. The vignettes of classical imagery are of peace (top right) and justice (top left). The latter includes the Aztec calendar stone and drawings of a railway, ships, and port, presumably to represent Mexico's economic progress. At the bottom, there is a monument to Christopher Columbus. This was the work of the French sculptor Charles Cordier (1827–1906). It was shipped from France in 1875 and unveiled in August 1877 in the main avenue in Mexico City known as La Reforma where it still stands.[178] Finally, as noted earlier, the national emblem of the eagle and the serpent was designed by Tomás de la Peña.

The signatures are of Benito Gómez Farías as "El Director de la Deuda Pública" ("The Director of the Public Debt"), and of the General Treasurer and Head of Section, although these are not readily legible. The stamps and overprinted text (at bottom right) were later additions to the bond. In accord with the provisions of the 1885 law, the face value is expressed in British, U.S., and Mexican currencies.

Five million pounds' worth of the issue was sent to Britain for the conversion but only the higher values were thought necessary. These were series D (£100); E (£150); G (£250); H (£500); I (£1,000). For reasons unknown, F (£200) was not included.[179] The exact date of their arrival in London is also not clear but there was much speculation in the press at the time. Following the Mena agreement with the bondholders of June 1886, *The Statist* reported on 25 September that the bonds were being signed in Mexico and would soon be dispatched to London. Two months later, on 20 November, *The Money Market Review* reported that they were "now being signed but will certainly arrive before Christmas." Then, on 1 December, the Financial Agency announced details of the conversion.[180] Bondholders were asked to present their existing stocks for examination at the Agency on Mondays and Thursdays between 10:00 A.M. and 2:00 P.M. They had to complete printed forms already prepared for each type of bond or certificate, listing series, numbers, and values. Finally, they had to add their names and addresses because "holders will be advised by post when the new bonds are ready for delivery."[181]

In fact, the bonds were probably received in London early in January 1887, soon after which they were distributed to the various categories of bondholders. As already explained in earlier sections of this work, holders of the 1837 Deferred received 15% of their nominal value in the new 1886 Three per Cents. The 1843 Five per Cents were given 29% while the 1864 Empire bonds were exchanged at 50%. Coupons and interest due on the 1851 Three per Cents for the twenty years from 1 July 1866 to 1 July 1886 were accepted at 15% and other outstanding dividend certificates were similarly exchanged for the new bonds.

There are various estimates of the total number of 1886 Three per Cents used for the Dublán conversion. For example, according to the Corporation of Foreign Bondholders *Report* for 1887, there were 11,200 distributed, with a face value of £4,650,000.[182] The Corporation's 1889 *Report* puts the figure at £4,585,000 and the London Legation's summary of 30 November 1888, cited above, also has £4,585,000.[183] With the lowest bond at £100, there were many instances where the value of the "old titles" did not equal that amount. Hence, fractional certificates for what were called "Residues" were given out by the Financial Agency. Bondholders who were able to acquire enough of these (they could be bought in the market) were able to exchange them for bonds. Those certificates still outstanding after 30 June 1888 were paid off in cash.[184]

The 1886 Three per Cents were granted an official quotation on 7 June 1887. The Stock Exchange Committee had delayed its decision because of a surge of protests against the new bond issue. As noted earlier, within a week of the Mena agreement of 23 June 1886, Foss and Ledsam protested against the terms offered to the 1837 Deferred bondholders and against the absence of any offer to those holding the 1843 Five per Cents. Their demands were settled by negotiation with the Financial Agency but there were many other protests. An unexpected one came from Francis Perry.[185] He was the brother of the late Edward Joseph Perry, who had been the bondholders' agent in Mexico from 1868 until his death in 1883. The bondholders' committee had promised to meet his late brother's claim for expenses of £5,000 by giving him bonds to the nominal value of £15,000. Nothing had been done, however, and he now asked the Stock Exchange not to approve any new Mexican bond issue until the claim had been settled.

Perry's case was obviously individual and personal. Far more serious was a vociferous campaign on behalf of unpaid dividend certificates originally issued by Facio in 1851. In the Dublán conversion, the problem centered on the total debt represented by the certificates. The Financial Agency's calculation was rejected by the holders as inadequate and they took their case to the Stock Exchange. Protests against the issue of new bonds until their claim was settled arrived from Amsterdam, where most of the certificates seem to have been held, and from Belgium. In London, the Coupon Agency Ltd. complained on behalf of themselves and their clients. The stockbrokers, W.T.F.M. Ingall & Co, acting, they said, on behalf of many Dutch holders, added their protest. Formal notice of opposition to the granting of a quotation for the new bonds "when it is applied for" was lodged with the Stock Exchange in November 1886. Faced with this wave of protests, the Stock Exchange Committee decided to defer its decision.[186] Eventually, the Financial Agency reached agreement with the 1851 certificate holders (see Chapter 2). Whether Mr. Perry reached agreement with his claim is not known. Finally, on 4 May 1887, another request for a quotation was submitted by the Financial Agency, accompanied by a com-

Table 12
1886 Three per Cents

		J	F	M	A	M	J	J	A	S	O	N	D
1887	H						29	28	27	30	33	34	34
	L						28	27	26	27	30	31	32
1888	H	33	36	37	37	37	40	38	40	40	40	39	40
	L	32	33	34	36	37	38	38	38	39	39	38	39
1889	H	40	40	40	41	41	41	41					
	L	39	39	39	40	40	41	41					

plete, very colorful, and almost certainly unique specimen set of each of the nine series of bonds and dividend coupons, all of which are now in the Stock Exchange archive.[187] As indicated earlier, the official quotation for the 1886 Three per Cents was granted on 7 June 1887. (Table 12 gives the prices.)

1888 SIX PER CENTS

The result of the Dublán conversion was that Mexican bonds with a nominal value of £14,891,650 remained in the market. Most of the "old titles" and dividend certificates had been cancelled and the debt was now almost entirely represented by the 1851 Three per Cents at £10,241,650 and the 1886 Three per Cents at £4,585,000.[188] Interest was payable, and was paid, on both these stocks at the rising rates set out in the 1885 law. It was also the case, however, that Mexico had reserved the right in the same law to redeem all outstanding bonds at 40% before the end of 1890. Rumors began to circulate in London in early November 1887 that a new loan was imminent and that the funds raised were to be used to buy in all the Three per Cents.[189] Their price in the market rose accordingly toward 40% of their par value.

The market rumors were confirmed when, in December 1887, the Mexican Congress passed a law authorizing the Executive to negotiate a loan for a sum not exceeding £10,500,000 and an interest of no more than 6%. Talks had proceeded for some time with European bankers and these had brought agreement with the German financier, Gerson Bleichroeder, representing a group of leading bankers. Bleichroeder, a financial adviser to Bismarck and former agent of Rothschilds in Berlin, put forward various proposals which, after approval by the Mexican cabinet on 7 December, formed the basis of the Executive's initiative to Congress and the law of 13 December.[190] Negotiations continued and with agreement on the details of commission concluded, a prospectus was published in London on 21

March 1888.[191] This was for the first tranche of the "Mexican Government Consolidated External Six per Cent loan, 1888—Issue of £3,700,000 sterling, being part of £10,500,000 sterling (authorized by Law of Congress of 13th December 1887)."

The terms of the loan were set out in this prospectus. The bonds were offered at £78 10s. per cent, payable in the usual installments. Interest of 6% was payable quarterly and the principal was redeemable in ten years or in 1898. Subscriptions were to be opened simultaneously on 23 March in London, Berlin, and Amsterdam where the bankers were, respectively, Messrs. Antony Gibbs and Sons; Herr S. Bleichroeder; Messrs. Lippman Rosenthal and Co. Revenues assigned to servicing the loan were 20% of import and export duties and the net proceeds of Federal District taxes on real estate and industry. The purpose of the initial offering of £3,700,000 was "to extinguish the interest bearing floating debt" and, if any funds were left, for the construction of public works. The remainder of the £10,500,000, or £6,800,000, "will be applied to the redemption of the Three per Cent Bonds of the Consolidated Debt of London, amounting to about £15,000,000."

The aim, therefore, was to complete the final redemption of the debt which had originated sixty-four years earlier, in 1824. Mexican credit in Europe was now so strong that the loan was vastly oversubscribed. According to a notarized statement sworn by Herbert Gibbs in London on 6 April 1888, the total amount of stock applied for in London, Berlin, and Amsterdam was £81,142,635. The whole of the issue had been allotted.[192] It had been, as Luis Camacho put it in a telegram to his Finance Minister, "un magnífico éxito" ("an outstanding success").[193]

The £6,800,000 remaining from the overall loan of £10,500,000 was taken up by the bankers at 85% and the bonds were released into the market in stages. The total issue comprised 93,000 bonds in the following series:

2000 bonds numbered 1-2000 each of £1000	£ 2,000,000
6000 bonds numbered 1-6000 each of £500	3,000,000
47,500 bonds numbered 1-47,500 each of £100	4,750,000
37,500 bonds numbered 1-37,500 each of £20	750,000
	£10,500,000[194]

Unfortunately, no example of any of these bonds has been found and the design cannot, therefore, be illustrated.[195] On the other hand, there is a notarized copy of the wording on each one in the Stock Exchange Quotations file. This shows that they had the text of the congressional decree of 13 December 1887 which authorized the Executive to raise the loan. Also included were the first five articles of the contract signed with the bankers. As usual, the different series, numbers, and values of the whole issue were printed on each bond. Interest was payable in sterling or in marks. Finally, payable to Bearer, they were all signed by the Mexican Treasurer-General, the Treasury Accountant, and Antony Gibbs & Sons. The text was in English, Spanish, and German.[196]

At the time of the issue of the first tranche of £3,700,000, Scrip certificates were given to buyers because the bonds were not yet available. Fortunately, there are specimen copies of these certificates in the Gibbs archive and one is reproduced in the next illustration (15).[197] They were produced by the printers Skipper & East.

These Scrip certificates served as bonds for the next few months because of a delay in the arrival in London of the new Six per Cents which possibly were printed by Skipper & East. They would have been sent to Mexico City for signature and then by train to Veracruz for dispatch to Europe. On 18 December 1888, Gibbs announced that "the exchange of Scrip certificates against the definitive bonds cannot be effected until January, due notice of which will be given."[198] The reason for the delay was "a breakdown on the Mexican Railway." A month later, the bonds had finally arrived and in *The Times* of 25 January 1889, Gibbs reported that the exchange for the Scrip would be carried out on and after Monday, 28 January.

The 1888 Six per Cents, therefore, entered the London market from January 1889. Apparently, most of them quickly found their way to Germany where one estimate placed three-quarters of the whole issue of 93,000 bonds.[199] Among the buyers was Bismarck who, on the advice of Bleichroeder, invested 232,000 marks.[200] The lower denominations in particular, that is, the £20 series, were more popular on the continent than in Britain where it was said "no bond for less than £100 finds much acceptance."[201]

After the initial £3,700,000 was used for the floating debt, the remaining £6,800,000 was available for the redemption of the 1851 and 1886 Three per Cents. These were gradually bought in by the bankers with the proceeds of the sale of the Six per Cents. By April 1889, the amount of Three per Cents still outstanding was £3,997,600. Two announcements appeared in the press.[202] The first was by Gibbs which offered to convert the outstanding Three per Cents into Six per Cents at the rate of 40% plus the value of one dividend coupon:

The Bonds of the 3 per cent Mexican External Debt of 1851 and 1886, with the coupons due 30th June and 1st July respectively, and all subsequent coupons attached, will be received at £41 5s. for every £100 Bond deposited, and the Bonds of the 6 per cent External Loan, 1888, will be delivered in exchange, with the quarterly coupon due July 1st, 1889 attached, at the rate of £97 for every £100 nominal.

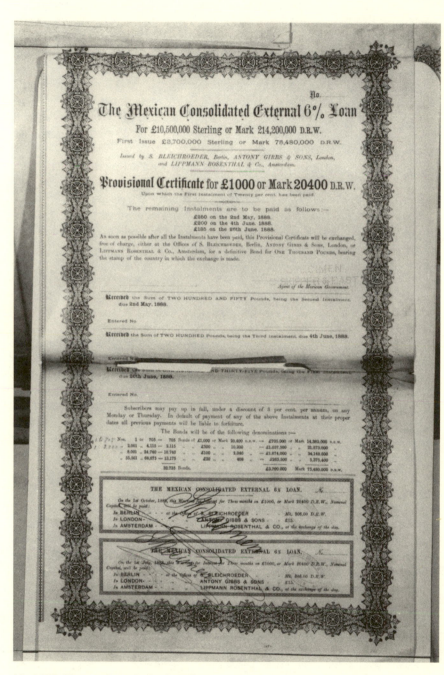

15. 1888 Six per Cent Scrip Certificate.

Table 13
1888 Six per Cents

		J	F	M	A	M	J	J	A	S	O	N	D
1888	H							92	94	94	92	90	93
	L							91	91	93	89	89	89
1889	H	93	93	94	98	97	97	96					
	L	91	92	93	93	96	95	95					

Fractional differences in the exchange would be paid in cash. One week only, from Monday, 29 April to Saturday, 4 May was allowed for the conversion.

On the same day, 27 April 1889, an announcement was also placed in the press by the Mexican Financial Agency:

Notice is hereby given, that in accordance with Article 6 of the agreement of 23rd June, 1886, all BONDS outstanding of 1851 and 1886, converted and issued by this Financial Agency of the Government of Mexico, will be PAID off on the 1st July next, at the rate of Forty per cent (40 per cent) of their par value. From 1st July, 1889, interest will cease on such outstanding bonds.

These two announcements offered bondholders the choice of taking cash or 1888 Six per Cents.[203] Not all took advantage of either offer, even though interest payments on their Three per Cents ended on 1 July 1889. The deadline for conversion was extended more than once by the Financial Agency but, finally, it was announced in *The Financial Times* (31 October 1889) and elsewhere that no more of the Three per Cents would be exchanged for cash after 27 May 1890. Even this last deadline did not persuade all the holders to come forward and by 1893, some £46,850 of the 1851 Three per Cents remained in circulation.[204] As for the 1886 Three per Cents, a Mexican Treasury report for the fiscal year 1893–1894 states that only £200 worth of those issued in London were still outstanding.[205] In 1895, the Financial Agency made the offer already referred to with reference to the "old titles," to buy in any outstanding bonds at a price to be agreed upon. How many bondholders took advantage of the offer is not known.

Table 13 shows the market prices of the 1888 Six per Cents from July 1888 when they were given an official quotation by the Stock Exchange until July 1889 when the Dublán conversion terminated.

ENGLISH CONVENTION BONDS

There was one remaining entry in the Corporation of Foreign Bondholders' statistical summary of the Dublán conversion. This referred to what was known as the English Convention debt. While of little direct concern to the bondholders as a whole, the subject was of material interest to the Committee of Mexican Bondholders in its negotiations with the British government.[206] The debt had its origins in several diplomatic Conventions agreed upon between Britain and Mexico. The first of these was the so-called Pakenham Convention, signed in October 1842 by Britain's Minister Plenipotentiary to Mexico, Richard Pakenham, and Mexico's Ministers of Finance and Foreign Relations. In the first two decades after independence in 1821, British citizens had suffered from forced loans, confiscation, and damage to their businesses and property as a result of the frequent military rebellions and civil strife which had afflicted the new republic. They demanded compensation and, faced with Mexican refusals to oblige, they naturally turned for help to their diplomatic representatives. The Pakenham Convention was the first formal recognition by Mexico of several of the claims against it. Under its terms, it acknowledged a debt of 250,000 pesos owed to the three main claimants, Mackintosh and Marshall; J.P. Penny & Co.; Martínez del Río Hermanos. The owners of the latter, it should be explained, although Panamanian in origin, had become naturalized citizens of Britain and successfully claimed British protection. It was agreed that the debt would be paid by a special levy of 2% on the Veracruz customs dues and of 1% on those of Tampico.[207]

Other similar Conventions were signed in following years but little cash was actually paid to the claimants, and by the end of the 1840s additional claims had accumulated. These led to another Convention arranged by the British Chargé d'Affaires, Percy Doyle. The Doyle Convention, dated 4 December 1851, was more detailed than its predecessors, which were incorporated into it.[208] Mexico acknowledged claims amounting to 4,984,214 dollars or £996,842. It agreed to amortize the principal at 5% per year and in the meantime to pay 3% interest on the remainder with payments made at six monthly intervals. After four years, the rates were to increase to 6% and 4%, respectively; 12% of the maritime customs dues were assigned to service the debt. Martínez del Río was appointed the creditors' agent to receive and distribute money or credits received from the customs houses.

As security, creditors were to be given bonds for the amount of their claim. The bonds were produced in four series or values: 1,000, 5,000, 10,000, 20,000 dollars.[209] Unfortunately, no example of the bonds of the English Convention has been found. Mexico, however, signed similar agreements with France and Spain at around the same time and bonds of the Spanish Convention are available. It seems likely that in terms of design, they were similar to those given to the English creditors. (Illustration 16 reproduces a Spanish Convention bond.)

This bond was printed by the Mexican firm of R. Rafael in a rather more ornate design than some of the earlier issues.[210] The reverse has the main articles from the Spanish Convention. Thirty dividend coupons were orig-

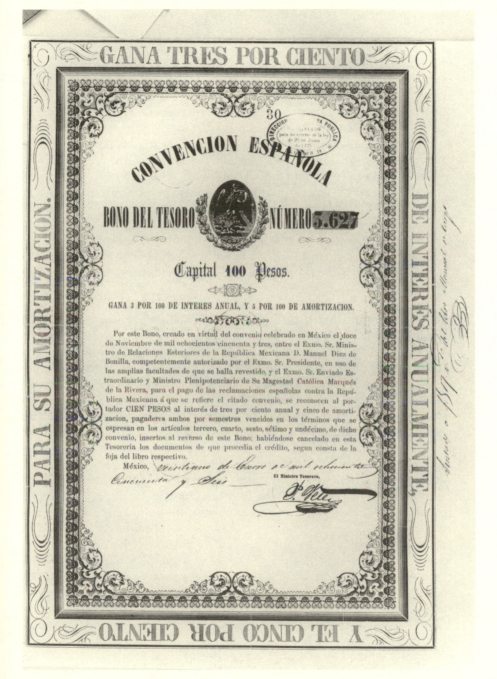

16. Spanish Convention Bond.

inally attached, corresponding to six monthly payments over fifteen years ending in February 1867.[211] Bonds of different values were printed in other colors.

Adjustments to the Doyle Convention were made in 1852 and 1853 which raised the charge on the customs dues to 16%. While some payments were made, the fund was soon in arrears which, by October 1854, had risen to 466,000 dollars. Political events and especially the War of the Reform meant that payments were again suspended. The British government's response was to send warships to Veracruz to demand that whichever party was in control of the port (control fluctuated between liberals and conservatives), Mexico's obligations to creditors, accepted by diplomatic Convention, must be faithfully observed. The result of this gunboat diplomacy was three more Conventions—known respectively as the Otway Convention; Dunlop Arrangement; Aldham Arrangement.[212] The details of these need not concern us, especially as in the prevailing chaos of the civil war, none was observed by Mexico. In all of them, the Mexican authorities of the day at Veracruz again agreed to ensure that the customs assignments were delivered to Martínez del Río, and in the Dunlop agreement of 1859 the charge on the customs was raised to 24%.

The Mexican bondholders in London were not at first concerned with these Conventions but their Committee, especially after David Robertson became chairman, waged a vigorous campaign for parity of treatment. Robertson pressed the Foreign Office to negotiate a Convention which would include all the debts owing to the London holders of Mexico's foreign debt bonds. His campaign failed to achieve a separate Convention but some of the claims of his members were included explicitly in the Dunlop Arrangement and implicitly in the adjustments subsequently negotiated by Captain Aldham. Henceforth, Robertson and his successors argued that the foreign debt bondholders and those of the English Convention debt enjoyed the same status. As he put it in a letter of June 1858, "The British Convention creditors are in the same boat." "We are," he went on, "the older creditors, and, of course, the first and best entitled by the acknowledged law of nations as national creditors; but we are quite satisfied to be put altogether."[213]

Part of Robertson's case for parity of treatment by the British government was based on the identity of the Convention debt bondholders. The Convention bonds were saleable securities and they were used in financial transactions in Mexico, and probably in London. In August 1858, for example, Martínez del Río ceded sixty-nine of its bonds with a face value of 1,200,000 dollars to the firm of Hermenegildo Viya & Co. Viya subsequently resold some of them to the Lizardis.[214] By 1861, of the original principal debt of almost 5,000,000 dollars accepted in the 1851 Doyle Convention, 75% of the bonds were in the hands of Spaniards, Mexicans, and other foreigners; 20% were held by naturalized British subjects "or standing in their names"; and only about 5% were owned by "British native subjects." These details were included in the 1861 *Report* of the Mexican Committee and they were certainly taken from an open letter sent to Lord Russell by the barrister and Committee member Richard Garde.[215] He told the Foreign Secretary that he had before him the names and amounts claimed of all those included in the Convention debt: "Among thirty-one names, I find those of only four Englishmen, and the amount of those claims is a mere trifle." Unfortunately, Garde does not reveal the names but his point, also made repeatedly by Robertson, was that the British government was giving its protection essentially to foreigners while neglecting its own citizens. "In what respect," asked Garde, "are the claims of the Mexican Bondholders entitled to less support, legally or morally?"[216]

The Mexican Committee's campaign for official diplomatic recognition of its claims against Mexico in the form of an intergovernmental Convention was superceded by events. The Allied occupation of Mexican ports in 1862 with the ostensible purpose of collecting customs dues owed to British, Spanish, and French creditors brought about the first remittances to London for several years for both the foreign and Convention debt bondholders.[217] Even after the British and Spanish withdrawal, money continued to be taken from the customs houses and given to Viya Hermanos, who was now the agent for the Convention bondholders. By 1865, the recently formed London Bank of Mexico and South America was acting as agent for those who lived in Mexico. It invited holders resident in Britain to apply to participate in the arrangements it had concluded with them. According to the Bank, bonds to the value of 4,175,000 pesos remained unredeemed. It was estimated, however, that as the customs assignments were being paid, all the bonds would be redeemed at par within four or five years.[218] A few months later, the Bank announced the receipt from Mexico of £7,296 for the interest and amortization payments due on the Convention bonds.[219]

What turned out to be the penultimate stage in the Convention bonds occurred soon after the collapse of the Maximilian Empire and the restoration to power of the liberal government led by Benito Juárez. In July 1867, Mexico declared null and void all international agreements with those countries which had aided the Maximilian regime. Included in this declaration were the English Conventions which were deemed to be "nonexistent." In a letter to the Mexico-based company Barron & Forbes, which was acting as the temporary agent of the Convention creditors, the Finance Minister indicated his intention "to achieve the gradual extinction" of the Convention bonds by buying them in public auctions. Barron & Forbes held a meeting of the Mexico City holders and protested, but to no avail.[220] The first auction was held on 10 February 1868 and 90,000 dollars in cash was offered to those willing to surrender the largest quantity of bonds of the English and Spanish Convention debts. English debt bonds to the value of 168,073 dollars were surrendered for 48,615 dollars in cash. Another 316,780 dollars' worth of the Spanish bonds fetched 41,385 dollars.[221]

With the suspension of diplomatic relations between Mexico and Britain in 1867, nothing further happened on any official level regarding the Convention bonds until the negotiations for the renewal of relations began in 1883. They led to an agreement between the Special Commissioners appointed by both countries, which was signed in August 1884. It provided for the renewal of relations and for payment of the Convention debt.[222] Further talks in Mexico City led to an agreed rate for the redemption which was settled at £150 of the new 1886 Three per Cents for each £100 of the Convention bonds, including all interest arrears. According to the calculations of the Corporation of Foreign Bondholders, of the original £996,842 worth of bonds issued after the Doyle Convention, some £599,999 remained outstanding. By the end of the Dublán conversion in 1888, bonds with a nominal value of £581,257 had been surrendered in exchange for £871,886 of 1886 Three per Cents. Bonds worth a nominal value of £18,742 were not presented and, it is to be hoped, may yet be found.[223] The identity of the holders who benefited from this conversion is not known but strong rumors at the time suggested that former President Manuel González and his brother-in-law, Ramón Fernández, had acquired up to half of the bonds.[224]

NOTES

1. For more details, especially for the later decades of the nineteenth century, see D.C.M. Platt, "British Bondholders in Nineteenth Century Latin America: Injury and Remedy," in M.D. Bernstein, ed., *Foreign Investment in Latin America. Cases and Attitudes* (New York, 1966), pp. 81–102.

2. W.J. Reader, *A House in the City. A Study of the City and of the Stock Exchange Based on the Records of Foster & Braithwaite* (London, 1979), pp. 16–17.

3. See J. Rodríguez O, "Mexico's First Foreign Loans," in J. Rodríguez O, ed., *The Independence of Mexico and the Creation of the New Nation* (Los Angeles, 1989), pp. 215–235.

4. There is a useful discussion of the role of contractors in the rather more sophisticated loan market of the 1870s in C. Marichal, *A Century of Debt Crises in Latin America from Independence to the Great Depression, 1820–1930* (Princeton, N.J., 1989).

5. Platt, "British Bondholders in Nineteenth Century Latin America: Injury and Remedy," pp. 92–93.

6. F.G. Dawson, *The First Latin American Debt Crisis. The City of London and the 1822–1825 Loan Bubble* (New Haven, Conn. and London, 1990), p. 105. For Disraeli's Mexican investments, see Chapter 5.

7. Marichal has interesting examples of the corrupt practices used in the 1870s; Marichal, *A Century of Debt Crises*, pp. 114–119.

8. Ibid., pp. 222–223.

9. For details, see R.M. Burch, *Colour Printing and Colour Printers* (Edinburgh, 1983), pp. 121–122; P.A.H. Brown, *London Publishers and Printers, c.1800–1870* (London, 1982).

10. The original is in the copies of manuscripts from the Barings Archive housed in the public archives of Canada, at Ottawa: Barings Papers—D—Printed Matter, 1781–1891. I used the microfilm copy in Reel C. 1439.

11. Copy kindly provided by Herr Joachim Block.

12. I. Smith, "Security Printing," *International Bond and Share Society Journal* (November 1997), p. 36.

13. *The Times*, 20 November 1838, 14 October 1846.

14. Correspondence in Secretaría de Relaciones Exteriores Archivo "Genaro Estrada" (Mexico City)—henceforth SRE—40.11.7, 1844 file. Occasionally, there are no fol. numbers on the manuscripts in this archive.

15. T. Murphy to Minister of Foreign Affairs, 1 December 1844, SRE, 3.11.4716, fol. 126. There is a file of documentation on the Tebbutt case in the Archivo General de la Nación (henceforth AGN), Galería 6, Deuda Externa, vol. 14. Copies of his letters are also in SRE, L.E. 1230, 1822–1844, vol. 1. His correspondence with the British Foreign Office and a copy of his memorial are in Public Record Office (henceforth PRO), F.O., 50/160, 169, 179.

16. On the early negotiations for the loans, see Rodríguez O, "Mexico's First Foreign Loans," and Borja's correspondence in *La Diplomacia Mexicana* (Secretaría de Relaciones Exteriores, Mexico, 1910–1913), vol. 2, pp. 181–196.

17. Cited in E. Turlington, *Mexico and Her Foreign Creditors* (New York, 1930), p. 38.

18. AGN, Galería 6, Deuda Externa, vol. 12.

19. Deposit Book, 1813–1824, Bank of England Archive/Museum, 85/87–15, fol. 179. All future references to Deposit Books refer to those in the Bank of England Archive/Museum.

20. Migoni to Minister of Finance, 22 March 1824, AGN, Galería 6, Deuda Externa, vol. 12, fols. 128–133.

21. The legal opinions are in AGN, Galería 6, Deuda Externa, vol. 12, fols. 120–126.

22. Deposit Book, 1813–1824, Bank of England Archive/Museum, 85/87–15, fol. 179. The Goldsmidt contract has been printed in various works; see, for example, J.M.L. Mora, *Obras sueltas* (Mexico, 1963), pp. 437–444.

23. The copies of the bonds are in the PRO, F.O. 97/275, fols. 119–129.

24. *The Times*, 19 July 1824.

25. Rodríguez O, "Mexico's First Foreign Loans," p. 222.

26. See Deposit Books, 85/87–15, fols. 180, 181; 85/87–16, fols. 8–9, 12, 19–20, 24–25, 28–29, 30.

27. Dawson, *The First Latin American Debt Crisis*, p. 39.

28. Turlington, *Mexico and Her Foreign Creditors*, p. 44.

29. H.F. Barclay & A.W. Fox, *A History of the Barclay Family* (London, 1934), p. 286. In 1844, Barings referred to David Barclay of "Barclay Bros. & Co." as being the loan contractor in 1825: Barings to T. Murphy, 1 May 1844, SRE, 40.11.7. He may also have been M.P. for Penryn (1826) and later for Sunderland.

30. Some of Herring's correspondence at this time is in the English Papers, County Record Office, County Hall, Ipswich.

31. E.H. Plumptre to Messrs. Sweet and Carr, 2 January 1832, ING Barings Archive (henceforth Barings), HC4.5.3, fol. 8: AGN, Deuda Externa, vol. 12, fol. 235.

32. Plumptre's correspondence with Michelena is in SRE, 40.11.7.

33. For example, *The Times*, 18 November 1824.

34. The advertisement appeared daily in *The Times*, from 31 January 1825 onwards. This had been agreed at a meeting with Michelena on 7 January 1825: see the minute of the meeting in SRE, 40.11.7.

35. *The Times*, 8 February 1825.

36. Ibid.

37. Deposit Book, 85/87–16, fol. 12.

38. Correspondence in SRE, 40.11.7.

39. David Barclay and Vicente Rocafuerte made the first deposit of the cancelled Six per Cents in the Bank of England on 21 February 1826: Deposit Book, 85/87–16, fol. 30.

40. *The Times*, 15–22 February 1826.

41. B. Goldsmidt & Co. to M.E. de Gorostiza, 14 May 1830, SRE, L.E. 1230, 1822–1844, Deuda de México a Inglaterra. Tomo 1, fols. 2–3. The company was still listed in the 1830 *Robson's London Commercial Directory* (London, 1830) as B.A. Goldsmidt & Co., at 5 St. Helen's Place.

42. The liquidation of Barclay's accounts lasted for several years—see the file in SRE, 40.11.9.

43. *The Times*, 9 November 1826.

44. Deposit Book, 85/87–17, fol. 105. In a letter of 1 June 1844, Murphy said there were 15 boxes, but in a later letter of 1 December 1844, he said 14; both letters are in SRE, 3.11.4716, fols. 64, 124–130.

45. Correspondence in ibid., fols. 64, 89.

46. Deposit Book, 85/87–18, fol. 61. The words in italics are printed and are the standard wording on the forms in the Deposit Books—the other words are handwritten entries made at the time of the deposit.

47. SRE, 3.11.4716, fols. 124–126.

48. S. Herbert to J.M. Mendoza, 10 September 1850, SRE, 40.11.7.

49. These letters are in the Stock Exchange Quotations collection (henceforth Stock Exchange/Quotations) in the Guildhall Library (London), Ms 18000, 13B 240; 19B 437.

50. The translated text of Alamán's letter is in *Proceedings of the Committee of the Holders of Mexican Bonds, appointed at the General Meeting of Bondholders, held at the City of London Tavern, the 26th of May, 1830* (London, 1830), pp. 4–9. Henceforth the Committee of Mexican Bondholders' reports will be referred to as CMB *Report* followed by the year of publication. Where more than one report appeared in a year, the month of publication is also given.

51. The formation of the Committee of Mexican Bondholders is examined in Part II.

52. For the bondholders' relations with the British government, see Part II.

53. Details and quotations from CMB *Report* (1830), pp. 26–33.

54. See the correspondence in AGN, Deuda Externa, vol. 14, fols. 694–756.

55. The terms were published in the form of a three-page leaflet. There is a copy in Barings Archive, HC4.5.4, no.14.

56. J.D. Powles to E. de Gorostiza, 21 September 1831, SRE, 40.11.7.

57. R.T. Wilson to E. de Gorostiza, 30 June 1831, ibid., 40.11.7 There seems to have been no reference to tax liability on the higher value coupons, as had been the case with the 1824 bonds.

58. T. Murphy, *Memoria sobre la deuda exterior de la República Mexicana desde su creación hasta fines de 1847* (Paris, 1848), pp. 7–9.

59. Barings, HC4.5.4., fol. 8.

60. Barings to E. de Gorostiza, 5 November 1831, SRE, 40.11.4.

61. AGN, Deuda Externa, vol. 3, fols. 120–122.

62. See SRE, 40.11.4., vols. 2 and 3.

63. Murphy gives a slightly larger number, 11,946, in a letter of 1 June 1843 to his Minister of Foreign Affairs. Apparently, Barings issued a few without Gorostiza's signature: SRE, 3.11.4715.

64. Correspondence published in *The Times*, 17 June 1836.

65. *The Times*, 15 February 1873. Santa María's recommendation is in SRE, 3.11.478.

66. Chapman, *The Rise of Merchant Banking*, pp. 39, 41. Chapman mistakenly describes the firm as Anglo-American of European origin (p. 11).

67. Reports of the Lizardi court case are in *The Times*, 15, 18, 19, 25 February, 5 May 1873.

68. The Lizardi bankruptcy papers have disappeared. The case was clearly entered in the Bankruptcy Registers (PRO, B6 187 and 201) but there are no papers except those concerning a dispute over the forfeited recognizances in PRO, TS 25/ 1880.

69. Borja Migoni's will is in PRO, Prob. 11/1793.

70. Turlington, *Mexico and Her Foreign Creditors*, p. 70.

71. The various laws and other documents relating to the 1837 conversion were collected together and published as *Acts of the Mexican Congress relating to the conversion of the foreign debt. 1837–1839* (London, 1839).

72. Turlington, *Mexico and Her Foreign Creditors*, pp. 70–72.

73. There is a detailed report of the proceedings of the meeting in *The Times*, 10 August 1837.

74. Ibid.

75. PRO, F.O. 50/111, fol. 250.

76. *The Times*, 6 September 1837.

77. One signed copy is in SRE, 40.11.8. See also *Report of the Committee of Spanish American Bondholders, presented at a General Meeting of the Bondholders, held at the London Tavern, May 8, 1839* (London, 1839), pp. 3–11. Future references to this Committee will be CSAB.

78. *Acts of the Mexican Congress*, pp. 13–16.

79. J. Van Sommer to Lizardi & Co., 23 November 1842, published in *Conversion of Mexican Bonds. Report of the Committee of the Stock Exchange* (London, 1842), p. 1.

80. Deposit Book, 85/87,18, fol. 209.

81. Ibid., 85/87, 19, fol. 6.

82. Lizardi & Co. to T. Murphy, 13 November 1841, SRE, 40.11.8. There are

several lists of the numbers of the certificates signed by Murphy in this file and in 3.11.4712. See also L. Alamán, "Liquidación general de la deuda esterior de la República Mexicana hasta fin de diciembre de 1841," in *Obras: Documentos diversos*, vol. 9 (Mexico, 1945–1947), pp. 323–472.

83. Alamán, "Liquidación," p. 456.

84. Regulations for the issue of the certificates were included in the presidential order of 29 July 1839, published in English in *Acts of the Mexican Congress*, pp. 13–16.

85. R.C. Wyllie, *To G.R. Robinson, Esq., Chairman of the Committee of Spanish American Bondholders, on the present state and prospects of the Spanish American loans* (London, 1840), p. 10.

86. Robinson's letter is in SRE, 3.11.4712, fols. 12–14.

87. Murphy's letters were published in *The Morning Chronicle*, 24, 26 March 1840. See also his letter of 15 April 1840 to his Foreign Secretary in SRE, 3.11.4712, fols. 18–20.

88. Correspondence in ibid.

89. The agreement was also printed as a separate leaflet. There is a copy in ibid., 3.11.4714, fol. 32.

90. SRE, 3.11.4714, fols. 16, 28–34.

91. The list of Debentures presented by Mr. Smythe to the London Legation is in ibid., 3.11.4716, fol. 92.

92. The correspondence was published by the Stock Exchange as *Conversion of Mexican Bonds. Report of the Committee of the Stock Exchange* (London, 1842).

93. *The Times*, 10 May 1843.

94. The letter was published in ibid., 16 September 1843.

95. See the reports of the meetng in ibid., 7 October 1843, and *The Morning Chronicle*, 7 October 1843. All the newspapers carried details of the meeting and published correspondence concerning the dispute.

96. PRO, F.O. 50/170, fols. 87–95.

97. The newspaper cuttings are in SRE, 3.11.4715.

98. D.W. Walker, *Kinship, Business and Politics. The Martínez del Río Family in Mexico, 1823–1867* (Austin, 1986), p. 181.

99. SRE, 40.11.8.

100. Stock Exchange, Committee for General Purposes. Minutes of meetings of 26 February; 4, 13 March 1844, Guildhall Library, Ms. 14600, 18, pp. 349–350, 359–360.

101. Murphy, *Memoria sobre la deuda exterior*, pp. 64–69.

102. Correspondence in SRE, 40.11.7.

103. Ibid., L.E. 1231, fol. 266b.

104. M. Ortiz de Montellano, *Apuntes para la liquidación de la deuda Contraída en Londres* (Mexico, 1886), p. 209.

105. The letter was published in the *The Standard*, 22 September 1884.

106. AGN, Galería 6, Deuda Externa, vol. 10.

107. *The Times*, 28 June 1886.

108. The resolutions taken at the meeting and the Foss and Ledsam correspondence with the Stock Exchange Committee are in Stock Exchange/Quotations, Guildhall Library, Ms. 18000, 13B 240.

109. *The Times*, 16 November 1886.

110. Mexican Legation (London) report to Minister of Foreign Affairs, 30 November 1888, SRE, L.E. 1035, fol. 136.

111. SRE, 40.11.8.

112. Information supplied by Companies House, Cardiff.

113. Details are in J.D. Casasús, *Historia de la deuda contraída en Londres, con un apéndice sobre el estado actual de la Hacienda Pública* (Mexico, 1885), pp. 195–203.

114. See G. O'Brien to T. Murphy, 19 January 1827, SRE, 40.11.9.

115. Murphy was later accused of exceeding his powers and acting against Mexico's best interests in the 1846 conversion. He published various documents to refute the allegations: *Documentos oficiales relativos a la conversión de la deuda mexicana exterior verificada en 1846* (London, n.d. but probably 1846).

116. *The Morning Chronicle*, 19 May 1846; *The Times*, 19 May 1846.

117. *The Times*, 22 May 1846.

118. M. Payno, *Mexico and Her Financial Questions with England, Spain and France* (Mexico, 1862), p. 16.

119. Murphy, *Memoria sobre la deuda exterior*, p. 115.

120. Manning and Mackintosh Papers, Benson Latin American Collection, folder 93.

121. *The Times*, 12 January 1847.

122. Ibid., 6 July 1846.

123. Respectively in SRE, 40-11-5, fol. 45; Shropshire Record Office, Marrington Collection, 631/3/2591; and PRO, F.O. 50/224, fols. 142–143. The bond in SRE may be the specimen sent by Mora with his letter of 6 September 1848: see SRE, 3.11.4720, fol. 416.

124. Deposit Book, 85/87-19, fol. 2.

125. CMB *Report* (January 1853), p. 11.

126. Payno, *Mexico and Her Financial Questions*, Appendix E; Ortiz de Montellano, *Apuntes*, p. 74.

127. Mexican Legation (London) report, SRE, L.E. 1035, fols. 135–138; Corporation of Foreign Bondholders (henceforth CFB) *Report* (1888), p. 108.

128. Lizardi & Co. to G. Robinson, 30 November 1842, in *Conversion of Mexican Bonds. Report of the Stock Exchange*, p. 3.

129. Deposit Book, 85/87-18, fol. 107

130. Schneider & Co. to Minister of Finance, 30 June 1849, SRE, 3.11.4720, fols. 107–108.

131. Sheppard & Son to J.M. Mendoza, 21 January 1847, SRE, 40.11.7.

132. Ibid., 3.11.4721, fols. 1–2.

133. Ibid., fols. 107–108.

134. CMB *Report* (1855), p. 17.

135. List given in Casasús, *Historia de la deuda*, p. 297.

136. Stock Exchange/Quotations, Ms. 18000. 13B 240.

137. Table published in *The Times*, 17 September 1887.

138. Ibid., 2 May 1895.

139. Ibid., 14 October 1846.

140. Ortiz de Montellano, *Apuntes*, pp. 155–160.

141. The debate was fully reported in *The Times*, 7 July 1847 and in Hansard: *Parliamentary Debates*. 3 ser. 93: 1285–1307.

142. There is a printed copy of Palmerston's circular in PRO, F.O. 97/273, fols. 16–17. See also Chapter 6 of this study.

143. B. Tenenbaum, *The Politics of Penury. Debts and Taxes in Mexico, 1821– 1856* (Albuquerque, 1986), p. 98.

144. CSAB, *Statement of Proceedings in relation to the Mexican Debt* (London, 1850), p. 15.

145. J.D. Powles to Lord Palmerston, 14 January, 12 July 1848, PRO, F.O.50/ 225, fols. 9, 131–132.

146. The exchange of letters with Mora and the text of the legal opinion are in CSAB, *Proceedings*, pp. 17–28.

147. The letter to Mora is dated 13 October 1848. A draft copy is in SRE, 3.11.4720, fol. 69.

148. *The Times*, 16 October 1826.

149. The text of the agreement is in ibid., 19 September 1849.

150. For the full text of the law, see M. Dublán and J.M. Lozano, eds., *Legislación mexicana* (Mexico, 1876), vol.5, pp. 743–744. There is an English translation in the CMB *Report* (1856), pp. 16–17.

151. CMB *Report* (December 1850), p. 12.

152. J. Bazant, *Historia de la deuda exterior de México (1823–1946)* (Mexico, 1968), pp. 71–73.

153. Correspondence in *The Times*, 14, 19 May 1851.

154. M. Payno, *Memoria en que Manuel Payno da cuenta al público de su manejo en el desempeño del Ministerio de Hacienda* (Mexico, 1852), Appendix 3, pp. 51–52.

155. *The Times*, 19 February, 23 March, 13 April 1852.

156. CMB *Report* (1856), p. 15.

157. An English translation of the law was published by the Corporation of Foreign Bondholders under the title *United States of Mexico. Law for the Consolidation and Conversion of the National Debt. 22nd June 1885* (London, 1885).

158. The text of the Mena agreement was published by the Corporation of Foreign Bondholders as *Arrangement agreed upon between the undersigned . . . as representatives of the Holders of Mexican Bonds, to fix the mode of payment of the unpaid interest of the Mexican debt of 1851 . . .* (London, 1886).

159. Glyn's announcement is in *The Daily Telegraph*, 2 September 1886.

160. Corporation of Foreign Bondholders to Secretary, Share and Loan Department, Stock Exchange/Quotations, Ms. 18000, 13B 240.

161. *The Bullionist*, 18 September 1886.

162. Table published by Mexican Financial Agency in *The Times*, 17 September 1851.

163. CFB *Report* (1889), p. 114.

164. Ibid., (1895), p. 214.

165. Announcement in *The Times*, 2 May 1895.

166. Barings' letter, dated 12 March 1864, and the report by G. White are in PRO, F.O. 97/281, fols. 1–3, 18–20.

167. *The Times*, 14, 16 March 1864.

168. Ibid., 21–22 March 1864; Turlington, *Mexico and Her Foreign Creditors*,

pp. 153–155. There is a copy of the contract in the Royal Bank of Scotland Archive, GM/399. I am grateful to the Deputy Group Archivist, Mr. Philip Winterbottom, for providing me with a photocopy.

169. The bondholders' meeting was first summoned for 30 March and then postponed several times. For press reports of the negotiations, see *The Times*, 24, 28, 30 March, 9 April 1864.

170. A copy of the letter to James Capel is in PRO, F.O. 97/281, fols. 181–182.

171. Slight discrepancies in the arithmetic are due to the omission of shillings and pence.

172. Turlington, *Mexico and Her Foreign Creditors*, pp. 154–155. The Imperial Six per Cents were converted into a new issue in 1865, see ibid., pp. 156–157.

173. Reproduction by kind permission of ING Barings of original bond in its archive.

174. For illustrations of the coupons, see Chapter 2.

175. For Romero's letter and related documents, see CMB *Report* (1869), pp. 25–39. The Juárez government's agent in Europe had warned in June 1864 that no arrangements with the imperial regime would be recognized. See Turlington, *Mexico and Her Foreign Creditors*, pp. 155–156.

176. Author's calculations based on table in Corporation of Foreign Bondholders (henceforth CFB) *Report* (1888), p. 114. The Mexican Legation report of 30 November 1888 has slightly different figures, £4,792,200 and £71,800; SRE, L.E. 1035, fols. 135–138.

177. An English translation of the regulation was published in *The Mexican Financier*, 6 February 1886. The quotations which follow are from this translation.

178. B.A. Tenenbaum, "Streetwise History. The Paseo de la Reforma and the Porfirian State, 1876–1910," in W. Beezley et al., eds., *Rituals of Rule, Rituals of Resistance. Public Celebrations and Popular Culture in Mexico* (Wilmington, Del., 1994), pp. 127–150.

179. The bond series to be offered in London were listed in the application to the Stock Exchange for an official quotation; see Stock Exchange/Quotations, Ms. 18000 15B 237.

180. *The Times*, 8 December 1886 and printed notice, dated 1 December 1886 published by the Financial Agency. There is a copy in the CFB Newspaper archive, vol. 9, p. 214.

181. Ibid.

182. CFB *Report* (1888), p. 109.

183. Bazant, *La deuda exterior*, p. 269 has £4,585,000.

184. For information on the fractional certificates, see *The Daily Telegraph*, 26, 29 March 1887; *The Times*, 11 October 1888.

185. Perry's letters to the Stock Exchange are in Stock Exchange/Quotations, Ms. 18000, 13B 240.

186. All these protests are in the Quotations file 13B 240.

187. Ibid.

188. I have basically adopted Bazant's calculations (pp. 122, 124, 269) but there are others which differ slightly in the totals. For example, the Legation report of November 1888 puts the 1851 debt at £10,142,400, giving a total of £14,727,400.

189. *Financial News*, 10 November 1887.

190. Bazant, *La deuda exterior*, p. 126.

191. There is a copy of the prospectus/application form in the CFB Newspaper Archive, vol. 11, p. 58.

192. Stock Exchange/Quotations, Ms. 18000 19B 437.

193. M. Dublán, *Informe que el Ministro de Hacienda, Manuel Dublán presenta al Congreso sobre el empréstito contratado en Europa de £10,500,000* (Mexico, 1888), p. 25. Dublán included similar telegrams received from Mexico's agents around Europe.

194. Stock Exchange/Quotations, Ms. 18000 23B 459.

195. It is something of a mystery why these particular bonds should have disappeared so completely since examples of all the others issued from 1886 onwards are available. They were redeemed in 1899 but the cancelled bonds have disappeared. Fruitless searches were made by the author, or on his behalf, in the archives of banks, stockbrokers, and printers such as the American Bank Note Company of New York and Bradbury and Wilkinson, which were possible designers and producers. The records of the Bleichroeder Bank have disappeared and those of the Berlin Stock Exchange where an example of the bond might have survived were either destroyed during World War II or removed thereafter to Russia. The Amsterdam Stock Exchange archive has examples of several Mexican bond issues of the 1890s but there is no sign of the 1888 bond.

196. Stock Exchange/Quotations, Ms. 18000 23B 459.

197. The Gibbs archive is in the Guildhall Library. The Scrip certificates are in Ms. 11090. There is no sign of the bonds.

198. *The Times*, 18 December 1888.

199. *Mexican Financier*, 10 August 1889.

200. F. Stern, *Gold and Iron. Bismarck, Bleichroeder, and the Building of the German Empire* (London, 1977), p. 288.

201. *Mexican Financier*, 25 October 1890.

202. *The Times*, 29 April 1889. See also Stock Exchange/Quotations, 19B 40.

203. CFB *Report* (1890), p. 104.

204. Foreign Office. Annual Series. No. 1150 (1893), p. 22.

205. "Treasury Statement for the Fiscal Year, 1893–1894," published in *Mexican Financier*, 1 June 1895.

206. See Chapter 6 of this study.

207. Walker, *Kinship, Business and Politics*, pp. 38, 179.

208. There is a bilingual text of the Doyle Convention in PRO, F.O., 50/246, fols. 210–216.

209. The bond values are given in a notice published by the London Bank of Mexico and South America in *The Times*, 16 August 1865.

210. The original is in the author's collection.

211. There are fourteen coupons left on the bond, the first payable on 14 August 1860.

212. Turlington, *Mexico and Her Foreign Creditors*, pp. 194–195.

213. D. Robertson to L.C. Otway, 30 June 1858, in CMB *Report* (1861), p. 153.

214. Walker, *Kinship, Business and Politics*, pp. 210–211.

215. CMB *Report* (1861), p. 3: R. Garde, *A letter to the Right Honourable Earl Russell, on the absolute right of the Mexican Bondholders, who are subjects of her Most Gracious Majesty* (London, 1861).

216. Garde, *Letter*, p. 24.

217. See the correspondence in PRO, F.O., 97/280, fols. 423–427.

218. Notice in *The Times*, 16 August 1865.

219. *The Times*, 23 January 1866.

220. Details from reports and copies of correspondence in PRO, F.O., 97/282, fols. 31–35.

221. Details from a printed document issued by the Interior Ministry in Mexico in PRO, F.O., 97/282, fol. 13. The English bonds were sold by a Sr. Cancino.

222. Turlington, *Mexico and Her Foreign Creditors*, pp. 200–201.

223. Corporation of Foreign Bondholders' *Report* (1889), p. 114.

224. Turlington, *Mexico and Her Foreign Creditors*, p. 207; Bazant, *Historia de la deuda exterior*, p. 125.

Chapter 2

Dividends, Coupons, and Certificates

On 7 February 1861, Reverend John Hemery Carnegie, vicar of Cranborne, near Salisbury, wrote from his vicarage to the British Foreign Secretary, Lord John Russell.[1] The story he told was already familiar to the Foreign Office. He was, he said, "a considerable holder of Mexican bonds," many of which had been purchased by his late father (a doctor at Wimborne, Dorset) as far back as the year 1826. Neither he nor his father were speculators in foreign stocks. Nor were the numerous other middle-ranking professional people of moderate income in Dorsetshire who, he knew, were in a similar position to himself. Like his, their bonds had been bought as a bona fide investment when they were first offered for sale, or they had inherited them. They had seen their capital "ruinously depreciated" and they had agreed to reduced interest, but still dividends were not paid. Yet, he personally, only last year, had been compelled "to pay a considerable sum for Probate and Legacy Duties" on his inherited Mexican bonds. As tax was taken from Mexican bondholders like himself, was he not entitled to "look to the British Government for assistance and protection."

Reverend Carnegie's letter was not untypical of many such pleas for help made to the Foreign Office. Bondholders like himself were disappointed and frustrated that the dividends they had been repeatedly promised by the Mexican authorities had failed to materialize. Many claimed, and there is no reason to doubt them, that they were financially dependent on their dividend income and that they had been forced into penury and hardship by Mexico's failure to honor its agreements. This chapter is concerned with these dividends, both paid and unpaid. In particular, it seeks to explain how Mexican taxes paid in silver pesos at, for example, remote Pacific coastal ports, were turned into dividends paid in pounds, shillings, and pence to bondholders like the Reverend Carnegie.

Additional to a general mortage on all its revenues, the Mexican government hypothecated several taxes to the payment of dividends on its foreign debt. Foremost among these were the taxes on trade or the so-called customs duties levied on imports and exports. Throughout the nineteenth century, these provided the Mexican Treasury with its main source of income. However, as expenditure always exceeded income before the Díaz regime in the 1880s, all governments were forced to borrow heavily in order to meet even their basic daily expenses. It became normal practice to pledge or mortgage future customs revenues as security for the repayment of both foreign and domestic loans. As we have seen in previous sections on the bond issues and conversions, interest payments were guaranteed by specific assignments on the customs duties. Dividends on the 1824 and 1825 bonds, for example, were secured by one-third of the taxes on imports through the Gulf ports of Veracruz and Tampico. Subsequent guarantees included varying proportions of both import and export taxes together with money from the tobacco revenue or from taxes on silver exports. Under the terms of the 1850 agreement, payment of dividends was promised from 25% of import duties at both maritime and frontier customs; 75% of duties on exports out of Pacific coastal ports; and 5% of those on exports from Gulf ports. Forty-six years later, the Dublán conversion again promised dividends on the 1886 bonds out of customs revenues.

Interest payments on the foreign debt, therefore, always seemed well secured and the bondholders went to considerable lengths to calculate the potential yield of the customs and other taxes they were promised. The customs in particular, however, were subject to many variable and to some degree, unpredictable, factors. These included, for example, the wars against the French in 1838 and the United States in 1846–1848, both of which seriously affected commercial activity. Frequent tariff changes and internal conflict often in or around the ports, especially Veracruz, had similar disruptive effects. It was soon clear that the calculations which the bondholders made on the basis of Mexican Treasury reports were unreliable and that estimates of future revenues were at best haphazard.

These and many other general considerations affected the volume and value of trade and the revenues derived from it. But there were also three more specific factors of immediate concern to the bondholders which directly influenced remittances to the dividend fund. The first of these was contraband. Mexico's maritime ports were located along its extensive Gulf and Pacific coasts. Some central government control was possible over the major Gulf ports like Veracruz and Tampico through which the majority of imports passed. Elsewhere, at more distant places like Guaymas, Manzanillo, San Blas, Acapulco, Sisal, or Campeche, little effective supervision was exercised. The frontier posts at Matamoros and elsewhere along the northern and southern borders were even more isolated. Tenenbaum quotes a good example of the situation at Mazatlán in 1824 when it was reported that "there was one Custom House officer at this port and he was blind. In January 1825, the Port was composed of 2 huts of mud and 4 of straw."[2] Improvements to the installations were certainly made in later years but smuggling remained endemic. Underpaid customs officers, dishonest traders, and venal local politicians and military combined to defeat every attempt at reform which the authorities in Mexico City introduced. As the Minister of Finance said in 1830, "on coasts so desert(ed), and of such an immense extent as ours, it is utterly impossible to prevent a clandestine trade."[3]

The bondholders, some of whom were merchants with long experience in the transatlantic trade, were well aware that every tax dollar evaded cost them interest on their bonds. Their solution to the problem of corrupt officials and contraband was to have their own agents at the ports and frontier posts. In return for a commission, usually around ½%, they would check cargoes, bills of lading, and duties paid. They would ensure that the dividend fund's promised share of the proceeds of trade was collected and they would remit it to London on the monthly packets. The first agents appointed in 1830 were John Welch at Veracruz and Joseph Crawford at Tampico. Both were British vice-consuls at the ports, although the Foreign Office insisted that in their paid work for the bondholders they could only act in a private capacity.[4]

In later years, the bondholders repeatedly pressed the Mexican authorities to allow agents or commissioners at other places but it was not until 1850 that many more were allowed. By then, in addition to the firm of Manning and Mackintosh, which had acted for the bondholders in Mexico City since 1830, there were agents in the following locations:

Veracruz	Manning, Markoe & Co.
Tampico	Stewart L. Jolly & Co.
Guaymas	John A. Robinson
Mazatlán	Messrs. Kunhardt & Ewart
San Blas	Barron & Forbes
Colima	José Sarmiento
Acapulco	Custodio Souza
Altata	Jorge Lebrún, of Culiacán[5]

The bondholders' commissioner, Francis Falconnet, later admitted that he had been unable to find anyone in the more remote ports and frontier posts willing to accept appointment "for a commission of ½%."[6]

The presence of these agents had some effect and for a couple of years, as the Committee of Mexican Bondholders noted with satisfaction, "the revenues of the Bondholders have been collected and remitted with some approach to regularity."[7] The Mexican government, however, had always been reluctant to allow this foreign supervision of its most important revenue source and its sanction of the agents was soon withdrawn. Remittances to the dividend fund suffered an immediate decline and the bondholders pressed for the reinstatement of their agents. After "nearly four years' incessant and persevering efforts," Mexico agreed in 1857.[8] Customs taxes had always been payable in cash or bills payable at one-, three-, or six-month dates. Henceforth, customs collectors were to draw separate bills from importers for the 25% assigned to the dividend fund. These notes were to be handed over to the agents, together with the same percentage of any duties paid in cash.

To quote the Committee of Mexican Bondholders again, this new arrangement was followed by "vexatious and mortifying disappointments."[9] The War of the Reform devastated much of Mexico from 1857 to 1860 and control of all the main ports fluctuated between the contending liberal and conservative armies. The idea that either of the belligerent parties would take taxes from the few importers who risked their cargoes and then give them to distant European creditors was something which even the most optimistic bondholder recognized as improbable. British military intervention and blatant gunboat diplomacy with the arrival at Veracruz of warships persuaded the Mexicans then in control of the ports to agree to "interventors" or inspectors in the customs houses, but again political circumstances prevented implementation. Finally, when Juárez won the war, he found that no less than 92% of the customs revenues collected at Veracruz and Tampico were pledged to foreign and domestic creditors.[10] The decree of July 1861, which suspended all debt payments and triggered the Allied Intervention and Maximilian Empire, followed.

The bondholders' attempts, therefore, to ensure that they received their promised share of the customs revenues by placing their agents in the ports were rarely successful. They had similar difficulties in collecting the other taxes assigned to them. In the 1846 agreement, for example, export taxes on silver shipped out of Pacific ports were allocated to the dividend fund. The bondholders had high hopes of substantial sums flowing into their pockets because despite the damage caused to the silver mining industry during the war of independence, output had soon recovered, due partly to British investment. Silver again became Mexico's most important export, and by the 1850s it was producing 600 tons or about two-thirds of the world's total output of 900 tons.[11] Thirty years later, it remained the world's second largest producer after the United States.[12] The silver dollar, which has been aptly described as the traveller's check of the time, was accepted throughout the commercial world, and especially in China where there was a strong demand for both bullion and coins.[13] It was, as *The Times* (4 September 1835) put it, "the coin of commerce." European merchants depended on it for their international trade, and month after month they anxiously awaited the arrival of the ships bringing their supplies from Mexico. In the first decade after independence, before trading companies were well established in Mexico City and Veracruz, there was little or no credit system in which bills of exchange or other forms of credit could be widely used. Hence, to quote *The Times* (16 June 1824) again,

merchants and capitalists are driven to the clumsy expedient of remitting specie from America to England, and from England to America, as their respective transactions may require. Vessels laden with dollars are now constantly passing each other on the Atlantic.

Monthly amounts varied and there are no complete statistics of totals involved. In later years, however, shipments or 1 or even 2 million dollars in a single month were not unusual. In September 1860, the Royal Mail Steam Packet Company's vessel *The Tasmanian* brought to Southampton the largest amount recorded to that time—5,638,455 dollars' worth £1,127,691 sterling and weighing 154 tons. Of this cargo, 4,568,702 dollars came from Mexico.[14]

It was in the knowledge of this substantial trade in silver that the bondholders in 1846 welcomed the addition of the taxes on silver exports to their dividend fund. They calculated that silver worth between 6,000,000 and 8,000,000 dollars was dispatched from Pacific ports each year. The export tax was 3% (it was raised later), which should have yielded between 210,000 and 280,000 dollars for the dividends.[15] Instead, only negligible amounts were received. The cause was again contraband. Merchants, customs officials, British diplomats, and above all, British naval captains, were involved in widespread tax evasion. Silver, in specie and bullion, was usually shipped on British warships from Pacific ports such as San Blas, Mazatlán, and Guaymas. These provided security for valuable cargoes but just as significant, "the whole point of shipping via the Royal Navy was the avoidance of duties."[16] Naval captains and resident consular officials were rewarded by merchants for their cooperation and such "commissions" had long been a welcome perquisite of their jobs. Mexican customs officials also actively participated, even using their own boats to smuggle silver out at night to waiting British ships.[17]

The bondholders protested to the Foreign Office. Writing to Lord Palmerston on 30 October 1849, they drew his attention to the recent arrival of HMS *Calypso*. It had brought from the Pacific approximately 3,000,000 dollars in gold and silver on which export taxes of almost 120,000 dollars should have been paid. The amount actually paid, the bondholders noted, had been 1,245.[18] Further letters to the Foreign Office persuaded Palmerston to refer the matter to the Admiralty but its enquiries brought a denial of any wrongdoing from the *Calypso*'s captain, H.C. Worth. The bondholders persisted with their campaign and they were aided by Mexican officials in London and Mexico City, demanding that the Admiralty put a stop to all smuggling on its ships. They insisted that "no bullion be received as freight by British men-of-war, nor by the packets, without proof that the duties had been paid."[19] They wanted captains to be required to refuse any cargo of silver unless it was accompanied by a certificate signed by both customs officials and the bondholders' agents, confirming that duties had been paid. Foreign Office officials prevaricated but, eventually, they sent the file back to the Admiralty. Its response was a good example of civil service evasion. No formal complaint, it said, had been received from the Mexican government and hence the matter would not be considered because,

My Lords (of the Admiralty) have not recognized the right of British subjects to make complaints in the name of a Foreign Government on the grounds that they may have advanced monies to such Governments, and their Lordships consider that such an admission, if once made, might lead to inconvenient precedent.[20]

In short, aside from claiming that appropriate instructions had already been circulated to naval captains, the Admiralty refused to cooperate. No effective action was taken and as Dr. Mayo concluded, the Royal Navy continued to play "an essential role in the export of contraband silver."[21]

The bondholders found, therefore, that they were powerless to stop or even diminish the effects of smuggling on their interest payments. They were equally impotent in respect of another frequent assault on their funds. Several Mexican administrations, for what they deemed to be national emergencies, unilaterally reduced or suspended totally all payments to their foreign creditors. The bondholders soon discovered that what they thought to be binding legal agreements, which they often tested in the courts, held little sway when presidents like Santa Anna achieved control in Mexico. In 1833, for example, he reduced the agreed charge on the customs for the dividends from one-sixth to 6%. In 1846, another government appropriated over 600,000 dollars already collected for the dividends and ready for dispatch to London. On other occasions, funds destined for the bondholders were seized by military chieftains.

There were many such seizures of bondholders' funds in the 1830s and 1840s but they were especially frequent during the civil war from 1857 to 1860. Both sides in the conflict had no hesitation in confiscating money and supplies whenever and wherever they could. Silver trains, known as *conductas*, transporting to the ports bullion from the mines or specie from the mints, were seized on the highway, and merchants in areas controlled by bandits or rebels were forced to make contributions in cash or goods to the dominant faction. The most notorious example occurred in Mexico City in 1860, just a few weeks before the war ended. Control of the ports, especially Veracruz and Tampico, was essential to both sides and much of the fighting took place in and around those areas. Consequently, few of the merchants who risked their cargoes in or out of the ports paid their import or export duties in cash. Indeed, in an attempt to deprive the liberals (who controlled Veracruz for much of the war) of money which they could use to pay their supporters, the conservative government in the capital decreed that no customs duties were to be paid in cash. Instead, they were entirely settled in bills which were sent to Mexico City for payment. The bondholders' share of the proceeds was stored in the British Legation at 11 Calle de Capuchinas.

The military situation was such that it was too dangerous to send the money back to the coast for shipment to London. As mentioned earlier, silver trains had been robbed by bandits or rebels and even if strong military escorts could be found, the bondholders' agents and British diplomats concluded that it was better to leave it where it was, under lock and key, and British diplomatic protection. The cash accumulated in the Legation. It was placed in "large wooden chests" in a padlocked room on the first floor and the British Consul, George Mathew, "placed his official seal on the lock, and had taken the key."[22]

The precautions were futile. On 16 November, on the orders of the conservative government headed by Miguel Miramón, army officers searched the premises, demanding money. The next day, in the presence of the Spanish ambassador and British and American diplomats who had been called to be witnesses, the soldiers returned, bringing with them blacksmiths and carpenters. Ignoring the assembled diplomats' protests and warnings of the gravity of what they were about to do, the workmen cut the padlock. They managed to do this without breaking the "official seal," much to the satisfaction of the army officer in charge, but the diplomats present warned him that it was a meaningless achievement.

Another lock was forced and the carpenter opened the door "by cutting the frame." The soldiers entered the room, forced open the boxes, and found more than 600,000 dollars or £120,000. The bondholders' agent described the scene which followed: "the whole treasure was carried away in carts, an operation which continued till two or three of the following morning—the streets in the meantime were guarded by a military force."

Vociferous protests and official outrage at this violation of diplomatic protection followed for weeks in both Mexico City and London. The bondholders demanded a powerful response from the British government to "the most flagrant of robberies ever committed in the recent history of civilized nations."[23] Although the "Legation theft," as it became known, became an important factor in the British decision to join the Allied Intervention in

1861, at first the Foreign Office was not helpful. Its officials blamed the bondholders for leaving the money in Mexico City.

Smuggling and the other factors influencing trade, such as unilateral suspension or reduction of interest payments and illegal seizure of dividend funds, all meant that payment of dividends in cash was a comparatively rare event. During the sixty-two "dividend years" from the first bond issue of 1824 to the start of the Dublán conversion in 1886, the bondholders received some cash payments in only twenty years and even within those, whole dividends were rarely paid. Some of the arrears were covered by means other than cash, for example, capitalization into new bonds or the issue of special certificates. These will be explained later in this chapter. For the time being, we turn to the dividends that were paid.

Although the arrival of cash from Mexico for the dividend account rarely matched what the bondholders expected, in some years the shipments were regular. Usually within twenty-four hours of the arrival of the monthly packets at Falmouth or later Southampton, the Committee of Mexican Bondholders published details of the amount brought for the dividend fund. The following table shows the ships and dollars they brought in 1850 from Veracruz, Tampico, Mazatlán, Guaymas, and San Blas.[24]

			Veracruz	Tampico
1850	January	*Great Western*	66,613	—
	February	*Trent*	36,758	44,633
	March	*Thames*	80,882	10,715
	April	*Avon*	61,107	20,398
	May	*Clyde*	55,391	15,641
	June	*Severn*	49,727	10,997
	July	*Thames*	42,000	14,889
	August	*Tay*	30,652	6,235
	September	*Great Western*	40,559	10,202
	October	*Trent*	30,067	5,000
	November	*Dee*	30,000	—
	December	*Clyde*	42,000	17,000
1850	July	*Argo* (Mazatlán)	2,000	
		Amphitrite (Mazatlán)	5,000	
	August	*Cockatrice* (Guaymas)	14,625	
	October	*Inconstant* (San Blas)	4,674	
		Inconstant (Mazatlán)	1,806	
	December	*Clyde* (Mazatlán)	4,000	

The dollars were kept in deposit boxes at the Mexican ports until they were ready for shipment. Then, for the journey across the Atlantic, they were probably transferred into sealed barrels which was the usual method of carrying silver specie.[25] A separate bill of lading was normally drawn up for money destined for the foreign debt dividend account. Illustration 17 provides one example of a bill for two boxes containing 5,173 dollars which were shipped on 4 March 1840 from Veracruz to Falmouth by the bondholders' agents, Manning and Marshall, to Lizardi. The ship was the *Delight* and the captain, William Lory.[26]

In the early years of trade with independent Mexico, British Admiralty rules had dictated that specie or bullion could only be carried on ships sent specifically for that purpose. As the ships used were often from the British West Indies station, the main beneficiaries of this system were the captains, who collected a 2½% commission. Cargoes of silver, however, were insufficient to fill the holds and the captains often spent days or weeks sailing around the Caribbean looking for other cargoes. Long delays ensued before the silver reached Britain and the mercantile community in London soon began to protest.[27] In response to demands from merchants, Canning had agreed in October 1826 to the establishment of a monthly packet service to Mexico.[28] Within a few months, the merchants began to press that the packets should be allowed to transport silver. Again, their wishes were eventually met. In future years, it was the packets arriving first at Falmouth and later at Southampton, after the introduction of steamships in the early 1840s, which brought to Europe the vast amounts of silver extracted from Mexican mines.

At the port of arrival in Britain, the boxes or barrels containing the silver were unloaded and transported to London. Usually, they were taken directly to the Bank of England where they were "repacked into strong canvass bags, each containing 1000 coins."[29] On other occasions, they went to another bank, often Barings, where they were checked and counted.

The net value of the dollars depended on several things. There were charges for boxing and freight, for example, which were usually met by Mexico. Insurance was another cost, sometimes paid in Mexico, and sometimes in London. The rates varied over the years. In 1826, Barings paid £1,137 to insure an expected cargo of specie estimated to be worth £70,000.[30] The next year, however, in April 1827, the British warship *Tweed*, which had left Veracruz on 5 March with 2,000,000 dollars and 200 bags of cochineal, was several days overdue. Merchants who were awaiting its arrival began to panic and take out emergency insurance. Rates quickly rose to five, ten, and even twelve guineas per cent compared, as *The Times* pointed out, to the normal rate of 15 shillings.[31] In 1850, the Committee of Mexican Bondholders took out a policy for £20,000 on specie due to arrive from Veracruz and Tampico. It cost £150 at the rate of 15 shillings per cent plus an extra £5 for "Policy duty."[32]

By order of the Mexican Government

SHIPPED, in good order and well-conditioned, by A. Man Wm. Steger himself, to the merchant freighted, and Manning March &c..., called the Golorosa, whereof on board the Hamburgh Steamship, called the Golorosa, whereof _____ is Master, now lying in the Port of Vera Cruz, and bound for Falmouth.

To say: —

Two boxes containing Stars and cents D One hundred and seventy four dollars seventy three cents D

being marked and numbered as in the margin, and are to be delivered in the like order and condition, at the Port of Falmouth _____ (the dangers of the seas only excepted) unto Messrs. Mesgs. Wm. Cigarette &c. _____ or to their assigns, they paying freight for the said of 1½ being fifteen Cents _____

with _____ primage and average accustomed. In witness whereof, the Master or Purser of the said Vessel hath affirmed to _____ Bills of Lading, all of this tenor and date; one of which being accomplished, the others to stand void.

Dated in Vera Cruz, the fourteenth day of March A D 1840

Wm. Loy

43
73

17. Bill of Lading (1840).

There were a number of other costs and in 1826, the Mexican Chargé d'Affaires in London, Vicente Rocafuerte, asked Barings to explain what they were. The company's reply provides a good summary:

We have to inform you that Mexican and all other foreign monies and coins must be sold at the market price which is, of course, subject to variation, and that all foreign coins and bullion are sold by the English ounce and weighed; the present price of dollars is 4s. 8¾d. provided the standard of the metal and weight is the same as that of the old Spanish dollar. The charges on the sales of coin and bullion are Freight per agreement, generally 2½ per cent; the carriage from Portsmouth is usually about 5s. 3d. per $1,000 but this depends upon circumstances and if the Bill of Lading is filled up, deliverable at the Bank of England, this expense is then paid out of the freight, to which must be added Brokerage, ⅛ per cent and commission ½ per cent.[33]

The price of a Mexican dollar, as Barings noted, depended on its standard and weight. There was some variation according to the mint which produced the coins, but by and large there seems to have been a reasonable consistency throughout the nineteenth century. In 1834, the British Minister in Mexico, Richard Pakenham, reported to the Foreign Office that Mexican silver coin was "260 parts fine" and "28 parts alloy."[34] Almost sixty years later, another British Foreign Office report noted that "the weight of a dollar may be set down at 417.79 grains troy, and that of its fine silver contents at 377.139 grains."[35] Occasionally, there were difficulties with forged or "adulterated" coins. In 1842, one John Sutton was acquitted at York Assizes on a charge of counterfeiting Mexican "piastres."[36] A few years earlier, in 1835, "adulterated" coins were discovered in the market and had to be returned to the Guadalajara mint which had produced them. *The Times* (4 September 1835) remarked that it was a serious matter becuse Mexican coins were accepted "in confidence in the high character they have attained all over the world." Sometimes, design or specification changes caused problems. In 1862, for example, there was a shortage in the market caused by the recent War of the Reform and the Allied Intervention with the result that the price rose to 62¼d. per ounce. Part of the shipment that had arrived in September, however, only fetched 59¾d. per ounce. This was because the coins were from the Hermosillo mint and "these dollars, although better in weight, quality and appearance than the usual coinages, are rejected by the Chinese in consequence of their being milled on the edge, like English currency, and hence they have from necessity either been melted or sold for their equivalent value, 59¾d per ounce."[37]

The sale value of the dollars reflected these various factors and also was largely determined by the market price of bar silver of standard fineness. Despite all the variables in the market, the price remained fairly stable for much of the period and the exchange rate followed. As it was expressed in a Foreign Office report of 1893, "from time immemorial," the custom had been to value the dollar at 4 shillings or 5 to the pound sterling.[38] But in 1886, the price of silver suffered a dramatic fall and the exchange rate dropped correspondingly, remaining for some time "within a fraction of 36d."[39] Fortunately for the bondholders, the 1886 Three per Cents issued under the Dublán conversion paid dividends in sterling and the cost of the fall in the exchange rate therefore fell on the Mexican Treasury. On the other hand, the market price of the stocks also fell. On 19 October 1892, *The Financial Times* commented that "All Mexican securities, even the Sterling loans, rise or fall with the silver market. As a rule, they exaggerate its fluctuations."

Most of the above points can be illustrated with an actual example. Mention has already been made of the 2,500,000 dollars of the United States indemnity money which Mexico agreed to pay to the bondholders. That sum, in Mexican currency, was taken out of Mexico City, under guard, on 18 June 1852. A couple of days later, it reached Veracruz where it was stored until the arrival of the branch packet *Medway*. It was then loaded together with various other sums belonging to merchants and on 5 July 1852, the *Medway* steamed out of Veracruz with 2,673,697 silver dollars on board.

The *Medway* called at various ports on the mail route and eventually arrived at St. Thomas for its connection with the Royal Mail Steam Packet Company's ship *Orinoco* and the final stage of the journey to England.[40] The money was transferred to the *Orinoco* which brought it to Southampton on 2 August. From there, it was transported to London and deposited at Barings' counting house. The 2,500,000 dollars were in 876 boxes or barrels. When these were opened, they were found to contain 2,499,709 coins which weighed 2,168,506 ounces. With silver at 58⅝d. an ounce, the gross value was estimated at £529,702 15s. 4d. A further 243 coins were found to be counterfeit but, when melted down, still produced £18 8s. worth of silver, less 4 shillings for the cost of melting and assays. Forty-eight coins were missing. The final total yield was £529,720 19s. 4d.[41]

From this gross yield, all the costs had to be deducted. Barings' accounts list these as follows:

Charges in Mexico and Veracruz

Carriage from Mexico to Veracruz ½ per ct.	$12,500
Bags, Counting etc.	$516 45
Premium on $140,000 changed from gold to silver ½ per ct	$700
Cartage and expenses on same	$45 25
Receiving and shipping at Veracruz	$2,846 56

Carriage to Veracruz ½% on $3,591			$17 96
Commission at Mexico for advancing and paying above at 1½%			$249 39
Total			$16,875 61

Charges in London

Insurance on—

£367,000 @ 15s.% & duty	£ 2,845	10	0
£50,000 @ 20s.% & duty	£ 512	10	0
£47,000 @ 25s.% & duty	£ 611	0	0
£57,000 @ 15s.% & duty	£ 487	10	0
£3000 @ 20s.% & duty	————	—	—
	£ 4,456	10	0
Freight 1⅛%	£ 5,959	7	3
Bags	£ 62	10	0
Brokerage ⅛%	£ 662	3	0
Commission 1%	£ 5,297	4	0
	————	—	—
	£16,437	14	3

Adding commission paid to Falconnet, the total charges came to approximately £21,980. Hence, from the gross sum of £529,720, the net proceeds were £507,740 8s. 5d.

At times, the dollars were left on deposit at the Bank of England if it was judged that the silver price was likely to rise in the future. In December 1850, for example, there was 1,040,878 dollars in the dividend fund at the Bank. This sum had accumulated from the monthly remittances but it could not be paid out to the bondholders because of a dispute between Schneider & Co. and the Mexican government. Silver prices, however, were considered high at the time and the bondholders' representatives sought and obtained agreement from the Financial Agent, Facio, to take advantage of this by selling the dollars. The coins were sold at 59½ pence per ounce which produced £5,600 more than would have been obtained before the rise in the silver price. The money in sterling was returned to the dividend account at the Bank of England.[42] The success of the operation was due in no small way to the fact that the bondholders' chairman who arranged the sale was Isaac Lyon Goldsmid. He was probably the most experienced bullion dealer in the city of London and his company, Mocatta and Goldsmid, had been the Bank of England's bullion suppliers for many years. He was also one of the major holders of Mexican bonds.

Once the amount of dollars on deposit at the Bank of England was calculated to be enough to provide the pounds sterling needed for a dividend, they were sold in the market. The Financial Agency, or the contractor acting for the Mexican government, advertised the payment. The format of the advertisement changed little over the course of the nineteenth century. The following example appeared in *The Times* on 13 March 1826, together with a similar announcement for the Five per Cent loan dividend:

MEXICAN SIX PER CENT LOAN. The FIFTH QUARTERLY DIVIDEND, due on 1st day of April next, will be paid on that and on the succeeding days between the hours of 10 and 2, at the Countinghouse of Messrs. Barclay, Herring, Richardson and Co., 11 New Broad Street Mews. The Dividend Warrants, with lists thereof numerically arranged, are requested to be left for examination one day previous to payment.

Sixty-five years later, the advertisement was much the same, for example:

MEXICAN GOVERNMENT CONSOLIDATED EXTERNAL SIX per CENT LOAN, 1888. The QUARTERLY COUPON of the above loan, due 1st July next, will be PAID on that or any subsequent day, at the Counting House of Messrs. Antony Gibbs and Sons, 15 Bishopsgate-street, within, between the hours of 11 and 2 (Saturdays, 11 and 1).
   Coupons must be left four clear days for examination.
   15th June 1891.[43]

The advertisement was usually placed in all the main newspapers and repeated several times. This was partly because those bondholders living outside of London, in Europe or beyond, needed time to send their stocks or to contact their London agents or bankers who collected the dividends on their behalf. In those cases where large holdings were involved, specially printed forms were provided on which the numbers and series of the bonds on which dividends were being claimed had to be entered.

Every bond had a sheet of dividend coupons attached. The number of coupons depended on the duration of the loan—usually twenty or thirty years—and whether the dividends were paid quarterly or half-yearly. Each was numbered and carried the date when payment was due and the amount. Few of the coupons have survived, probably because they were destroyed once payment on them had been made. Fortunately, some have been found and the next illustrations (18 and 19) are the 1837 Five per Cents; 1851 Three per Cents; 1864 Three per Cents; 1886 Three per Cents. The first two, those of 1837 and 1851, are of simple design and printed in black ink on white paper. The other two, 1864 and 1886, are considerably more ornate and colorful.

As can be seen in these illustrations, all of which reproduce original coupons, there was little variation in the wording.[44] The exception, of course, is the 1886 Three per Cent coupon which is written in Spanish and which has its value given in the three currencies—Mexican, U.S., and Brit-

18. Dividend Coupons: 1837 Five per Cents; 1851 Three per Cents.

19. Dividend Coupons: 1864 Three per Cents; 1886 Three per Cents.

ish. There were forty such coupons attached to each of the 1886 bonds, the first being dated 30 June 1886 and the last, 31 December 1905. There is a complete set of coupons with each of the nine bonds issued in what is almost certainly the unique set found in the Stock Exchange Quotations archive.[45] These coupons are also very unusual, and again possibly unique for Mexican stocks, in that they bear the portrait of the hero of the war of independence, José María Morelos.[46]

As explained earlier, dividend payments through the use of these coupons were few and far between but they were not the only source of a cash return for the bondholders on their investments. Coupons in arrears, or not yet due, could always be sold to speculators, although at a discount. In 1844, for example, *The Times* (11, 13 March) reported that half-yearly coupons due on the 1837 Five per Cents were selling in the market at 6 to 7 shillings in the pound and one stockbroker, a Mr. West, advertised "a quantity" of coupons for sale at 10 shillings in the pound. In 1858, A. Schwareschild & Co., of 21 Lombard Street, London, advertised its readiness to buy the unpaid sixth coupon of the 1851 Three per Cent bonds.[47] The practice was still common in the 1880s when a company known as the Coupon Agency Ltd., of 20 Bucklersbury, London, was active in buying up dividend certificates, making "large purchases for ourselves and clients."[48]

Also, as we have seen in the section dealing with the bond issues, there were several occasions on which unpaid dividends were capitalized into new bonds. The 1831 bonds were given in exchange for the coupons in arrears since 1827. After the 1837 rescheduling of the debt, unpaid dividends were met in part with the customs certificates and then with Debentures. The 1864 Three per Cents covered the ten years of arrears on the 1851 Three per Cents. For the most part, the bondholders suffered a loss on these capitalizations because the par value of the new stocks they were given was less than the total par value of the coupons they replaced. But there were exceptions. In the 1831 agreement, £62 10s. of 5% coupons received a £100 bond. The 1864 Three per Cents gave an enhanced value of 40%, that is, £60 of coupons brought a new £100 bond. These new securities could be sold in the market, thus allowing bondholders to realize some cash. Again, there were always speculators willing to take a risk in buying up even the most discredited stock. In December 1876, Mexican bonds were near their lowest ever price with the 1851 Three per Cents at around 7 and the 1864 Three per Cents at 3–4. At such almost unsaleable levels—very few deals were made—*The Money Market Review*'s advice to bold investors was to follow the market dictum of "Always buy rubbish."[49]

Another alternative to the payment in cash of the dividends was the issue of special certificates. These were similar to the fractional certificates explained earlier but rather than replacing bonds, they were usually offered when only part of a dividend was being paid. Cutting a coupon in half to show that half its value had been paid, which was done in 1831, was not a satisfactory procedure. Instead, certificates were printed which showed how much of a particular dividend remained to be paid. Again, these became negotiable securities which were bought and sold in the market. Like the coupons, few have survived, but three examples have been found and can be illustrated.

The first (Illustration 20) is a certificate issued by Lizardi in 1843. It was printed, and presumably designed, by Whiting. The background to this certificate relates to the 1843 dividends. In October 1843, Lizardi offered to pay the half-yearly dividend of £2 10s. due the previous April on the 1837 Five per Cent Actives with one-third in cash and two-thirds in bonds, using for the purpose the 1837 Deferred Five per Cents. In other words, for each coupon from a £100 bond, bondholders were offered 16s. 8d. in cash and £1 13s. 4d. in bonds. The minimum face value of the bonds was £100. Many bondholders did not have enough coupons to exchange for a bond and hence, they were given certificates. The example reproduced is number 619 and worth £18 6s. 8d. Although it could have been derived from a number of combinations of coupons, it is also possible that its holder had presented eleven coupons from a £100 bond. At £2 10s. interest per coupon or £27 10s. in total, he would have received one-third in cash or £9 3s. 4d. and the remainder or £18 6s. 8d. in the form of the certificate. As the text states, "on presentation of a sufficient number of these Certificates," he would receive a bond "in Mexican Consolidated Five per Cent Stock." He could have bought similar certificates in the market to reach the minimum required value of £100 or equally, he could have sold his own in order to raise more cash.[50]

The next certificate was issued by Barings in August 1867 (Illustration 21).[51] It may be recalled that Barings had resumed the job of representing the bondholders in 1862, after the Committee of Mexican Bondholders had been wound up, albeit temporarily. Following the 1864 agreement with Maximilian whereby the dividend arrears were capitalized into the so-called 1864 Three per Cents, dividends had been paid using money raised from the sale of other bonds, mostly in France—the Six per Cents. By July 1866, however, no more funds were available and the dividend due on the first of that month was not paid. Nevertheless, despite the mounting problems faced by the imperial regime in Mexico, some remittances were sent to Europe. By March 1867, there was approximately £130,000 in the dividend fund on deposit in the Bank of England in the joint names of Barings and Maximilian's interim Chargé d'Affaires, Angel Nuñez Ortega.

After various disputes between the bondholders themselves over the distribution of this dividend fund (see Part II), it was finally agreed that it should be used to pay a partial dividend. Barings made the payment using certificates such as the one illustrated which was given to an 1851 bondholder. These certificates, which became known as the Barings Certificates,

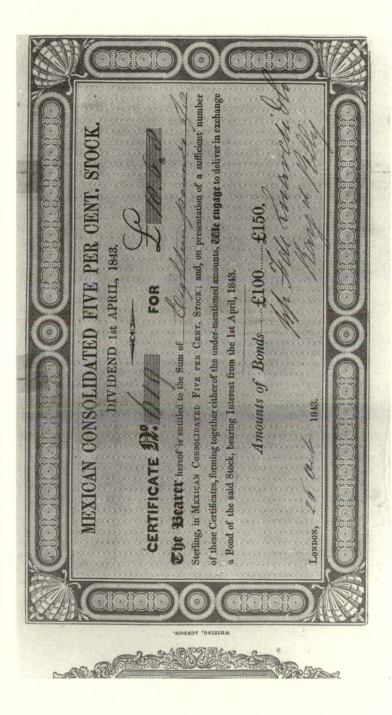

20. 1843 Dividend Certificate.

No. 3252

MEXICAN CONSOLIDATED 3-₩-CENT. BONDS OF 1851.

DIVIDEND DUE 1st JULY, 1866.

We hereby certify that the Mexican Government is indebted to the Bearer hereof in the sum of *Three Pounds fifteen shillings* being the Balance remaining due and unpaid on Mexican Consolidated 3-₩-Cent. Coupons for the Half-year's Dividend due 1st July, 1866, amounting to ... £ 11 : 5 : —

of which two-thirds have been paid, say ... „ 7 : 10 : —

Balance as above ... £ 3 : 15 : —

And we declare and certify that these Coupons have been delivered to us on account of the Mexican Government, and that this Certificate is issued in lieu of the unpaid balance thereof, and entitles the Bearer to all the rights and claims which attach to the Coupons which have been thus delivered.

LONDON, *12th August,* 1867.

21. 1867 Barings Certificate.

were also negotiable securities bought and sold in the market. Nothing further was paid on them in the form of dividends but they remained valid and in circulation until the 1886 Dublán conversion. Under the terms of the Mena agreement with the bondholders of June 1886, they were to be accepted at 20% of their face value against the 1886 Three per Cents—in other words, for each £100 nominal value of certificates, the holder received in exchange £20 in the 1886 Three per Cents. By the end of the conversion in 1889, certificates worth £37,675 had been presented and their holders given new bonds with a face value of £7,535. According to the Corporation of Foreign Bondholders, that left outstanding some £37,859 of certificates. In sum, only half of those issued were converted. Whether the remainder were presented later is not known.[52]

Finally, there are the 1851 certificates. These had a rather more controversial history and for reasons which are not entirely clear, many found their way into the hands of Dutch owners. They originated in 1851 as part of the rescheduling of the debt which brought the 1851 Three per Cents to the market. A brief recap may be useful at this point. The 1846 conversion had fixed the principal of the debt at £10,240,651. Annual interest of 5% was promised, payable in half-yearly dividends. For many reasons, not least the war with the United States, only one dividend was paid and that was the one due on 1 January 1847, which was settled in two instalments in 1849 and 1850. By the time agreement was reached, therefore, on the 1850/1851 conversion which was to start paying dividends on 1 July 1851, there were eight coupons in arrears on the 1846 Five per Cent bonds. Each coupon from a £100 bond had a face value of £2 10s., making in total £20.

The law of 14 October 1850, which set out the terms of the conversion of the debt, proposed to settle all outstanding arrears with the payment of 2,500,000 dollars of the United States indemnity, and the following, stated in Article 2 (ii):

> That with the said two million five hundred thousand dollars, and with what has been received up to the date of the present law, and also with that which may be received up to the approval of the settlement which is proposed to them today, the creditors shall consider themselves paid for all the arrears of dividends up to the day of their agreement with this settlement.

The meaning of this clause is imprecise and it was to be the cause of considerable dispute for almost the next forty years. For the time being, however, the bondholders were anxious to have their arrear coupons paid as soon as possible. They accepted the terms offered and awaited distribution of the assets promised in the clause quoted above. These included more than a million dollars already on deposit in the dividend fund in the Bank of England; the two and a half million dollars from the indemnity; and several other substantial sums expected from Mexico. They calculated the total offered in satisfaction of the arrears as £868,111.[53]

The bondholders voted to accept the terms of the new conversion at a meeting on 23 December 1850. A week or so later, on 4 January 1851, the Financial Agent, Facio, announced that he was prepared to make an interim payment of £2 per £100 bond toward the arrears. Bondholders were required to leave with him the eight unpaid coupons from their 1846 bonds.[54] At first, it seems that the intention was to give them a receipt for their coupons but then it was decided that special certificates should be prepared. Facio announced on 25 January that these would be available from 1 March. Those bondholders, or their agents, therefore, who took their coupons to the Financial Agency at 32 Great Winchester Street, were eventually given a certificate. Illustration 22 reproduces one of the certificates, found in the London Stock Exchange archive. It was produced by Letts, Son & Steer and again, it is almost certainly a unique original example.[55]

This certificate was given in exchange for the eight coupons in arrears attached to the 1846 Five per Cent £100 bond, number 2019, of the A series. At the same time, the holder was given £2 in cash. It is dated 5 March 1851, and must have been one of the first to be presented to Facio. His signature appears, as does that of James Capel who, at the time, was deputy chairman of the bondholders' committee.

It may also be noticed that the certificate bears a stamp which states "Paid £5 :3 1852." This refers to payments made from the 2,500,000 dollars of the United States indemnity money. This cash arrived in London at the beginning of August 1852. For months before this, the bondholders had considered how they would distribute it once it was safely in their hands. After much discussion in private and public meetings, an arrangement was reached with Barings. As soon as it was satisfied that the Mexican government would honor the agreement, it would make an advance payment of £4 10s. per £100 bond to any holder who so desired. Those who wanted cash quickly could get it while others could wait until the money had arrived and had been converted into sterling. The bondholders accepted this offer, for which Barings received a commission. On 5 April 1852, Facio invited holders to present their certificates to him for authentication. He would stamp them with the amount due, that is £4 10s. per £100 bond, and higher amounts for the higher value series. Barings would then pay the cash.[56] By August, the indemnity money had arrived and as indicated earlier, had yielded £507,740, after all expenses had been deducted. Together with some money already on deposit at the Bank of England, that allowed a further payment of 13s. or a total of £5 3s. On 26 August 1852, Facio announced that Barings would pay 13 shillings to those who had already received the £4 10s. advance, and £5 3s. to those who

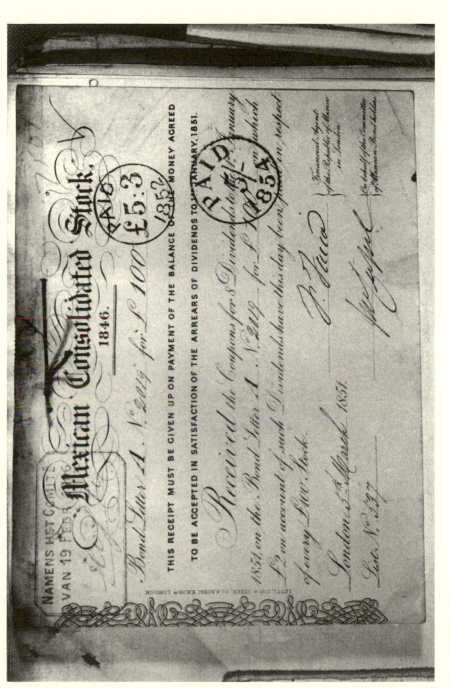

22. 1851 Certificate.

had not.[57] Hence, the certificate illustrated was taken to Facio for stamping and to Barings for payment of £5 3s.

Finally, there is another stamp on the certificate indicating that 5 shillings was paid in 1854. This payment was again made by Barings in April 1854 from money which had accumulated in the dividend fund account. By that time, the bondholders were engaged in what was a protracted and acrimonious dispute with Facio and the Mexican government over the meaning of the clause cited above from the October 1850 law. The imprecise wording had not escaped the vigilant eye of the bondholders' committee when the text of the law had first been received. Baron Goldsmid wrote in December 1850 to the Mexican Minister of Finance to seek confirmation that all monies received for the dividend account in Mexico as well as in London were included. In other words, money collected in cash or bills at the ports, or from the taxes on silver, or any other source assigned to the dividend fund between the date of the law (14 October 1850) and its acceptance by the bondholders (23 December 1850), even if not yet remitted to London, belonged to the bondholders.[58] That was the interpretation which the bondholders put on the clause but it was not shared by the Mexican authorities. Their position was that only money received in London by the deadlines indicated was for the arrears. Any funds awaiting remittance from Mexico were not included and they could be, and were, appropriated.

The bondholders protested to Mexico and appealed for help to the British Foreign Office, but to no avail. Mexico refused to accept any further liability for the arrears on the 1846 bonds and future remittances were made exclusively for interest payments on the 1851 Three per Cents. Not for the first time, nor the last, the bondholders sought legal opinion on their case from prominent attorneys, notably Dr. Robert Phillimore, who had advised them on previous occasions. They were assured that the law was on their side and that their claim was justified. As part of their evidence, a detailed account was prepared of the various monies which, it was claimed, Mexico owed the certificate holders. The total amounted to 900,000 dollars or £180,000.[59]

No progress was made on the claim and with the outbreak of civil war in Mexico in the mid-1850s, the bondholders recognized there was no point in pursuing it for the time being. Barings presented its accounts in July 1856. The certificate holders had received in total £754,853, leaving just £3,028 to be collected.[60] The total face value of the certificates which represented four years' interest on a capital debt of £10,241,650 was £2,048,330. Hence, assuming the £3,028 was collected later, there was an outstanding sum of £1,293,477 of interest arrears. In short, on a certificate representing eight coupons of £2 10s. from a £100 bond or £20, £7 8s. had been paid, leaving £12 12s. outstanding.

Political events, the War of the Reform, the Allied Intervention and the Maximilian Empire, all preoccupied the bondholders in the next few years and no more was heard of the 1851 certificates until 1864. It was in that year when Maximilian's advisers reached an agreement with the bondholders over the interest arrears on the 1851 Three per Cents. The 1851 certificates had circulated in the market as negotiable securities and some had been acquired by Dutch investors. Anxious to take advantage of Maximilian's early enthusiasm and misguided generosity, the Amsterdam Stock Exchange tried to persuade him to settle the claims of their "Arrear Certificate Holders." They formed a committee to press their case and asked to cooperate with the London Committee of Mexican Bondholders. Nothing came of their efforts.[61]

After the failure to persuade the Maximilian regime to pay off the 1851 certificates, nothing more was achieved until the several negotiations of the early 1880s. In these talks between sundry Mexican representatives and the Committee of Mexican Bondholders various proposals were made to redeem them. In 1883, for example, the so-called Rivas agreement envisaged the exchange of £32 worth of new bonds for each nominal £100 of certificates. The following year, under the Noetzlin proposals, the sum offered was less generous at £24 per £100 but the total nominal value of the certificates was accepted as £1,260,000.[62]

These negotiations produced no result until the 1885 law on the foreign debt and the subsequent Dublán conversion. The Mena agreement with the bondholders of 23 June 1886 for the conversion of all recognized securities included the 1851 certificates. The rate of exchange for the new 1886 Three per Cents was to be 20%, "that is to say, for each £100 nominal of those Certificates, the holder shall receive £20 in Bonds of the New Issue."[63] The Mena agreement, however, did not specify what the total nominal value of the certificates was and difficulties soon arose. The problem was partly caused by the wording on the certificates. As can be seen in Illustration 22, no nominal cash value is stated. Instead, it reads, "This receipt must be given up on payment of the balance of the money agreed to be accepted in satisfaction of the arrears of dividends to 1st January, 1851." Two interpretations were applied to this wording. The first, adopted by Mena, was that "the balance of the money agreed" was £180,000 which was the sum the bondholders had calculated in 1854. The second, pressed by some of the holders, was that as each certificate had been issued to represent eight unpaid dividends of £2 10s., or £20, and as £7 8s. had already been paid, there remained to be paid £12 12s. per cent. Higher sums pertained to the higher-value certificates. On that basis, the total value of all the certificates was approximately £1,260,000 which was the amount accepted in the unratified Noetzlin agreement of 1884.

When the details of the Dublán conversion were published, the holders discovered that they were not going to receive 20% of £12 12s. in new stock. Instead, the Mexican Financial Agency insisted that the bondholders had agreed upon a figure of £180,000. Converting that sum at 20% meant that new stock of only £36,000 would be offered in exchange for the certificates. The effect was that a certificate from a £100 bond was valued at £1 15s.1d. and as this was to be converted at 20%, holders would receive new stock to the value of a fraction over 7s. The other certificates were valued as follows:

B (ex £150 bond)   £2 12s.   8d.
C (ex £250 bond)   £4   7s. 10d.
D (ex £500 bond)   £8 15s.   8d.

Holders would also receive one-fifth of these values in 1886 Three per Cents.[64]

When these figures were absorbed in city circles in London and Europe, irate letters to the press soon appeared.[65] Holders in London, Amsterdam, Brussels, and elsewhere also wrote to the Stock Exchange to demand that its approval of the 1886 Three per Cents, on which the whole Dublán conversion rested, should be withheld.[66] One of the protesters from Holland enclosed the certificate in Illustration 22 which the Stock Exchange, fortunately from our viewpoint, failed to return. The chairman of the Amsterdam Stock Exchange added his weight to the protests in a letter to Porfirio Díaz. The Mexican president replied that he would not interfere with the Mena agreement but that he had instructed the Financial Agency in London to find a solution to the problem. Then W.T.F.M. Ingall & Co. (stockbrokers), of 6 Drapers' Gardens, London, announced that it represented a large number of the holders, both in London and Amsterdam.[67] It also protested to the Stock Exchange and sent memorials to the Finance Ministry in Mexico City. Another company with what seemed like good grounds for complaint was the Coupon Agency Ltd. It had received a written assurance from one of the Mexican Financial Agency's officials that the £100 certificates were to be accepted at £12 12s. face value. On that basis, the company had bought a substantial number of them in the market. It joined the protests to the Stock Exchange.[68]

In view of the volume of protests received, the Stock Exchange Committee decided to defer its decision on granting an official quotation to the 1886 Three per Cents until it had time to consider the arguments. Among the submissions to it was one from Mena, who made several points. First, that in all his discussions with the bondholders' representatives, the figure of £180,000 had been accepted by all parties. Second, there had never been any intention of paying 20% of £1,260,000 as the Coupon Agency claimed. The misunderstanding with that company had arisen because of a difficulty between himself and his officials caused by the fact that when he arrived in London, he did not speak English.[69]

After consideration of all the evidence, including a long report on the history of the certificates since 1851 by one of its own officials, and letters from anxious bondholders urging it to ignore the protests, the Stock Exchange Committee resolved to grant a quotation to the 1886 Three per Cents on 7 June 1887. Some certificate holders had already accepted the Financial Agency's offer of 7 shillings per cent and 3,404 certificates had been "converted" by 19 May. Notwithstanding these factors, the bond-holders' representatives continued to press the Mexican authorities for a more generous settlement and they had some success. It was agreed that a further £36,000 worth of the new bonds would be made available to the certificate holders, doubling the amount originally offered and enabling the conversion rate to rise from 20% to 40%.[70] The basic certificate from the original £100 was thus paid off with 14 shillings. By the time the conversion closed on 23 June 1888, certificates to the value of £135,251 had been presented and exchanged for new bonds worth £54,100.[71] Although we do not know exactly how many of the 51,742 certificates originally issued (one for each of the 1846 bonds) were eventually redeemed, it seems likely that more were brought to the Financial Agency in later years. Certainly, the offer made in 1895 to accept unredeemed stocks at a price to be negotiated included the 1851 certificates.

NOTES

1. Carnegie's letter was published in CMB *Report* (April 1861), pp. 191–193.
2. Tenenbaum, *Politics of Penury*, p. 24.
3. BSFP, vol. 17, p. 1026.
4. See the correspondence in CMB *Report* (1830), pp. 16–19; and BSFP, vol. 28, pp. 971–972.
5. CMB *Report* (June 1850), p. 31.
6. CMB *Report* (1854), pp. 13–14.
7. CMB *Report* (1855), p. 9.
8. CMB *Report* (April 1861), p. 18.
9. Ibid., p. 19.
10. Turlington, *Mexico and Her Foreign Creditors*, p. 124.
11. J. Grant to Barings, 2 September 1858, Barings Archive, HC4.5.31, fol. 7.
12. *The Financial Times*, 19 October 1892.
13. T. Green, *Precious Heritage. Three Hundred Years of Mocatta and Goldsmid* (London, 1984), p. 18.
14. *The Times*, 28 September 1860.
15. CMB *Second Report* (April 1850), p. 19. This *Report* is undated but seems to have been released on 9 April. See *The Times*, 10 April 1850.
16. J. Mayo, "Consuls and Silver Contraband on Mexico's West Coast in the Era of Santa Anna," *Journal of Latin American Studies* 19 (1987), p. 405.
17. P. Doyle to Ld. Palmerston, 5 December 1851, PRO, F.O. 50/246, fols. 233–248.
18. J.D. Powles to Ld. Palmerston, 30 October 1849, ibid., 50/234, fols. 293–295.

19. Correspondence in ibid., 50/234, fols. 346–348; 50/240, fols. 116–148; 50/241, fols. 6–20.

20. Ibid., 50/249, fols. 142–143.

21. Mayo, "Consuls," p. 402.

22. Details of the Legation theft are from a "public instrument of protest" sworn at the British Consulate in Mexico City on 23 November 1860 by Charles Whitehead, commissioner of the bondholders. The text is in CMB *Report* (April 1861), pp. 54–59.

23. D. Robertson to Ld. Wodehouse, 16 December 1860, in Kimberley F.O. Correspondence, Bodleian Library, Oxford (henceforth Kimberley F.O. Correspondence), Ms. Eng C. 4006, fols. 23–24.

24. Figures from CMB *Report* (December 1850), appendix no. 2.

25. Green, *Precious Heritage*, p. 31.

26. The document illustrated is in AGN, Galería 6, Aduanas, vol. 1051, n.f.n.

27. *The Times*, 13, 25 April 1827.

28. Correspondence in PRO, F.O. 50/40, fols. 234–317.

29. Green, *Precious Heritage*, p. 31.

30. Barings to V. Rocafuerte, 27 October 1826, SRE, 40.11.4.

31. *The Times*, 9 April 1827.

32. CMB *Second Report* (April 1850), pp. 26–27.

33. Barings to V. Rocafuerte, 27 October 1826, SRE, 40.11.4.

34. PRO, F.O. 50/83, fols. 163–165.

35. F.O. 1893. Misc. Series no. 302. Mexico. *Report on the Effect of the Depreciation of Silver on Mexico* (London, 1893), pp. 3–4.

36. PRO, F.O. 50/157, fols. 1–8.

37. *The Times*, 30 September 1862.

38. F.O. Misc. Series no. 302, p. 3.

39. *The Financial Times*, 22 June 1888.

40. The *Orinoco* was 2,901 tonnage and 800 horsepower; *The Times*, 13 October 1854.

41. Details of the 2,500,000 dollars are from the CMB *Report* (1853), p. 30.

42. *The Times*, 7, 21 December 1850.

43. Ibid., 15 June 1891.

44. Illustrations are from originals or photocopies in the possession of the author.

45. Stock Exchange/Quotations, Guildhall Library, Ms. 18000 15B 237.

46. I am grateful to Dr. Anne Staples, Carlos Rodríguez, and Harim Gutiérrez, all of the Colegio de México, for help in identifying the portrait of Morelos.

47. *The Times*, 2 October 1858.

48. Stock Exchange/Quotations, Guildhall Library, Ms. 18000 15B 237.

49. *The Money Market Review*, 29 December 1876.

50. This certificate is in the author's collection.

51. This certificate was kindly donated to the author by Mr. Brian Mills.

52. CFB *Report* (1889), p. 114. The Mexican Legation report of 30 November 1888 has slightly different figures; SRE, L.E. 1035, fol. 136.

53. CMB *Report* (December 1850), p. 12.

54. *The Times*, 4 January 1851.

55. Stock Exchange/Quotations, Guildhall Library, Ms. 18000 15B 237.

56. *The Times*, 5 April 1852.

57. Ibid., 26 August 1852.

58. Correspondence in PRO, F.O. 50/256, fols. 170–177.

59. CMB *Report* (1854), pp. 28–31.

60. CMB *Report* (1856), pp. 4, 14.

61. *The Times*, 24 May 1865. For more details of the Amsterdam Committee, see Ortiz de Montellano, *Apuntes*, pp. 227–263, and Part II of this study.

62. For details of the Rivas and Noetzlin proposals, see CMB *Report* (1883); *The Times*, 19 September 1884: Part II of this study.

63. Clause 3 of the Mena agreement; CFB *Report* (1887), pp. 85–90.

64. Details from correspondence in *The Bullionist*, 12 February 1887.

65. For example, *The Times*, 16 November 1886; *The Bullionist*, 12, 19 February 1887.

66. Correspondence in Stock Exchange/Quotations, Guildhall Library, Ms. 18000 15B 237, and Amsterdam Stock Exchange Archive, file 40.

67. *The Daily Telegraph*, 11 December 1886.

68. Stock Exchange/Quotations, Guildhall Library, Ms. 18000 15B 237.

69. Mena's submission is in ibid.

70. Benito Gómez Farías sent a telegram to the Amsterdam Stock Exchange to inform its members of the extra allocation; Amsterdam Stock Exchange Archive, 40, fol. 156.

71. CFB *Report* (1889), p. 114; SRE, L.E. 1035, fol. 136.

Chapter 3

A Brief Postscript: The Fate
of the Bonds

Disregarding the extensions which latecomers among the bondholders were allowed to present their bonds, the Dublán conversion ended in June 1888. It had achieved its objective of redeeming and cancelling virtually all the outstanding Mexican stocks which had accumulated in European markets since the first bond issue of 1824. The Corporation of Foreign Bondholders calculated that "98.7 per cent of the old securities has been converted."[1]

The cancellation meant that, in numerical terms, tens of thousands of Mexican securities were withdrawn from circulation, to be added to those already stored in the Bank of England from all the earlier conversions. An exact calculation of the total number is difficult but it is unlikely to have been much less than 200,000 documents of one sort or another. The question arises: What happened to this large volume of paper? The answer almost certainly lies in an exchange of correspondence between the Financial Agent, Mena, the Ministry of Foreign Affairs, and the Finance Minister himself, Manuel Dublán. On 7 May 1887, Mena wrote to Foreign Affairs to ask what he should do with the ever-increasing quantity of cancelled securities. His letter was referred to Dublán who replied on 15 June. He wrote as follows: "all the Mexican Debt securities for which there have been the various conversions including the most recent carried out in accord with the law quoted are in fact of no use; these certainly may be destroyed." At the same time, he added, a record must be kept of the "number, series, value, colour and other features which identify each of the documents."

In short, Dublán authorized the destruction of all the cancelled bonds and certificates, not just from the current conversion but also from previous ones. Before this decision was received, however, and perhaps in anticipation of it, the Financial Agency had sent one of its officials to the Bank of England to retrieve the cancelled stocks. This was Román de Olano and on 27 May 1887, having presumably already gone through the deposit books to locate the relevant entries, he withdrew, or "received back," as the entries record it, all the wooden and tin boxes deposited during the previous sixty-three years since 20 March 1824. Against each entry, Olano signed the receipt to confirm that he had removed the box. Those he "received back" were as follows:

1. Box containing the General Mortgage Bond and Goldsmidt contract for the 1824 Loan, deposited by Migoni and Goldsmidt on 20 March 1824.

2. Box containing redeemed 1824 Five per Cent bonds, deposited by Migoni and Goldsmidt on 6 April 1824.

3. Box containing redeemed 1824 Five per Cent bonds, deposited by Migoni and Goldsmidt on 5 October 1824.

4. Box containing the General Mortgage Bond and Barclay contract for the 1825 Loan, deposited by David Barclay on 14 June 1825.

5. 15 boxes containing redeemed 1824 Five per Cent and 1825 Six per Cent bonds deposited by Mexican representatives and Goldsmidt or Barclay on various dates in 1825 and 1826.

6. 14 boxes containing cancelled 1824 Five per Cent; 1825 Six per Cent; 1831 Five per Cent; 1831 Six per Cent bonds, deposited by Murphy and Lizardi on 22 October 1844.

7. 2 boxes containing 1846 E Bonds, deposited by Murphy and Schneider on 20 August 1846.

8. 15 boxes containing cancelled 1837 bonds and 1842 Debentures, deposited by Mendoza on 14 April 1851.

9. Box containing 1837 Five per Cent bonds, deposited by Facio and Schneider on 26 April 1853.

10. 21 boxes containing cancelled 1846 Five per Cent bonds, deposited by Facio on 12 January 1853 (these were removed by Olano on 8 October 1886).

Olano removed from the Bank of England's vaults, therefore, 72 boxes containing many thousands of the bonds and certificates which had formed the basis of Mexico's foreign debt. We can assume that the load was transported by carriage or cart from the Bank in Threadneedle Street back to the nearby offices of the Financial Agency at Blomfield House, London Wall.

Mena received Dublán's decision early in July 1887 and on the thirteenth of that month, he wrote to Foreign Affairs that "I am informed that the old bonds and titles may be destroyed." He promised to tell the Ministry when the destruction had taken place. Unfortunately, at this point the trail goes cold. These letters quoted above are in Mena's personal file in the Foreign Ministry archive but there is no further reference in it to the fate of the bonds.[2] A few months later, he was succeeded as director of the Financial Agency by Benito Gómez Farías but again, there is no mention in his papers of the bonds being destroyed. Were they, therefore, destroyed? Was there a bonfire in the grounds of Blomfield House some time after July 1887? The fact that none of the cancelled bonds have ever been found suggests that there was. It also seems certain that subsequently the cancelled 1851 Three per Cents, 1864 Three per Cents, and 1886 Three per Cents would also have been incinerated or otherwise destroyed. On the other hand, the Mexican clerk who was given the job of disposing of the pile of "useless" paper, possibly Olano, may have decided to retain a few examples as souvenirs. Perhaps at some time in the future, particularly when Mexico has found the resources to catalogue the still largely uncatalogued archive of the Finance Ministry, a few of the bonds may be found. If not, we can only hope that somewhere in an attic or solicitor's or stockbroker's office, the few 1824, 1825, and 1831 bonds which were never presented for cancellation by their holders await discovery.

NOTES

1. CFB *Report* (1889), p. 114.
2. SRE, L.E. 1035.

Part II

The Bondholders

Chapter 4

The Committee(s) of Mexican Bondholders, 1830–1887

It is necessary to get a lot of men together, for the show of the thing, otherwise the world will not believe. That is the meaning of committees. But the real work must always be done by one or two men.
> —A. Trollope, *The Claverings* (1867) (reprint, Oxford University Press, Oxford, 1986), p. 338

SOME PRELIMINARY OBSERVATIONS

For scholars who seek to study the history of its origins and development, the Committee of Mexican Bondholders offers some curious and unexpected difficulties. In the first place, apart from occasional passing reference to it in books on Mexico's foreign debt, nothing of substance has been written about it. This is surprising in several respects. For example, the Committee existed for a long time, lasting, with only one short interruption, for almost sixty years from 1830 until 1887 when it seems to have been fully absorbed into the Corporation of Foreign Bondholders. Throughout much of this period, it was a well-funded organization, with offices and secretary/administrator in the heart of London's financial district. Its members were invariably from the social and financial elite of Britain's capital city. They included peers of the realm, prominent politicians and Members of Parliament, Admirals, Generals, millionaire financiers and businessmen, together with leading city figures from the merchant banks, and stockbrokers. Few special interest groups can have been better represented or have had more esteemed figures to press their case. Access to the corridors of power, notably the British Foreign Office, if not instant, was always rapid. Successive Foreign Secretaries were ever willing to receive and listen to delegations putting their case on behalf of the bondholders, even though they always refused to give the full support requested. Questions to Ministers in Parliament, debates, and commissions of enquiry on their claims were regularly achieved by the bondholders' lobby, benefiting, as the Committee's secretary put it in 1850, from "friends in the House of Lords and also in the Commons."[1] Yet, even in the light of such characteristics, no historian has deemed the Committee's membership, organization, financing, or activities worthy of study.

This neglect of an organization which acted on behalf of thousands of bondholders, who themselves represented a good cross section of Victorian England's "Upper Ten Thousand," may be due to another odd feature of the Committee.[2] With one or two exceptions, its archive or records accumulated over those years has disappeared. There is no trace of the letter books or copies of its very extensive inward and outward correspondence with both the British and Mexican governments. In 1850, its secretary was specifically ordered to keep "books in which all correspondence shall be entered with the least possible delay after receipt or dispatch."[3] None of these books have been discovered. Similarly, what was certainly a substantial volume of letters from the countless bondholders who wrote for information or complaint is nowhere to be found. All manner of memorials, protests, legal depositions, and reports were composed by the Committee's secretaries or chairmen and while those that were printed have been located, there is now no trace of the original drafts. With one exception, the Committee's minute books of what were hundreds of meetings have disappeared—the Committee met more than 200 times in just three years between 1850 and 1853, "besides numerous meetings of sub-committees."[4] The exception is the minutes for the years 1874 to 1883, recorded in a single manuscript volume found in the Corporation of Foreign Bondholders' archive.[5] For many years, the Committee employed agents who were sent to Mexico to press the case for dividend payments or redemption of the bonds. Those agents sent back their progress reports on the monthly packets together with confidential assessments of political and other developments as far as they affected debt payments. Once again, there is no sign of them.

The disappearance of what must have been a very substantial collection of papers remains a mystery. Some outgoing correspondence, however, is available in British, European, and Mexican archives. For the most part, this consists of letters written by the successive chairmen of the Committee. As the copies of these letters, and the replies to them, are not to be found in any central repository, it seemed possible that they might be found in the personal papers of their authors. Not all the chairmen, of course, left any papers but of those who did, once again there is nothing to be found relating to their activities for the bondholders. Sir Robert Wilson, for example, was chairman from 1830 to 1836. He had enjoyed a long and distinguished career in the British Army participating in campaigns in many countries, including Argentina and the Iberian peninsula. He rose to the rank of general, was awarded many honors including an Austrian baronetcy and knighthood, served as a Member of Parliament for thirteen years from 1818 to 1831, and ended his career as governor of Gibraltar.[6] His personal papers are scattered throughout various repositories but from those which it has been possible to consult, aside from an occasional reference to his general interest in Hispanic and Spanish American affairs, he left nothing related to his activities concerning his personal investments in Mexican bonds nor his years as chairman of the bondholders' committee.[7]

Wilson was succeeded as chairman by George Richard Robinson who led the Committee of Spanish American Bondholders, which included the Mexican, from 1836 until 1850. He also was a man of considerable distinction and prominence in the city of London. A partner in the firm of merchants, Hart & Robinson, his fortune was made in the Newfoundland trade.[8] In addition to his political career as Member of Parliament for Worcester and later Poole, he became a leading figure in financial circles and in particular at Lloyd's, the insurance brokers, where he was also chairman for sixteen years from 1834 to 1850. Indeed, one of Lloyd's historians describes him as "the saviour of Lloyd's" in the 1840s after the ruinous fire which had destroyed their premises in 1838. The same writer, however, notes another perhaps odd fact, which is that Robinson was "a man whose memory (it may be thought) has not been honoured at Lloyd's in proportion to his deserts."[9] He is one of the few chairmen, for example, of whom there is no portrait. Likewise, there appears to be no record of his work for the Mexican and other Spanish American bondholders from 1828, when he attended the first meeting of bondholders, to his demise in August 1850. The originals of the certainly very large volume of correspondence which he wrote on behalf of the bondholders and the "masses of letters" which he himself said he received from them, together with minutes of meetings and memoranda he composed, have all disappeared without trace.[10] Nor have any of his personal or business papers survived. This may be attributable to his rather unconventional personal life. A lifelong bachelor, he nonetheless managed to father three sons by one woman and a daughter by another. In his will, signed on 1 July 1850, just a few weeks before his death and after several months of illness, he left most of his £157,000 estate to friends and business partners. The "natural sons," led by his namesake, George Richard, challenged the will in the Court of Canterbury where testamentary cases at the time were heard. The various submissions made to the Court reveal that Robinson's private life had been far from harmonious.[11]

Robinson's immediate successors as chairmen of the Committee of Mexican Bondholders included Sir Isaac Lyon Goldsmid and James Capel. Both were major figures in financial circles and founders of companies which still exist to this day. Goldsmid was a partner in the firm of Mocatta & Goldsmid, bullion brokers to the Bank of England and to the East India Company. He was also a director of many other companies including the London Dock Company and the Globe Insurance Company, and he had interests and investments in several Spanish American enterprises such as the Imperial Brazilian Mining Association. His estate was valued at the immense sum (for the time) of "£1,000,000 and upward," and his will reveals that he was a large investor in stocks and shares. He had at least £10,000 in Mexican stocks. Hence, his interest in the bondholders' committees. He was first elected to the Mexican Committee in 1830 and he remained for the next twenty years, accepting the chairmanship with some reluctance in 1850. Again, however, those of his papers which have been seen contain nothing related to his Mexican interests or to his work for so many years on the Committee. The same applies to the stockbroker, James Capel, who became chairman after Goldsmid in 1853. Like his predecessor, he was a major holder of Mexican bonds on his own account (at least £10,000) but also represented clients with holdings in excess of £500,000. He also served on the Committee for many years and yet there appears to be no trace of his personal Mexican interests in the records of his company.[12]

Another chairman, certainly the most active and vociferous on behalf of the bondholders' interests, was David Robertson. He was the fourth son of Sir John Marjoribanks, of Lees, Berwickshire, but he assumed the name Robertson in 1834 in compliance with the will of his wife's maternal grandfather, William Robertson. By that time, Robertson had already become a prominent financier in London. He had started his career in the stockbrokers' firm of Sir Philip Antrobus & Co., for which James Capel also worked. The two became firm friends and later business partners in the firm of Marjoribanks, Capel & Co.[13] Both shared an interest and enthusiasm for the Hispanic world. Robertson, in particular, invested much of his fortune (he left almost £250,000) in both Spanish and Spanish American stocks. At the time of his death in June 1873, he had substantial holdings in Spanish, Costa Rican, Chilean, New Granadan, Paraguayan, and above all, Buenos Aires and Mexican stocks. With £100,000 of the latter in the 1850s, he had been the second-largest individual holder of Mexican foreign debt bonds and his Argentine holdings were "the best stock, I think, in the world."[14] With such large personal investments, Robertson was soon an active member of several of the bondholders' committees, especially after he retired from business in 1837. For example, he joined the Committee of Spanish American Bondholders in the same year of his retirement, remaining on it until 1850 when he was elected to the newly formed Committee of Mexican Bondholders. He became chairman of the Mexican Committee in 1856, continuing to hold that office until the Committee was temporarily wound up in 1862. He also served on the committees of Spanish, Buenos Aires, and Venezuelan bondholders, presiding over many of their public meetings until well into the 1860s. Finally, he was also the Liberal Member of Parliament for Berwickshire from May 1859 until 1873 when he was dubbed Lord Marjoribanks, just a week before his death on 19 June of that year.

Robertson's name will figure prominently in other sections of this book, but for the time being it is sufficient to note that he was an exceptionally active chairman of the Committee. He personally lobbied politicians and Ministers constantly, writing so many letters and petitions that one Foreign Office official was moved to describe him as "that indefatigable bore."[15] Many of his letters have survived in the Foreign Office records and uniquely, in his case, a substantial number were included in one of the Committee's published reports.[16] In a preface to the letters, however, addressed to the bondholders and almost certainly written by Robertson himself, there is the following:

The Correspondence which our Chairman has had with the authorities at home and in Mexico, and with other influential parties, for your welfare, would of itself fill an ordinary volume. Much of it was necessarily of a *private* and *confidential* nature, without which it is impossible to approach or to acquire the confidence of men in office; and as many of the said letters are of that character, and the replies to them marked *private* (which last he considers one of the most binding and sacred of human obligations, to be preserved inviolate), it is of course impossible to publish them.

More than 100 printed pages of letters follow and as the preface states, much more was left unpublished. The question arises, therefore, of what happened to this very substantial correspondence together with all the other miscellaneous documentation which Robertson must have accumulated during more than twenty years as a Committee member and six as chairman. As he emphasized in a letter to Lord Wodehouse at the Foreign Office, he seems to have taken some pride in the fact that rather than relying on the Committee's secretary to compose them, "I, as you may suppose, always write my own letters."[17] Most were written from his country estate in Berwickshire, known as Ladykirk. The estate still exists to this day and remains in the ownership of Robertson's descendants. The present owner, Henry Askew, kindly permitted the author to examine all the family records. At first, very few of Robertson's papers were found but subsequently, a large wooden chest was located in the stables which Robertson had built after his horse "Little Wonder" won the Derby in 1840.[18] The chest bears Robertson's name and in it there is his briefcase together with a mass of papers concerning many aspects of his life: personal accounts, dinner invitations, family correspondence, checkbooks, cash books recording his expenditure, letters to his bankers such as Coutts, and all the ephemera of a long and busy life. Yet, with the exception of a couple of references to his Buenos Aires investments, there is nothing related to his lifetime interest in Spanish America. In particular, there is nothing to do with his investments in Mexican bonds, which he began in the mid-1820s, and nothing to do with his years of participation in the Committee of Mexican Bondholders.[19] All of his correspondence (inward and outward) related to Mexican bonds and bondholders has disappeared. There is, in short, a total absence of all traces of his Mexican interests.

Other chairmen, of course, followed Robertson, but for the first few years they held office for only a short time and there is perhaps no reason to suppose, or hope, that their Mexican-related papers would have survived. In 1868, however, another Member of Parliament was elected chairman. This was Henry Brinsley Sheridan. Born in London in 1820, and apparently no relation to his more famous namesake, the playwright Richard Brinsley Sheridan, he first came to public attention as a poet. One of his compositions in 1845 attracted praise in the literary magazine *The Athenaeum*, as "a piece of metrical elegance."[20] At the age of thirty-one, he decided to study law and he was called to the Bar in November 1856.[21] The following year, he was elected to Parliament for Dudley, a constituency he represented for almost thirty years until 1886. An active parliamentarian on the Liberal benches, he continued his career as a barrister, appearing as such in the London directories until the mid-1870s.[22] Sheridan remained chairman of the Mexican Committee for almost twenty years during which time he vigorously promoted the bondholders' claims both inside and outside of Parliament. He participated in almost continuous negotiations with Mexican representatives and chaired regular, at times, weekly meetings of the Committee. In addition, he participated in the work of the Corporation of Foreign Bondholders to which the Mexican Committee was affiliated in 1876. In short, like his predecessors, he must have accumulated a voluminous personal archive of correspondence, reports, and memoranda, together with all the details of the proposed conversions of the Mexican debt that were advanced in the 1870s and early 1880s. None of it appears to have survived, although there is one possible source which has not been available. This is the archive of the Corporation of Foreign Bondholders. Its activities were terminated in 1988 at which time its large archive was partly dispersed and partly deposited at the Guildhall Library in London. While some parts of it have been catalogued and made available to scholars, some have not and remain locked away in storage. It is possible that it contains some of the Mexican Committee's missing archive, especially relating to the years when Sheridan was chairman.

The Committee was perhaps inevitably dominated by London-based bondholders, together with bankers and stockbrokers who held substantial amounts of Mexican stocks on their own account or on behalf of their clients. Membership tended to be by invitation and even though such invitations were always confirmed by general meetings of bondholders, accusations of nepotism and cliquism were often made. As one newspaper put it, "A little junta of persons have assumed the right of nominating coadjutors or successors."[23] This charge was denied by the Committee but it does appear that its members were drawn from a very small group of entrepreneurs, merchants, and stockbrokers prominent in the London business community. Some, like Charles McGarel and David Robertson, had large personal investments in Mexican bonds. Indeed, one of the qualifications for membership adopted in the early 1850s was ownership of at least £10,000 worth of bonds. Others, with perhaps smaller personal stakes, were heavily involved in companies trading with Mexico or had shares in one or more of the many British enterprises that were established to invest in the Mexican mining industry.

The fact that so many of the Committee members had such large personal interests at stake gave rise to another persistent accusation. This was that the members used what was called "priority of information" for speculation in the market. It was alleged that when news of political events or any other information which might affect the bond price was received by the Committee, it was withheld to allow the privileged clique to buy or sell their stocks; in short, insider trading. As early as 1828, when discussions had only just begun about the possible formation of a Committee, *The Morning Herald* (2 May 1828) openly accused Alexander Baring, John Capel, and others of favoring the establishment of a Committee so that they could speculate in the market, investing in stocks on the basis of information which had not been released to the bondholders at large. What was the point, asked the editor with obvious sarcasm, of being a member of a committee if there was no profit in it? In 1843, *The Standard* (12 September 1843) attributed recent sharp price fluctuations in Mexican securities to market uncertainty "mixed up with the suspicion that all is not fair and above board, but that parties intrusted [*sic*] to look after the interest of the bondholders have been taking advantage of the knowledge they have acquired in that capacity."

The Committee members strongly denied such accusations against their integrity, insisting that they were "wholly destitute of foundation." All information, except that given in confidence, they said, was always released as soon as possible: "The Committee have transmitted to the newspapers, on the day of its arrival, the substance of whatever intelligence has been transmitted."[24] Certainly, the main London newspapers always carried noticeable amounts of information on the Mexican debt and on all the negotiations for the various conversions that took place. Reports from the Committee's agents in Mexico appeared regularly, as did details of the cargoes, and especially any funds for the dividend account, brought by the monthly packets. All the papers gave space to detailed summaries of public meetings of bondholders and frequently published statements and correspondence sent to them by the Committee. The press, therefore, provided an important link between the Committee and its constituents. As *The Money Market Review* (13 March 1880) noted, "Bondholders are spread all over the country; no lists of them are to be had; and no means exist of conveying information to them except through the medium of the Press."

Those bondholders who lived in London also had access to the Committee's office where letters and other documents received (including translations where necessary) were laid out on tables for their perusal. Most, however, did not live in the metropolis. They could not attend the public meetings held to consider proposals affecting their stocks nor could they visit the Committee's office to consult the latest information. Mr. J. Small of Guisbrough, Yorkshire, provides a good example of the problem. On 3 February 1844, he wrote to the Mexican Minister, Tomás Murphy. He owned, he said, several of the £100 bonds which he had bought some years earlier. He knew vaguely of the 1837 conversion and the Deferred bonds which were due to become active in 1847. He also had some of the Debentures issued in exchange for unpaid dividends but he had not received a penny on them. What he now wanted was information on the details of the 1837 agreement and on what was happening about the dividend arrears. He continued, "I reside at a distance of nearly 300 miles from London and only glean my information from the newspapers on these matters and the information they give is very meagre and not always to be depended upon."[25] We do not know if Mr. Small received any answer from Murphy but the problem of disseminating information remained. There are numerous similar letters to him in the Mexican Legation archive from bondholders in many parts of Britain. While the newspapers provided them with some details of conversions, dividend payments, and other matters, the constraints of space always meant that their coverage was limited or "meagre," as Mr. Small stated. The Committee was aware of the problem and, anxious to avoid the charges of cliquism or insider trading, devoted much time, industry, and expense to compiling very detailed reports of its activities. These reports are packed with data on every aspect of the debt negotiations, dividends, campaigns, agents' activities, correspondence, and financial statistics. Usually, they were prepared, printed, and distributed in advance of a public meeting of the bondholders. The contents were then put to the assembly for approval.[26] The proceedings and resolutions adopted at public meetings were also often printed separately.

The published reports provided the most comprehensive source of information for the many bondholders who lived outside of London, either elsewhere in Britain or in Europe, if not even further afield. We do not know the size of each print run, but given the importance of the information, the number of interested bondholders, and their geographical spread, it would seem reasonable to conclude that hundreds, if not thousands, were produced. If that is a correct conclusion, it is all the more surprising that, in most instances, almost all copies have been lost. The first, for example, of 37 pages, was printed in London in 1830, by Effingham Wilson, Royal Exchange. Only three copies have been found, one each in Yale University Library, Barings' archive, and Mexico's Foreign Ministry archive. The second, 19 pages printed in 1831 by R. Clay in London, is even scarcer with only two copies known, again one each in the latter two archives. The third was issued by the Committee of Spanish American Bondholders in 1839. Given that the Committee represented not just the Mexican bondholders but also the investors in all the other Spanish American stocks as well, the print run was presumably substantial. Yet, only a single copy is known to have survived and that is in the Louisiana State University Library at Baton Rouge. Similarly, there seems to be only one extant copy of a printed report of the proceedings of a meeting held on 4 June 1846 to discuss the terms of the 1846 conversion. That sole copy was found among a bondholder's papers now housed in Kendal Record Office.[27] Even more perplexing is the almost total disappearance of the several reports published by the Committee of Mexican Bondholders between 1850 and 1862. In those years, the newly established, independent Committee, separate from the Spanish American Committee, was exceptionally active. The 1851 conversion was agreed upon and implemented, negotiations on the Lizardi Deferred 1837 bonds continued, there were diplomatic Conventions, and campaigns were waged to persuade the British government to intervene. Finally, the whole episode of the Allied Intervention was initiated. These myriad events and complex negotiations over the debt, allied with the Committee's anxiety to be seen to be working on behalf of the bondholders as a whole rather than themselves in particular, resulted in the publication of no less than fifteen reports and several other documents. In addition, the Committee of Spanish American Bondholders produced an account of its own activities. While some of these reports are relatively small at between 20 and 40 pages, others are in excess of 200 pages. All except the first, which cost Threepence, were priced at Sixpence, compared to the Two Shillings charged for the 1830 *Report*, in what seems to have been a deliberate attempt to achieve a wider circulation. Yet once again, with the exception of some of the shorter reports of which there are copies in the British Foreign Office archive, only a handful of copies of the others is known to exist. There seem to be only two copies of the April 1861 *Report*, at Yale University Library and the Bancroft Library, University of California. The only known copies of the 1862 *Reports*, dated January and February, are also in the Bancroft. These apparently unique examples are bound in a three-volume collection of reports and other documents concerning the Committee.

The Committee was wound up in 1862 but resurrected in 1868. The new, at first "Provisional" Committee at once began to produce and publish its own reports in 1868, 1869, and 1870. Copies of these are in the British Library which, inexplicably, has none of the earlier ones. The annual reports of the Corporation of Foreign Bondholders, starting in 1874, are more generally available. The Mexican Committee, however, although affiliated to the Corporation in 1875, continued to produce its own separate reports and once again, very few copies have survived. In fact, in the case of the 1876 *Report*, only four have been found. Consisting of 47 pages, printed by Wertheimer, Lea & Co., and dated 31 March 1876, it was prepared for submission to a general meeting of bondholders held at the Corporation's offices at 10 Moorgate Street on 4 April 1876. According to contemporary press accounts, the meeting attracted a large attendance. It was certainly a very lively session, with much criticism of the British goverment's failure to support the bondholders and even talk that they might themselves finance the dispatch of a warship to Mexico to collect what they were owed.[28] Most of the newspapers carried summaries of the report in the days preceding the meeting and they had presumably been sent or had purchased copies. It also seems reasonable to assume that a substantial number were available to the bondholders themselves either before or at the meeting. Almost all have disappeared. Of the four known copies, two are in the British Library and one is in the Public Record Office (F.O. 50/429, fols. 145-170). The other was discovered by the present author in the London Stock Exchange archive. It was sent to the Exchange in 1886 by Francis Perry. As indicated in an earlier section, he was the brother of the by then deceased Edward Joseph Perry who had been the bondholders' agent in Mexico from 1868 until his death in 1883. According to Francis Perry, his brother had been promised £15,000 worth of Mexican bonds by the Mexican Committee in compensation for some £5,000 of expenditure he had incurred in Mexico. These had not been paid and despite promises to do so, the Committee had failed to honor the commitment. Perry, therefore, asked the Stock Exchange not to sanction any new Mexican bonds, in particular, the 1886 Three per Cents, until the debt owed to his late brother had been settled. As evidence for his brother's work, he submitted his own personal copy of the 1876 *Report*. It has many complimentary references to his brother's efforts on behalf of the bondholders, which Perry underlined for the benefit of the Stock Exchange Committee. We do not know what success Perry had in his personal campaign but again, fortunately, his copy of the 1876 *Report* was not returned and has thus survived.[29]

Several other reports were published in the 1880s but in almost all cases, no more than one or two copies have been located. Like the Committee's archive of sixty years of accumulated correspondence and other documentation, what must surely have been hundreds, if not thousands, of copies issued between 1830 and 1886 have inexplicably disappeared. We can only presume that they suffered the same fate as the cancelled bonds which, as we have shown earlier, were almost certainly destroyed in the late 1880s. Fortunately, at least one copy of every report has been found, and a substantial volume of correspondence and other documentation located in archives and the press. These sources have provided the basis for the following synopsis of the Committee's foundation, membership, and activities. It is to these topics that we now turn.

ORIGINS, 1827–1830

Mexico defaulted on its loans in October 1827. It was by no means alone. Chile, Colombia, Peru, and Guatemala had already failed to pay dividends on time and when Buenos Aires did the same in January 1828, all the six Spanish American republics which had floated loans in London were in default. In the absence of registers of bondholders, we have no way of knowing how many investors were affected by this situation, although Dawson estimates that the total Latin American debt of £21,000,000 "was owned initially by at least 25–30,000 bondholders."[30]

For the disillusioned bondholders, and for the many others who had lost the money they had invested in the numerous speculative companies formed at the time to exploit the assumed wealth of Latin America, the news of events was not good. Wars, domestic political strife, constitutional chaos, and economic stagnation were prevalent across the continent. Mexico, in particular, seemed to be rapidly descending into anarchy. After a period of relative calm following the fall of the Iturbide Empire in 1823, and the establishment of a federal republic in October 1824, revolutions against the elected government began in 1827 with the so-called Tulancingo revolt led by the nation's vice president, General Nicolás Bravo. His revolt was largely inspired as a protest against recently issued laws which expelled Spaniards from the country. The anti-Spanish legislation reflected the bitter internal divisions between rival masonic factions which in turn led to more revolts and counterrevolts. Pessimistic reports of the worsening situation of the country soon found their way into the British press. The federal government, it was said, had run out of money. Its civil servants, and more importantly, the military garrisons in Mexico City, were not being paid. Attempts to raise funds with internal loans had failed miserably and the expulsion of the industrious Spaniards, who were allowed to take their capital with them, could only harm the economy.[31] Even more worrisome for the bondholders were persistent rumors that Ferdinand VII of Spain was determined to reconquer his lost colony of New Spain. The Spanish king had never accepted the loss of his empire in America and it was no secret in the royal courts of Europe that he intended to raise an army to invade Mexico. It was known that men and materiel were being assembled in Cuba in preparation for the invasion.[32] Finally, British diplomats warned that in the prevailing circumstances, "There does not appear to be the least prospect of any remittances being made to England for the Dividends, for a long time to come."[33]

Mexico's bond prices reflected the market's disillusion. From a high of around 83 in early 1825, the Five per Cents were down to 29 by February 1828. The Six per Cents had declined from a peak of 86 to around 40. Early in March, news of the Tulancingo rebels, and their defeat by military forces loyal to the government, reached the London press and seemed to confirm the growing instability in the country. The bond prices declined even further to 24 and 31, respectively. All the other Spanish American bonds had experienced similar falls. Then, on 25 March 1828, *The Times* reported that a group of several Members of Parliament had met the previous week to consider calling a general meeting of all the creditors of the Spanish American debtor nations. Prominent people had already signed the requisition to summon the meeting, which had been sent around the city offices, and a leading merchant had offered to take the chair. Some of the bondholders of particular countries had already held meetings and set up committees to press their claims. They had been ineffective, according to *The Times*, because by themselves they were too small to be taken seriously, especially by the British government. A meeting of bondholders of all the defaulting states was likely to be much more effective.

The meeting took place in the "great room" at the London Tavern on 1 May 1828.[34] It began promptly at 2:00 P.M. in the presence of about 120 bondholders, including the following Members of Parliament (constituency in parentheses):

Alexander Baring (Callington)

John Capel (Queenborough)

Thomas Henry Davies (Worcester)

John Easthope (St. Albans)

George Robinson (Worcester)

William Thompson (London)

William Ward (London)

In addition to their parliamentary status, these men, who included both Liberals and Conservatives, were all very prominent figures in mercantile circles in London. Baring was the senior partner in his family's bank. Capel, whose cousin James was to have a leading role among the Mexican bondholders in later years, was a stockbroker. Easthope was the director of several companies, including the United Mexican Mining Association, and subsequently proprietor of *The Morning Chronicle*. Thompson, a wealthy iron-master from Grayrigg, near Kendal, was a director of the Bank of England and Lord Mayor of London. Ward, also a director of the Bank of England, was a financier and expert in Foreign Exchange markets. He was the cousin of Henry George Ward, Britain's first Chargé d'Affaires in Mexico from 1825 to 1827. Davies was a company director and retired army colonel who had fought at Waterloo. Finally, there was Robinson, a merchant and shipowner, who, as indicated earlier, later became chairman of the Committee of Spanish American Bondholders.

The first business of the meeting was to choose a chairman and on a motion put by Ward, Baring was elected. After opening remarks from the chair, in which Baring declared that he had no personal interest in any of the bonds, Robinson put resolutions which he said had been hastily prepared in advance of the meeting. The first of these referred to the size of the total debt which was calculated to be over £17,000,000 and which should have been yielding annual interest of £985,960. The second was that a committee should be formed with instructions to approach the British government for assistance in persuading the debtor nations to pay. Members of the committee were to be as follows: Capel, Davies, Easthope, Milbank, Robinson, Thompson, Ward.

In his remarks, Robinson urged that recriminations would be futile and that what mattered was the future. Other speakers followed, including Mr. D. Salomons, Mr. Hammond, Mr. Kemple, Mr. Davis, and Mr. Young. Some attacked Spain and its threats which were forcing the Spanish Americans to spend their resources on defensive measures. One made the point that without the bondholders' money, the new republics would not have achieved their independence. Several insisted that the British government was obliged to help them. Baring summarized the discussion from the chair, introducing a cautionary note to the proceedings. He was not surprised, he said, that the new nations had defaulted. They were inexperienced, lacked financial expertise, and were plagued by internal dissension. Moreover, he reminded the meeting, all investors knew that the high interest rates offered on the bonds at the time of issue implied a higher level of risk. Notwithstanding their obvious problems, however, as far as he was aware, not one of the debtor nations intended to repudiate their debts. An approach to the British government would certainly be heeded although with what practical effect remained to be seen.

The resolutions were approved with some amendments. The British government was to be asked for help but "without at the same time implying a fixed distrust of the honour of the Republican States." Membership of the committee was likewise agreed. Unfortunately, we have scant details of any discussions with the British Foreign Office as a result of the meeting. We can only assume that the Committee made its case for British intervention, but despite the involvement of so many Members of Parliament and other influential personalities from London's financial community, no promises of official support were forthcoming.

The first general meeting of the Committee of bondholders, therefore, failed to have any noticeable impact on the British government. On the other hand, the publicity arising from the meeting, which was widely reported in the press with all the London papers carrying detailed summaries, certainly raised the profile of the issue. Also, it served to reassure those bondholders who lived elsewhere in Britain and Europe that their claims had not been forgotten. As those present at the meeting had hoped, their activities did not escape the attention of Spanish American diplomats. Just a few days later, Vicente Rocafuerte, Mexico's Chargé d'Affaires, felt it politic to write to the Foreign Secretary, the Earl of Dudley. Having referred to the bondholders' recent meeting, he offered a long explanation, in French incidentally, of the causes of his country's failure to meet its obligations. He promised that Mexico would resume payments on its debts. Ten days later, he wrote again to say that 400,000 dollars was being sent for the dividend fund.[35]

Rocafuerte's confidence probably reflected the fact that he knew of a decree about to be approved by the Mexican Congress. This was released on 23 May 1828. It ordered that one-eighth of the net proceeds of the maritime customs and of export duties on gold and silver should be assigned to the payment of dividends and redemption of principal of the London debt. News of this decree reached London in July and translations of it were quickly published in the press.[36] If the bondholders' hopes were raised by it, they were soon to be disappointed once again because although the monthly packets continued to bring hundreds of thousands of dollars from Mexico, all was for private mercantile accounts and none for the dividend fund. "It is painful to be compelled to state," as *The Times* (6 June 1828) expressed it, "that there was almost no chance of dividends being paid in the near future. Its pessimism was justified when on 28 October, it reported that the money set aside at the Veracruz customs for the dividends had been seized to pay the local garrison.

It was on 28 October 1828 that the Mexican Congress approved the first measure for the capitalization of the dividend arrears. It proposed to exchange the unpaid coupons of both the 1824 Five per Cents and 1825 Six per Cents for new bonds and also, that regular payments for the dividends "shall be remitted, without fail, every three months." The law envisaged that the "assent of the parties interested in the overdue dividends" would be obtained and Rocafuerte was instructed to consult Barings on how best to proceed with the bondholders. Barings' reply was direct and unequivocal. There was no point in seeking to capitalize the arrears with new bonds until such time as regular and punctual payment of dividends could be assured. Too many promises had been made and not kept for the bondholders to accept the present proposals. Furthermore, Alexander Baring added, "I cannot consent to risk my name when I see no positive indication of the actual fulfilment of the promises and pledges which would be given through my intervention as agent of the government."[37] A few months later, in June 1829, further Mexican requests to Barings to summon the bondholders to consider the capitalization proposals met with similar refusals.[38]

THE FIRST COMMITTEE OF MEXICAN BONDHOLDERS, 1830–1836

After the general meeting of bondholders of all the Spanish American republics in default, no further attempts at any kind of umbrella organization seem to have been made. Instead, the bondholders of individual countries formed their own committees to lobby the British government and the authorities of the nation which owed them money. Some 200 Colombian bondholders, for example, met in November 1828 at a meeting chaired by Sir Robert Wilson. Guatemalan creditors also met and formed their committee in September 1829 and there were similar committees representing the interests of Spanish, Portuguese, and other national bondholders. The formation of the first Mexican Committee in 1830 followed the trend but it was also the direct result of events and decisions taken in Mexico. The two years 1828 and 1829 had seen continued political upheaval in the republic. The laws expelling Spanish residents had been implemented and large amounts of capital had been taken from the country as a result. Serious riots in Mexico City in December 1828 had destroyed several million dollars' worth of property, greatly alarming property owners who feared popular revolution by the impoverished masses. The result of the presidential election held in 1828 had been challenged by military revolt and the elected candidate, Manuel Gómez Pedraza, had been forced to flee, arriving in Britain in April 1829. The new government was headed by Vicente Guerrero, a semi-literate half caste, despised by the white creole elite in control of the country's economy. Guerrero, however, was a popular hero of the wars of independence and his administration was dominated by radicals, in particular his Finance Minister, Lorenzo de Zavala, who promptly introduced, or tried to introduce, all manner of taxation on property and income. Despite his efforts, which were largely unsuccessful, the government's deficit of expenditure over income continued to increase and it was reported that "With respect to finance, the state of affairs in Mexico was nearly as bad as possible."[39] Finally, the long-expected Spanish attempt at reconquest took place in July 1829. Almost daily reports of its progress appeared in the press and although the invasion army was described as a "Quixotic enterprise" led by "an ignorant boatman," Mexican bonds fell to their lowest point at around 15–16 for the Five per Cents and 17–18 for the Six per Cents.[40] It was not until December 1829 that news of the defeat of the Spanish army was confirmed. The market responded with rises in the bond prices to 21 and 26, respectively.

The situation facing the bondholders, therefore, was bleak. In December 1829, however, the vice president of the Guerrero administration, General Anastasio Bustamante, at the head of a reserve army intended to fight the invading Spaniards, used his opportunity to rebel against his own government. Guerrero was soon forced to flee Mexico City which Bustamante entered in triumph in January 1830. A pro-clerical conservative, Busta-mante at once set about instituting a strongly reactionary regime, in an attempt to suppress the radicalism and anti-clericalism of his predecessors. Among his first cabinet appointments was Lucas Alamán. As indicated in an earlier section, he had travelled widely in Europe where he had many personal contacts. He was very pro-European, as opposed to pro–United States, and could be aptly described as an Anglophile. Strongly conservative, and later monarchist in his political views, one of his main priorities was to sort out the national financial crisis. In particular, he saw the need for Mexico to attract foreign capital investment into its ailing economy and he fully appreciated that to do so, it was essential to resolve the question of the unpaid foreign or London debt. Literally within weeks of his taking office, therefore, he sent a set of proposals to London. These led to the 1831 capitalization and as they have already been explained in some detail, there is no need to repeat them here. One of his points, however, was of particular relevance to the formation of the Committee of Mexican Bond-holders. In his letter of 5 March 1830, addressed to the Mexican Minister, Manuel Gorostiza, he suggested that the best way of making his ideas known was by "calling a meeting of the principal holders of the bonds in London."[41] In a later letter to Barings of 5 May, he was even more specific when he suggested that a committee of bondholders should be established.[42]

Gorostiza received Alamán's letter on the packet which arrived on 1 May. Within days, he had explained the contents to leading bondholders in London and held detailed discussions with Alexander Baring. Bondholders in Holland, France, and Germany were also consulted.[43] Barings wrote to Alamán on the same date expressing its "Great hopes of persuading them to accept a reasonable settlement."[44] On 5 May, Gorostiza posted a notice in the Foreign Stock Exchange announcing the receipt of the proposals, promising to publish them in translation as soon as possible. The translation appeared in the press on 7 May, by which time the bonds had risen to around 30 and 40, respectively, or about double their price of just a few months earlier. Rumors of privileged information and insider trading were reported and there were questions asked as to why, with the arrival of the packet on 1 May, there had been a delay of four days before the public disclosure.[45] Then, on 13 May, the following advertisement was placed in the press:

A Meeting of the Holders of Mexican Bonds will be held at the City of London Tavern, Bishopsgate-street, on Wednesday, the 26th inst. for the purpose of taking into consideration the communication recently made to the Bondholders by His Excellency the Mexican Minister. The chair will be taken at one o'clock precisely.

This notice was dated 13 May and was issued from the North and South American Coffee House but it has no signature or name of the person or persons responsible for it.

The meeting took place at the scheduled time but neither press accounts nor the subsequent printed *Report* of its proceedings indicate the number or identity of all the bondholders in attendance. The printed *Report*, however, does tell us that the following six Members of Parliament were present: Alexander Baring, George Robinson, William Thompson, William Ward, John Marshall, Robert Wilson.

The first four of these parliamentarians have already been mentioned as participants in the general meeting in 1828. The final two, Marshall and Wilson, seem to have been newcomers to the Mexican lobby. Marshall was a Leeds mill owner and linen manufacturer who represented Yorkshire in the House of Commons. Born in 1765, the son of a draper, he had built a highly profitable textile business. By 1813, with more capital than he required for his company, he had begun to speculate in Exchequer bills and foreign stocks. In 1822, he had £31,000 in Spanish American bonds and he continued in following years to invest heavily in foreign issues, including Mexican.[46] Having lived in London for the season for several years, he decided to seek a parliamentary seat and he was returned in June 1826 as a county candidate for Yorkshire.[47] We have again already briefly encountered Wilson and further biographical details are unnecessary except perhaps to note his increasing prominence at meetings of bondholders.

The meeting chose Alderman Thompson as chairman. It considered Alamán's proposals and approved various resolutions. Some of these were in part formalities. For example, thanks were presented to the Foreign Secretary, Earl of Aberdeen, for his expressed willingness to assist the bondholders in pursuit of their claims. Similar thanks were voted to Gorostiza, Alexander Baring, and to Robert Wilson "for his communication of this day" although there is no indication of what this was.[48] On a more general level, the principal resolution welcomed Alamán's proposals and resolved to set up a committee "to represent the general interests of the Bondholders." In addition, it was to confer with Gorostiza on the proposals on the table and to suggest measures which could be put to the Mexican government with a view to restoring the nation's credit. Also, it was "to take such steps as may be necessary for securing the influence and cooperation of the British government."[49] Finally, the Committee was to consist of the following members who were empowered to increase their number to fifteen, with three being accepted as a quorum:

John Marshall, M.P.	John Moxon
G.R. Robinson, M.P.	Henry Patteson

Alderman William Thompson, M.P.   John Diston Powles
Sir Robert Wilson, M.P.   Gabriel Shaw
Charles Buisson   Herman Sillem
Isaac Lyon Goldsmid

Thus, the first Committee of Mexican Bondholders was formally established. It was immediately accepted by both the British and Mexican authorities as a negotiating body on behalf of the bondholders as a whole. There are indications, however, that the meeting considered what legal powers the Committee would have, given that only a small proportion of bondholders had been present. Gorostiza was told a week or so later that the Committee was not empowered

in any legal or authorized manner, to release the Mexican government from any responsibility under which it at present lies towards the Bondholders. There are no less than forty thousand of these bonds in circulation, dispersed all over England, Scotland, and Ireland—in France, Holland, and Germany—and some of the holders are even resident in the East Indies. Any agreement to release the Mexican government from responsibility of any kind, must have the assent of every individual Bondholder; an object which is, under these circumstances, utterly unattainable.[50]

The Committee, therefore, was to be a representative body, with strictly limited executive powers. We do not know for certain that all of those chosen to serve on it were present at the meeting but it seems likely that most would have been. Among those we have not so far encountered are the last seven names. Nothing is known about Patteson. Buisson probably was part of the merchants, Buisson & Morlet, whose business was at 23 Fenchurch Street, and Shaw may have been a banker in the company known as John Perring, Shaw, Barber and Co., which failed in February 1826.[51] Moxon was a stockbroker and he remained a member of the Committee and its successor until the 1840s. A Thomas Moxon, who was almost certainly his son, joined the Committee in 1856. Sillem also remained for several years, representing Dutch holders of £800,000 worth of Mexican bonds.[52] His business, known as Herman Sillem, Son & Co., ceased trading in 1857. According to *The Times* (25 November 1857), it was "a house of more than fifty years' standing," with extensive business interests in Europe as well as North and South America. Isaac Lyon Goldsmid, the bullion dealer and noted financier, has been briefly described earlier. Finally, there was John Diston Powles. He was to have a very long career and prominent role in several of the bondholders' Committees until the 1860s. His involvement in both Spanish and Spanish American securities appears to have started in 1822 when together with Charles Herring and William Graham, described as "an association of merchants trading with the Caribbean," he won the contract for a Colombian loan.[53] In later years, he was a leading member of the Committees of Mexican Bondholders, Spanish American Bondholders, and Spanish Certificate Holders, and he also participated, usually as chairman, in meetings of Venezuelan, Ecuadorian, and Central American bondholders. Apart from these financial interests, he was also the founder or director of many companies, especially in the mining industry. These included the Anglo-Mexican Mining Association, Zacatecas Mining Company, English and Australian Copper Company, Mariquita and New Granada Mining Company. In connection with these industrial and commercial interests, he was also vice-chairman and later chairman of the South American and Mexican Association, a group formed to represent merchants across Britain who were trading with Latin America. Its members included several of the notable bondholders, including Alderman Thompson.

Powles was clearly an exceptionally active and energetic entrepreneur and his prominence on so many committees confirms his effectiveness and popularity among his peers in London's mercantile and financial circles. On the other hand, many of his businesses failed with the loss of investors' money. Not surprisingly, he made enemies, one of whom chose to publish a vitriolic attack on his career and his honesty. This was Christopher Richardson whose forty-page pamphlet, published in 1855, denounced Powles, his brothers, son, and diverse other relatives for every kind of exploitation, nepotism, corruption, dishonesty, and "reckless wrongdoing."[54]

There are no extant minute books recording the new Committee's meetings but within a week of the general meeting, the Yorkshireman, John Marshall, had been named as the chairman (see Illustration 23). His first letter, signed as "Chairman of the Committee of Mexican Bondholders," was dated 3 June 1830 and it was written from his home address at 34 Hill Street. It was sent to the Earl of Aberdeen and concerned the use of British vice-consuls at Mexican ports as receiving agents for dividend funds. Over the next few days, a series of letters on the topic were exchanged with the Foreign Office. Marshall also began discussions with Gorostiza on the use of agents in Mexico, as suggested by Alamán, and on the details of the proposed capitalization of dividend arrears. He put various suggestions for the collection and remittance of customs dues, for the rate of capitalization of arrears, and for the issue of new bonds. Gorostiza promised on 12 June that all the ideas would be sent to Mexico for evaluation.

This correspondence with the Foreign Office and Gorostiza, together with a translation of Alamán's letter of 5 March, were published in the newspapers. They were also collected together and issued in the form of a report or *Proceedings* of the Committee, dated 27 June 1830, and priced Two Shillings. It was produced, as it states on the cover, "FOR THE INFORMATION OF THE BONDHOLDERS, BY ORDER OF THE COMMITTEE."[55]

Marshall soon gave up the chairmanship of the Committee. His health

23. John Marshall, Chairman, Committee of Mexican Bondholders, 1830. Photograph reproduced by courtesy of the University of Leeds Art Collection.

had not been good for some time and he had decided to resign his seat in Parliament, which he did after the dissolution later in 1830. He was followed as chairman by Wilson who by December 1830, always writing from the North and South American Coffee House which was now used as the Committee's office, was consulting with Gorostiza and others over the proposed capitalization (see Illustration 24). The Mexican government had agreed to most of the changes suggested by the Committee and an appropriate decree was approved by Congress on 2 October. This reached London on the December packet. The Committee considered its terms and concluded that the new bonds to be used in payment of arrears should be issued immediately rather than in 1836, as the decree stipulated. On 24 December, Wilson, describing himself as "Chairman of the Committee," wrote to Gorostiza stating the Committee's demand. He also wrote to Manning and Marshall, who had been appointed agents for the bondholders in Mexico City, asking them to put the case to the government for an amendment to the 2 October law. Eventually, the change was agreed upon. More talks with Gorostiza on the detail of the capitalization and bond issue followed and with their successful conclusion, a partial dividend was paid in July. The Committee decided that it was time to issue a second report for "the Information of the Bondholders." This was signed by Wilson, at the usual Coffee House, and dated 6 July 1831. It contains the text of the Mexican decrees, copies of correspondence with Gorostiza, and explanations of the financial arrangements and how much each bondholder was to receive for his arrear coupons.[56]

Once again, the absence of minute books or other records of the Committee's meetings means that we do not know how often they were held, nor who attended. On the other hand, from Gorostiza's correspondence in Mexico's Foreign Ministry archive, it is clear that much of the negotiation was conducted privately with leading bondholders and with Barings. Gorostiza refers to lengthy meetings held in his home where there were "many hours of discussion."[57] Among those present was Alexander Baring who although retired, in his own words, from "speculation or commercial operation of any sort" since 1829, had agreed to help both Gorostiza and the bondholders.[58] Wilson was frequently involved as was Powles, described by Gorostiza as "the most influential member of the Committee."[59]

Following the 1831 capitalization and the issue of the new bonds from November onwards, there was little for the Committee to do. The monthly packets brought cash for the dividend fund and although never enough, advances from Barings enabled the 1832 dividends to be paid. As a result, the bond prices remained, at least for the first few months of the year, fairly stable at between 25 and 28 for the Five per Cents and between 30 and 35 for the Six per Cents. The packets, however, also brought news of events, including details of Santa Anna's revolt against the Bustamante regime. The rebellion was centered on Veracruz and bondholders and mer-

24. Sir Robert Wilson, Chairman, Committee of Mexican Bondholders, 1830–1836. Photograph reproduced by courtesy of the National Portrait Gallery, London.

chants alike feared that trade and the taxes on it would be disrupted, not just by a decline in imports and exports but also by seizures of the money by the rebellious troops. Santa Anna apparently tried to seize the dollars already set aside for the dividend fund early in the revolt but intervention by the British Consul at Veracruz persuaded him for the time being to desist.[60] By June, the news was more pessimistic and letters from Mexico City confirmed that "business was in a paralysed state throughout the country."[61]

The rebellion ended in December 1832 with the victory of Santa Anna's forces. The prospect of peace after almost a year's conflict brought optimism to the London market and Mexican stocks rose a couple of points. Reports from Mexico that "large remittances of specie to England were in progress" raised the bondholders' hopes that the January 1833 dividend, which had not been paid, might eventually be honored.[62] Then, about the same time as these reports, came the news that the new administration in office in Mexico City had concluded that it could not afford to do without the one-sixth of the customs dues assigned to the dividend fund. Instead, it proposed to allow just 6%. This decision, taken on 18 February, reached London toward the end of April 1833 and *The Times* soon noted that "it is quite clear that unless the bondholders can induce the Government to return to the old arrangement of setting aside 16 instead of 6 per cent of the duties, they cannot expect to obtain more than a fourth part of the interest due on their bonds."[63]

The Committee had already protested in a long letter which Wilson sent to Gorostiza on 3 May. He condemned the breach of a solemn contract entered into in good faith by the bondholders who had already made substantial sacrifices to help the Mexican government. Mexico's credit in Europe had now been destroyed. Gorostiza, he said, should make known to his government "the extreme disappointment of the bondholders." It was essential for the credit and national honor of Mexico that the agreed payments to the dividend fund should be restored.[64] Similar letters followed over the next few months and all were dutifully referrred to Mexico by Gorostiza. The British Minister in Mexico, Richard Pakenham, added his weight to the protests, but all to no avail.[65] By 14 September, *The Times* concluded:

The Mexican and South American stocks are declining, and seem to be threatened with a further fall. It would appear that the breach of its engagements committed by the Mexican government in regard to the remittances for the dividends has materially shaken the confidence of those who have been anxiously watching of late for signs of a regeneration of the credit of the other Spanish American states.

The year 1834 brought better news for the bondholders. Whether or not in response to their complaints or pressure by Pakenham, the assignment of the agreed one-sixth of the customs dues was resumed. Ferdinand VII of Spain had died in September 1833 and within weeks there were strong rumors that negotiations for Spanish recognition of Mexican independence, and that of other Spanish American republics, was about to start. The bonds rose to their highest price for several years at 36 and 46, respectively. In March, the packet *Lady Mary Pelham* brought 1,000,000 dollars for merchants and news of a plan being aired in the Mexican Congress to expropriate 40,000,000 dollars' worth of Church-owned property. In May, the British Consul at Tampico wrote that "I am induced to believe the dividends will be punctually paid."[66] Finally, perhaps to take advantage of what seemed to be an improving situation in Mexico, Wilson wrote directly to the Foreign Minister. The Committee, he said, expected that the "Government will cause to be remitted to its agents here Messrs Baring Brothers & Co such a sum as may represent the amount of the portion of the Duties which would have been remitted if the law of 2 October 1830 had been continued to be observed."[67]

The optimistic mood continued throughout 1835, even though no dividends were paid. In a letter to Barings, subsequently published in the newspapers, the Mexican Finance Minister promised that the "just and due payment" of the dividends would soon resume.[68] When the federal system of government was abandoned later in the year in favor of a centralized republic, press reports predicted improved business conditions and in August it was claimed that "commercial matters were assuming a better tone."[69] A proposed settlement of the Colombian debt, which was to be divided between New Granada, Venezuela, and Ecuador, helped the market for Spanish American stocks, and in April there was a consistent rise, as follows:

Chilean   +13%

Colombian   +11%

Mexican   +6%

Peruvian   +9%

By the end of the year, *The Times* was able to report that Mexican stock "has been comparitively neglected for some time past but the disposition to do justice to the foreign creditor shown lately by the Mexican government, though it has produced as yet no result, has acted favourably on their credit in this market."[70] Even the news that Texas had rebelled and declared its independence had little impact on bond prices.

No public meetings of Mexican bondholders were held during 1835 and there is no evidence of any activity by their Committee. In January 1836, however, Wilson resigned as chairman. His reasons are unknown but he seems to have continued as a member of the Committee. He wrote to Lord Palmerston at the Foreign Office on several occasions to protest about Mexico's "scandalous infraction of engagements." In another letter of 21 May 1836, he complained of Texas land sales being advertised in London. Land agents and speculators had been quick to take advantage of the Texas rebellion. For example, a Mr. Geo. Robins offered for sale "at the Auction Mart, opposite the Bank of England," 100,000 acres of valuable freehold land in the Province of Texas, "being part of the Grant made to the New Arkansas and Texas Land Company." From the bondholders' viewpoint, put forcibly by Wilson, they held a mortgage on all of Mexican territory as part of the security offered to guarantee the original loans. No part of the country could be disposed of in any way without their consent. Such land sales were, therefore, illegal and invalid.[71] Finally, Wilson proposed a scheme whereby European exporters to Mexico should pay at their European ports of departure the one-sixth of their import taxes due to the bondholders. His idea was forwarded to Mexico but elicited no response.[72]

Wilson's resignation as chairman was first referred to in a letter of 30 January 1836 from Captain J. Warrington to Lord Palmerston. Warrington had been a bondholder since the 1820s and he now told the Foreign Secretary that as Wilson had resigned, "it devolves upon me" to write on behalf of the bondholders. He proceeded to condemn Mexico's failure to honor its pledges and to demand immediate British government intervention. If, he said, the British government would not stand up for its own citizens, it should not object if the bondholders were to fit out their own armed vessels to enforce their just rights on the Mexicans. Palmerston's reply firmly rejected the notion of armed reprisals.[73]

The irate tone of Warrington's letter may have simply reflected his own attempts to put pressure on the Foreign Office, but it was also a firm sign that the bondholders were becoming impatient with Mexico's failure to honor its agreements. Another bondholder, signing himself "A Friend to Truth," in a letter to *The Times* (4 March 1836) maintained that "Mexico has ample means to pay her creditors at home and abroad." The British government must constantly remind Mexico of the consequences of "her suicidal contempt of good faith." Barings, still the Financial Agent, was becoming equally unhappy. On 1 March, it reminded the Chargé d'Affaires that on 1 April the terms agreed in the 1831 conversion became operative. These included the renewal of interest payments on all the stocks as well as the issue of new bonds in exchange for the receipts that had been distributed for dividend coupons. Barings' letter was sent to Mexico but it produced no more than the usual promises.[74] Barings resigned its commission.

THE COMMITTEE OF SPANISH AMERICAN BONDHOLDERS, 1836–1850

By the spring of 1836, therefore, the Mexican bondholders lacked a chairman for their Committee, Barings had resigned the Financial Agency, and there was no sign that Mexico was going to honor the pledges it had made in 1831. The bond prices fell accordingly with the Five per Cents down to around 22 in June and the Six per Cents at 32. The situation facing creditors of the other Spanish American republics was no better. The agreement on the Colombian debt had not been ratified and all the republics remained in default on their dividends. The city editor of *The Times* (21 January 1836) painted a dismal picture. The combined debt had risen to £25,000,000, recovery of which was a matter of national importance, requiring "energetic interference" by the British government. Even military intervention was justified. The republics could well afford to pay their debts, especially now that recognition by Spain, expected any time, removed their need to maintain large armies. The moment had arrived "for some new and urgent representations" by both the government and the creditors.

The Committees of the bondholders of the various countries had continued to press their case, occasionally holding public meetings and often sending deputations to the Foreign Office to ask for help. Some bondholders had urged a general meeting of all the creditors "for the purpose of a joint representation on behalf of their claims," as had been done in 1828, but for the time being nothing was achieved.[75] Then, in June 1836, a general meeting was finally summoned for the twenty-eighth of the month. Again, the identity of the organizers and promoters is not known for certain but when the assembly opened, in the presence of what press reports described as a large number of bondholders, the first speaker was Robert Wilson.[76] He proposed that George Robinson should take the chair. Among those who spoke in the subsequent discussions were James Young, who had attended the 1828 meeting, Mr. R.P. Lowther, and Mr. Bailey. The main speech, however, was by Robinson. He made several points which became the basis of much of the case put by the bondholders in later years. Spanish America, he argued, would not have achieved its independence without the loans. While they were private transactions, they had been encouraged by the British government which was obliged to help its citizens recover their money. Other nations, for example, the United States, supported its citizens and they had a right to expect the same. As for the Spanish American republics, they were rich enough to pay their debts but chose to spend their money on other things because they were aware of the British government's indifference. A "combined effort" was necessary to get justice.

Robinson put several resolutions to the meeting and after debate, they were all approved.[77] In general, these reiterated the existing situation with regard to the loans. Mexico, Colombia, Peru, Chile, Buenos Aires, and Central America had contracted loans in Britain and all had failed to honor their commitments. Revenues assigned for interest payments had been diverted to other purposes, dividends had not been paid, and the total accumulated debt of principal and interest arrears exceeded £25,000,000. The meeting expected the "active support of His Majesty's Government, to which they humbly consider themselves entitled on every principle of justice and protection." Finally, it was essential that the bondholders should unite "for the purpose of taking more decided measures than have yet been adopted" to ensure the debtor nations met their obligations. It was resolved, therefore, to form immediately a General Committee to pursue the bondholders' claims. Its members were to be as follows, "with power to add to their number":

G.R. Robinson, M.P.	Charles Herring
William Marshall, M.P.	J.D. Powles
Lieut.-Gen. Sir Robert Wilson	J. Easthope
Colonel T. Davies	Henry Coape
Isaac Lyon Goldsmid	James Henderson
Herman Sillem	Thomas Hammond
James Young	John Moxon
W.C. Damant	William Hammond
John Field, Jun.	John Capel

Thus, the Committee of Spanish American Bondholders was formed on 28 June 1836 by a voluntary amalgamation of the various regional committees. Its founder members included representatives from each of the regional committees, several of whom had investments in the bonds of more than one country. Mexican bondholders were strongly represented in the persons of Robinson, Wilson, Goldsmid, Moxon, and Sillem. Over the next few years to 1849, another seventeen members were co-opted. These included leading Mexican bondholders such as future chairmen David Robertson and James Capel, merchant George Rougement, and businessman R.C. Wyllie.[78] The prominence of some of the others indicates the importance of the Committee. There were, for example, four titled members: Lieutenant-General Sir H. Cumming, Sir William Heygate, Sir Robert Campbell, and most notably, Admiral Sir Thomas Cochrane, the naval commander whose role in the emancipation of Chile and later events in America had brought him both fame and fortune, some of which he had obviously invested in the Spanish American loans.[79]

The Committee began its work very quickly. Within a week, Robinson had sent a copy of the resolutions to the Foreign Office and a delegation from the Committee had a face-to-face meeting with Palmerston in which they presented the Foreign Secretary with a statement of their claims.[80] They pressed him for "a more active and efficient interference on behalf of a numerous body of British subjects." Palmerston responded with further instructions to British diplomats in all the debtor republics. In Mexico, Pakenham warned the Foreign Minister that "the British government cannot be indifferent to the interests of the numerous subjects of his Majesty whose fortunes are involved in the transactions." A month later, he was even more direct:

a strong feeling of indignation has arisen in England at the manner in which the South American States continue to withhold payment of the interest on their debts and this feeling may at no distant period compel the British government to take the matter up.[81]

The formation of the Spanish American Committee, and the more energetic attitude of the British Foreign Office which followed, had the desired effect on Mexican diplomats. In particular, Miguel Santa María, Mexico's Minister in London, emphasized the critical need for his government to sort out the debt problem. Writing from Madrid where he had gone to negotiate the terms of Spanish recognition of independence, he told his Foreign Minister that he had tried to stop the general meeting of bondholders because he knew the adverse publicity that it would generate. The bondholders were justifiably angry and they had lost faith in Mexican promises. In his own corrrespondence with Robert Wilson, he had pledged his personal word that interest payments would be resumed. He went on to recommend the appointment of Lizardi & Co. as Financial Agents in place of Barings, and he urged that their proposals for converting the debt be given every consideration.[82]

Santa María was a respected and influential figure in Mexico's ruling circles and his advice, together with the British diplomatic pressure in Mexico City, persuaded the Mexican government to address the debt issue. The 1837 conversion was the result and may justifiably be described as the Spanish American Committee's first success. It was soon involved in negotiations with other debtor republics and it was promptly recognized as "a representative organ" by the governments of Venezuela, New Granada, Ecuador, Chile, Peru, and Mexico, as well as by the British authorities. Although the General Committee continued to exist until well into the 1860s, by which time it was usually chaired by Powles, it was involved directly with Mexican affairs only until 1850 when dissident Mexican bondholders chose to reestablish their own organization. At that time, the Spanish American Committee chose to publish an account of its work or proceedings on behalf of Mexican bondholders since its foundation in 1836. Included in that 122-page report are details of the membership of the Committee, its meetings, and its various campaigns.[83] Between the years 1836 and 1849, twenty-eight public meetings of bondholders were arranged by the Committee, of which all but one related to the business of a particular country. One general meeting of the bondholders of all the defaulting States was also held for which a printed report, that of 1839, was prepared.[84] Again, there are no extant records such as minute books of the ordinary Committee meetings but from press references to them, they seem to have been frequent, bearing in mind the range of business involved in all the debtor republics. Especially when reschedulings of the debt were under consideration or when disputes with Financial Agents over dividend money were in progress, the meetings were very frequent. In September 1843, for example, there were three meetings in a single week.[85]

The membership and activities of the Committee covered the entire Spanish American debt but the affairs of each group of bondholders were kept separate because, as it was put in the 1850 report,

The Committee are not aware that it would have tended to the dispatch of business, or to the convenience of the Bondholders, to have called together the Bondholders of six different States, when a proposition was to be considered affecting only one of those States.[86]

For that reason, therefore, the Mexican debt was the subject of eight special meetings between 1837 and 1849 at which the various conversions of 1837 and 1846, together with the issue of Debentures in 1842, were discussed. Much of the Committee's time during those years was taken up with the controversial activities of Lizardi & Co., which have been referred to in earlier sections of this work. Counsel's opinion was sought on more than one occasion and cases against the company were brought before the courts. The protracted issue of the excess 1837 Deferred bonds which Lizardi placed in the market was a source of constant attention and the disputes over interest payments or non-payments by both Lizardi and its successor, Schneider & Co., absorbed more time and effort. As will be discussed later in this study, the Committee also maintained its pressure on the British government, repeatedly demanding its intervention and support.

The events leading to the separation of the Mexican bondholders in 1850 began with the Committee's attempts to persuade the Mexican government to allocate at least some of the United States indemnity payment to the foreign debt. As indicated in the section on the 1851 Three per Cents, the Committee had engaged in acrimonious debate with the Mexican Minister in London, Mora, who had rejected any claim on the indemnity money. Legal opinion had been obtained in support of the bondholders' case and their agents in Mexico, Manning and Mackintosh, had been instructed to press the claim at every opportunity.[87] In September 1848, the Committee decided to send a Special Commissioner to Mexico, in effect to demand that a portion of the indemnity money should be allocated to the payment of dividend arrears. A meeting of the bondholders was held on 6 September to approve this decision and it was resolved that the expenses of the mission should be met out of the first dividend payment made in the future. The person chosen as Special Commissioner was William Parish Robertson. He had been co-opted to the Committee on 2 May 1848, presumably on the grounds of his long and varied experience in Spanish American affairs. He was the younger brother of John Parish Robertson who, together with his father, a Glasgow-based merchant, had first travelled to South America in 1806. In later years, the two brothers experienced many adventures and vicissitudes in their business affairs in Paraguay, Buenos Aires, and elsewhere. Eventually, they built a substantial and profitable business trading in hides and on their return to England, they established an import-export company with connections in London, Liverpool, Glasgow, and Paisley.[88] In addition to their commercial activities, they were soon involved in finance and were contractors for the 1824 Buenos Aires loan (see the signature on the bond shown in Illustration 3). The elder brother, John, lost his fortune in 1826 and subsequently wrote, sometimes with his brother, several works relating to their experiences in Paraguay and Argentina. Little is known about the career of William in the 1830s and early 1840s but his connections with Spanish America remained very strong. By 1847, for example, he held the largely honorary position of Consul General for Ecuador.

William Parish Robertson, therefore, was appointed as the Special Commissioner to Mexico. He was given a detailed set of instructions by the Committee. In sum, these ordered him to proceed to Mexico where he was to cooperate with Manning and Mackintosh and the British Minister in pressing the case for at least some of the indemnity money. He was authorized to offer in return a reduction in the interest rate on the debt from the current 5% to 3% a year in cash and 2% in bonds. He requested and was given assurances from the Foreign Office that it would support his mission and, armed with his credentials, copies of the 1846 bonds, and various letters of introduction, he left Southampton on 2 December 1848.[89] He was accompanied by his daughter. The journey to Havana proceeded normally and on 12 January they left for Veracruz on the branch packet *Forth*. Two days later, on Sunday, 14 January, the ship was struck by what the captain described as "an inexplicable current" and was driven aground on the Alacranes reef in the Gulf of Mexico. Fortunately, the thirty-four passengers and 126 crew survived. They were quickly taken off the reef by a passing ship but had to be left for two days on a nearby deserted island. Eventually, a Yucatán ship arrived to rescue them and take them to Campeche, a voyage which lasted some thirty-three hours.[90]

Robertson lost all his papers in the wreck and had to write to London from Campeche to request that the Committee should send him duplicates. He had also been slightly injured from "a dangerous fall" on the ship and he had to spend three weeks recuperating at Campeche. Finally, he was fit to travel and he and his daughter arrived at Veracruz on 9 February where their host was Frederick Jonson, a partner in the firm of Markoe, Price &

Co. They stayed with him for a few days and left for Mexico City where they arrived on 26 February, to be met by Ewen Mackintosh.[91]

Over the next few months, Robertson pursued his goal of achieving a settlement of the debt. He was helped by the British Minister, Percy Doyle, by Mackintosh, and by Manuel Escandón, the country's leading entrepreneur. Numerous meetings took place with Mexican officials and partly through an intermediary, Sr. Olarte, who was promised commission, an outline agreement was worked out. Robertson sent progress reports back to London on every packet and the Committee in turn sent him its views on the proposals being discussed.[92] At first, his relations with the Committee (its letters were usually written by Robinson or Powles) seemed amicable, but gradually, difficulties arose. After weeks of what he described as intense work and negotiation, Robertson signed an agreement on 6 July 1849 with the Finance Minister, Francisco de Arrangoiz.

The Arrangoiz-Robertson Convention, as it was called, was subsequently rejected by both the Mexican Congress and by the bondholders' Committee. Its rejection by the Committee, which viewed it as a poor and unacceptable offer in some respects, confirmed its disappointment with Robertson's efforts. Several areas of disagreement had arisen. For example, Robertson had urged for weeks that a permanent commissioner should be resident in Mexico to keep up the pressure for the collection and payment of dividends. He repeatedly recommended that his son be given the job and just as insistently, the Committee had refused his advice on the grounds that it was not authorized by the bondholders to make such an appointment nor did it have funds to pay for it. Second, Robertson had negotiated a separate agreement in which he accepted the appointment of Colonel Facio as Mexico's Financial Agent in London. He was to have joint control of the dividend fund, with the Committee. Again, various objections were raised but the main point was that Robertson had no authority to make such an agreement. Third, there was the issue of the cotton licenses or permits. The origin of these, briefly, was in 1846 when the Mexican government had assigned to the bondholders' agents, Manning and Mackintosh, permits to import cotton. The import of raw cotton was restricted and the government used the permits as a means of paying off its more pressing creditors. Each permit allowed the import of one quintal of cotton with a nominal value of 4.5 dollars. Those given to the bondholders had a total nominal value of almost 680,000 dollars which was the sum of dividend money previously appropriated by the government or its agents and diverted to other purposes. The idea was that the owner or possessor of the permits could sell them to importers or textile manufacturers who, for whatever reason, found that the supplies of domestically produced cotton did not meet their needs. The more hard-pressed permit owners, however, anxious to realize some cash, sold the permits for significantly less than the nominal value and the more the government released, the lower the market price. Robertson found that they were being sold at around 3 pesos. He decided to accept an offer from Manning and Mackintosh of 250,000 dollars, payable in three annual installments. Subsequently, Manuel Escandón bought them from Manning and he agreed to pay Robertson a commission of 25,000 dollars.[93]

The Committee strongly objected to these deals, arguing that the loss of 430,000 dollars on the nominal value of 680,000 was unacceptable. Moreover, the commission that Robertson received was obviously open to misinterpretation. It was not the only charge or suspicion of financial malpractice levelled against him. One unnamed member of the Committee alleged that he had been sending confidential information to his friends regarding conditions in Mexico and the progress of his negotiations. They had used this knowledge to their advantage in the market, speculating in Mexican stocks. There were said to be "three parties who continually receive letters from Mr. Robertson." While he did not deny writing to his son and other friends, he fiercely rejected the accusation of insider trading. It was, he said, "a preposterous allegation," with no foundation whatever. Any information which he had given his friends was available to all who read the newspapers.[94]

There were several other disputes between Robertson and the Committee, most notably over the question of his expenses. He left Mexico in October, travelling on the return journey via New York, and he arrived back in London on 13 December 1849. Two days later, with the obvious intention of bypassing the Committee, he personally called a meeting of bondholders at the London Tavern for 20 December at which he would report on his mission.[95] Rumors promptly circulated that there was to be a proposal at the meeting for the establishment of a new and independent Mexican Committee. Again, a large number of bondholders assembled on the twentieth and with James Capel in the chair, Robertson gave a long account of his mission. He answered questions from the floor and after a dispute between Powles and Levy which caused some disorder, a vote of thanks to Robertson was agreed. The idea of a new committee does not seem to have been raised.[96]

Exactly what transpired over the next few weeks is unclear but it seems that Robertson began to talk confidentially with other bondholders about a separate Mexican Committee, independent of the general Committee of Spanish American Bondholders. Nothing was disclosed in public, probably because of the likely effect on the bond prices and for the time being, Robertson said nothing to his colleagues on the Spanish American Committee. He attended its meeting on 26 December and again on 21 January 1850, immediately after which he was part of a delegation which went to discuss the situation at the Foreign Office. Twenty-four hours later, apparently having given no indication of his intentions, he resigned from the Spanish American Committee. In his resignation letter of 22 January, published in *The Times* the same day, he specified two of what he said were several reasons. The first concerned Colonel Facio. The Committee had refused to recognize the contract he had signed agreeing to Facio's appointment as the Financial Agent. It had declined, therefore, "to recognize him in his official capacity." As Robertson put it, "I could not stultify my own deed" by denying the competency of his appointment. Second, as Consul General of Ecuador, he had received instructions to commence negotiations with that nation's bondholders. He intended to summon a meeting and to ask them to form a Committee of their own. "You will, accordingly, please inform my late colleagues that I have today ceased to be a member of their body."[97]

THE COMMITTEE OF MEXICAN BONDHOLDERS, 1850–1862

The W.P. Robertson Committee, 1850

Robertson resigned from the Committee of Spanish American Bondholders on 22 January 1850. The next day he chaired a crowded and, by all accounts, rowdy meeting of the Mexican bondholders at the London Tavern.[98] The meeting had been summoned, anonymously at first, but later with the name of Henry Guedalla attached. Haim Guedalla (he preferred to be known as Henry) belonged to a Jewish merchant family. In his early years (he was born in 1815) he worked in the family business, but by 1845 he is listed in the London Directory as a merchant operating from the North and South American Coffee House. Connected by marriage with the Montefiore family, he became a leading figure in London's Jewish community. He was, as *The Times* (4 October 1904) put it in its obituary, "a picturesque figure" and "a voluminous writer on religious and financial topics." He was also a prominent bondholder, with investments in Mexican and other stocks—he chaired the Turkish bondholders' Committee from 1876 to 1881—and he was to remain active in pressing the bondholders' claims for almost the next forty years.[99] His name will reappear often in later pages of this study. For the time being, his role was behind the scenes in persuading the bondholders that their needs were not being met by the Spanish American Committee and that a separate, independent body was required. After long debate, with some speakers attacking Robertson and others defending him, the bondholders agreed to set up a new Committee. The approved resolution was as follows:

That a Committee, consisting of not less than five members, be now elected by this meeting, to act as the executive of the Mexican bondholders in England, who shall conduct all necessary correspondence, and receive the remittances from Mexico, on account of the dividends, in conjunction with the agent appointed by the

Mexican Government, and generally to take cognizance of all matters and things considered to be conducive or prejudicial to the interests of the bondholders.

Eleven other resolutions were adopted.[100] These included the opening of an office and the appointment of a secretary. He was to keep copies of all correspondence and to be available in the office for "a reasonable number of hours per day" to answer bondholders' questions. In particular, to avoid any suspicion of privileged information being used by the Committee members, he was to compile a summary of the contents of all despatches as soon as received and to send it to the Stock Exchange and the press. Office and secretarial expenses were to be met by levies on future dividend payments. Robertson's expenses incurred on his Mexican trip were also to be met from the dividend fund, once his accounts had been examined and approved by the Committee. Finally, general meetings of bondholders were to be held every six months, in January and July.

The meeting nominated nine names of those who were to be invited to form the new Committee. These were:

Baron de Goldsmid	Thomas Thornton
Francis Mills	Capt. Thomas Ross
W.P. Robertson	Rowan Ronald
Henry Guedalla	James Rhodes
James Capel	

Some of these names are already familiar to us. Goldsmid and Capel, for example, were members of the Committee of Spanish American Bondholders and, for the time being, they refused to serve on the new body. Thornton was also a member of the Spanish American Committee but he accepted the invitation. He was the nephew of Richard Thornton, one of the largest individual bondholders and one of the richest men of the Victorian age.[101] Ronald was a director of the National Bank of Ireland and Rhodes was a director of the London & County Joint Stock Bank. Captain Ross may have been the North Pole explorer. Mills was a member of the bankers, Glyn, Mills, Currie & Co. He himself was apparently never a partner in the Bank but he brought considerable business to it through his promotion of railways in France and Italy. He was also chairman of the Minerva Life Assurance Company and among other things, he was one of the founders of the Garrick Club.[102]

An office was quickly found at 61 Moorgate Street, for £70-a-year rent, and a secretary, William Morgan, was appointed. The first meeting, attended by seven of the nine invited (Goldsmid and Capel declined), was held on 28 January. It named Robertson and Mills as chairman and deputy-chairman, respectively. Over the next few days, Robertson, assisted by the new secretary, tried to get his Committee recognized by all the relevant parties. Colonel Facio was contacted and he agreed to cooperate, as did Mora, head of the Mexican delegation.[103] Letters were also prepared and sent to Manning and Mackintosh in Mexico City, to all the other agents at Mexico's ports, and to Mexico's Foreign Minister. Lord Palmerston and the secretary of the Stock Exchange were informed that the Committee now claimed to be the properly constituted representative of the Mexican bondholders. Finally, attempts were made to obtain £10,367 from the dividend fund in the Bank of England. The hope in this respect was to complete payment of the January 1847 dividend which had previously been only partially paid by Schneider & Co. Facio agreed to release the money but no reply for the time being came from Schneider.[104]

Prompt recognition of the new Committee was essential for Robertson because of the reaction of the Spanish American Committee. He had written on 29 January to its chairman, Robinson, to tell him formally what had transpired at the meeting on the twenty-third and since. In particular, he emphasized that control of the dividend fund in the Bank of England, standing at over 500,000 dollars, was now vested in himself and his deputy, Mills, and the Financial Agent, Facio. In short, he was implementing the Agency agreement he had signed while in Mexico City the previous year. Robinson, who had been ill for months (he died in August), did not reply. Instead, the reply was from the Spanish American Committee's secretary, Alfred Godfrey. He flatly rejected Robertson's claims, especially with regard to the dividend fund. Neither he nor any member of the new body would be given access to it because "the moneys were remitted to the joint order of Colonel Facio and this Committee." Furthermore, it was the intention of his Committee to summon another meeting of Mexican bondholders to consider the whole situation.[105] The date was fixed for 18 February.

It was clear that the Spanish American Committee was not going to accept the formation of what may be labelled the Robertson Committee without a fight. Press articles attacking its record were refuted and counter-articles were sent to the newspapers. Robertson was attacked for failing to achieve a settlement during his mission to Mexico and the bondholders were reminded that Mora had constantly opposed claims to the indemnity money. Both sides hastily prepared written reports in anticipation of the meeting scheduled for 18 February. The 122-page Spanish American report or *Proceedings* was completed on 4 February and published two days later. The Robertson Committee *Report*, rather shorter at 23 pages, is dated 14 February.

The meeting on 18 February was very well attended and widely reported in the press. As *The Times'* correspondent wrote, "It was evident some time before the discussion commenced that there would be a strong struggle between the two parties."[106] Tempers were soon raised with "much strong language" as speakers for both sides made their case. The chairman was William Marshall, M.P. and as a member of the "old" committee, he defended its record. Nobody had complained about its efforts and he did not believe that the majority of Mexican bondholders agreed with the decisions taken on 23 January. Powles supported him and a Mr. Waley called for the restoration of the Spanish American Committee's authority. That brought "a burst of disapprobation" and "violence of feeling" from the floor. Then, Edward Moriarty, described as a Barrister at Law of the Inner Temple and Foreign Jurisconsult, spoke strongly in favor of a separate Committee for the bondholders of each of the debtor republics. Goldsmid, seconded by Alderman David Salomons, another prominent Jewish merchant and banker, tried to conciliate the two groups, suggesting an amalgamation. More intemperate language followed and "a scene of great confusion was the result." Eventually, a vote was taken and the resolutions adopted on 23 January were approved. "Hearty applause" followed and after thanks to the chairman, "mutual apologies were made by all parties for any recriminatory language indulged in."

Hence, the Mexican bondholders removed their affairs from the general Committee of Spanish American Bondholders. The new group, however, was unable to consolidate its position. Much of its time and attention was devoted to getting the cash from the Bank of England to complete payment of the 1847 dividend. There were four other interested parties: Facio, Schneider, Bank of England, and the Spanish American Committee. Facio had already sided with the new Committee but Schneider and the Bank were reluctant to cooperate until they were certain that control of the dividend fund had been transferred from the old Committee. Letters passed between all the parties, and eventually it was agreed that delegations from each Committee should meet to resolve the matter. Their conference was held on 5 March at the Moorgate Street office and it was agreed to ask the Bank to sell enough dollars from the dividend fund to produce £10,367. This sum was to be handed over to Schneider who would in turn pay the dividend. Mocatta and Goldsmid, the Bank's bullion dealers, handled the sale and the bondholders finally received their money in early April, less the levy deducted for the Committee's expenses and those of Robertson.[107]

Another area to which the new Committee turned its attention was the duties on silver exported from Mexican ports. A proportion of these had been assigned to the dividend fund but as smuggling was so rampant, very little of what were often large cargoes of silver was actually taxed. The main culprits were known to be the British naval officers who acted in collusion with Mexican exporters and smugglers. The new Committee appealed to the Foreign Office, urging it to persuade the Lords of the Admiralty "to put a stop to this fraud." They suggested various means of doing so and the Mexican Legation supported "the spirit of these resolutions."[108] As usual, the Foreign Office agreed to do what it could but in practice, nothing effective was achieved.

Finally, moves were made to strengthen the Committee. Three of the original seven members had already resigned—Guedalla, Ronald, and Thornton—but we do not know their reasons. Moriarty was elected on 26 February and on the same day, in an attempt at reconciliation with the Spanish American Committee, four of its members were invited to join. None of the four—Goldsmid, Marshall, Capel, and Tasker—replied. The remaining members of the Robertson Committee—Robertson, Mills, Ross, and Rhodes—prepared the *Second Report* containing their correspondence and efforts regarding the dividends, silver duties, and diverse other matters. In their conclusion, they recommended that "the Committee shall in future consist of not less than ten members, three of whom shall be a quorum." As for themselves, they all resigned.

We do not know why Robertson and his allies resigned. Their stated reason, which may have had some force, was that as "men engaged in business of their own," they simply did not have sufficient time to devote to the affairs of the bondholders.[109] There was almost certainly more to it, especially since the allegations of insider trading against Robertson and the issue of his expenses were as yet unresolved. Moreover, the agreement which he had signed with Arrangoiz in Mexico had not been ratified by the Mexican Congress. In his own defense, he prepared a densely packed 66-page report dated 4 April and published a few days later.[110] He included in this a stage-by-stage account of his mission to Mexico with copies of all his correspondence with the Spanish American Committee and the various governmental authorities in London and Mexico. Naturally, he firmly rejected all wrongdoing by himself or his son and daughter. Finally, business rivalries and perhaps conflicting personal interests may have contributed to what *The Times* described as the "wretched dissensions" among the bondholders.[111]

The Goldsmid Committee, 1850–1853

The next phase of the Committee of Mexican Bondholders began on 12 April at a general meeting summoned—it is not clear by whom—to consider the situation arising from the resignation of the Robertson group.[112] James Capel was elected to the chair. The bondholders considered various matters, including ways of attaching some of the indemnity money. The main resolution was to establish "a large and influential Committee" which would represent all classes of bondholders. The following were selected to form the Committee:

Baron de Goldsmid	David Robertson
Admiral Sir George Sartorius	Capt. Ross

William Marshall, M.P.   James Rhodes

John Sadleir, M.P.   E.A. Moriarty

J.L. Prevost   Charles Herring

Joshua Walke   Richard Garde

James Capel   John Clement Ruding

Charles McGarel

The second main resolution instructed the new Committee to consider and report on the account which Robertson (he attended the meeting) had published of his mission to Mexico.

Several of the above names were new to the Mexican Committee although some, for example, David Robertson, had been on the Spanish American Committee. Goldsmid and Capel, also still on the latter Committee, had previously refused invitations to join the Mexican counterpart, but whatever their reasons, they now relented. William Marshall had also served on the Spanish American Committee since 1836 but he does not seem to have shown any direct interest in the Mexican Committee and had not replied to earlier invitations to join it. He was the eldest son of the Leeds linen manufacturer, John Marshall, who had been the bondholders' first chairman in 1830. Rather than going into the family business, William had trained as a lawyer and then followed a parliamentary career. From 1826 to 1830, he represented Petersfield, a "rotten borough" purchased by his father for £5,000. Subsequently, he sat for Leominster, Beverley, and Carlisle until 1847 when he was returned for Cumberland East, which he retained until he was defeated in 1868.

Nothing is known of Ruding or Walke but the others were, or were soon to be, well-known figures in London's political and mercantile community. Charles McGarel, for example, was a wealthy businessman described by his friend David Robertson as "a real millionaire," as opposed to himself who was merely wealthy.[113] He was born in 1788 at Larne in County Antrim, one of four sons of a innkeeper.[114] At the age of sixteen, he and two of his brothers went to seek their fortunes in Demerara, British Guiana, which at the time had the reputation of being a place where "instant fortunes could be made."[115] He prospered, soon acquiring sugar estates, and by 1822 he was in business in London as a sugar merchant in the firm known as Hall, McGarel & Co.[116] He expanded his interests throughout the West Indies, acquiring more sugar plantations, and he later bought extensive estates, mines, quarries, and other properties in County Antrim. He became a major benefactor to his home town of Larne, funding its first Town Hall and many other charitable foundations. His estate at the time of his death in 1876 was valued at the enormous sum (for the time) of £600,000.[117] Richard Garde was a barrister living at Brighton "who has long held Mexican stock as an investment."[118] He was to serve intermittently on the Committee for almost the next twenty years. John Sadleir was soon to be a notorious figure in London. He was a solicitor and chairman of the London and County Bank where the Committee opened its account. A much respected figure, he was a Liberal Member of Parliament from 1847 until 1853 and rose to be a Lord of the Treasury. Then, in what became a sensational affair at the time, he was discovered to have engaged in fraudulent share transactions and he committed suicide on 17 February 1856.[119] Charles Herring had been a member of the Barclay partnership which had been the contractors for the second loan in 1825. In later years, he was connected with several of Powles' business activities and he had been on the Spanish American Committee since its formation in 1836. Finally, there was Admiral Sartorius, a naval officer with personal experience of Spanish America. Born in 1790 and retired from active service since 1843, he had enjoyed a long and distinguished career. After taking part in the Battle of Trafalgar, he had joined the British fleet which invaded the River Plate in 1806. In later years, having witnessed the surrender of Napoleon in 1815, he served in the Portuguese navy. On his return to the English navy, he rose to the rank of Rear Admiral in 1849 and in later years he was the senior Admiral of the Fleet. The origins of his investments or interests in Mexican bonds are unknown but his rank and seniority provide another good example of the status and influence of the Mexican Committee.[120]

The new Committee met for the first time on 16 April and elected Goldsmid and Capel to be chairman and vice-chairman, respectively. Over the next few months, it issued two *Reports* of its activities. The first, dated 11 June 1850, was presented to a general meeting of bondholders held on 25 June, again at the London Tavern.[121] Baron Goldsmid (see Illustration 25) took the chair and there were two main items on the agenda. The first was Robertson's report on his mission which a subcommittee had been set up to consider. It absolved him of some of the allegations made against him, for example, of insider trading, and it concluded that his claim for expenses amounting to the considerable sum of £5,215 was largely justifiable. On the other hand, in accepting a "present" of 25,000 dollars from Escandón, he had not acted "consistently with the position which he filled." Some of the bondholders present at the meeting were more critical. Press reports refer to "a very strong feeling of disapprobation" of his conduct and a large majority considered him to have been "at least indiscreet."[122]

The second main item on the agenda was the Committee's advice that the bondholders should appoint another commissioner to travel to Mexico on their behalf. It was known by this time that the Robertson-Arrangoiz Convention had not been approved by the Mexican authorities. Instead, it had been superceded by another set of proposals emanating from a congressional committee and these were under discussion in the Chamber of Deputies. A commissioner in Mexico City was required, the Committee

25. Sir Isaac Lyon Goldsmid, Chairman, Committee of Mexican Bondholders, 1850–1853. Photograph reproduced by courtesy of the College Arts Collections, University College London.

suggested, "to represent and watch over their interests there." It recommended the appointment of Francis de Palezieux Falconnet. He had considerable experience of the Hispanic world, having worked for Barings in Spain, Argentina, and in Mexico as recently as 1849. He was obviously held in high regard in the city of London because the contract which the Committee now suggested he should be offered was for three years at the substantial salary of £3,000 per annum. In addition, he was to be allowed £2,000 for his outfit, travel, and other incidentals, and £500 per annum for a secretary who was to accompany him to Mexico. Some bondholders felt it was excessive but Goldsmid replied that it was negligible when set against the £10,000,000 owed to them, which Falconnet was being charged with recovering. The meeting accepted the argument and Falconnet's appointment was approved. It was also agreed that the cost of his mission would be met with a levy of £1 8s. per cent from the next dividend distribution.[123]

A month later, a special general meeting of the bondholders was called. Again, there were two main items on the agenda. The first concerned a delay in the payment of a dividend which the Committee had earlier promised would be made from funds already on deposit in the Bank of England. Goldsmid explained that there were several causes of the delay, including a problem over certain monies raised by W.P. Robertson, and continuing difficulties with Schneider & Co. The Mexican government had now cancelled Schneider's commission but the company was refusing to hand over the books to Facio. Without them, he could not authorize any release of funds from the Bank of England.

The non-dividend payment led to the second agenda item which was that there was no money to pay Falconnet. Hence, he had not yet left for Mexico. Goldsmid announced, however, that such was the urgency of his mission that several Committee members had agreed to subscribe a total of £6,000 to pay his expenses and his first year's salary. The subscribers were Goldsmid himself with £1,000; Capel and friends, £2,000; David Robertson, £1,000; Herring, Moriarty, Richmond, and Ross, £500 each.[124] That provoked more criticism from the floor about the amount being paid to Falconnet and others expressed doubts about the effectiveness of commissioners. Some felt it would be better to put the whole matter into the hands of Barings who already had its own agents in Mexico. The Committee defended its policy and insisted that Falconnet's appointment must stand. Once again voices were raised and

the harmony of the meeting was in the course of the discussion, grievously disturbed by a personal attack by Mr. Levi on the chairman and the refusal of the former to apologize or retract the offensive expressions drew forth strong disapprobation.[125]

Falconnet left for Mexico on the September packet, arriving in Mexico City on 14 October. It was on that same day that the Mexican government published the law which incorporated its final decisions on British claims to the indemnity money. The details of the law have been given in a previous section and need not be repeated here. Its provisions, in particular, the assignment of 2,500,000 dollars of the United States indemnity to cover dividend arrears; and the rescheduling of the debt with the issue of new bonds, the 1851 Three per Cents, were accepted by the bondholders at another general meeting on 23 December 1850. It was to that meeting that the Goldsmid Committee presented its second written *Report*.[126] This reviewed the work of the Committee for the previous few months. Most of its attention had been given to the terms of the proposed conversion which, it advised the bondholders, "it will be expedient to accept" in the "candid and liberal spirit" they had previously shown the Mexican republic.[127] No dividend payment had been possible because of continuing difficulties with Schneider but the Committee had established that the dividend fund was in future in the joint control of Goldsmid, Capel, and Facio. In order to achieve this, Goldsmid and Capel had been obliged

to give the late G.R. Robinson, Esq., the former Chairman of the Spanish American Committee, a full indemnity, in order to effect a transfer of 530,447 dollars, which stood in his name in the books of the Bank of England.[128]

That was not the only personal commitment which the Committee members had been called upon to make. With all the recent changes in the bondholders' representation, together with the ongoing disputes between Facio and Schneider over the Financial Agency, the legal position over who controlled the dividend fund was obscure. The Bank of England refused to make any transfers or allow any withdrawals until its legal advisers had been consulted. They demanded an Indemnity Bond for £300,000 before any sale or transfer of bullion was allowed. The Committee's solicitors, Messrs. Crowder and Maynard, prepared the bond which was "entered into" by Goldmid, Capel, McGarel, Moriarty, Ross, and Ruding.

The Goldsmid Committee continued until January 1853 at which time it recommended its own "reconstruction." It was obliged to do this because of the original sixteen members "two have since died—one has gone abroad—one resides at a great distance from London—three have ceased to attend, and five have resigned or intend to do so." Since its formation in April 1850, the bondholders were told at a general meeting held on 26 January 1853, it had organized seven general meetings. In addition, there had been over 200 Committee meetings and many more of the subcommittees. More than 5,500,000 dollars had been recovered and that alone was "proof that their labours have not been altogether in vain."[129] Three more *Reports* were produced and the secretary, now Nils Andreas Nilsen, "a Swede by birth," according to David Robertson, had diligently sent to the newspapers the regular monthly reports received from the Committee's agents in Mexico.[130] Much time and effort were expended on statistical data of dividend fund receipts and deposits in the Bank of England. When the amounts arriving on the packets were found to be insufficient or when there were signs that Mexico was not keeping to the terms of the 1851 conversion, more appeals for help were made to the British Foreign Office. These included a long and detailed statement of grievances, sent to the Foreign Secretary, Earl of Malmesbury, in August 1852.[131] Goldsmid told the Foreign Secretary that about one-quarter of Mexico's external debt was now held by French, Dutch, and United States citizens. He wanted the British government to invite the governments of those countries to instruct their diplomats in Mexico to join with the British "to obtain justice for the foreign creditors of Mexico." Finally, the long-established agents in Mexico City, Manning and Mackintosh, ceased trading in January 1851, owing large sums of money to many creditors, including the bondholders. On Falconnet's recommendation, agents were to be appointed in every port and frontier town where a Customs House was located.

The Goldsmid Committee also devoted much time and attention to securing the safe collection, shipment, and conversion into sterling of the 2,500,000 dollars from the United States indemnity payment. As explained in the section on dividends, the money arrived in August 1852. Falconnet had personally supervised the whole transaction in Mexico City where he had been a vigorous and energetic advocate of the bondholders' cause. His relationship with the Committee, however, was not always harmonious. It had refused to allow him to resume his work for Barings unless he took a salary cut, and he told Barings that the Committee was "a set of shabby people."[132] In order to avoid payment of tax on the export of the 2,500,000 dollars in silver coin, he had bribed, or said he had bribed, certain congressmen. Perhaps inadvertently, at a general meeting on 26 January, Capel disclosed the bribery which had cost 60,000 dollars. As *The Times* reporter put it, "This circumstance occasioned a lengthy debate and was strongly animadverted upon."[133] *The Daily News* concluded that "No doubt there was bribery but it was effectual." *The Morning Post*, which printed the full text of the Committee's report, recalled that during the debate, "the Government and Parliament of Mexico were called all sorts of bad names."[134] The bondholders had clearly not minced their words. A Mr. Waters, for example, had referred to "the baseness of an assembly which would accept a bribe of 60,000 dollars." In the end, after many somewhat pious expressions of disapproval, the bondholders accepted that Falconnet had acted in their best interests. They approved the resolution that "it is expedient to adopt this transaction, although this meeting may strongly disapprove of the principle which governed it."[135]

The main London papers were sent to Mexico on the monthly packet. Within days of their arrival in Mexico City early in March, Mexican editors had picked up the story of bribery in their national Congress. It caused nothing short of a sensation in the city. Ex-ministers, ex-deputies, and Falconnet himself rushed into print to deny any kind of wrongdoing. Fifty-two of the deputies, however, decided to bring a criminal prosecution against Falconnet for slander and corruption. He was arrested and incarcerated "in the vilest of jails, surrounded by assassins and robbers."[136] Eventually, he was released after a judge, in a neat compromise, ruled that "there was proof enough that he had said that the Deputies had been bribed but not that he had bribed them, and that he had been punished enough by his imprisonment."[137] In other words, no proceedings were required against the deputies. Not surprisingly, Falconnet was furious with the bondholders' "stupidity and ingratitude." Not a single one, he complained, had bothered to send him any note of sympathy or encouragement while he was imprisoned.[138] Doyle, the British Minister, was equally dismissive of the Committee: "The bondholders, or rather their Committee, have cut their own throats as far as we are concerned by their absurd speeches."[139]

The Capel Committee, 1853–1854

The January 1853 meeting was the last organized by the Goldsmid Committee. Given that most of its members had ceased to be active, it had recommended that a new committee should be chosen.[140] On a motion put by Guedalla, it was resolved that the next one should be restricted to seven members and "that the qualification of a Committee-man be £10,000 Stock." The following were then nominated and appointed:

James Capel

David Robertson

Charles McGarel

A.B. Richmond

Capt. Ross

Henry Guedalla

Charles Staniforth

Of these names, only Staniforth had not previously served on the Committee. He was a director of the Edinburgh Life Assurance Company and he was to remain a member for almost ten years. Clearly, with personal holdings of at least £10,000 in Mexican bonds, he was a person of some substance.

James Capel (see Illustration 26) was chosen to chair the Committee, a position he occupied for a year until January 1854 when he resigned on grounds of ill health, to follow his medical advisers' recommendation, as he put it in his resignation letter, "to keep myself very quiet and free from excitement."[141] He remained prominent in the Stock Exchange for a number of years, retaining his chairmanship of the Spanish bondholders' Committee until at least the mid-1860s. During his year in charge of the Mexican bondholders' affairs, he had pursued what the Committee's own

26. James Capel, Chairman, Committee of Mexican Bondholders, 1853–1854. Photograph reproduced by courtesy of HSBC Holdings plc.

printed reports now regularly described as being under "the usual three heads." These were matters relating to dividend arrears, current interest on the new or 1851 bonds, and "sundry collateral matters." Under the first "head," the Committee achieved a further payment of 5 shillings on the 1851 certificates. It also initiated a claim against the former agents, Manning and Mackintosh, for 253,645 dollars. During the process of liquidating the company's assets following its failure in 1851, it had offered to transfer to the bondholders mortgages which it held on a rural property in the state of Veracruz and on "certain public lands in the state of Tamaulipas." The estate, named Uvero, was 43,384 acres, "not in cultivation but valuable on account of its great capabilities." It had been put in the name of Mrs. Mackintosh. The public lands amounted to some 5 million acres. Manning and Mackintosh had a joint interest in the latter with a Mr. Alexandre de Gros, who had been granted colonization rights in them. Expensive complications arose with the bondholders' claims. First, there was "an interminable law-suit" over rival claims to the rural estate. Second, about 3.5 million acres of the Tamaulipas lands were found to be within the territory conceded to the United States in the 1848 peace treaty. Le Gros had started legal proceedings for compensation in Washington. Third, the Tamaulipas authorities declined to survey the territory remaining in Mexico. Falconnet had signed various agreements, in particular, a 250-dollar-a-month fee to Le Gros "to defray the expenses of that gentleman's stay in Mexico, for the management of the concern." Other costs were also incurred, including a 1,000-dollar retaining fee for two lawyers in Washington.[142]

No progress was made with these claims although the Committee persisted for several more years. Eventually, in 1861, it accepted that after spending some £1,500 in prosecuting them, there was "but a poor prospect of ultimate success."[143] The Capel Committee was similarly unsuccessful in another of its initiatives. In March 1853, Santa Anna was restored to the Mexican presidency after a period of foreign exile. Notoriously venal in his financial dealings, he was nevertheless recognized as energetic and unusually effective in raising funds for his Treasury. The bondholders welcomed his return with effusive praise but also reminded him of the three half-yearly unpaid dividends on the London debt. Santa Anna's response was conciliatory. The bondholders' claim, he said, was "perfectly just" and he would use his best efforts "to acquit myself of these sacred obligations."[144]

The Committee's letter to Santa Anna, dated 1 February 1854, had been timed to correspond to reports of an extensive land sale to the United States which the Mexican government was said to be negotiating. This turned out to be the so-called Gadsen purchase. James Gadsen was the United States Minister to Mexico and in talks with Santa Anna in September 1853, he raised the possibility of buying the desert region known as the Mesilla Valley, which was on the route of a proposed transcontinental railway.

There were rumors of offers of millions of dollars to be paid to Mexico and eventually, a treaty was agreed in December 1853 by which Mexico sold the area south of the Gila River to the United States for 10,000,000 dollars.[145]

The bondholders' hopes were naturally raised by the news of the sale and as in 1848 with the United States indemnity money, they believed that their claim should and would be given priority by the Mexican Treasury. To press their case, they made a point which became an essential plank of their argument for the next thirty years. At this time, several schemes for the construction of railways in Mexico were being discussed, in particular, from Mexico City to Veracruz. The Committee warned Santa Anna that while the railway scheme was excellent in principle, in practice foreign investors would not be willing to risk their money on such a project while Mexico's credit rating was so low "in consequence of the treatment which the foreign creditors of Mexico have experienced."[146] In short, they told Santa Anna that if Mexico hoped to attract foreign capital investment in such projects as the railways, it was essential first to restore the national credit by at least paying current dividends on the London debt. As will be explained in following sections, part of the Committee's strategy in future years was to try to deny Mexico access to capital markets in Europe by protesting to Stock Exchange authorities in London, Paris, Amsterdam, and elsewhere against the flotation of any new loans by a defaulting nation. For the time being, the threat proved to be futile and despite Santa Anna's encouraging words, all that was obtained from the Gadsen money was a "pittance of $180,000."[147]

Another of the Capel Committee's initiatives proved equally disappointing. Falconnet's contract with the bondholders ended in September 1853—he returned to England a year later. The Committee decided, however, that it was still essential to have an agent or commissioner (both words were used) in Mexico City. No doubt recalling the protests against the cost of Falconnet's mission (the final bill eventually came to almost £17,000), it advised the bondholders that an agent could be found "on a more economical scale than before."[148] The person appointed was John L. Rickards. He had already spent several years in Mexico as a businessman and was strongly recommended to the bondholders by firms such as Rothschild & Co. and Murrieta & Co.[149] He was engaged on an annual basis, renewable for three years, at a salary of £1,000 per year. His priority, he was told, was to secure some of the Gadsen money for the unpaid dividends. He failed to achieve this and spent over 12,000 dollars on what the Committee described, without giving details, as "wholly unauthorized expenses." He was persuaded to return to England to explain his conduct but although the Committee accepted his explanation, his contract was terminated. He was soon replaced as the bondholders' representative by Charles White-head, another British businessman, long resident in Mexico City.

Finally, the Committee also entered into an acrimonious dispute with Colonel Facio, still Mexico's Financial Agent in London. There were several areas of disagreement. Facio's salary and office expenses (the office was at 32 Great Winchester Street) had been set by Mexico at 15,000 dollars annually. This sum was taken from the dividend fund held at the Bank of England but, as the bondholders frequently protested, their bonds entitled them to dividends free of all charges. Second, the arrangement whereby the dividend fund had been under the joint control of the Financial Agent and the Committee's chairman and deputy-chairman had been rescinded by the Mexican government. Facio had been given sole control of the bank account. In its published *Report* to the bondholders, the Committee was unusually frank in its views. Facio was not the right man for the job. He was guilty of arbitrary and illegal acts "adopted chiefly for the pleasure of annoying the bondholders." It was time for "all false delicacy" to be set aside. Facio was "constitutionally incapable" of carrying out a conciliatory and sensible policy and he must be replaced. In his place, Mexico should appoint as agent a mercantile house which enjoyed the full confidence of the British public.[150]

The McGarel Committee, 1854–1856

Capel resigned as chairman in January 1854. For the next few months, his role was fulfilled by the deputy-chairman, McGarel, and he chaired the general meeting on 15 May 1854 at which the Committee reported on its activities (see Illustration 27). Following what had now become normal procedure, a new Committee was chosen by the meeting. On this occasion, however, the incumbent members were reelected together with two new names. The first was Samuel Herbert Ellis. He had been on the Spanish American Committee from 1837 to at least 1850. Nothing is known of his career but he was probably connected to the stockbrokers, Edward Ellis & Co. The other newcomer, however, was a much more prominent figure. This was Rear Admiral Sir Provo William Parry Wallis. He was to remain on the Committee, with one short break, for the next thirty years until the final Dublán settlement of 1886. Dubbed by *The Times* on 15 April 1890, in an article to mark his one-hundredth birthday, "The Father of the Royal Navy," Wallis was for many years the senior ranking officer in the English navy. Born in Halifax, Nova Scotia, in 1791, he enjoyed a long and very eventful naval career. Full details of his life are readily available elsewhere and there is no need to repeat them here. Like Admiral Sartorius, he had some personal experience of Spanish America. He served on a British warship which was sent to Veracruz in 1838 to protect British interests there during the so-called Pastry War between France and Mexico. Although we do not know the origin or extent of his investments in Mexican stock, it is interesting to note that his second wife, whom he married in 1849, was

27. Charles McGarel, Chairman, Committee of Mexican Bondholders, 1854–1856. Photograph reproduced with the kind permission of Larne Borough Council Museum Service (negative SG 139).

Jemima Mary Gwyne. She was the daughter of Sir Robert Wilson, whose name we have already encountered as the chairman of the Mexican Committee from 1830 to 1836. It was by no means the only family connection among the bondholders.[151]

The appearance of Admiral Wallis undoubtedly added weight and standing to the Committee but when it presented its next *Report* to the bondholders at a general meeting on 27 February 1855, it did not have much good news. The claims against Manning and Mackintosh continued without result. Dividends were still in arrears and despite many requests, accounts of funds collected and shipped from Mexican ports could not be obtained. Facio was still uncooperative and refused to provide the information the Committee had requested on various matters concerning the 1851 conversion. The difficult issue of the Lizardi excess Deferred bonds, excluded from both the 1846 and 1851 conversions, was unresolved. At every public meeting, those who held them pressed the Committee for action but there was little it could do. As indicated earlier, the Mexican government's proposal of September 1854 to pay off the outstanding Deferred bonds with an additional issue of Three per Cents was dismissed by the Committee as a ruse to raise money.

There were two slightly more positive matters. Mexico had recently authorized domestic textile manufacturers to place their own inspectors at Customs Houses to supervise the collection of excise taxes on various types of textile imports which a new tariff had permitted. These inspectors were entitled to examine all goods imported and exported, to scrutinize documentation relating thereto, and to keep records of such transactions. It was expected that their presence would significantly contribute to a reduction in contraband at the ports and frontier customs. As dividends on the foreign debt were paid from the import and export duties, the bondholders would benefit from the reduction in smuggling. Hence, the manufacturers' representative, Pablo Martínez del Río, had invited the bondholders to contribute to the cost of employing the inspectors. The Committee recommended a positive response to the invitation on the grounds that it could produce a significant increase in the dividend fund.[152]

The second matter concerned Yucatán. The Gadsen purchase had not produced the hoped-for lump-sum payment but the Committee told the bondholders that it had good reason to believe "that the cession of Yucatán by Mexico to her great northern neighbour, is contemplated and actually on the *tapis*." If Mexico could obtain the price "commensurate with its political value," it would have ample funds to pay off the overdue dividends and a large part of the principal debt. Moreover, the bondholders had a mortgage on the whole of Mexican territory and Yucatán could not be ceded without their concurrence.[153]

Nothing came of the Yucatán "prospect," as it was described, and when the bondholders assembled at the London Tavern on 26 February 1855, it was announced that the Commitee was reluctant to continue in office. The *Report* was adopted and the meeting approved two resolutions. The first called on the Mexican government to close its Financial Agency in London. The second was as follows:

The Committee having well discussed and considered the matter in all its bearings after an experience of some years, are of opinion, that the best instrument for conducting the affairs of the Mexican Bondholders, for attending to their interests in Mexico, and receiving the money due to them there, and for the payment of dividends in this country, is a respectable House of Agency who have the confidence of the British Public and the Government of Mexico.

Although the formal resolutions do not make it clear, both had the same objective. The press accounts of the meeting confirm that the "respectable House" referred to was Barings and that the idea was that it should assume both the Financial Agency and the representation of the bondholders' interests. In fact, the newspapers all indicate that Barings had already agreed to at least the latter.[154] Hence, the Committee tendered its resignation, offering to remain in office for only a few more weeks "in order to put matters in proper train."[155]

Talks with Barings presumably continued over following weeks but no reference to them has been found in the company's archive. We do not know exactly what happened, therefore, except that the negotiations were not successful. At the next general meeting, held on 16 October 1855, McGarel announced that the Committee had "virtually ceased after the last meeting" on the assumption that Barings would assume its functions. This had not proved possible, however, "in consequence of Santa Anna and his Government having entirely disappointed the just expectations of your Committee."[156] Santa Anna had failed to keep his promises to the bondholders' agents as well as to British diplomats. Money set aside for the dividend fund at the ports had been seized and Santa Anna had imposed "an arbitary suspension of the payment of all assignments on the revenues of the republic."[157] His own corruption and financial extravagances, allied to his arbitrary, dictatorial rule, had provoked widespread opposition and he was forced from office in August 1855, for the last time in his long career at the center of Mexican politics.

In such unsettled and unpredictable circumstances, it was not surprising that Barings was reluctant to take on any commitments to do with Mexican financial affairs. That left the Committee in a difficult position. As McGarel reminded the bondholders, he and his colleagues had "all absolutely resigned" at the February meeting and had only continued on a temporary basis. Reluctant as they were to remain, they would not now "desert our post." On the other hand, he suggested that consideration be given to the idea that "your affairs would be better conducted in the hands of one individual, a man of integrity, talent, and ability, with a fixed salary." He added, "my experience tells me that large committees are not calculated to promote your interests."[158]

We do not know if McGarel had any individual in mind when he made this suggestion but it was not well received by the bondholders. Hence, he and his Committee continued in office for a few more months until August 1856. Their final *Report* was presented to a general meeting on 6 August. Again, it was arranged "under the usual heads" of arrears, current interest, and other matters. Little had been achieved. "The troubled course of politics in the Republic," and especially the continual and rapid changes in Ministers of Finance, had made it impossible to persuade the Mexican government to give priority or even attention to the bondholders'claims. Six dividends were now overdue on the 1851 Three per Cents and with a seventh due on 1 January 1857, the arrears amounted to £1,074,373. There was only £30,349 in the dividend account at the Bank of England and little prospect of significant further remittances. On the other hand, the political changes that had taken place in Mexico offered some grounds for hope. In particular, a new liberal government under the presidency of General Ignacio Comonfort had taken office and its Minister of Finance was Miguel Lerdo de Tejada. He was someone of "great talent and industry, as well as spotless purity of character." "No happier choice" could have been made from the viewpoint of Mexico's many creditors.[159]

Even more interesting to the bondholders were certain measures which the new Mexican authorities had taken against the Roman Catholic Church. The vast property holdings of the various ecclesiastical corporations in Mexico had long been seen as a target for the impoverished governments. There had been talk, and sometimes concrete proposals for some form of confiscation or nationalization of this Church wealth for many years. Now, with the establishment of a radical liberal administration in power, the issue returned to the forefront of national politics. To punish the clergy for having allegedly financed a rebellion against it, the government imposed in March 1856 an "intervention," or attachment, of ecclesiastical property in the diocese of Puebla to the value of 1,000,000 dollars. In London, the bondholders noted these developments with particular interest. They were well aware of the controversy surrounding Church wealth and many of them had personal acquaintance with the man whose writings on the subject largely formed the basis of liberal policy toward the clergy. This was Dr. Mora, the former Minister in London. He had written extensively on Church wealth and advocated the amortization of the public debt by means of the sale of ecclesiastical property. The Committee was clearly familiar with his work and especially with his calculations of the value of Church assets. Even though these included several demonstrably erroneous assumptions, the bondholders were advised that they were based on what appeared to be "authentic data." It was, the Committee admitted, a tempting prospect, and if the "intervention" being implemented in Puebla were extended to all Church property, it would yield enough to restore Mexican finances "to a highly prosperous condition." Mora's figures were quoted to show that the clergy's property was valued at 179,163,754 dollars. Even allowing for a proportion of this sum to be used to finance the clergy, enough would remain for the redemption of the whole of Mexico's domestic and foreign debt and "still retain a surplus of some consideration for the construction of roads and other public works."[160]

Church wealth soon became a subject of even greater interest to the bondholders as the Juárez *Reforma* was implemented in Mexico but, for the time being, they were confined to approving various resolutions commending the work of their Committee. They also condemned Santa Anna's conduct toward them, repeated their pleas for assistance from the British government, and composed a memorial to General Comonfort asking for his cooperation. Finally, McGarel announced his resignation as chairman and following the established practice, the whole Committee resigned. McGarel, however, also nominated his successor. This was his deputy, David Robertson. He expressed his willingness to assume the office, provided the departing Committee was replaced "by one likely to insure [sic] unanimity of views and action."[161] The meeting agreed and it was resolved that the next Committee should consist of the following:

David Robertson	Charles Staniforth
Charles McGarel	Thomas Moxon

The D. Robertson Committee, 1856–1862

The years of David Robertson's (see Illustration 28) chairmanship from 1856 to 1862 were among the more eventful in the history of the Mexican Committee. In Mexico, following the fall of Santa Anna in August 1855, a Liberal regime began the implementation of a reform program involving, among many other changes, the disestablishment of the Roman Catholic Church and the expropriation of its substantial assets. The challenge posed by the radicals, enshrined in a constitution in 1857, provoked violent reaction by those clerical and Conservative forces most adversely affected. A bitterly fought civil war followed. The Conservative faction gained control of Mexico City where General Félix Zuloaga was installed as president on 22 January 1858. The Liberal, or Constitutional, regime, established first at Guanajuato, later took Veracruz under the leadership of Benito Juárez. The subsequent conflict brought economic disruption and many instances of the forced confiscation of money and property, some of which belonged to foreign nationals, including the bondholders. Mention has already been made of the theft in 1860 of dividend funds held at the British Legation in

28. David Robertson, Chairman, Committee of Mexican Bondholders, 1856–1862. Photograph reproduced by courtesy of the Trustees of the Paxton Trust.

a last-ditch attempt by the Conservative regime to acquire the resources to buy a few more weeks in control of the capital. There were many similar incidents and most commercial activity ground to a halt.

As the fortunes of both sides fluctuated, all semblance of law and order collapsed in many regions where local military chieftains imposed their own arbitrary rule. In the circumstances, neither the Liberal nor the Conservative administration was in any position to honor its international obligations, but both still desperately sought to raise funds, especially from the United States, and both were willing to negotiate the possible sale of territory in return for financial aid. In addition, there was talk of annexation by the United States or at least the establishment of some form of Protectorate to suppress the feuding factions, and to safeguard the United States' strategic and commercial interests. Finally, there was the series of events leading to the Allied Intervention during which the combined forces of Britain, France, and Spain occupied the Gulf ports to enforce the collection of the customs dues assigned to Mexico's foreign creditors. The Committee's relationship with the British government and the various diplomatic conventions agreed upon with Mexico on behalf of the bondholders will be dealt with in Chapter 6 of this study. For the time being, we turn to Robertson's other activities and especially his myriad attempts to get payment of both dividends and principal.

There was little public activity by the Committee. An office was maintained in London, at 10 Basinghall Street, and the secretary, still Nilsen, looked after the bondholders' affairs in the capital, regularly publishing the agent's reports from Mexico. He was aided by the deputy chairman, McGarel, and by Charles Staniforth, but there is infrequent mention of the other member of the Committee, the stockbroker, Thomas Moxon, whose father, John, had been on the 1830 Committee. Prior to 1861, when the pace of events leading to the Intervention dictated otherwise, there was only one public meeting, held, as always, at the London Tavern, on 28 May 1858.[162] Robertson makes it clear in his correspondence that he was always reluctant to give in to demands from some bondholders for more frequent meetings because he felt that their business was more appropriately conducted in private. On the other hand, he did prepare, with Nilsen's assistance, three exceptionally long and informative *Reports* dated, respectively, 29 April 1861, 23 January 1862, and 25 February 1862. The Committee also financed the publication of other documents including a collection of Mexican legislation on the foreign debt since 1850.[163]

To a large extent, therefore, the business of the Committee after 1856 was directed from rural Scotland. It was from his country estate at Ladykirk, Berwickshire, that Robertson wrote his voluminous correspondence on behalf of the bondholders, or rather dictated it to one of his estate workers, George Denholm, whose handwriting he had discovered to be much superior to his own almost illegible script. He spent comparatively little time in London until 1859 when he was elected to Parliament, the only Liberal success, he proudly remarked, in an entirely Tory Scotland, and one which was particularly gratifying to him since his opponent had been his nephew, Sir John Marjoribanks.[164] He was kept informed of developments in Mexico by Nilsen who sent him copies of the agents' reports, by letters from his correspondents, and from the newspapers which carried extensive coverage of the civil war.

In addition to many ongoing topics such as dividend arrears, customs assignments, the position of the 1837 Deferred bondholders and 1851 certificates, Robertson's efforts and attention were concentrated on several main areas. The issue of Church property in Mexico had already been noted by the McGarel Committee and Robertson continued to see the ecclesiastical assets as one source of money for the bondholders. Various laws were passed by Liberal governments in Mexico to dispossess the Church of its real estate and invested capital. The Lerdo Law, so-called after the Finance Minister Miguel Lerdo de Tejada, was passed in July 1856. It provided for the transfer of Church urban and rural properties to their tenants. Much more severe were the laws of 1859 which nationalized the wealth of the Church. All clerical properties were ordered to be sold either to tenants or in public auction with payment being made partly in cash, and partly in bonds of the internal public debt. The details need not concern us. What mattered to Robertson was how he could persuade the Mexican authorities to assign at least some of the confiscated property to the foreign debt. In many letters to the British Foreign Office, he pleaded for help and that British diplomats in Mexico City should be instructed to support his demands. He made two general points. The first concerned the value of Church wealth. Using Mora's estimate as a base, he revised the figure upwards arriving at a total of £60,000,000 or 300,000,000 dollars, more than enough, he argued, to service both the internal and external debt. Second, he emphasized the Spanish precedent. Some years earlier, Spain had also expropriated much of the wealth of its Church and had devoted some of the proceeds to the redemption of its foreign debt. The result was its stock had risen from 17% to 40% and its credit worthiness had been restored. Hence, Robertson told Lord Wodehouse at the Foreign Office, "we have a precedent in the mother country in which Church property is held so sacred and of the same Roman Catholic Church."[165]

Exactly how the clerical property would be assigned to the foreign debt was the subject of much discussion and various suggestions were advanced. In 1858, for example, and before the nationalization, it was reported by the bondholders' agent in Mexico City that there was a plan for the Church "to take upon itself the payment of the dividends on our debt."[166] Robertson welcomed the idea, adding that he would also be willing to accept Church real estate provided full and indisputable title was transferred to the bondholders. Other schemes for the transfer of clerical assets either toward payment of the principal or dividends were discussed and it was reported in 1860 that a "distinct proposal" had been made by the Juárez government at Veracruz "to make over the whole of Church property as security for the London debt in return for British recognition."[167] In a letter to Lord Wodehouse on 6 March 1860, Robertson said that Lerdo de Tejada had sent a confidential note stating that, if England would acknowledge the Juárez government, "the Church property will be assigned for the payment of the English Debts and Dividends."[168] Another less ambitious proposal was that Church property to the value of £2,500,000 should be provided as security for the payment of interest arrears. This envisaged that "Lands and houses of that fee-simple value should be vested in trustees, to be appointed by the Bondholders, and be held by them as security for the payment of the arrears."[169] The rents from the properties, which Robertson estimated at between £120,000 and £140,000 a year, would be used to pay one of the half-yearly dividends. There was also a proposal that the 1851 certificates should be given the same status as internal debt bonds and accepted in part payment for the purchase of Church properties when they were put up for auction. Finally, Robertson was aware that a substantial proportion of the Church's wealth was invested capital rather than real estate. He demanded that the Sinking Fund deficit—£200,000 at £50,000 a year since 1857 under the terms of the 1850 conversion—should be paid out of "the nationalized money investments of the Church."[170]

None of Robertson's hopes regarding the Church assets were realized. While the Mexican authorities were always willing to use the possibility as a negotiating ploy, it is clear in retrospect that there was never any likelihood of significant amounts of money from the nationalization program ever reaching the distant bondholders in Europe. Robertson's estimates of the value of Church wealth were much inflated and his informants in Mexico failed to apprise him of the difficulties faced by the government in realizing any cash from the nationalization. By 1862, when he realized this, he was naturally "astonished and dismayed." The entire wealth of the Church appeared to have been wasted and where it had all gone "remains a riddle." He told the bondholders that "a property which had been looked to as the means of freeing the republic of debt, both at home and abroad, was, through reckless mismanagement, collusion, and fraud, or for political ends, converted into smoke." So complete and expeditious a destruction of so immense a property, he added, was without parallel in the history of any nation.[171]

Another area to which Robertson devoted much time and attention involved the United States and its ambitions toward its southern neighbor. Since its emancipation from Spain in 1821, Mexico had endured more or less continuous political instability. Governments and constitutions changed with sometimes bewildering frequency and the chaos was at times such that some Mexicans concluded that their nation was incapable of self-government, especially in the form of a republic. Following the catastrophic war against the United States in 1846–1848, one group of politicians began to argue the case for the restoration of a European monarch as the only solution to the country's problems. They were to reach their ascendancy in 1864 with the foundation of the Maximilian Empire. For the time being, however, the monarchist solution remained a minority interest of no real political significance. More prominence was achieved by another group with an alternative solution. These were the annexationists or those who concluded, especially after the end of the war, that the best hope for Mexico was incorporation or annexation by the United States, or some form of protectorate.

The annexationists never achieved any real power in Mexico but particularly after the fall of Santa Anna in 1855 and the outbreak of civil war which accompanied the Reform, their ideas achieved prominence in Washington and elsewhere. Various schemes were discussed, usually involving substantial cash payments to Mexico by the United States. For example, in November 1856, the United States ambassador, John Forsythe, reported that the Comonfort administration was willing to consider a treaty of defensive and offensive alliance with the United States, which amounted to a virtual protectorate, in return for a substantial cash payment. Over the next few months, more talks were held which resulted in the signing of several documents, including a treaty of reciprocity, a postal treaty, a claims convention, and a treaty of commerce and loans. Under the terms of the latter, the United States was to advance 15,000,000 dollars.[172] None of these treaties were approved in Washington and Forsythe's other ideas on the same lines came to nothing, but before details of what was being proposed and their rejection were known, all sorts of rumors had reached London. The bondholders' Mexican agent reported in January 1857 that annexation was being openly discussed "as their only salvation."[173] Two weeks later, Robertson told Foreign Secretary Lord Clarendon that annexation was being negotiated with a 15,000,000–20,000,000–dollar payment.[174] At the same time, he wrote to the newly installed United States President, James Buchanan. Buchanan had visited London the previous year and had met Roberston at a dinner at McGarel's house in Wimpole Street. He told the president that in Mexico "the great plan of seeking the protectorate of the United States was openly discussed and fondly desired." Such a development, he thought, was sooner or later inevitable but then he went on to press the point which was to preoccupy him for the next few years. This was that if the United States were to absorb Mexico or even only part of its territory, it was duty bound, both morally and under international law, to pay off the country's debts. All of Mexican territory, he added, was mortgaged to the bondholders. A fair price for their stocks would be 60% of their par value and he hoped that the United States would guarantee that at least some of the 20,000,000 dollars to be paid to Mexico would be used to pay overdue dividends.[175]

The rumors of annexation deals persisted throughout 1857 and Robertson restated his case for compensation to the United States Secretary of State and to its ambassador in London. Then, in May 1858, a letter was received from General Sam Houston. He sent the the text of a resolution he had introduced in the United States Senate requesting an enquiry into the expediency of establishing a protectorate over Mexico. The bondholders welcomed his ideas at their meeting on 28 May 1858 and Robertson was asked to reply. He did so on 3 June. He also praised Houston's initiative but reminded him that whatever arrangement was reached with Mexico, the United States must be "responsible for the mortgage or pay it off before assuming possession."[176] A few days later, assuming that Barings would be involved in any United States payment to Mexico, he wrote to the company asking it to ensure that the bondholders' capital was repaid out of any "purchase money."[177]

Once again, of course, nothing came of the various annexation or protectorate talks but Robertson continued to promote the idea for several more years in his correspondence with British Ministers and diplomats. In 1859, for example, he told Lord Malmesbury that in his opinion, as far as the future of Mexico was concerned, "the only permanent remedy, the only one that can prove the salvation of that rich and fine country, and of the property and everyone in it—namely, its annexation to, or the protectorate of the United States."[178] Two years later, in 1861, he was still pressing his point on the United States ambassador in London.[179]

Annexation was not the only hope for the bondholders. Both sides in the civil war in Mexico were in desperate need of money and both saw the sale of territory to the United States as a possible source. Again, there were various schemes and deals arranged. Under the terms of the McLane-Ocampo Treaty of December 1859, for example, the Juárez government agreed to the sale of Lower California and granted various other rights of access to the United States. The Senate rejected the proposals but two years later, the ambassador to Mexico, Thomas Corwin, was still promoting similar schemes. One was of special interest to the bondholders. This involved the payment by the United States of the dividends on the foreign debt for five years—the cost was about £400,000 a year—in return for a mortgage on all public lands and mineral rights in Lower California, Chihuahua, Sonora, and Sinaloa. If the money was not repaid by Mexico, the mortgaged territories would become the property of the United States.[180]

Corwin's aim was to persuade the British government to desist from any armed intervention in Mexico, and by promising the bondholders their dividends he clearly indicated his belief that British policy was being influenced, if not determined, by their campaigns. His plan made no progress, nor did his other proposals for substantial loans in return for mortgages on public lands. Details of another perhaps more unusual idea also reached the bondholders early in 1862. Barings' agent in Mexico reported that a government minister had told him "in strictest confidence" that the United States wanted to buy land in Mexico "for the purpose of locating some 200,000 free negroes." If the plan ever materialized, he was assured, the money would be used to pay the bondholders.[181]

Another topic which had long interested the bondholders was also revived by Robertson. Under the terms of the 1837 conversion, the Deferred bonds and fractional certificates issued at the same time could be used to purchase vacant lands in northern Mexico at the rate of 5 shillings an acre. Events in Texas and its de facto independence, never recognized by Mexico, prevented any use of these land warrants for some years, but by 1842, George Robinson, on behalf of the Spanish American Committee, told the British Foreign Office that it was their intention to start the process of acquiring lands in Upper California.[182] Again, no progress was made and no actual lands handed over to bondholders, but over the next few years, the issue was raised from time to time. Then at their meeting on 23 December 1850, at which the bondholders voted to accept the terms offered in the 14 October law, a resolution was passed to the effect that, as compensation for their sacrifices in accepting reduced interest and writing off some of the debt, they expected to be given "unappropriated lands of the Republic." Talks were started with the Mexican government but again without success and in 1853, the Committee reported that "the prospect of obtaining a free grant of public lands is a good deal more remote and doubtful."[183]

Robertson took up the land question again when he became chairman. He first adopted a suggestion from one of the 1851 certificate holders that public lands be offered in exchange for the certificates.[184] Again, nothing happened because of circumstances but he returned to the matter in the 1861 *Report*. According to his calculations, since 1837 the bondholders had suffered losses on their stocks of £11,887,644. A generous price for land in Mexico would be £200 per square league, which meant that the bondholders were entitled to 60,000 square leagues or rather more than half of Mexico's total territory. That possibility, he accepted, was unrealistic but the claim remained valid. He also noted that public lands in the northern region had not been surveyed. The Mexican authorities, however, had announced a scheme whereby companies which carried out surveys at their own expense could keep one-third of the land surveyed. The other two-thirds would be retained by the government, giving it ample means to compensate the bondholders "by the grant of selected lands of ascertained value." In his view, the scheme offered "sufficient inducement" for an English company to take it up and he invited companies to put proposals to the Committee.[185]

Excluding relations with the British government which, as indicated earlier, will be discussed later, these were the principal areas of interest for the Committee from 1856 until 1862. At the general meeting on 11 July 1861, the main resolutions concerned requests for assistance to the British government. Two other resolutions, however, were also adopted. The first invited the following persons to join the Committee:

Admiral Wallis	R.F. Gower
Colonel Sir Henry Baily	A.F. Wood
Richard Garde	Chair of Stock Exchange Committee, ex-officio

Although their names do not appear in the text of the formal resolution, two other bondholders were also invited to join the Committee, namely, John Norbury and Reverend J.H. Carnegie.[186]

Admiral Wallis, it may be recalled, had first joined the Committee in 1854, but soon afterwards he had resumed his naval duties when in 1857 he was appointed commander-in-chief on the southeast coast of South America. He was recalled from that post on his promotion to Vice-Admiral in September 1857 and hence was able to resume his role on the Committee. Richard Garde, a barrister, had first been elected to the Committee in 1850. In 1861, using the form of "A Letter" to Earl Russell, he wrote a forty-three-page pamphlet on the rights of Mexican bondholders who were British subjects. The following year, 1862, he wrote a series of letters to Lords Palmerston and Russell, and to United States and Mexican diplomats in London. In these, he protested against what he had learned from the *New York Tribune* was a scheme to mortgage all public lands in Mexico to the United States in return for a payment of 11,000,000 dollars. He reminded them that "the public lands of Mexico, are already under a mortgage for principal and interest, of a very long standing, to the subjects of Her Most Gracious Majesty." This correspondence was published and circulated by the Committee. Later in the same year, he also penned a letter to Lord Palmerston, again published by the Committee, in which he defended the claims of the bondholders against those of the English Convention creditors.[187] Rev. Carnegie had come to Robertson's attention when he wrote to the Committee in January 1861. Robertson encouraged him to write directly to the Foreign Secretary "as an ill-used Englishman" and the letter already referred to (see Chapter 2) was the result.[188] Norbury was a stockbroker and a senior partner in Capel & Co. Wood and Gower were also stockbrokers and Baily was a retired army officer.

The new enlarged Committee, still chaired by Robertson, did not serve for very long because another resolution was "That Messrs. Baring, Brothers, and Co. be respectfully requested to accept the agency of the Mexican Bondholders." For several years, both McGarel and Roberston had tried to persuade Barings to take on the representation of the bondholders. They also wanted the company to resume the role of Financial Agent for the Mexican government. Colonel Facio, still officially the Financial Agent, remained in control of the dividend fund in the Bank of England but as remittances dried up, the bondholders saw little point in his continuation in office. They particularly objected to the fact that his annual salary of £3,000 was paid from the dividend fund or, as they saw it, from their money. With the exception of a partial payment in 1858 to complete the 1854 dividend, interest was not being paid, and as a result, he was receiving his "annual large salary for doing absolutely nothing."[189] In many letters to the Foreign Office and to British diplomats in Mexico City, Robertson urged that the Mexican government be persuaded to replace him with Barings. In a letter of 30 June 1858 to Loftus C. Otway, British Minister to Mexico, for example, he wrote that

Colonel Facio, who, although I believe a good man himself, is only to the bondholders an enormous expense, a hindrance, a mockery and a delusion. The money is ours, and not Mexican. We desire it no longer to get into Mexican hands, in Mexico, or in England.[190]

Otway did what he could in Mexico City and by September 1858, it seems that Barings was to be offered the Financial Agency. Disagreements with the company over existing accounts, however, caused the Mexican government to suspend its decision.[191] Facio had been ordered to accept a diplomatic posting to the Hanse Towns but he declined on the grounds of ill health, preferring to remain in London.[192] He retained his post and his salary for several more years.

Barings seems to have been reluctant to resume responsibility for representing the bondholders, perhaps in the light of its earlier experience. The company was heavily involved at the time in new loans for Chile, Peru, and Venezuela as well as European and North American issues. Robertson persisted, however, using his friendship with Thomas Baring, and eventually, agreement was reached in January 1862. No doubt the initial success of the Allied Intervention and what seemed likely to be the resumed flow of dividends across the Atlantic, and the commissions to be earned thereon, were factors in the decision.

The agreement with Barings was reached on 17 January 1862 when a memorandum of understanding was signed by McGarel and the company. The Committee, with McGarel, Garde, Staniforth, Wallis, and Wood in attendance, had met on that day to approve the document which McGarel then personally took to Barings for its signature.[193] According to its terms, Barings accepted the "Agency of the Mexican Bondholders." It undertook to seek the resumption of regular dividend payments; the restitution of the money stolen from the Legation in 1860; the recovery of interest arrears, amounting to £2,457,996; and a settlement of the claims of the Deferred

Bondholders. In return, the company was to receive a commission of 1% on all money remitted from Mexico and was further authorized to make a "sufficient deduction" to meet expenses such as freight and insurance, as well as the costs incurred by the Committee in London up to that time. Finally, it was agreed that all official communications on matters relating to the bondholders' claims with both the English and Mexican governments were to be made through Barings.[194] Charles Whitehead, the Committee's agent in Mexico, resigned and Barings announced that in his place, one of its own senior managers, George White, would be leaving for Mexico on the next packet.

The Committee reassembled on the next day, 18 January, to approve the agreement and resolved to summon a public meeting for 28 January for final ratification.[195] At the meeting, the assembled bondholders unanimously approved a resolution to ratify the agreement "with the highest satisfaction." Robertson, who chaired the meeting, explained that in adopting the resolution, "the functions of the Committee would, from that moment, absolutely cease." Although it would continue for as long as needed to wind up its business, it would have no further interference in the direction and management of the affairs of the bondholders. As the 1862 *Report* puts it, this statement was "Passed by acclamation."[196] The bonds—1851 Three per Cents—quickly reached 35, the highest price since they entered the market.

Thus, the Committee of Mexican Bondholders was voluntarily and unanimously dissolved. Effusive thanks for their help over the years were voted to Lords Palmerston, Russell, Wodehouse, and to Seymour Fitzgerald, Under Foreign Secretary in the administration of Lord Derby. Similarly, thanks were offered to the "Press of England" and especially to the city editors of the London newspapers for "able and unflinching advocacy" of the bondholders' claims. Finally, on the motion of James Capel, it was resolved that each member of the Committee should be presented with a piece of plate, varying in value from £525 for Robertson to £52 10s. to those who had joined in July 1861. A gratuity of £1,000 was also voted to the secretary, Nilsen, on his retirement after twelve years' service.[197]

Robertson returned to Scotland immediately after the meeting and the final winding up of the Committee was left to McGarel and Nilsen.[198] A Schedule of Assets and Liabilities was drawn up for the twelve years since the Committee's reestablishment in 1850. The Assets page shows a balance in the dividend account in the Bank of England of £19,925, and several smaller entries including £3,744 still due from W.P. Robertson. Liabilities included the £1,000 gratuity voted to the secretary, Nilsen, and a "Falconnet award" of £3,000, although it is not clear what this refers to. The Balance sheet which follows shows receipts of £714,986 to the dividend fund, of which £657,882 had been paid to bondholders.[199]

The final meeting of the Committee was held on 26 May 1862 with

McGarel, Baily, Garde, Staniforth, and Wood in attendance. They formally resolved to transfer everything to Barings. In a letter to the company of the same date, Robertson, who seems to have missed the meeting, explained that the accounts had been audited by an accountant—a Mr. Major—and that there was a small balance in the Committee's account at the London and County Bank. He added that the gratuity to Nilsen, and the cost of the plate voted to members of the Committee, had still to be met.[200]

BARINGS; THE COMMITTEE OF DEFERRED BONDHOLDERS; THE DUTCH COMMITTEE, 1862–1867

Barings retained the bondholders' agency for six years. Its main achievement was the capitalization of interest arrears into the Imperial Three per Cents which have been explained in an earlier section. The bondholders also benefited in other ways, at least initially, from the establishment of the Maximilian Empire. Dividends were paid and some dividend remittances once again began to reach the account in the Bank of England. Confidence in Maximilian's ability to consolidate his regime, and enthusiastic support for him by *The Times*, combined to persuade the market that at last Mexico's potential for economic development and wealth were about to be realized.[201] The Mexican bond price increased rapidly, rising to 48 by April 1864, its highest level since the 1820s.

One particular group who also expected to have their claims finally met were the so-called Deferred bondholders. They were the holders of the excess bonds sold by Lizardi in the 1837 conversion. Although all parties agreed that they had been the innocent victims of fraud by Lizardi, nobody, and not least successive Mexican governments, had been willing to buy in the excess bonds. Hence, they were excluded from both the 1846 and 1851 conversions and also from all dividend distributions. For their part, the bondholders themselves waged a persistent and at times vociferous campaign. They wrote letters to the newspapers, attended and spoke up at public meetings of the bondholders, and continually addressed pleas and petitions to the Foreign Office. The Committee of Mexican Bondholders was at first reluctant to take up their cause, but eventually it did include their claim in its reports and in its own petitions to the British and Mexican governments.

Several of Barings' own clients had substantial amounts of the Deferred stock, including the largest single holder with bonds to the value of £60,600.[202] Not surprisingly, therefore, when the company took over the task of representing the bondholders, it was expected that it would press the Deferred case. Its agent, George White, who had gone to Mexico in February 1862, promptly presented a detailed memorandum on the subject to the British ambassador in May 1862.[203] Also, in response to more petitions from holders, the Foreign Office promised diplomatic support.[204]

Events intervened for a time—the French invasion and the establishment of Maximilian—and nothing was achieved in 1863. Then, in early 1864, the financial negotiations which led to the capitalization of the interest arrears on the 1851 Three per Cents were successfully concluded. The Deferred holders saw their opportunity and renewed their claims. Maximilian responded by agreeing to set up a special committee (the Baring Committee) to consider their case.[205] It was composed of Thomas Baring, James Capel, and George Glyn. Their report, released in May 1864, recommended that the 1837 Deferred bonds should be exchanged for bonds of the new £8,000,000 Six per Cent loan that was about to be raised in the European markets. The rate of exchange was to be £75 worth of the Six per Cents for £100 of Deferred.[206] The Deferred holders accepted the offer and, after some delay, it was approved by Maximilian. Interest on the Six per Cents was promised from 1 October 1864 with the first payment on 1 April 1865.

The Baring Committee's proposals to settle the Deferred claim were considered at a public meeting on 19 May 1864.[207] Those holders who were present not only voted to accept the offer but also to set up a Committee to represent their interests in the future. The following were elected to the first Committee of Deferred Bondholders:

I. Gerstenberg   Albert Levy

A. Cohen   J. Searle

T. Moxon

Gerstenberg was a stockbroker with investments in several of the Spanish American bonds. He is first mentioned in 1856 when he contacted the Committee of Mexican Bondholders regarding his 1851 certificates. By 1862, he was chairman of the Ecuador Land Company and he was becoming increasingly prominent in city circles. In following years, in addition to his Mexican interests, he was an active member of the Venezuelan bondholders' Committee, becoming its chairman in 1866. He also seems to have been the contractor for a new Chilean loan in February of the same year.[208] Subsequently, he was one of the leading financiers on the new Mexican Committee and then he became chair of the Corporation of Foreign Bondholders. Cohen was a stockbroker whose firm represented several foreigners with holdings of almost £3,000 of the Deferred bonds. Moxon we have encountered earlier as a member of the Mexican Committee in 1856. Although not a Committee member before, Levy had attended and spoken at bondholders' meetings since 1843. Finally, nothing is known of Searle.

The Deferred Committee's brief was to ensure that the agreement with Maximilian's representatives was implemented. Unfortunately, despite many further meetings and renewed assurances by Mexican authorities in both Paris and Mexico "to settle the Deferred Bondholders' claims without delay," no dividends were paid and the promised new bonds were not forthcoming.[209] Pleas for aid to the British government and diplomatic pressure in Mexico City followed. The Imperial government Ministers promised more than once that they would attend to the matter and that the Deferred holders should be accorded "equal footing with the rest of the bondholders."[210] Finally, on 21 November 1865, Barings announced that it had received confirmation from Mexico that Maximilian had approved the settlement proposed the year before by the Barings Committee.[211] Ignacio Ibarrondo was to travel to London to implement the conversion. A few days later on 28 November, the Deferred bondholders met to hear the latest news. Gerstenberg, who chaired the meeting, announced that he had on that same day received word from Barings that the agreement could not be honored. Ibarrondo had gone to Paris to liaise with the Mexican Financial Commission only to be told by its director, Count de Germiny, that there were no Six per Cent bonds available to convert the 1837 Deferred.[212]

Further appeals were sent to Mexico but no further offer was made before the collapse of the Maximilian Empire in 1867. The Committee of Deferred Bondholders remained in existence for several more years. Unlike the Committee of Mexican Bondholders, however, it does not appear to have opened an office or employed a secretary and there are no extant minute books of any meetings. Gerstenberg's correspondence as chairman was always written from 11 Warnford Court, which was probably his business address. Also, there are no printed reports of its activities and in the absence of any reference in the newspapers, it seems that no more public meetings were held. In 1875, reporting on its activities in the previous year, the newly established Corporation of Foreign Bondholders noted that "The Mexican Deferred Committee, acting in co-operation with the Council, have lost no opportunity of pressing their claims on the Government and its representatives."[213] As indicated, Gerstenberg had also become chairman of the new Corporation and it appears probable that the interests of the Deferred holders were absorbed by it.

One other development took place during Barings' tenure of the bondholders' agency. In 1865, members of the Amsterdam Stock Exchange sought the cooperation of the London bondholders in pressing their own claims against the Mexican government. In the first instance, these involved the 1851 certificates, many of which had been acquired by Dutch investors. Around February 1865, the president of the Amsterdam Bourse addressed a letter to the chairman of the still active Committeee of Spanish American Bondholders. His letter was passed to Gerstenberg who replied on 22 March, welcoming the suggestion of cooperation and giving the names of the Deferred Committee's members.[214] More correspondence passed between London and Amsterdam and in May 1865, Gerstenberg wrote to the Mexican Minister in Paris in support of Dutch proposals.[215] In brief, the Dutch investors, who seemed to have formed themselves into a subcommittee of their Bourse, had proposed that the Maximilian government should offer land warrants of 100 hectares for each £100 worth of 1851 certificates.

Nothing came of the land warrant idea but contacts between the London Deferred Committee and the Dutch group continued. In May 1868, for example, replying to more documents sent by the president of the Bourse, L. Weetjen, the secretary of the London Stock Exchange assured him that they would be passed on to the "Committee of Mexican Deferred Bondholders."[216] In later years, the Amsterdam Committee continued to cooperate with the Mexican bondholders in London until the final Dublán conversion. More details will be found below.[217]

THE PROVISIONAL COMMITTEE OF MEXICAN BONDHOLDERS, 1867–1868

The Provisional Committee issued one published *Report* on 27 March 1868. It is signed by the following:

Henry Brinsley Sheridan	Henry Guedalla
Richard Bridgeman Barrow	J. Corbett Irving
Henry Brouncker	B. Poulson

Sheridan (see Illustration 29) had been appointed chairman in February 1868. His appearance is surprising in as much as no reference has been found to any previous participation by him in the affairs of the bondholders. As indicated earlier, despite almost thirty years in the House of Commons, few traces of his political or legal career have survived. Very unusually, he appears to have died intestate, leaving no will at his death in 1906, and we have no details of his estate nor, in particular, of any investments in Mexican bonds. We do not know, therefore, of his business interests or if he continued the line of those wealthy bondholders who had emerged to lead the Committee since its original formation in 1830. On the other hand, it may be that he was recruited by the bondholders at least in part because of his parliamentary position. He was the fifth Member of Parliament to chair the Committee since its formation in 1830 and certainly, over the years of his chairmanship (which also lasted until 1886), he was to raise the bondholders' claims in the House of Commons on several occasions.

Guedalla had served on earlier Committees and he also was to remain a member, albeit intermittently, until 1886, as did James Corbett Irving, who was a partner in the stockbrokers Irving & Slade, who had emerged to represent some of the bondholders in March 1867. Brouncker was from an old Dorsetshire family and one of the principal landowners in the

29. Henry Brinsley Sheridan, Chairman, Committee of Mexican Bond-holders, 1868–1886. Photograph reproduced by courtesy of the Clerk of the Records, House of Lords Record Office.

county. His country residence was Boveridge House in the parish of Cranborne where Reverend Carnegie, who joined the Committee in 1861, was the incumbent vicar. Brouncker resigned within a few months.[218] Nothing is known of Poulson, who also seems to have left soon afterwards. Finally, Barrow was on the Committee until his death in 1876.

The first indication of the formation of the Provisional Committee was in March 1867. Some bondholders, holding nearly £1,000,000 of Mexican stock between them, were unhappy with the way in which Barings had been representing their interests.[219] Apparently led by Edward Thomas Wilson and the firm of Irving & Slade, acting on behalf of their clients Schwabacher & Salmon who had holdings of £550,000, presumably also for clients, the bondholders decided in March 1867 to form a new Committee. They had two complaints against Barings. The first related to the lack of information which the company released to the press about its activities on their behalf. The second related to dividends. Maximilian's agents had agreed to provide sufficient funds from the proceeds of the Six per Cent loan to pay the dividends due in 1864 and 1865 on both the 1851 and 1864 Three per Cents. With those dividends covered by this agreement, the Mexicans ceased to collect or set aside the bondholders' share of the customs revenues. Remittances from Mexico stopped. In November 1865, Barings asked the British Foreign Secretary, Lord Clarendon, to take "such steps as may be deemed expedient" to secure the resumption of the collections from the customs.[220] Some occasional remittances were subsequently received and by early 1867, the dividend fund, still kept on deposit in the Bank of England, had reached £130,000.

The dissident bondholders asked Barings to use the £130,000 to make a partial dividend payment. Barings, however, promptly found itself in dispute with both the Mexican Legation in London and with the bondholders. The Mexican Minister was Angel Nuñez Ortega. He insisted that the dividend fund could not be used without his consent and that he was entitled to a commission of ¾% on any sum distributed. Barings disagreed and refused to release the money. Nuñez was replaced in the Legation soon afterwards by Juan Nepomuceno Almonte, who assured Barings that the dividend could and should be paid, apparently without any commission to himself. £80,309 of the £130,000 in the Bank of England was then paid out to the 1851 bondholders as a partial dividend.[221]

All of the money available in the Bank was not paid out immediately because of another complication which had arisen when some 1864 holders, represented by the noted banker Baron David (or Herman) Stern and stockbroker Louis Cohen, insisted that they were entitled to a share of it.[222] The 1851 holders objected, arguing that the money was exclusively intended for interest on their bonds and should not be used to pay dividends on the 1864 Three per Cents. Their case was that there was no reference on the 1864 bonds to interest payments from customs or any other specified revenues.

Barings was caught in the middle of this dispute and refused to act until the whole matter had been resolved by a test case in the Court of Chancery. The case was arranged amicably by leading bondholders and the company, and it was brought before the Court as "Guedalla versus Barings." Henry Guedalla apparently held substantial investments in the 1864 bonds. The Court's decision was delayed until December 1868 and it was that the 1851 and 1864 bondholders had equal rights to the dividend fund.[223] With the dispute thus amicably resolved, Barings distributed £48,648 to the 1864 holders as a partial dividend.

The dividend distribution was Barings' final direct involvement in the bondholders' affairs. The company had offered to resign as their agent in April 1867, transferring the Agency "to such firm or person as may be mutually agreeable to the Bondholders and the representative of the Mexican Government."[224] The offer was not taken up for the time being by the Provisional Committee but then in February 1868, Sheridan wrote to say that it had been decided that the interests of the bondholders would be best served by "the maintenance of a permanent committee."[225] It was their intention to call a public meeting of the bondholders to express their wishes and "give effect to the same by a recorded vote." In the circumstances, Sheridan assumed that Barings "would consent still to conduct the financial business of the Bondholders." Barings replied two days later. It resigned and declined "to act further as agents for the Mexican bondholders."[226]

THE COMMITTEE OF MEXICAN BONDHOLDERS, 1868–1876

The decision to resurrect a permanent Committee seems to have coincided with the appointment of Sheridan in February 1868 as the Provisional Committee's chairman. A few weeks before, an approach to the British Foreign Office for help had been rebuffed. Edmund Hammond, the officer responsible for Mexican affairs, told the bondholders, in his customary abrupt fashion, that Mexico's refusal to communicate with British diplomats "precludes the possibility of compliance with your request."[227] The Provisional Committee decided that in the circumstances there was no reason why it should not communicate directly with the Mexican government and on 24 December 1867, it addressed an appeal to the Mexican Foreign Minister, urging a resumption of dividend payments. A few days later, Henry Guedalla wrote a similar letter on his own behalf asking for confirmation that Mexico's announced repudiation of any bonds issued by the Maximilian regime did not apply to his holdings of the 1864 Three per Cents.[228] Then, on 8 February 1868, *The Times* printed a statement from Sheridan. He announced that a memorial to British Foreign Secretary Lord

Stanley had been prepared pleading for "the resumption of consular intercourse between the two countries." All bondholders were asked to sign the memorial personally or to authorize their London representatives to sign on their behalf. They were also asked to indicate by letter or in person whether they wished to see the formation of a permanent Committee.[229]

The letters which the bondholders sent to express their views on the desirability of a new permanent committee have not survived but they were said to be unanimously in favor. Consequently, the decision was taken by the Provisional Committee to call a public meeting for 27 March 1868, to be held as usual at the London Tavern. Sheridan duly presented the Committee's *Report* of its activities to the meeting and then, on a motion made by Guedalla and Charles Capper, it was resolved to set up a permanent Committee. Its functions were to superintend and manage the bondholders' interests; negotiate a settlement of their claims, subject to approval in a public meeting; appoint and remove agents; all expenses being paid out of the first available assets.[230] On another motion, put by Gerstenberg and McGarel, the following were appointed to the Committee:

H.B. Sheridan	Henry Guedalla
R.B. Barrow	J.C. Irving
H. Brouncker	Admiral Wallis
C. Capper	

The only new face was that of Capper who was made vice-chairman. He was a merchant and shipowner, chairman of several public companies, and at the time Member of Parliament for Sandwich, although he resigned his seat soon afterwards. He died in March 1869 and hence had little time to participate in the bondholders' affairs.

The first period of what may conveniently be called the Sheridan Committee lasted until 1876 when the bondholders, after some hesitation, decided to affiliate to the recently formed Corporation of Foreign Bondholders. An office was first opened at 1 Copthall Court or Chambers, which was the premises of Irving & Slade, and later, in 1872, at 35 Finsbury Park. William W. Holmes had been appointed as Honorary Secretary in 1867 and he looked after the general administration and correspondence. An agent was also appointed in Mexico City. Sheridan had held private talks with the Spanish General Prim regarding a suitable person for the post and he had recommended one of his own staff, a General Millans, who was personally acquainted with President Juárez. Millans attended several of the Committee's meetings to discuss the mission but then apparently demanded a £1,000 fee for his services, a sum which the Committee decided it neither had nor would pay.[231] Subsequently, another candidate was found for the Agency. This was Edward Joseph Perry, described as "a

British merchant of twenty-five years standing in that country."[232] He agreed to represent the bondholders without remuneration until his efforts had produced a settlement. Finally, there were some changes to the Committee in the years from 1868 to 1876. As noted previously, Brouncker resigned within a short time because of other commitments and Guedalla, who was always a volatile character, soon fell out with his colleagues and also resigned in October 1868. They were replaced by former member Richard Garde who died soon afterwards, and by Edward Wright, a prominent member of the Stock Exchange and a bondholder since at least 1849. Finally, the vacancy caused by Barrow's death in 1876 was filled by the mercurial Guedalla the following year.

The Sheridan Committee was engaged in what it aptly described as "six years of uninterrupted negotiation."[233] There were several areas of activity, fully described in three published *Reports*, those of 1869, 1870, and 1876; for example, relations with the British government, particularly Sheridan's attempts to raise the bondholders' case in Parliament. There were more or less continuous negotiations with Mexico involving various proposals for converting the debt. Attempts were made to block investment in Mexican railways and finally, there was the Committee's relationship with the Corporation of Foreign Bondholders.

After the British Foreign Office's rejection of the bondholders' appeal for help in December 1867, on the grounds that there was no diplomatic contact between the two countries, both the Committee and Henry Guedalla had written to Mexico in an attempt to open negotiations on the debt directly with the Mexican government. At first, the response was not discouraging. In May 1868, a reply was received from the Finance Minister, Matías Romero, offering to open talks and suggesting the appointment of an agent in Mexico City. After Perry's appointment, negotiations were started but then early in 1869, the Committee received the devastating news of the Mexican cabinet's decision not to recognize the existing debt. In sum, Romero argued in his letter of 28 December 1868 that by cooperating with the Maximilian regime, and especially by accepting the Imperial 1864 bonds in exchange for the dividend arrears, the bondholders had invalidated all prior agreements existing between themselves and the Mexican government. It would not recognize, therefore, any obligations toward the bondholders, such as, for example, the terms of the 1851 bonds relating to the general mortgage of Mexican revenues and the specific assignments on the customs revenues. Mexico did not repudiate the debt, although it refused to recognize the validity of the 1864 bonds, but it insisted that negotiations must start on the basis of a clean sheet of paper.

The Committee vehemently rejected Mexico's position and took legal opinion both in London and in Mexico in their efforts to refute it. Although the lawyers supported their case that Mexico was in contravention of both national and international law, in practical terms, the judicial reports had no effect. Similarly, more petitions to the British government brought no assistance. Romero kept to his position, telling Perry in February 1869 that his government "will willingly treat with you respecting the liquidation and payment of the debt represented by the Mexican Bondholders in London, provided that the latter, and you as their representative, should be disposed to enter on the negotiation on the bases indicated."[234]

The bondholders, therefore, while always refusing to accept the Mexican position, had little choice but to negotiate on Mexican terms. The talks, largely conducted by Perry in Mexico City, soon brought a variety of proposals.[235] One involved the transfer of land and mineral rights to the bondholders but that was soon found to be impractical. Another concerned the the formation of a National Bank of Mexico. The bondholders were to be offered the charter for the establishment of the Bank but the Committee rejected the idea on the grounds that they would have had to provide the subscribed capital of £600,000, and because "your abandonment of your customs' hypothecations was again made a condition of settlement."[236]

A more discussed, and more contentious, proposal was the construction of an interoceanic canal across the Isthmus of Tehuantepec. For years there had been talk in Mexico and elsewhere of the feasibility and desirability of constructing a canal to provide direct access to the Pacific Ocean and to the trade routes to the East. Companies had been formed and engineering surveys carried out, but domestic and international political factors had always prevented any progress. Then, in 1870, the idea was resurrected and the concession was offered to a United States company. The news arrived in London on 10 May, and four days later Sheridan swore out a formal protest before a Public Notary against "the proposed unqualified alienation by the said Government of Mexico, of certain national properties and rights known as the Concession of the Tehuantepec Canal Route across the Isthmus of that name."[237] Sheridan argued that the concession contravened the bondholders' "right of lien upon every and all the national property of that Republic."[238] In other words, he reasserted the general mortgage of all Mexican territory originally included in the 1824 bonds and repeated in subsequent issues.

A copy of the notarized protest was promptly sent to the United States Secretary of War, General W.S. Rosecrans, who was one of the promoters of the United States company, and also to the New York Stock Exchange where it was assumed capital for the canal might be sought. A few weeks later, at the request of the Mexican government, Perry forwarded a detailed set of Mexican proposals which offered the bondholders participation in the whole project. In short, Mexico proposed that the 1851 Three per Cents, the nominal value of which was £10,241,650, should be converted at 50% into new Six per Cent bonds. Half of the £5,120,825 worth of the new Six per Cent stock would be Active, paying interest from 1871, and half Deferred, paying no interest for ten years or until 1881. All the other outstanding securities of the London debt, including the 1851 certificates, the Lizardi Deferred 1837 Five per Cents, and the English and other Convention bonds were likewise to be exchanged for the new Six per Cents. The 1864 Imperial Three per Cents and all interest arrears were to be converted into shares in the Tehuantepec Canal Company. Finally, the general mortgage on Mexico and the specific hypothecations on the customs revenues were to be renounced in exchange for a mortgage on the Canal Company's assets; the concession of land plots along the course of the canal; canal dues; and £1,500,000 worth of shares in the company.[239]

Details of the proposal were published in the London newspapers on 1 July, but it seems that rumors of a possible settlement had been circulating for some time beforehand. Henry Guedalla, who was not on the Committee of Mexican Bondholders at the time but who had his own informants in Mexico, summoned a meeting of bondholders at the London Tavern for 21 June. The purpose of the meeting, the costs of which were met by Guedalla personally, was to discuss what should be done in the light of the "improved aspect of their position and future prospects."[240] The meeting was chaired by Mr. R. Hodgson. During what was described as "a long and personal discussion," Guedalla accused Sheridan and his colleagues of withholding information about the offer, which they used for their own benefit in the market. He moved a vote of censure on the Committee and proposed the appointment of an independent body to protect the bondholders' interests. Sheridan, who was present throughout, defended his Committee and denied the charge of insider trading. He also pointed out that the unofficial meeting would be seen by Mexico as indicating divisions among the bondholders. Finally, he announced that the full terms of the proposal were expected on the next West Indies mail packet and that once they were received, a report would be prepared and a public meeting of the bondholders summoned to discuss it.[241]

The public meeting was scheduled for 12 July at the London Tavern. Meanwhile, Guedalla studied the proposals and he did not like them. First, he prepared and swore before a notary another protest against the conduct of the Mexican government and its failure to honor its obligations to the bondholders, which he sent to all the European Bourses. Second, he composed a long letter or memorandum to the bondholders in which he denounced the Tehuantepec offer and urged them to reject it. The canal, he said, would take at least ten years to construct and would cost £40,000,000. "It will never be made in my opinion," he added, and even if it were, it would never yield even 1% profit to the shareholders. "Look at the Map," he proclaimed, "and note its relative position and that of the Suez Canal."[242] He then proceeded to offer his own detailed "Bondholder's Proposal" in which he suggested that Mexico should adopt a schedule of graduated interest payments starting at 1½% for five years and rising to 3% over fifteen years. He also resurrected the old idea that British merchants exporting to Mexico should pay their customs dues in London. Finally, he rejected criticism of his campaign. He had made sacrifices for the benefit of Mexico in the conversions of 1837, 1846, and 1851, and he was not going to be diverted from his cause by speculators and "satirical personalities" who attacked his motives. "I will continue to follow," he wrote, "my usual independent course for the benefit of my brother sufferers."

The public meeting took place as announced on 12 July. Sheridan presented the Committee's *Report* with all the documents relating to the Tehuantepec proposal. The Committee's view was that while it was "far from satisfactory," especially with regard to the arrangement offered for the 1864 bonds, which was "manifestly inadmissible," it should not be dismissed. Rather, it involved "interests of the most serious character" and negotiations should be continued with the Mexican authorities.[243] Several speakers, including Wright and Guedalla, urged the bondholders not to give up their rights, especially their mortgage on the customs revenues. Provo Wallis argued that if the Mexican government refused to recognize the 1864 bonds, it should return the arrear coupons for which they had been exchanged. Other speakers included Messrs. Taylor, Hyde Clarke, Hudson, and Greene. Eventually, it was resolved to adopt the *Report* and to continue the negotiation. Another resolution put by Guedalla and F. de Lizardi concerning expenses was passed, and Sheridan, seconded by Charles McGarel, moved a vote of thanks to the agent in Mexico, Edward Perry.[244]

Talks on the details of the Tehuantepec proposal were continued in Mexico City for a few more weeks but by September 1870, no progress had been made and the scheme was abandoned, at least as far as the bondholders were concerned. Their attention promptly turned to another topic. For a number of years, one of the tactics adopted or threatened by the Committee had been to warn the Mexican government that failure to honour its obligations would have the effect of closing all European capital markets to the republic. As a nation in default, Stock Exchange rules already precluded the possibility of floating new government loans in the markets. Now the bondholders tried to ensure that no more private capital for Mexican government–sponsored enterprises could be raised in any of the British, European, or United States stock markets. Their main target was the Mexican railway industry. The development of the country's railways had been delayed by internal domestic conflict, but gradually companies were formed to build particular lines. Railway construction, however, was both risky and expensive and as an incentive to investors to put their money into the railway stocks, the Mexican government guaranteed the companies generous annual subventions. The companies in turn raised their working capital by the sale of their bonds in the European markets. The Mexican Railway Company had been set up in London in 1864, largely but not entirely by British entrepreneurs, to build a line from

Veracruz to Mexico City, via Puebla. It received an annual subvention of 560,000 dollars or £112,000.[245]

The company's bonds were redeemed regularly and on 19 October 1870, it announced that £10,000 of its Class A Mortgage Bonds were to be paid off. That was the signal for the bondholders to begin their campaign. Three days later, Sheridan served formal notice on the railway company, holding it responsible for £254,342 received from the Mexican government. He reminded the directors that the money had been paid from revenues already mortgaged to the bondholders because, under the terms of their bonds, "the whole and entire revenues of Mexico, from whatever source derived, were solemnly hypothecated as guarantee for the payment of the interest, and also for the redemption of the principal of the debt due to the London bondholders." He warned them not to part with any of the money except to the bondholders and that they would be held responsible for it. Finally, he required them not to employ any of the money in the construction of the Mexican railway "or for the purposes of the Mexican Railway Company (Limited)."[246]

It is not entirely clear what Sheridan hoped to achieve by this procedure, which was widely publicized in the newspapers, other than to reassure the bondholders that the Committee was being vigilant on their behalf. He subsequently admitted that nothing more was done because no financial resources were available to pursue the matter in the courts.[247] A few months later, however, another opportunity arose. In June 1871, the Mexican Railway Company announced a new loan of £1,180,000 to be raised by the sale of interest-bearing bonds secured in part by assignments on Mexican government revenues. Again Sheridan and his Committee lost no time in protesting that the revenues offered as security were already mortgaged to the bondholders. Another formal protest, witnessed by the Committee's solicitor, Frederick Stanley, was drawn up and sent to the newspapers. At the same time, representations were made to the London Stock Exchange Committee which was asked to refuse an official quotation "to render the bonds of the loan unmarketable."[248] The request was refused, despite support from the Amsterdam Bourse, with the result that Mexico was allowed to evade, in the words of the Mexican Committee, "that ostracism which has hitherto, even on the less scrupulous of Continental Bourses, invariably been visited upon defaulting states."[249]

This initial failure did not deter the bondholders. In November 1872, the Committee wrote to the recently elected Mexican president, Sebastián Lerdo de Tejada. Rumors were circulating in London and New York, they said, of another railway concession about to be granted by the Mexican government to a group of United States investors. It was being claimed that customs revenues would be assigned to them. That was not acceptable and "in the unfortunate event of the rumours being confirmed," the Committee "shall feel themselves bound to put on record a formal protest against such a proceeding, and publish the same monthly on every Bourse in Europe and America, so long as the malversation continues."[250]

Railway investment resurfaced in 1874, again, at first, concerning the same Mexican Railway Company. In February, it offered for sale a further tranche of its 7% Mortgage Bonds. The Committee, now aided by the Corporation of Foreign Bondholders with which it was by then cooperating, at once started a campaign to block the issue. First, the following telegram was sent to the Amsterdam Bourse: "London Mexican Committee request Council oppose Mexican Railway new issue. This concurs with your previous notification to us." The Amsterdam Bourse obliged and resolved not to allow the sale of any Mexican stocks on its exchange.[251] The London Stock Exchange was less helpful to the bondholders. Once again, it rejected their case and the new stocks were allowed an official quotation. Several factors probably influenced the decision. As Hyde Clarke, secretary of the Corporation of Foreign Bondholders, explained to the president of the Amsterdam Bourse, "From the Press here, we received little support."[252] Most of the London newspapers had opposed any action against the Mexican Railway Company on two grounds; first, because it was largely a British company and it was therefore British investors who would lose money if it were prevented from carrying out its legitimate business. As one investor, James Gray, put it in a letter to *The Money Market Review* (28 February 1874), the company was English and not "the Mexican government in disguise." Second, the construction of railways in Mexico would result in greatly improved economic performance which in turn would generate the wealth required to pay the nation's creditors, including the bondholders.

The Committee's campaign against the Mexican Railway Company had clearly failed, but Hyde Clarke reassured the Dutch bondholders that "we will oppose all future issues and invite your cooperation."[253] Just a few months later, the campaign was renewed and this time with more success. Various schemes for the construction of lines were being planned, largely by United States companies. Using their contacts in the London Stock Exchange, the bondholders' Committee persuaded what was said by *The Times* (3 June 1874) to be "all the principal members of that establishment" to sign a memorial protesting against official sanction of any further issue of the Mexican Railway Company bonds or those "of any other Company formed for the furtherance of any Mexican enterprise" until the Mexican governemt had settled its debts.[254] The Amsterdam Bourse gave its full support and forty-one of its members signed their own memorandum in which they agreed

to oppose by all means in their power, the issue on the markets of Europe of any shares or bonds of any Railway company or other association formed for the execution of any public work in the Republic of Mexico [255]

These memoranda were submitted to the London Stock Exchange Committee and were circulated throughout the European Bourses. On this occasion, and for reasons which are not clear, most of the London newspapers supported the bondholders. *The Daily Telegraph* (3 June 1874), for example, stated that Mexico should not be permitted to borrow more money until it had paid its existing creditors and there was no sign that the republic was about "to stray unawares into the paths of honesty." Some railway company shareholders did protest but most opinion seemed to share the view of C. Rowlands who, in a letter to *The Financier* (15 June 1874), wrote that nations which failed to pay their debts must be "sent to commercial 'Coventry.' "[256]

Although the Stock Exchange Committee deferred any decision at its meeting on 22 June, and does not seem to have reached a decision subsequently, the pressure worked and it was reported that "the concessionaires of the new Mexican Railway system failed in their efforts to receive any assurances of aid in London, Paris and Frankfurt." The financiers in those cities had all insisted that Mexico's foreign debt must be settled before further capital could be raised. Such a position was "neither surprising nor unjust."[257] The bondholders were told by their Committee that after consultation with the continental Bourses, the Mexican government had been informed "that Mexico would no longer be allowed to avail herself directly or indirectly, of the European markets for the purpose of raising capital."[258]

The effects of Mexico's exclusion from the European capital markets, according to the Committee, were immediate. The Mexican president was sufficiently concerned that he asked friends who were visiting Europe "to ascertain unofficially the lowest terms upon which a settlement could be obtained." These presidential envoys were initially led by William Barron and José de Jesús Cervantes, both Mexicans, and Nathaniel Davidson, a British subject and merchant, who had spent many years in Mexico. They contacted the Committee and attended several of its meetings at which various terms for a settlement were discussed.[259] Eventually, after further consultations with Mexico, a proposal was put on behalf of the Mexican government. In short, this amounted to a a reduction of the principal of the 1851 debt to one-half of its value compensated for by an increase in the interest rate to 6%. Interest arrears were to be capitalized and again reduced by half but bearing 6%. The 1864 debt, reduced by 40%, was to be similarly treated. New Six per Cent bonds would be issued in exchange for the existing stocks but the interest rate was to start at 1¼%, rising by ½% yearly until, in 1885, the full 6% should be attained.

The Committee's reaction to these terms was not positive. It pointed out that among several disadvantages, the bondholders were being asked to give up half their capital without "any counterbalancing advantage."[260] Also, the 1851 bonds, with the mortgage rights embodied in them, were to be given up, and the interest rate offered was very low, at least in the early years. It put various counterproposals, including that the 1851 bonds should be placed in trust in the Bank of England. The talks continued in London but no settlement was reached and Barron returned to Mexico in November 1874. The bondholders' agent in Mexico City, Perry, continued to discuss the details and "active communciations by letter and by telegraph were maintained," but all to no avail.[261] No agreement was concluded. In its 1876 *Report* to the bondholders, the Committee advised that if no settlement were approved in the next session of Mexico's Congress, the choice before them was either to continue to negotiate, "undaunted by previous disappointments," or to approach the Crown "by that procedure known as 'Petition of Right' by which the subject obtains a judicial sanction for the pertinence of his demand for governmental protection and assistance in the enforcement of his rights."[262]

The failure of the negotiations was confirmed by the Committee's secretary, Holmes, in a letter published in the press on 19 January 1876.[263] The news provoked angry reaction. *The Daily Telegraph* (19 January 1876) denounced Mexico's conduct as "shabby and discreditable" for sending Cervantes "on what has since proved to be a thoroughly Quixotic enterprise." The bondholders were urged to ensure that Mexico was "financially outlawed on every Bourse in the civilized world." *The Bullionist* (22 January 1876) attacked recent speculation in Mexican stocks by those who had gambled on a settlement being reached or "foolish people who have gone on dabbling in Mexicans." Several bondholders expressed their frustration in letters to the newspapers. One, writing as "A Mexican Bondholder," demanded a parliamentary enquiry into the Mexican loans.[264] Christopher Rowlands again condemned the Mexican Railway Company for taking the bondholders' money "which is not saying much for the Directors who accept it."[265] Henry Guedalla circulated a pamphlet, advocating once again his own proposed terms for a settlement. He was also very critical of the Committee, which had not called a public meeting for five years. He favored the appointment of a Board of Management of well-paid people to look after the bondholders' interests.[266]

It seems to have been in response to this reaction that the Committee took two decisions. First, it was announced that there was to be a public meeting on 4 April 1876 at which a detailed account of its activities would be presented.[267] The *Report*, dated 31 March 1876, was quickly written and printed in time for the meeting. Second, in response to pressure from several bondholders, the decision was taken, and approved in due course at the meeting, to enter into formal links with the Corporation of Foreign Bondholders. A few words about its origins are appropriate at this point. It had been formed at a meeting of foreign bondholders held in London on 11 November 1868. The earlier umbrella organization or Committee of Spanish American Bondholders, formed in 1836, had continued until at least 1865, but thereafter (and lack of research means we cannot be certain) it seems to have ceased to function. The separate national committees for the debtor countries such as Ecuador, Venezuela, and the former Central American republics, however, had continued and several of their members were present at the November 1868 meeting. Also present were prominent Mexican bondholders, for example, Provo Wallis, Sheridan, Moxon, and Gerstenberg. It seems that the Spanish American bondholders in general had concluded that an association of bondholders of all debtor countries, including those in Europe and many of the states of the United States, would be more effective than the separate national committees. The meeting was chaired by Mr. G.J. Goschen and the resolution to set up the new body was put by Gerstenberg. It was approved, as were others concerning membership and finance. Finally, it was agreed that those who had convened the meeting should form the inaugural committee and that they should prepare a detailed plan to be put to a general meeting of bondholders.[268]

A few months after the inaugural meeting, the bondholders reassembled on 2 February 1869 to hear the interim committee's report. They accepted the various proposals and voted to form a twelve-member Council. Those elected to it included Sheridan, Provo Wallis, Moxon, and Gerstenberg. In addition to Sheridan, there were two other Members of Parliament, George Cavendish Bentinck and Charles Bell.[269] A secretary, Hyde Clarke, was quickly appointed and Gerstenberg was chosen to be the first chairman. The new body was welcomed and membership rapidly expanded. By 1872, it was decided to formalize the hitherto ad hoc rules into a formal Association of Foreign Bondholders with a fund of £100,000 to be provided by 1,000 members, each subscribing to a £100 bond. According to *The Times* (15 January 1872), leading merchants and financiers had already guaranteed the whole sum and many members of the Stock Exchange had joined. As the amount of business already being conducted was increasing rapidly, larger offices were taken at 10 Moorgate Street.[270] The following year, 1873, the Association or "old" Council was registered as a Corporation under the Companies Act of 1862. The success of the new Corporation can be seen in its first published *Report*, dated 17 February 1874. It indicates that it was already concerned with the affairs of twenty-six countries and eight states of the United States.

For the time being, the Sheridan Committee of Mexican Bondholders preferred to continue to operate independently of the Corporation. In 1874, there was an agreement between the two bodies for joint action but "afterwards the Committee thought it more desirable to act alone."[271] Then, apparently at the request of several bondholders, further consideration to closer cooperation was discussed. Sheridan reported to his colleagues in March 1876 that he had discussed the matter with the chairman of the Corporation and it was agreed that two of its members should be invited to join the Mexican Committee.[272] Further talks took place and eventually, at the public meeting of Mexican bondholders held on 4 April 1876, the decision was taken in favor of a formal association with the Corporation. Four of its members were to join the Mexican Committee. It closed its office at 35 Finsbury Circus and henceforth all of its business was conducted from the Corporation's offices at 10 and, subsequently, 17 Moorgate Street.

THE SHERIDAN COMMITTEE, 1876–1886

For the final decade leading to the Dublán conversion, the Committee of Mexican Bondholders operated under the auspices of the Corporation of Foreign Bondholders. It retained its autonomy, however, meeting regularly as a separate body and conducting its own negotiations with various Mexican government representatives. The membership changed only inasmuch as the representatives of the Corporation attended meetings. Sheridan continued as chairman throughout and Irving, Wallis, and Wright, together with Guedalla who rejoined in 1876, all remained on the Committee. The formal link to the Corporation in 1876 brought new faces which, until 1883, were in the persons of Francis Bennoch, who acted as vice-chairman, and Lionel Bonar. In addition, the chairman of the Council of the Corporation, Edward Pleydell Bouverie, attended meetings as an ex-officio member of the Committee. Finally, in 1883, another five names, including two Members of Parliament, appeared as members but in the absence of minute books, it is not known what they contributed. They were George Augustus Cavendish-Bentinck, a Conservative M.P. for Whitehaven; Peter McLagan, a Liberal M.P. for Linlithgowshire; Roger Eykyn, a stockbroker; Benjamin Newgass, described as an "adventuring entrepreneur" and "a keen operator" in his Stock Exchange dealings; and finally, D. Castello, also a stockbroker.[273] Holmes continued throughout as secretary and Edward Perry was the agent in Mexico until his death in January 1883.

The Committee's only extant minute book reveals the number of meetings and attendance. From July 1876, when the first meeting was held with the Corporation's representatives present, to 27 April 1883, when the last meeting recorded in the minute book was held, the Committee met seventy-three times. With the exception of 1877 and 1878, when there were only four and six meetings, respectively, there was about one a month. Sheridan, Irving, and Wright were exceptionally diligent, rarely missing a meeting. Guedalla was rather more erratic, although he did send letters and telegrams expressing his views on the matters under discussion. Similarly, Admiral Wallis was not a regular attender, being present on three or four occasions a year. This is perhaps not surprising given his age—ninety in 1881—and he was at the final recorded meeting on 27 April 1883, just two weeks after his ninety-third birthday. Of the Corporation's representatives, Bennoch, and especially Bouverie, were rarely absent. Bonar, who had been put on the Committee in 1876, does not seem to have appeared for three years, but from July 1880 he was also usually present. It is not known if the Corporation's representatives had personal holdings of Mexican bonds. It is unlikely, since there is no mention of them in earlier years and it seems more probable that their presence was to add weight to the Committee. Certainly, they were prominent figures in London's social, political, and financial circles. Bouverie, for example, was the second son of the Earl of Radnor, and a substantial landowner in Wiltshire. He was a Liberal and had held various high offices of state, in addition to being a Member of Pariliament for thirty years until 1874. Cavendish-Bentinck, a Conservative, was from similar aristocratic background, being the son of Lord Frederick Bentinck, and he also had occupied senior government posts.

The work of the Committee was revealed to the bondholders within the annual *General Reports* issued by the Corporation. For the most part, the Mexican Committee's entries were brief summaries of about a page, offering no more than an outline of negotiations or ideas under consideration. The hundred-page-or-more presentations of the past were no longer thought necessary. From time to time, however, especially when proposals for settling the debt were provisionally concluded, separate publications were issued. In 1879, for example, Sheridan published a *Letter of the Chairman* to inform the bondholders of a particular scheme that the Committee was recommending.[274] In later years, several protracted and difficult negotiations with Mexican representatives brought complex offers for converting the debt and these were also published separately. When the Dublán conversion began, the relevant Mexican legislation, translated into English, as well as details of the proposals, were issued as separate publications.

The volume of printed material issued by the Committee, therefore, was substantial but it did not stop criticism. As the attempts to reach a settlement failed repeatedly in the 1870s and early 1880s, despite many initial reassurances by the Committee that success was near at hand, many bondholders became disillusioned. They vented their anger in letters to the press and no doubt in private letters to Sheridan and his colleagues. Some complained of lack of information and the failure of the Committee to report to their constituents in public meetings at which questions could be put. One who wrote to *The Times* (4 April 1879) and who said he had £1,000 invested in Mexican stocks, wanted a meeting of "bona-fide" bondholders like himself, rather than speculators, to find out what, if any, talks were in progress. In November 1880, a meeting of bondholders representing approximately one-fifth of the total debt resolved to seek an interview with Sheridan to urge a more energetic policy by his Committee.[275] Others, for example, Christopher Rowlands, put forward their own ideas and demanded that a meeting be called to discuss them.[276] "A Constant Reader" suggested that the United States might be persuaded to buy the bonds "with their lien on Mexican customs duties," as a means of obtaining a foothold in Mexico. After all, he said, Britain had established its presence in Egypt by buying up shares in the Suez Canal.[277] Another bondholder wanted Mexico to allocate mines to them which could then be rented to a mining company and the rent used to pay dividends.[278]

Holmes usually responded to the above criticism on behalf of the Committee but the most vociferous voice was always that of Guedalla. He had rejoined the Committee in 1876, and over the next few years he sent dozens of letters to the newspapers, sometimes defending his colleagues and sometimes attacking them. He became the unofficial spokesman and as such, he said, he was besieged with letters from bondholders wanting to know if the rumors of imminent agreements were accurate.[279] He always pressed his own proposals, warning his fellow bondholders to beware of "busybodies and undertakers now amusing themselves by drawing up schemes." His own sources in Mexico, he insisted, provided him with accurate information and he added, in a somewhat enigmatic phrase,

I am very much in the position of the two performers on the stage with a pig. The one who imitated that animal was lustily cheered, whereas the sounds made by a live pig in the hands of the other were loudly hissed[280]

On some occasions, Guedalla was anxious to defend the work of the Committtee. In 1877, for example, referring to a rumor that influential London companies might help in negotiations with Mexico, he wrote that "We are masters of the situation and want no influential firms to act for us."[281] Later, he complained publicly that his colleagues did not always inform him of developments. A telegram had arrived from the agent Perry "with which I was kept unacquainted (although the most active of the Committee) till Friday, when all the cream had been taken off the milk."[282] Two years later, in a similar situation of the arrival of a telegram which he had not been shown, he condemned the "preposterous mystery and silence" shown by the Committee.[283]

Guedalla was an eccentric character whose colorful language at least amused the readers of his many letters to the press. Of more serious concern for the Committee was probably the attitude of some of the newspapers. Most were critical from time to time of the failure to make any real progress in the continuous talks, and none more so than *The Bullionist*. It attacked Sheridan personally, accusing him of nepotism when his son, Dudley, was sent to Mexico as the Committee's agent, following the death of Perry in 1883. It accused the Committee of inertia and incompetence, advising the bondholders that "nobody should put their faith in them." When the 1883 negotiations collapsed, it alleged that the main reason was the greed of members of the Committee who had demanded that Mexico compensate them with £400,000 to cover their past expenses.[284] Other papers joined in the attack. *The Statist* (17 November 1883) wrote that "One of the greatest stumbling-blocks in the way of a settlement seems to have been the extraordinary amount of commissions, blackmail, or hush-money which attached to the scheme." The weekly magazine *Money* (21 November 1883) openly accused the Committee of corruption and self-interest, claiming that there was "something mysterious about the whole business" and "there is a black wash over this strange affair that imperatively calls for an enquiry."

This barrage of criticism culminated in November 1883 when leading firms of brokers on the London Stock Exchange, together with other companies holding or representing bondholders, petitioned Barings to resume the job of representing them in negotiations with Mexico, "without the interposition of any Committee." There are ninety-one signatures on the memorial presented to Barings and although some are not readily legible, others include leading names in the city such as James Capel & Co., Cazenove, Louis Cohen, Foster & Braithwaite, Woodall & Co., G. Jacobson, L. Messel & Co., Hope & Co., and W.O. Dodgson.[285] The text of the memorial, although not the signatures, was published in most of the newspapers. *The Times* (16 November 1883) expressed the hope that if Barings agreed, that would "thus put an end to the hopeless confusion and mismanagement with which the business connected with the settlement of the debt has hitherto been conducted."

Barings refused to accept the agency in a brief letter to Foster & Braithwaite dated 19 November 1883.[286] Three days later, on the evening of 22 November, in an obvious attempt to defuse the attacks being made against it, the Committee published a 24-page account of its recent negotiations.[287] In its comments, *The Times* noted that the *Report* "shows signs of having been drawn up in some haste." In general, however, the newspapers accepted the Committee's defense of its labors and even though *The Standard* described it as "an exculpatory statement," *The Bullionist*, rather grudgingly, concluded that it offered "a plausible tale." *The Daily Telegraph* was much more enthusiastic. The *Report* provided, it said, "a complete vindication of the Committee from the charges recklessly made against them of mismanagement, ignorance, and self-seeking."[288] On the same day it was released, what seems to have been a conciliation meeting took place in private at the Corporation of Foreign Bondholders' office between Sheridan's Committee and members of the Stock Exchange. Sheridan's explanation was accepted by the brokers and he was thanked for the clarity of his statement.[289]

The origin of the widespread discontent with the Committee's work lay in the collapse of a series of negotiations held with diverse Mexican representatives who arrived in London, claiming to have official Mexican authorization to negotiate a settlement of the debt. All manner of people approached the Committee with offers to act as intermediaries. For example, Thomas Morrison, manager of the London Bank of Mexico and South America, pressed, in strict confidence, for his Bank to be appointed as the bondholders' agent in Mexico. After considerable consultation with Stern Brothers and other leading bankers in London, the proposal was rejected because Bouverie was doubtful if the Bank was as influential in Mexico City as Morrison had claimed.[290] An American lawyer, Wallace McFarland, introduced by Sheridan to the Committee, was made its confidential agent in New York to report on the activities of American capitalists who at the time (1881) seemed to be investing heavily in Mexican stocks. He was paid a retaining fee of £100.[291] Various other offers to help were made, always on the basis of commission, payable in the event of success. The negotiations, and the intermediaries, however, also seem to have required the payment of "douceurs." In a letter to the Committee, Admiral Wallis expressed his total opposition to "all forms of settlement based or relying upon the payment of douceurs by the Bondholders to the intermediaries engaged in obtaining their acceptance by the Government of Mexico."[292] His stand was not shared by all his colleagues. "The question of douceurs," the Committee was told at its meeting on 16 November 1882, "met them on every occasion of serious proposals being submitted to them for the settlement of the Debt." Sheridan favored their use, arguing that "douceurs were influential and decisive" in the recent grant of a charter to establish the National Bank of Mexico. Furthermore, referring to Cervantes, who was still involved in trying to negotiate an agreement, "he was in a position to approach the most influential people in the Mexican Administration with offers of douceurs which it would probably be dangerous for strangers to hint at."[293]

Cervantes had been the main intermediary for several years. After the collapse of his initial scheme in June 1876, he had gone briefly to Mexico but returned to London with more proposals in July. By August, a provisional agreement had been reached and Cervantes promptly returned to Mexico to seek the approval of the Mexican authorities. The scheme involved converting the debt into new Six per Cent stock but the bondholders were to concede a proportion of it for the funding of a National Bank of Mexico in which they would also become shareholders. Perry continued the talks in Mexico City throughout the next two years (1877 and 1878), but for various reasons, including internal political events, especially the rise to power of Porfirio Díaz, no progress was made. Then, finally, in November 1878, Perry reported that a deal was about to be concluded. The terms reached London in January 1879 but the Committee was bitterly disappointed. Perry had agreed to changes and concessions, the most notable of which was the abandonment of the idea of a Bank in favor of the bondholders' participation in the construction of a railway. Bennoch felt that the terms "were inadmissable and could not be for one moment entertained." Admiral Wallis agreed, saying they were "unworthy of consideration."[294] Telegrams were sent to Mexico rejecting the proposed arrangements.

Once again, by early March 1879, Cervantes was back in London to renegotiate. On 29 July, Sheridan decided to publish his chairman's *Letter* in which he set out the renegotiated terms. These were briefly as follows:

> The scheme for adjustment as at present proposed, and which your Committee believe they may have to submit to you, embodies the conversion of the 1851 debt, with its arrears of interest, into a 6 per cent Stock (at 50 per cent. of its nominal value), but subject to the contribution by you of a surrender of your claim to an amount nearly equal to such arrears towards the construction of a Railway from Mexico city [*sic*] to the Pacific seaboard of the Republic.

Other clauses provided for a settlement of the 1864 Three per Cents which were to have their nominal value reduced to 60%. Half of this reduced value would be converted into the new stocks. No railway could be built, Sheridan warned, without substantial capital investment, but he had assurances that "the building and equipping of the line, as well as the financial part of this great enterprise, have been secured by respectable and responsible firms."[295]

Unfortunately (for the bondholders), this new scheme was rejected by the Mexican Congress in September 1879. The repeated failure of the negotiations, however, now continuous for almost a decade, did not deter the ever-hopeful Committee nor the various intermediaries who came to London to press their ideas on the debt. Again, more or less throughout the early 1880s, there were renewed negotiations with several parties. In January 1881, in one of his frequent letters to the press, Guedalla identified five separate syndicates "formed during the last six months for the purpose of arranging the debt."[296] The circumstances seemed particularly propitious. The first Díaz administration (from 1876 to 1880) and its successor headed by his close ally, President Manuel González (1880–1884), received very favorable press in Europe. British observers noted with approval Díaz's emphasis on economic development and his presidential speeches to Congress and elsewhere were widely reported. *The Times* (2 November 1881) lavished praise on him, emphasizing again and again Mexico's inexhaustible natural resources which, in the age of peace which Díaz had inaugurated, were now ready to be exploited. Investors might expect that "A pound invested in the country may yield double and, perhaps, tenfold." Other papers adopted the same tone. Mexico was "a country teeming with natural wealth" and the amount needed to service its foreign debt was "a mere bagatelle for a rich and large country."[297] According to *The Daily Telegraph* (22 May 1879), Mexico was "weary and ashamed of her twelve years' banishment to the City of Ostracism, metaphorically known as Coventry."

While formal relations between Britain and Mexico remained suspended, despite many calls in the press that they should be resumed forthwith, full diplomatic ties were resumed with France in October 1880. Other developments noted with keen interest by the Committee included a Mexican congressional law calling for the consolidation of the whole of the national debt. Then, after considerable maneuvering and intrigue between competing parties, including discussions with the Committee, the contract for the creation of the National Bank of Mexico was awarded, in August 1881, to a Paris-based syndicate led by Edward Noetzlin, representing the Franco/Egyptian Bank. Its formation brought more rumors that one of the new Bank's priorities was to sort out the foreign debt. *The Standard* (14–17 September 1881) claimed, for example, that a deal had already been agreed upon to redeem half the debt with new Five per Cent bonds and the other half "by large annual drawings." Guedalla once again hastened to deny the rumors.[298]

All these developments, against the background of the optimistic scenario of Mexico's future depicted in the newspapers, must have made the bondholders hopeful that an agreement would be reached. Nothing, however, was achieved by the Committee in 1880 or 1881 and it seems to have decided that a more aggressive attitude was required. Various railway concessions were being granted in Mexico, mostly to North American groups, and from time to time, there were rumors that they were searching for investment funds in European markets. In July 1882, one such group of "United States capitalists" announced that they were seeking to raise £2,000,000 by way of mortgage debentures secured, in part, by charges on Mexican customs.[299] The Committee at once dispatched a protest to *The Times* (4 July 1882), warning investors that the bondholders had a first charge on all Mexican revenues. Furthermore, that as Mexico was still in default, the public should know that "a quotation in the official list of the Stock Exchange can hardly be anticipated for this new issue." Copies of the protest were promptly sent to the London Stock Exchange Committee and to the provincial exchanges at Liverpool, Manchester, Birmingham, Glasgow, Dublin, and throughout the British Isles. Other copies went to the continental exchanges at London, Amsterdam, and Paris and organizations such as London banks were also notified, as were "the Financial Papers."[300] The Mexican Railway Company's solicitor was promptly in touch to warn the Committee that it would be held responsible for any losses incurred. In turn, the Committee chose to seek counsel's opinion on the legality of the bonds and it also considered whether to institute formal legal proceedings against the company.[301] Finally, Sheridan raised the matter in the House of Commons, seeking the British government's protection of the bondholders' assets.

Although some papers, notably *The Times* (6 July 1882), dismissed the protest as unnecessary and counterproductive because it could inhibit Mexico's economic growth, the Committee's campaign seems to have worked. The railway promotors made no application to the Stock Exchange for an official listing and the Committee was able to report that "the bonds in question (were) virtually withdrawn from the European market."[302]

Sheridan enjoyed more success later in the same year of 1882. Shares in the recently formed National Bank of Mexico were offered for sale in the London market and early in December 1882, an application was made for an official quotation on the Stock Exchange. Sheridan promptly went in person to the Exchange to register his Committee's opposition and as a result of his protest, "consideration of the whole question had been deferred until the 19th inst."[303] Accompanied by Bennoch and Holmes, Sheridan put his case in person to the General Purposes Committee on 19 December—the Bank's case was put by Mr. Crews—and again the matter was deferred.[304] A few weeks later, Noetzlin himself travelled from Paris to attend a Mexican Committee meeting but he failed to persuade Sheridan and his colleagues to withdraw their opposition to the sale of the Bank's shares and the General Purposes Committee left the application in abeyance.

The success of the Committee's campaign seems to have persuaded the Mexican government to reopen negotiations on the debt. The much-travelled Cervantes had more discussions with the Committee in the final months of 1882 and then he returned to Mexico. He came back to London in April 1883 and was accompanied by Carlos Rivas, a congressional deputy and private secretary to President González. Rivas claimed to have full authority to arrange a settlement of the debt and he submitted his credentials to the Committee. These consisted of letters to him from President González. They were examined at the Committee's meeting on 27 April 1883 and deemed to be authentic. Hence, talks began at once and within less than two weeks, a "Heads of Proposed Arrangement" was signed on 12 May. Briefly, the terms were that a new loan of £20,000,000 in Three per Cent bonds was to be floated; £15,300,000 of the new stock was to be used to convert the London debt, including the 1851 Three per Cents, 1864 Three per Cents, and several of the outstanding certificates. The remaining £4,700,000 was to be retained by the Mexican government for other purposes, including "payment of the remuneration and expenses of the Committee since its formation."[305]

The Committee quickly published a *Report* setting out the details of the proposed settlement and summoned a public meeting of bondholders for 18 May at the Cannon Street Hotel. Meanwhile, press reaction to the terms was mixed. *The Times* (12 May 1883) thought that the offer to settle was the result of pressure from United States railway promotors who needed to raise capital in European markets. The weekly *Money* (16 May 1883) was much more critical. The whole deal, it argued, was simply a ruse by Mexico to raise another loan on which it would certainly default, as it had always done. It warned the bondholders to beware of anything to do with "the insolvent and bandit republic." *The Echo* (15 May 1883) told them that "Once bit, twice shy, should be their maxim."

The public meeting was chaired by Sheridan. Although there was some opposition from the floor, notably by one Captain Pavy and a Mr. Bulman, most speakers supported the Committee's motion that the terms be accepted. Mr. Van Raalte added his voice in support, saying that he represented the Dutch bondholders who were unanimously in favor. Another speaker was W.H. Bishop, who soon afterwards went to the trouble and expense of having his own history of the debt printed.[306] Eventually, after what was a long discussion, the Committee was authorized to take the necessary steps to implement the conversion. The meeting was extensively reported in all the main newspapers but several advised caution against optimism that a settlement had finally been reached. *The Bullionist* (19 May 1883), in its customary colorful style, compared the Committee to "the drowning man who catches at a straw."

Over the next few weeks, the bondholders waited for their money but it soon became clear that complications had arisen. In June 1883, the Mexican Congress approved a law for the consolidation of both the internal and external debt. Some of the terms of the law conflicted with the terms of the Rivas agreement with the bondholders. Rumors began to spread that Rivas had not been properly authorized to negotiate and there were conflicting reports that the agreement had been rejected in Mexico or that it required major changes. The Committee published letters and telegrams received from Mexico which seemed to refute the rumors and it was reported that Messrs. Murrieta & Co. had been appointed by Mexico to carry out the conversion.[307] The rumors of problems continued, and in July Sheridan felt obliged to publish a telegram allegedly from the Mexican president asserting that "the settlement made with the bondholders by Sr. Rivas and accepted by the Chambers is irrevocable."[308]

In fact, despite the public reassurances, the Committee was very concerned. Rivas had retired to Paris after the bondholders' meeting on 18 May. Over the next few months, several of the Committee's members pursued him across Europe in a forlorn attempt to ascertain the true status of their agreement with him. Holmes was the first to go to Paris, only to discover that Rivas had left for Carlsbad to take the waters. He was followed by Dudley Sheridan who travelled to Carlsbad to find that Rivas had returned to Paris the night before. Dudley made his way to the French capital but again missed his quarry who had gone to the country for the weekend. Finally, on 20 September, the Committee received a letter from Rivas, confirming that changes to the agreement were required. He asked that Chairman Sheridan should travel to Paris for talks. Sheridan, accompanied by Irving, "at great personal inconvenience," duly went to Paris. The talks continued both in Paris and in London, to which Rivas returned

for a few days. According to the Committee, the main reason for the difficulties was "a system of French intrigues that has its ramifications in this
country."[309] Apparently, a syndicate of French speculators, with the connivance, or at least cooperation of Rivas, had "from the commencement of
negotiations increasingly endeavoured to defeat the arrangement with the
Bondholders, and to depress the market in order to secure to themselves
the settlement of the debt."[310]

The failure to conclude the negotiations successfully provoked hostile
press reaction both against Mexico and the Committee. For example, under
such headlines as "The Mexican Collapse" (5 September), "The Mexican
Fiasco" (26 September), "The Mexican Scandal" (21 November), *Money*
announced on 21 November that "the great Mexican bubble has burst."
As indicated earlier, most of the newspapers blamed the incompetence, inefficiency, and nepotism of the Committee and there was the futile attempt
to persuade Barings to take over the job of representing the bondholders.
For their part, Sheridan and his colleagues defended themselves as best they
could, first in the November *Report*,[311] and then in letters to the newspapers. On 12 December, *The Times* published a long letter from Holmes on
behalf of the Committee in which he insisted that the agreement with Rivas
had been approved by the Mexican Congress and that all that remained to
settle were a few minor details. Rivas had returned to Mexico for talks
with his government, "with a view to remove such differences of form as
up to this time have prevented the completion of the conversion."

The very critical press which Mexico received in London was noted in
Mexico City. On 29 November 1883, the official government newspaper,
the *Diario Oficial*, published a twenty-three page article on the Rivas negotiations in order to refute the allegations being made in the European
press against Mexico's "sincerity and good faith." "Such statements and
mispresentations," it added, "are highly offensive to our national decorum,
and it becomes a necessity to deny them in a most convincing manner."
The text of three documents followed. These were the May agreement concluded with the bondholders; a "Project of a Contract" subsequently agreed
upon by the Committee and Rivas; and "Comments of the Mexican Government on the Proposed Modifications." Far from being rejected, the article insisted, the Mexican government confidently expected that although
the negotiations "have not yet arrived to a final term, it is hoped they will
attain it within a short time and in a most satisfactory manner."[312]

The Committee probably received its copy of the *Diario Oficial* in late
December. It had the text translated and composed a brief preface, and the
English version was published early in January 1884.[313] In the preface Sheridan left no doubt that "the remarkable Article" fully justified everything
his Committee had done and that "all the statements of the Committee,
made both before and since the departure of Señor Rivas from this country,
are fully supported and established." In an unequivocal attack on his critics,

the full text had been included, he said, "lest it should be said by the 'Opposing Party' that the statement is unfair and incomplete." The Committee, he concluded, had every confidence that the Mexican authorities intended "to honourably carry out the provisional Agreement of May last."

Sheridan's son, Dudley, had left for Mexico City in December 1883 to pursue the negotiations on the Rivas agreement. His reports back to London, however, soon began to indicate that "unexpected obstacles were being raised" to the ratification of the agreement and that modifications were being sought by "influential politicians." After months of indecision, the Mexican government decided to abandon the May agreement and "to open negotiations de novo through an Agent other than Sr. Rivas."[314]

The new agent appointed to negotiate with the Committee was Edward Noetzlin. As we have seen, he had been instrumental in arranging the foundation of the National Bank of Mexico. Now, he was asked to proceed to London to negotiate a settlement of the foreign debt. His credentials were issued on 10 June 1884 and he arrived in London about a month later. By now very suspicious of Mexican representatives who came to London claiming to have the authority to conclude any negotiation, the Committee went to considerable lengths to verify the authenticity of his credentials. Telegrams went back and forth to Mexico. After receiving confirmation from both President González and his successor, President Díaz, that they had sanctioned Noetzlin's mission, Sheridan and his colleagues agreed in August 1884 to restart negotiations. An agreement was quickly concluded and again the Committee took the precaution of telegraphing the details to Mexico, and in return both González and Díaz gave their approval of the proposed terms. These now envisaged a new issue of Three per Cent bonds to a value of £17,200,000. Of these, £14,450,000 were to be used in converting the debt and the remainder was to be for the "expenses of conversion, negotiation and Committee." Interest was payable on a rising scale, starting at 2%, for the first two years, the first coupon payable on 1 April 1885 and increasing to 3% in the fifth and following years. Included in the conversion at varying rates were the 1851 Three per Cents with arrears; the 1864 Three per Cents, with arrears; 1837 Deferred Five per Cents; various certificates, including those of 1851. As security for payment of interest, 10% of all import customs duties was assigned irrevocably.

Rumors of the negotiations quickly reached the newspapers and *The Money Market Review* reported on 16 August that "the prospects of the Bondholders have not been so favourable for seventeen years." The bond prices began to rise, with the 1851 Three per Cents reaching 24 compared to 20 at the beginning of the year. By early September, the Committee was meeting every few days to assess the terms and they were accepted at its meeting on 9 September. On 18 September, the formal arrangement was signed by Noetzlin and Sheridan. Some details had already been published in the newspapers and the full text was now printed.[315] Final ratification was left to a public meeting of the bondholders convened for 24 September, at the Cannon Street Hotel. In contrast to his other experiences at bond-holders' meetings, when Sheridan arrived to take the chair, he was received "with cheers." In a long introductory speech, he went through and rec-ommended the agreement, emphasizing that President Díaz was "the most able and reliable man in Mexico" and that he had personally approved the terms before the meeting. Bennoch seconded the motion to approve but other speakers opposed it. Mr. Bishop complained that the terms offered were worse than those in the Rivas agreement. Mr. Van Raalte, supported by a Mr. Jones from Maidstone, wanted a better deal for the 1837 and 1864 bondholders and he warned that the Dutch bondholders would not accept the agreement in its present form. Other speakers included W.C. Fretwell and Mr. Stoker. Also there was George Herring, a former book-maker, who had become one of the best-known and richest financiers of his day. A noted and very generous philanthropist, he was a "character" in city circles, known as "The Bloater."[316] Whether he was any relation to the earlier generation of bondholders, especially Charles Herring, one of the contractors for the 1825 loan, has not been established, partly because, as his entry in the *Dictionary of National Biography* puts it, George was "of uncertain birth." After much debate and the defeat of amendments put by Van Raalte and others, the motion to approve the agreement was ap-proved "amid loud cheers."[317]

With the restoration of diplomatic relations between Britain and Mexico formally confirmed shortly after the Noetzlin agreement, it seemed that at long last a settlement of the English debt had finally been achieved, but it was not to be. Like all those before it, the Noetzlin agreement failed to be ratified in Mexico, but on this occasion the causes were completely unex-pected. As the text was being taken through the Mexican Congress, popular protests in the streets of Mexico City demanded that it be rejected. The protesters objected to the export of Mexican money to foreign bondholders at a time when there was widespread poverty, unpaid or reduced wages, and increases in taxation. The size or extent of what were described as riots is not known, but according to *The Times* (20 November 1884), the dis-turbances were so serious that the military opened fire on the protesters, killing several of them.[318]

The effect of the demonstrations was that Congress suspended its dis-cussion of the debt question. To reassure the bondholders, and to correct various erroneous reports in the newpapers, Sheridan wrote to *The Times* (15 December 1884) to confirm that the agreement had been suspended but not rejected. He had every confidence, he said, that President Díaz, only just installed in the presidential office for his second term on 1 De-cember, would honor his promises to the bondholders. In fact, with the Congress not due to reassemble until 1 April 1885, Díaz and his new Fi-nance Minister, Manuel Dublán, took the opportunity to appoint a commission whose brief was to reexamine the whole issue of the national debt, both internal and external.

The enquiry into the public debt produced the law of 22 June 1885. Its terms have been indicated in previous sections of this work and only a brief recapitulation is given here. The whole of the recognized internal and external debt of Mexico was to be consolidated into new Three per Cent bonds and henceforth known as the Consolidated Debt of the United States of Mexico. Interest was to become payable in 1886 at the rate of 1%, rising by 1890 to the full 3%. The National Bank of Mexico was charged with servicing the debt with funds supplied directly to it from the maritime customs at Veracruz. Article 16 listed the claims that were admissible. These included the 1851 Three per Cents issued in London as a result of the law of 14 October 1850 and the English and other Convention bonds. Specifically excluded (Art.17) were claims arising from the "de facto Governments which ruled in Mexico from 17th December, 1857, to 24th December 1860, and from 1st June 1863, to 21st June 1867." This meant, of course, that the 1864 Three per Cents issued by the Maximilian regime in exchange for arrear coupons were excluded. Similarly, there was no direct reference to the 1837 Deferred, 1843 Five per Cents, and the various certificates such as those of 1851, although recognized securities not consolidated were to be converted at the rate of £20 per £100 nominal value. Interest arrears were to be the subject a special arrangement with the creditors. Finally, regarding the foreign debt, a Financial Agency was to be established in London to carry out the conversion.

Details of the June law were promptly available in London and included in the main newspapers from early July onwards. Recognizing its importance, the Council of the Corporation of Foreign Bondholders had the whole text of the law translated and published as a separate pamphlet.[319] Initial reactions were not especially favorable. *The Saturday Review* (4 July 1885), for example, in an article headed "The Mexican Crisis," claimed that the Mexican proposals were the direct result of the country's bankruptcy. *The Bullionist* (25 July 1885) said that reaction to "Mexico's latest step is decidedly unfavourable" and *The New York Herald* (n.d., July 1885) emphasized "the financial rottenness in Mexico." Sheridan and his Committee were similarly disappointed. Letters were dispatched to Díaz, reminding him of his commitment to the Noetzlin agreement and at its meeting on 14 August, the Committee recorded "its surprise and regret" at the June law. *The Times* (19 August 1885) published the Committee's correspondence with Mexico and Sheridan's explanation to the bondholders but only "as an act of courtesy to a body which, though incompetent, was well-intentioned, and until recently possessed a good deal of influence." Disappointed bondholders wrote their own letters to the newspapers, some attacking the Mexican Committee. Sheridan duly defended its efforts, pointing out that over many years its members had done their best and without any recompense.[320]

Early in September, a public meeting of bondholders to consider the June law was announced for 9 September, at the Cannon Street Hotel. On the day before the meeting, Guedalla, still active with his own views, wrote to the newspapers to urge acceptance of the proposals, provided arrear coupons could be converted into Deferred stock.[321] On the appointed day, about 45 bondholders assembled and what was described as a "thinly attended" meeting was held.[322] Bouverie took the chair and he told his audience that the terms on offer were not acceptable, mainly because of the vague nature of the offer to settle by future negotiation the question of dividend arrears which constituted about half the total debt. He proposed that an agent fluent in Spanish should be sent to Mexico to negotiate better terms.

Sheridan spoke at some length of Mexico's improved finances but he thought the Noetzlin agreement offered better terms. It was important, he said, to insist on recognition of the 1864 bonds and on the settlement of dividend arrears. The Committee's secretary, Holmes, had recently gone to the United States to see if there was any American interest in settling the debt and it would be a good idea to send him now to Mexico to renogotiate the offer. At this point, although it is not entirely clear what happened, there was a sharp disagreement between Bouverie and Sheridan. Bouverie scornfully dismissed the idea that Holmes, "a mere accountant," should be their agent. What was needed was someone skilled in the language and manners of diplomacy. Moreover, Holmes did not even speak Spanish, to which Sheridan responded that he could read the language and he could speak French which was the language of Mexican diplomacy. Bouverie warned that if Sheridan persisted, the Corporation of Foreign Bondholders would wash its hands of the whole affair. What one report described as "a lengthened and somewhat disorderly discussion ensued."[323]

Exactly what happened thereafter is not clear because the press reports of the meeting differ. According to some, the meeting voted to send Holmes to Mexico but others state that it was agreed that a joint deputation of Holmes and a nominee of the Corporation of Foreign Bondholders would form the agency.[324] More letters to the press were critical of Sheridan. W.H. Bishop had spoken at the meeting and in a letter to *The Times* a couple of days later (11 September 1885), he claimed the meeting had been dominated "by a compact body of adherents of Mr. H.B. Sheridan." *The Bullionist* (12 September 1885) alleged that it was an open secret, not revealed to the meeting, that the agent was to be Sheridan's son, Dudley. "Some means," it added, "must be contrived to get rid of the Sheridan faction."

The bitter dispute over the agents, the renewed dissensions among the bondholders, and the attacks on the Sheridan Committee obscured consideration of the June law, but it was clear that its terms were not acceptable.

More discussions between Sheridan and Bouverie seem to have resolved their differences and according to *The Bullionist* (28 November 1885), the Mexican Committee gave way on the question of the agent and "relinquished for the moment all participation in this matter." In fact, the Corporation of Foreign Bondholders encountered considerable difficulty in finding a suitable agent and eventually it decided to appoint its own Council's secretary, Mr. O'Leary, who had years of experience in Colombia as British Consul-General and some experience of similar negotiations in Colombia and Spain.[325] The whole exercise turned out to be unnecessary because soon afterwards, the Mexican government advised that its Financial Agency in London was about to be established and that its staff would conduct negotiations on the debt, as well as carry out the conversion. Hence, there was no need to send an agent to Mexico.

The Mexican law of 29 January 1886 formally established the Financial Agency in London "for the registration, liquidation and conversion of the debts" (Art. 2). General Francisco Z. Mena, Mexico's Minister in Berlin, was appointed the head of the Agency and Carlos Mexía, consul at Liverpool, as its secretary. Mena was also appointed Mexico's Minister Plenipotenciary to Britain but he delayed presenting his credentials until the debt negotations had been concluded.[326] These began soon after his arrival in London toward the end of February. The bondholders seem to have been represented largely by Bouverie, rather than Sheridan, and he set out his negotiating position in a long letter dated 19 May 1886.[327] Agreement was reached and signed on 23 June 1886, by Bouverie for the Corporation of Foreign Bondholders, Sheridan for the Committee of Mexican Bondholders, and Mena for the Mexican government. The next day, 24 June, reflecting the fact that Dutch investors still held large holdings of the bonds, Bouverie sent the details to the president of the Amsterdam Stock Exchange. The agreement, he said, had been reached "after some difficult and protracted negotiations" and he hoped it would meet with their approval.[328]

The specific terms of the Mena agreement have been indicated earlier and there is no need to repeat them. All that remained to be obtained was the approval of the bondholders in a public meeting. This was convened for 30 June and in the days before, all the newspapers carried summaries of the terms. On this occasion, Sheridan took the chair and after explaining what was on offer, he moved acceptance. Bouverie seconded the motion. There seems to have been some dissent, but not much. Philip Falk, for example, said he had held his stock for eighteen years and had hoped for better terms but he accepted that the offer was probably the best that could be obtained. In general, the other speakers favored acceptance, partly because of Sheridan's assurance that the first dividend, due on 1 July, would be paid within a few days by Glyn, Mills, Currie & Co. Finally, Sheridan also revealed that £50,000 worth of the new bonds was being allocated to cover expenses, including those of the Committee.

The Mena agreement was accepted unanimously by the assembled bond-holders and, as explained in the first part of this study, each of the outstanding Mexican securities arising from the original bond issues of 1824 and 1825 was converted into the new 1886 Three per Cents, which in turn were subsequently exchanged for the 1888 Six per Cents or redeemed for cash. The public meeting of bondholders of 30 June 1886 seems to have been the last to be held in the long series of such assemblies which had started with the first meeting sixty years earlier in 1828. Similarly, it appears that the Committee of Mexican Bondholders, if not actually disbanded at this point, more or less ceased to function as a separate body. More negotiations over the conversion rates for some of the securities, for example, the 1851 certificates, took place after June 1886 but these were conducted by the Corporation of Foreign Bondholders. In the absence of minute books for the Mexican Committee, we cannot be certain exactly when it ceased to function, but there are some indications. No reference to it occurs, or has been noted, in the press after 1886. Second, and perhaps more significantly, in the Mexican section of the annual general *Reports* of the Corporation of Foreign Bondholders, the names of the Mexican Committee members are always stated. The last time the names are given, however, is in the 1887 *Report*, which covers the events of the previous year. The Corporation continued for many more years to be actively concerned with Mexico's foreign debt, including each year in its *Reports* details of the current position, but for the rest of the nineteenth century there is no mention of the Mexican Committee or of its members.

It seems safe to assume, therefore, that the Committee of Mexican Bond-holders, originally established in 1830, terminated its activities in the weeks, or perhaps months, following the Mena agreement of June 1886. Some of its members had served continuously since the reestablishment of the Committee in 1868 and they were no doubt glad to retire. Sheridan, for example, had been chairman for almost twenty years, during which time he had suffered no small amount of personal abuse from irate and disappointed bondholders. Also, by coincidence, after representing the Dudley constituency since 1857, he lost his parliamentary seat in the election of 1886. It is tempting to think that, perhaps, he had spent too much of his time on the affairs of the bondholders. He was then 66 years old and he seems to have retired from public life. Even older, of course, was Admiral Wallis, who by the time of the Mena agreement was in his ninety-fifth year (he died in 1892, a few weeks short of his 101st birthday). Guedalla was also well advanced in years at 71 (he was still writing letters to the press in 1889), and he had acquired his first Mexican bonds over fifty years earlier in 1837. Similarly, Irving had been on the Committee for almost twenty years. Finally, Bouverie, although on the Mexican Committee as chairman of the Corporation of Foreign Bondholders, rather than as a Mexican bondholder in his own right, was always a regular and energetic presence. He continued on the Corporation for a couple of more years but died in 1889 at the age of 71.

FINANCE

Over the half century of its existence from 1830 to the mid-1880s, the Committee of Mexican Bondholders incurred many costs. There were office expenses, including rent and the cost of heating and lighting; administrative/secretarial costs such as salaries and stationery; the hiring of rooms for public meetings; advertising and printing costs; postage, travel, and various sundry expenditures. Finding the money to meet these at times substantial amounts was always a preoccupation of the various Committees and several methods were tried, with varying degrees of success.

The first Committee (1830–1836) seems to have incurred little expenditure. No secretary was appointed and the North and South American Coffee House provided an address for correspondence. Postage costs of the few letters that were sent were almost certainly paid by their author, Robert Wilson. Although we have no details, it seems likely that the other, more significant expenses, especially for the printing of the *Reports* of 1830 and 1831, were met by voluntary donations from either the Committee members or the bondholders at large. The foundation of the general Committee of Spanish American Bondholders in 1836 led to an increase in expenditure, and accounts for the first three years were included in the 1839 *Report*. Unfortunately, the page of "Disbursements and Receipts" of the only known copy of the *Report* is torn and some of the items are not legible. The surviving fragment shows that in the year 1836–1837 the following costs were incurred:

Sundry Office Expenses	£ 8 0s. 2d.
Rooms for Public Meetings	£ 8 7s. 0d.
Rent of Office	£ 7 10s. 0d.
Secretary	£37 10s. 0d.

Other entries are for £31 19s. 6d.; £2 17s. 5d.; £70 18s. 11d.; but the nature of the expenditure is on the part of the page that has been lost. The total for the year was £167 3s. 0d.. In the next two years (1837–1838, 1838–1839) the accounts show a similar range of costs, amounting, respectively, to £101 2s. 5d. and £124 6s. 3d.[329] In sum, therefore, the Committee spent £392 11s. 8d. in the first three years of its work. The income to cover this sum, as the accounts show, came from donations and subscriptions. At the inaugural meeting on 28 June 1836, the assembled bondholders had resolved "that a subscription be immediately entered into, and placed at the disposal of the Committee for the purpose of meeting their expenses."[330] Contributions, however, were never enough. In the enthusiasm of the first year, £167 3s. 0d. was received, but in the second year, this declined to just £30 3s. 6d., with the result that there was already a deficit of almost £71 over the first two years. Donations increased in the third year, but by the time the accounts were presented to the bondholders there was still a deficit of £49 13s. 2d.

It is not entirely clear how the deficit was paid but it seems that Committee members advanced the money. At any rate, they left the bondholders at large in no doubt that they were not willing to assume all the "pecuniary responsibility" for their affairs. The final page of the 1839 *Report* reminds them that there were inescapable costs and that there was already a deficit. "The Committee," it continues, "are quite willing to give the Bondholders their services without fee or reward, but they cannot at the same time consent to put themselves in a situation of pecuniary responsibility."[331]

Whether this appeal or perhaps threat to the bondholders had the desired effect of producing more donations is not known, and no more accounts of the Spanish American Committee have been found. It is clear, however, that significant expenditure, or lines of credit, were available to the Committee. For Parish Robertson's mission to Mexico in 1849, for example, £500 was placed for his account at Schneiders & Co. His son also received £100 and subsequently, a letter of credit for £500 was sent to Mexico but not used because Robertson had already left. Again, the sources of income to meet these costs are not clear and by the time the renewed Committee of Mexican Bondholders was formed by Robertson himself in January 1850, the need for a more secure income was obvious. Hence, at the meeting on 23 January 1850, the bondholders resolved that the Committee's expenses should be covered by "a subscription from the annual dividend pro rata not exceeding 1d. per £100 of the capital."[332]

The levy or deduction imposed on dividends became the accepted means of raising the money required to fund the activities of all subsequent Committees. It was soon evident that 1d. was insufficient and the usual rate was fixed at 6d. per £1 on dividends. It was also the case, however, that dividends were often not paid and there was no money to pay the Committee's expenses. The solution adopted, for the first time in June 1850, was to take money from the dividend fund in the Bank of England. When remittances for the dividends arrived from Mexico, they were placed on deposit at the Bank until such time as there was enough to pay all or part of a coupon. Interest on the deposit accumulated and not all bondholders claimed their dividends. Hence, there was almost always an unused sum in the dividend fund. Control of that money was a constant source of dispute with Mexico's Financial Agents and especially with Colonel Facio, whose own salary of £3,000 a year was taken from it. There were several agreements for joint control with the fund placed in the name of the Financial Agent and a representative of the Committee, but Facio was always reluctant to cooperate or to accept that it was bondholders' money. The first dispute with him occurred in 1850. At the meeting of 25 June of that year, it was agreed to send Falconnet to Mexico to press for the allocation of the United States' indemnity payment to the foreign debt. The meeting authorized the Committee to take £10,000 from the dividend fund "to meet the expenses of such mission, the Secretary's salary and the ordinary office expenses."[333] Facio refused to release the money and as Falconnet's mission was considered urgent, several Committee members provided £6,000 from their own pockets to ensure his prompt departure.[334]

The eventual total cost of Falconnet's mission at £16,889 was to be the biggest expense faced by the Committee. His successors as commissioners or agents to Mexico were paid considerably less at a basic £1,000 per year plus the promise of a bonus if their missions were successful. The money to pay them was raised by a levy of 6d. per £1 on dividends as agreed by the bondholders at general meetings in 1854 and 1855.[335] Throughout the 1850s, the usual administrative and personnel costs were also incurred. The W.P. Robertson Committee, which only lasted from January to April 1850, spent £111 on furniture and fittings; £72 on *Reports* and advertising; £198 on office expenses, rent, stationery, postage, and the salary of the secretary. The Goldsmid Committee spent even more, getting through £1,679 in the two years between April 1850 and April 1852.[336] When the Committee was wound up in 1862, the final balance sheet summarized all the expenditure for the previous twelve years. The entries for staff, premises, and administration include £1,160 on rent, coal, and housekeeping; £341 printing costs; £424 postage; £90 hire of rooms for public meetings; £4,737 salaries; and diverse miscellaneous costs such as legal fees, insurance, and advertisements.[337]

The restored Committee, first as the Provisional in 1867, followed by the permanent body chaired by Sheridan, faced the same problems as their predecessors in raising funds to cover running costs. On giving up the job of representing the bondholders, Barings handed over £950 left in the dividend account, but £650 of that was spent by the end of 1868 on office expenses, the cost of meetings, and sundries.[338] It was quickly evident to Sheridan and his colleagues that a source of income had to be found, but the former solution of a levy on dividends was no longer possible since no dividends had been or were likely to be paid for some years. Their solution was put to a general meeting on 12 July 1870. It was that a fund for defraying the Committee's expenses should be set up with contributions from bondholders of 6d. per cent on the nominal value of their bonds. Those present at the meeting agreed to this procedure but it seems that few of the bondholders at large responded positively, and soon afterwards the Committee resolved on a much more controversial tactic. A brief memorial was printed which bondholders were asked to sign. It was addressed to the chairman and Committee of the London Stock Exchange and it reads as follows:

> The Undersigned, being Holders of the Bonds of the Mexican Debts of 1851 and 1864, beg most respectfully to urge on your Committee the expediency of a separate quotation being accorded in your Official List for transactions in such of the above securities as have had the *pro rata* contribution of 6d. per cent paid on them, in conformity with the vote passed at our Annual Meeting in July last.

A dozen copies of this memorial were sent to the Amsterdam Exchange in December 1870, with a request that they be returned with signatures added by Dutch bondholders.[339]

Even though, according to the Committee, the memorial was "numerously signed," the Stock Exchange refused the request for a separate quotation and few bondholders paid the 6d. levy.[340] As a result, the Committee complained, it lacked the financial resources to pursue its actions against the Mexican Railway Company which in October 1870 had announced its intention to redeem some of its mortgage bonds. A "valuable opportunity" to bring a test case regarding "the right of the Railway Company to receive and retain revenues hypothecated to you" was thus lost.[341]

The Committee continued to function independently in the early 1870s but it was only able to do so because its members largely met sundry costs out of their own pockets and its employees worked without remuneration. The secretary, Holmes, received no salary after June 1871 and the agent in Mexico, Perry, agreed to continue on the basis that his remuneration depended on a satisfactory settlement of the debt. The voluntary 6d. levy produced only £163 16s. 0d. and all the usual costs of office, post, advertising, "costly telegraphic communications," and travel expenses for Committee members still had to be met.[342]

It is likely that part of the reason for the Committee's decision in 1876 to join the Corporation of Foreign Bondholders was financial. The Corporation's financial situation was much healthier. It had expanded rapidly and had a basic working capital of £100,000, provided by 1,000 members each subscribing £100. In contrast, the Sheridan Committee had several outstanding liabilities. The secretary, Holmes, had still not been paid and it was agreed in March 1876 that the £300 a year he was owed since 1871 should be met from the first available assets arising from a settlement of the debt.[343] Holmes was not the only one owed money. The Sheridan Committee's office was at 35 Finsbury Circus and its landlord was the Tolucca Mining Company Ltd. On 22 March 1876, aware that the Committee was about to vacate the premises to join up with the Corporation, the company wrote to Sheridan to remind him of the rental agreement. Under its terms, his Committee was to contribute £25 per annum toward the rental of the building and £5 toward office expenses. Nothing had been paid since June 1871 and the total owed on the two accounts, respectively £118 15s. 0d. and £23 15s. 0d., was £142 10s. 0d.[344]

The Sheridan Committee's liabilities were discussed with the Corporation's secretary, Hyde Clarke. Several items were found; the rent and office expenses debt of £142 10s. 0d. plus £34 6s. 2d. for advertising and telegrams; Holmes' unpaid salary; Perry's unpaid salary; not less than £500 and not more than £3,000 promised to the Mexican agent, Cervantes, if a settlement was reached; and "a somewhat larger arrangement with another Mexican" who was not named. Clarke refused to accept liability for the rental and office expenses debt, arguing that it should be met out of the agreed, but unpaid, levy on the bondholders. He did promise, however, to pay the money owed for advertising and it was also agreed that the Corporation would pay Holmes £100 a year "as a retaining fee."[345]

After 1876, therefore, the cost of representing the Mexican bondholders in their campaigns and negotiations with diverse Mexican representatives was met by the Corporation of Foreign Bondholders. Although we have no details, such costs as printing and advertising were presumably paid immediately to the suppliers. Similarly, travel expenses may also have been advanced to Dudley Sheridan for his mission to Mexico and to Holmes and others who went to France in pursuit of Rivas. The bills, however, were not forgotten and in the negotiations over the debt which took place with Mexican representatives more or less continuously after 1876, one item was always how the accumulated expenses of both the Committee and the Corporation were to be paid off. The method adopted was to allocate a proportion of the new bond issue to expenses. Clause 14 of the 1883 Rivas agreement, for example, included a commitment by the Mexican government to allocate bonds "for the payment of the remuneration and expenses of the Committee since its formation, and to defray also the remuneration and expenses of its agent, the late Mr. Perry, and the expenses of the negotiation of the conversion." When the agreement collapsed, several newspapers accused the Committee of having demanded excessive commissions and expenses. Notwithstanding such comment, a similar clause was inserted in the Noetzlin agreement and it again attracted criticism. Perhaps in the light of such hostile reaction, the successful Mena agreement was more circumspect and careful in its language. Article 11 covered the payment of expenses "strictly required" and limited the sum to £200,000 in bonds at par values. Again, details are lacking and we do not know how much was eventually paid to Sheridan and his colleagues to cover their Committee and personal expenses. Nor do we know if Holmes received his back pay. Finally, as noted previously, Francis Perry, brother of the deceased agent Edward Perry, asked the Stock Exchange not to sanction the new 1886 Three per Cents until the £5,000 owed to his brother had been paid with £15,000 worth of bonds.[346] Whether that debt was ever paid also remains unknown.

NOTES

1. W. Morgan to J.M. Mendoza, 11 March 1853, SRE, 40.11.6.

2. The phrase "Upper Ten Thousand" seems to have been coined by the American writer, N.P. Willis (1806–1867) and to have been in common use by the 1860s. See A. Trollope, *Can You Forgive Her?* edited by Stephen Wall, Penguin Classics, reprint 1987, p. 831, note 1.

3. CMB *Report* (February 1850), p. 4.

4. CMB *Report* (January 1853), p. 15.

5. The CMB Minute book is in the Guildhall Library, 15.795.

6. See DNB entry and A. Brett-James, ed., *General Wilson's Journal, 1812–1814* (London, 1964).

7. For the location of Wilson's various papers, see U.K. National Register of Archives.

8. *The Bristol Mercury*, 7 March 1825; R.B. Mosse, *The Parliamentary Guide: A Concise History of the Members of Both Houses of Parliament to March 26, 1836* (London, 1836), p. 205. Later in his career, Robinson had other business partners including John Bingley Garland, Thomas Holdsworth Brooking, and his son, George Thomas Brooking.

9. D.E.W. Gibbs, *Lloyd's of London* (London, 1957), pp. 102, 365. See also M. Stanton, ed., *Who's Who of British Members of Parliament: A Biographical Dictionary*, vol. 1 (1832–1885) (Sussex, 1976), p. 330.

10. See report of the bondholders' meeting in *The Morning Herald*, 19 May 1846.

11. The papers concerning the disputed will are in PRO, Prob. 37/618.

12. The Goldsmid and Capel records are in the Guildhall Library.

13. M.C. Reed, *A History of James Capel & Co.* (Bristol 1975), p. 20.

14. Details of Robertson's assets are from the manuscript copy of his will which is in the Scottish Record Office, Edinburgh, SC60/41/25, fols. 144–174. The quotation is from f. 164. There is also a slightly abbreviated printed version in the family papers preserved at Ladykirk.

15. Comment on draft letter in PRO, F.O. 97/275, fol. 239.

16. CMB *Report* (April 1861), pp. 113–223. Some of Robertson's subsequent correspondence is in CMB *Report* (January 1862), pp. 171–192.

17. D. Robertson to Ld. Wodehouse, 16 December 1860, Kimberley Papers, Ms. Eng C, 4006, fols. 23–24.

18. Among his other claims to fame, Robertson provided a Tweed Water Spaniel which was mated in 1868 with a yellow retriever, thus producing the Golden Retriever.

19. The archivist at Coutts informed the author that there are none of Robertson's papers in the Bank's records.

20. See the entry in S.A. Allibone, *A Critical Dictionary of English Literature and British and American Authors* (London, 1859–1871), vol. 2, n.p.n.

21. J. Foster, *Men at the Bar: A Biographical Handlist of the Members of the Various Inns of Court, Including Her Majesty's Judges* (London, 1885), p. 423.

22. *Who's Who of Parliament*, vol. 1, p. 326.

23. CSAB *Proceedings* (1850), p. 105.

24. Ibid., p. 111.

25. SRE., 40.11.7.

26. A full list of the *Reports* is given in the List of Sources.

27. This 1846 report has no printer or date. It is entitled *MEXICAN DEBT. Copy of Proceedings at the Meeting of Mexican Bondholders, held at the London Tavern, on the 4th June, 1846. Report of the Committee.* It is in the Proudfoot Papers, Kendal Record Office, WD/MM/175. These papers have not been indexed. For more information on them, see Chapter 5 of this work.

28. See *The Bullionist, The Standard, The Times, Hour*, all 5 April 1876, and *Investors' Guardian*, 8 April 1876.

29. Stock Exchange/Quotations, Ms. 18000, 13B 240.

30. Dawson, *The First Latin American Debt Crisis*, pp. 173, 213.

31. *The Times*, 8 February 1828.

32. M.P. Costeloe, *Response to Revolution. Imperial Spain and the Spanish American Revolutions, 1810–1840* (Cambridge, 1986), pp. 96–100.

33. C. O'Gorman to J. Bidwell, 25 January 1828, PRO, F.O. 50/46, f. 74.

34. See reports in *The Morning Chronicle, The Morning Herald, The Times*, all 2 May 1828.

35. Correspondence in PRO, F.O. 50/51, fols. 9–15.

36. *The Times*, 21 July 1828,

37. Cited in Casasús, *Historia de la deuda*, pp. 118–120; Turlington, *Mexico and Her Foreign Creditors*, p. 54, n. 2.

38. Casasús, *Historia de la deuda*, p. 121.

39. *The Times*, 6 July 1829.

40. Ibid., 1 August 1829.

41. The translated text of Alamán's letter is in CMB *Proceedings* (May 1830), pp. 1–9.

42. Barings Archive, H.C. 4.5.8., no. 76.

43. E. Gorostiza to L. Alamán, 20 May 1830, SRE, 3.11.4703.

44. Barings to L. Alamán, 20 May 1830, idem.

45. *The Times*, 6, 7 May 1830.

46. Marshall's holdings of Mexican bonds are discussed in Chapter 5.

47. W.G. Rimmer, *Marshalls of Leeds. Flax-spinners, 1788–1886* (Cambridge, 1960), pp. 92–96.

48. CMB *Proceedings* (May 1830), p. 13.

49. Ibid., p. 12.

50. Ibid., p. 24.

51. Dawson, *The First Latin American Debt Crisis*, p. 124.

52. E. Gorostiza to L. Alamán, 21 June 1830, SRE, 3.11.4703.

53. Dawson, *The First Latin American Debt Crisis*, p. 26.

54. C. Richardson, *Mr. John Diston Powles, or the Antecedents as a Promoter and Director of Foreign Mining Companies, or as an Administrative Reformer* (London, 1855).

55. CMB *Proceedings* (May 1830).

56. CMB *Report* (July 1831). Details of Wilson's correspondence are from this report.

57. E. Gorostiza to L. Alamán, 21 July 1831, SRE, 3.11.4704.

58. See A. Baring's letter in *The Times*, 20 January 1831. This letter was in reply to an earlier one by H. Hunt (*The Times*, 17 January 1831) who accused Baring of buying up all the tallow in London with the intention of raising the price of soap.

59. E. Gorostiza to L. Alamán, 21 July 1831, SRE, 3.11.4704.

60. *The Times*, 26 March 1832.

61. Ibid., 20 June 1832.

62. Ibid., 23 April 1833.

63. Ibid., 21 May 1833.

64. R.T. Wilson to E. Gorostiza, 3 May 1833, SRE, 3.11.4706.

65. Correspondence in ibid.

66. *The Times*, 3 May 1834.

67. R.T. Wilson to J.J. del Garay, 14 June 1834, PRO, F.O. 50/89, f. 107. The letter is addressed to Garay as Foreign Minister although he had in fact been Finance Minister.

68. *The Times*, 23 January 1835.

69. Ibid., 22 August 1835.

70. Ibid., 8 December 1835.

71. Wilson's letters are in PRO, F.O. 50/103, fols. 101, 102–4, 114–15.

72. *The Times*, 27 February 1836.

73. Correspondence in PRO, F.O. 50/103, fols. 45–48, 57–59, 61–66. Rodríguez refers to an English bondholder, Joel Warrington, writing to Rocafuerte in 1828: J. Rodríguez O, "Mexico's First Foreign Loans," p. 233, n. 46. I was unable to find the letter in the SRE at the location cited by Rodríguez.

74. Correspondence in SRE, 3.11.4708.

75. *The Times*, 26 September 1834.

76. The meeting was reported in all the London newspapers. The fullest report was in *The Morning Chronicle*, 29 June 1836.

77. The text of all the resolutions is in CSAB, *Proceedings* (1850), pp. 106–108.

78. Wyllie published a pamphlet on the loans in the form of an open letter to G.R. Robinson: *To G.R. Robinson, Esq. Chairman of the Committee of Spanish American Bondholders*. The Rougement firm consisted of two brothers, George and Francis Frederick. They were declared bankrupt in 1847 and Francis died two years later; see *The Times*, 2, 10 December 1847, 26 January 1848; and D. Morier Evans, *The Commercial Crisis, 1847–1848* (2nd ed., 1849, reprint, Devon, n.d.), Appendix, p. lxxi.

79. The other co-opted members were: W.S. Marshall, E. Chitty, H. Ellis, J.T. Robinson, J. Tasker, S. Samuel, T. Thornton, W.P. Robertson, H. Bland.

80. Correspondence in PRO, F.O. 50/103, fols. 138–39, 163–171.

81. Correspondence in SRE, 3.11.4798.

82. M. Santa María to Minister of Relations, 17 July 1836, ibid.

83. CSAB *Proceedings* (1850).

84. CSAB *Report* (1839).

85. *The Times*, 23 September 1843.

86. CSAB, *Proceedings* (1850), pp. 109–110.

87. G. Robinson to Manning and Mackintosh, 7 April 1848, in Baring Papers, Bancroft Library, folder 1, pp. 8–10.

88. DNB entry for John Parish Robertson: Dawson, *The First Latin American Debt Crisis*, p. 79.

89. Correspondence in PRO, F.O. 50/225, fols. 247, 258–264; 50/227, fols. 205–206; 50/228, fols. 129–133; ARE, 3.11.4720.

90. These details are from letters in *The Times*, 8 March 1849.

91. Details from W.P. Robertson, *The Foreign Debt of Mexico, Being the Report of a Special Mission to That State Undertaken on Behalf of the Bondholders by W. Parish Robertson* (London, 1850). Robertson also published a long account of his experiences in *A Visit to Mexico, by the West India Islands, Yucatan and United States, with Observations and Adventures on the Way* (2 vols.) (London, 1853).

92. Many of Robertson's letters were published in *The Times*. See, for example, the issues of 17 May, 12, 17 July 1849.

93. These details on the cotton licenses are from the CMB *Reports* (June 1850, pp. 7–8; December 1850, pp. 7–8); Robertson, *The Foreign Debt*, pp. 10, 40; CSAB, *Proceedings* (1850), pp. 91–93.

94. Robertson, *The Foreign Debt*, pp. 42–45.

95. Robertson announced the meeting in *The Times*, 15 December 1849; see also the note initialled "E" in PRO, F.O. 50/234, f. 339.

96. *The Times*, 21 December 1849.

97. CSAB, *Proceedings* (1850), pp. 113–114.

98. See the report in *The Times*, 24 January 1850.

99. For more details of Guedalla's life, see *The Jewish Chronicle*, 7 October 1904.

100. The text of all the resolutions is in CMB *Report* (February 1850), pp. 3–5.

101. More information on Richard Thornton is given in Chapter 5.

102. R. Fulford, *Glyn's, 1753–1953. Six Generations in Lombard Street* (London, 1953), pp. 80–84.

103. The correspondence with Facio and Mora is in *The Times*, 2, 6 February 1850.

104. Details from CMB *Report* (February 1850).

105. Correspondence in *The Times*, 1 February 1850.

106. Ibid., 19 February 1850.

107. CMB *Second Report* (April 1850), pp. 3–133. This *Report* is undated but seems to have been released on 9 April; see *The Times*, 10 April 1850.

108. Ibid., pp. 18, 22. For more details on the silver taxes and the Foreign Office, see Chapter 2.

109. Ibid., p. 31.

110. Robertson, *The Foreign Debt*.

111. *The Times*, 10 April 1850.

112. Ibid., 13 April 1850.

113. D. Robertson to Ld. Wodehouse, 16 December 1860, Kimberley F.O. Correspondence, fols. 23–24.

114. Biographical details of McGarel are largely from F. McKillop, *History of*

Larne and East Antrim (Belfast, 2000), pp. 123–125. I am also grateful to Joan Morris, Larne Museum, for help in finding information about McGarel.

115. A.H. Adamson, *Sugar without Slaves: The Political Economy of British Guiana, 1838–1904* (New Haven, Conn., 1972), p. 24.

116. In later years, McGarel's company was apparently named Bosanquet, Curtis & Co.: E.M. Hogg, *Quintin Hogg. A Biography* (London, 1904), p. 49.

117. McGarel, aged 68, married Mary Rosina, a daughter of Sir James Weir Hogg in 1856. Having no children, he left his Irish properties to his brother-in-law, James MacNaughton Hogg. Another beneficiary was Quintin Hogg, also a brother-in-law. As a condition of the bequest, the Hogg family was required to add the McGarel name to their own. The grandson of Quintin Hogg was Quintin McGarel Hogg, better known perhaps as the late Lord Hailsham.

118. D. Robertson, *The "Mexican Bondholders." Letters of Messrs. M'Calmont, Brothers, & Co., and Reply thereto, by David Robertson, Esq., M.P., Honorary Chairman* (London, 1861), p. 15.

119. *Who's Who of Parliament*, vol. 1, p. 339.

120. See obituary in *The Times*, 14 April 1885.

121. CMB *Report* (June 1850).

122. *The Times*, 26 June 1850.

123. For more information on Falconnet and his mission, see my article "The Extraordinary Case of Mr. Falconnet," *Mexican Studies* 15 (1999), pp. 261–289.

124. CMB *Report* (December 1850), p. 6.

125. *The Times*, 2 August 1850.

126. CMB *Report* (December 1850).

127. Ibid., p. 15.

128. Ibid., p. 5.

129. CMB *Report* (January 1853), pp. 14–15.

130. D. Robertson to Ld. Wodehouse, 16 December 1860, Kimberley F.O. Correspondence, fols. 23–24. Full details of the *Reports* are in the List of Sources.

131. PRO, F.O. 50/256, fols. 170–177.

132. F. Falconnet to Barings, 3 July 1852, Barings Archive, 4.5.25.

133. *The Times*, 27 January 1853.

134. *Daily News, The Morning Post*, 27 January 1853.

135. *The Times*, 27 January 1853.

136. F. Falconnet to Barings, 1 September 1854, Barings Archive, 4.5.25.

137. P. Doyle to Barings, 30 May 1853, ibid., 4.5.21.

138. F. Falconnet to Barings, 1 September 1854, ibid., 4.5.25.

139. P. Doyle to Barings, 3 May 1853, ibid., 4.5.21.

140. The resolutions taken at the January 1853 meeting were published separately; see List of Sources.

141. Capel's letter of resignation, dated 3 January 1854, is in CMB *Report* (May 1854), p. 40.

142. Quotations and details from CMB *Report* (April 1861), p. 40.

143. Ibid.

144. Santa Anna's letter was published in *The Times*, 21 April 1854.

145. O.L. Jones, *Santa Anna* (New York, 1968), pp. 127–128.

146. C. McGarel to A. López de Santa Anna, 1 February 1854, CMB *Report* (May 1854), pp. 38–39.

147. CMB *Report* (February 1855), p. 7.

148. CMB *Report* (May 1854), p. 17.

149. C. McGarel to Ld. Clarendon, 20 May 1854, PRO, F.O. 97/273, fols. 385–386.

150. CMB *Report* (February 1855), pp. 18–19.

151. DNB entry.

152. CMB *Report* (February 1855), pp. 11–12.

153. Ibid., p. 8.

154. For example, *The Morning Chronicle*, 27 February 1855.

155. *The Morning Herald*, 27 February 1855.

156. CMB *Report* (October 1855), pp. 1–2.

157. CMB *Report* (August 1856), p. 6.

158. CMB *Report* (October 1855), pp. 1–2.

159. CMB *Report* (August 1856), pp. 11–12.

160. Ibid., p. 11.

161. CMB *Report* (August 1856), p. 3.

162. The meeting was reported in *The Times*, 29 May 1858. The resolutions were published separately.

163. *Mexican National Debt, contracted in London. Decrees and regulations since the adjustment of October 14th/December 23rd 1850* (London, 1860).

164. D. Robertson to L.C. Otway, 28 May 1859, in CMB *Report* (April 1861), p. 172.

165. D. Robertson to Ld. Wodehouse, 17 March 1861, ibid., pp. 196–199.

166. D. Robertson to C. Lettsom, 30 March 1858, ibid., p. 137.

167. CMB *Report* (January 1862), pp. 18–19.

168. Kimberley F.O. Correspondence, fols. 11–14.

169. CMB *Report* (April 1861), p. 13.

170. Ibid., p. 25.

171. CMB *Report* (January 1862), p. 19.

172. Turlington, *Mexico and Her Foreign Creditors*, pp. 106–112.

173. D. Robertson to E. Hammond, 27 February 1857, in CMB *Report* (April 1861), pp. 113–114.

174. D. Robertson to Ld. Clarendon, 9 March 1857, ibid., pp. 114–115.

175. D. Robertson to J. Buchanan, 11 March 1857, ibid., pp. 115–119.

176. D. Robertson to S. Houston, 3 June 1858, ibid., pp. 147–150.

177. Ibid., pp. 125–127.

178. D. Robertson to Ld. Malmesbury, 21 February 1859, ibid., pp. 167–169.

179. CMB *Report* (January 1862), p. 189.

180. Turlington, *Mexico and Her Foreign Creditors*, pp. 136–143.

181. Barings Archive, H.C. 4.5.31–33.

182. G. Robinson to Ld. Aberdeen, 22 March 1842, PRO, F.O. 50/158, f. 60.

183. CMB *Report* (January 1853), pp. 13–14.

184. CMB *Report* (April 1861), p. 47; PRO, F.O. 97/275, f. 232.

185. CMB *Report* (April 1861), pp. 44–47.

186. CMB *Report* (February 1862), p. 19.

187. Full details of Garde's publications are in the List of Sources.

188. D. Robertson to J.H. Carnegie, 27 January 1861; J.J. Carnegie to Ld. Rus-

sell, 7 February 1861, in CMB *Report* (April 1861), pp. 190–193. The original of Carnegie's letter to the Foreign Office is in PRO, F.O. 97/280, fols. 7–9.

189. CMB *Report* (April 1861), p. 154.

190. Ibid., p. 153.

191. C. Whitehead to G. Matthew, 29 March 1861, SRE, L.E. 1234, fols. 339–341.

192. *The Times*, 2 September 1858.

193. The various documents concerning the transfer to Barings are in its archive at 204326 and AC 28.

194. The agreement was published in CMB *Report* (February 1862), pp. 24–26.

195. *The Times*, 18 January 1862.

196. CMB *Report* (February 1862), p. 17.

197. Ibid., pp. 16–19.

198. C. McGarel to Ld. Russell, 29 January 1862, PRO, F.O. 97/280, fols. 306–307.

199. These accounts are in Barings Archive, AC 28.

200. Ibid.

201. See, for example, *The Times*, 1 August 1864.

202. There is a list of Deferred bondholders in PRO, F.O. 50/249, f. 135.

203. PRO, F.O. 97/280, fols. 328–331.

204. Ibid., fols. 314–315.

205. Glyn Mills & Co. to James Capel, 11 April 1864, PRO, F.O. 97/281, fols. 117–118, 181–182.

206. For a copy of the report, see *The Money Market Review*, 28 May 1864.

207. *The Times*, 20 May 1864.

208. Ibid., 28 February 1866.

209. J. Gerstenberg to Editor, ibid., 23 October 1865.

210. Correspondence in PRO, F.O. 97/281, fols. 81–83, 103–104.

211. Correspondence in *The Times*, 24 November 1865.

212. For a report of the the the meeting, see *The Daily Telegraph*, 29 November 1865. See also the correspondence in PRO, F.O. 97/281, fols. 163–167.

213. *Second Annual General Report of the Council of the Corporation of Foreign Bondholders, for the Year 1874* (London, 1875), p. 45. Henceforth, the reports of the Corporation of Foreign Bondholders will be referred to as CFB *Report*.

214. I. Gerstenberg to President of Bourse, 22 March 1865, Stock Exchange Archive, Amsterdam 40, f. 4.

215. I. Gerstenberg to Sr. Hidalgo, 25 May 1865, ibid., 40, f. 11.

216. Ibid., 40, f. 25.

217. Ortiz de Montellano, *Apuntes*, pp. 227–263, has a section on the Dutch claims.

218. John Hutchins, *The History and Antiquities of the County of Dorset* (3rd. ed. Reprint, Wakefield, W. Yorkshire, 1973), p. 385.

219. *The Times*, 8 February 1868.

220. PRO, F.O. 97/281, fols.142–143.

221. Correspondence in Provisional CMB *Report* (March 1868), pp. 5–16.

222. There were two Stern brothers in London, David and Herman. Both had Portuguese viscountcies and were very prominent financiers—both were millionaires—but it is not clear which was involved with the Mexican bondholders; see

Chapman, *The Rise of Merchant Banking*, p. 45; W.D. Rubinstein, *Men of Property* (London, 1981), p. 93; and by the same author, "British Millionaires, 1809–1949," *Bulletin of the Institute of Historical Research* 47 (1974), pp. 202–223.

223. The court case was fully reported in *The Times*, 11 September, 8 December 1868.

224. Baring Brothers to Irving & Slade, 1 April 1867, Provisional CMB *Report* (March 1868), p. 11.

225. H.B. Sheridan to Baring Brothers, 20 February 1868, ibid., p. 23.

226. Ibid., p. 24.

227. CMB *Report* (March 1868), p. 18.

228. Ibid., pp. 18–20.

229. The signed memorial is in PRO, F.O. 97/282, fols. 27–29.

230. These details are from W. Holmes to Lord Stanley, 30 March 1868, ibid., fol. 19, and from the report of the meeting printed subsequently as *Report of the Proceedings of a Public Meeting of Mexican Bondholders, held at the London Tavern, 27th March, 1868* (London 1868). The only copy I found is in the Amsterdam Stock Exchange Archive, 40/23, where it was sent "With Messrs Irving & Slade's compliments, 26/5/68."

231. Report of public meeting held on 10 June 1869, in *The Bullionist*, 12 June 1869.

232. CMB *Report* (May 1869), p. 3.

233. CMB *Report* (March 1876), p. 20.

234. M. Romero to E. Perry, 20 February 1869, in CMB *Report* (May 1869), pp. 38–39.

235. Much of the Committee's correspondence of this time with Mexican Ministers is in AGN, Deuda Exterior, vol. 6 (volumes located in Galería 6). The same volume contains E.J. Perry's *Petición que hace el representante de los tenedores de bonos mexicanos en Londres al Congreso de la Unión* (Mexico, 1869).

236. CMB *Report* (July 1870), p. 9.

237. Ibid., p. 29.

238. Ibid., p. 30.

239. Ibid., pp. 11–12. For further details of Rosecrans' involvement, see Turlington, *Mexico and Her Foreign Creditors*, pp. 181–184.

240. *The Times*, 16 June 1870.

241. For a report of the Guedalla meeting, see ibid., 23 June 1870. A letter from the Committee correcting various statements is in the issue of 27 June 1870.

242. Guedalla's letter is dated 11 July 1870. There is a manuscript copy in the Corporation of Foreign Bondholders' Newspaper Archive, vol. 1, fol. 11.

243. CMB *Report* (July 1870), pp. 14, 15, 17.

244. For reports of the meeting, see *The Daily News*, 13 July 1870; *The Times*, 14 July 1870; *The Morning Post*, 13 July 1870. The F. de Lizardi present at the meeting was probably the son of the Lizardi firm's founder, Francisco.

245. Ortiz de Montellano, *Apuntes*, p. 233.

246. The text of Sheridan's "Notice" is in CMB *Report* (March 1876), pp. 23–24.

247. Ibid., p. 7.

248. Ibid., p. 8. The London Stock Exchange Archive, Quotations 18000, 1095 22A has the original ms. protest.

249. Amsterdam Stock Exchange Archive, 40/39; Ortiz de Montellano, *Apuntes*, p. 233; CMB *Report* (March 1876), pp. 25–26.

250. W. Holmes to S. Lerdo de Tejada, 30 November 1873, in CMB *Report* (March 1876), pp. 34–35.

251. The telegram and correspondence are in Amsterdam Stock Exchange Archive, 40/44.

252. Hyde Clarke to President of Bourse, 15 March 1874, ibid., 40/49.

253. Ibid.

254. Stock Exchange Archive, Committee for General Purposes. Minutes; meeting of 22 June 1874, Guildhall Library, Ms. 14,600.38, p. 294. The memorandum was published in *The Times*, 3 June 1874.

255. The Dutch memorandum is in Amsterdam Stock Exchange Archive, 40/59.

256. For a shareholder's protest, see *The Foreign Times*, 13 June 1874.

257. *The Financier*, 11, 26 May 1874.

258. CFB *Report* (1875), p. 44.

259. CMB Minute Book, Guildhall Library, 15.795. The first meeting recorded in the Minute Book was on 16 July 1874.

260. CMB *Report* (March 1876), pp. 16–17.

261. Ibid., p. 19.

262. Ibid., pp. 20–21.

263. *The Financier*, 19 January 1876.

264. Ibid., 14 February 1876.

265. Ibid., 26 January 1876.

266. Ibid., 25 February 1876.

267. For reports on the meeting, see *The Hour*, 5 April 1876; *The Times*, 5 April 1876; *Investors' Guardian*, 8 April 1876; *The Bullionist*, 8 April 1876.

268. *The Times*, 12 November 1868.

269. Ibid., 3 February 1869.

270. The first office was at 18 Palmerston Buildings.

271. CFB *Report* (1876), p. 26; CMB Minute Book, meeting of 23 July 1874.

272. CMB Minute Book, meetings of 8, 22 March 1876.

273. Chapman, *The Rise of Merchant Banking*, p. 77.

274. *Letter of the Chairman of the Committee of Holders of Mexican Bonds to the Bondholders* (London, July 1879).

275. *The Statist*, 20 November 1880.

276. *The Financier*, 12 June 1879, 20 April 1880.

277. Ibid., 6 March 1877.

278. Ibid., 10 April 1878.

279. Ibid., 23 August 1877, 18 March 1878.

280. Ibid., 12 October 1877.

281. Ibid., 28 June 1877; *The Bullionist*, 9 December 1882.

282. *The Financier*, 4 January 1881.

283. *Paris Bourse*, 28 August 1883.

284. *The Bullionist*, 20 January, 2 March, 17 November 1883.

285. The original signed memorial is in Barings Archive, 201814.

286. The letter was published in *The Daily Chronicle*, 20 November 1883.

287. *Report of the Committee of Mexican Bondholders on the state of the negotiations with the Special Envoy of the President of the Republic of Mexico, for*

carrying out the Agreement made with him, and approved by the Bondholders, on the 12th May, 1883 (London, 22 November 1883).

288. All quotations from newspapers of 23 November 1883, except *The Bullionist*, 24 November 1883.

289. W. Holmes to Editor, *The Standard*, 23 November 1883.

290. CMB Minute Book, 7 December 1880, ? February 1882.

291. Ibid., 20 April 1881.

292. Ibid., 6 June 1882.

293. Ibid., 16 November 1882.

294. CMB Minute Book, 24 January 1879.

295. *Letter of the Chairman*, pp. 6, 8.

296. *The Financier*, 4 January 1881.

297. Ibid.

298. *The Money Market Review*, 24 September 1881.

299. The prospectus is in *The Times*, 4 July 1882.

300. CMB Minute Book, 4 July 1882.

301. Ibid., 10 July 1882.

302. CFB *Report* (1883) p. 52.

303. CMB Minute Book, 14 December 1882.

304. Stock Exchange Archive, Committee for General Purposes Minute Book, Guildhall Library, Ms. 14,600.49, pp. 65–66.

305. CMB *Report* (May 1883), p. 13.

306. There is a copy of Bishop's account of the debt in the Newspaper Cuttings File of the Corporation of Foreign Bondholders, vol.6, pp. 140–148.

307. *The Bullionist*, 16 June 1883.

308. *The Times*, 17 July 1883.

309. CMB *Report* (November 1883), p. 22.

310. Ibid.

311. Ibid.

312. *Mexican Bondholders' Committee. Reprint of an article in the Mexican "Diario Oficial," of the 29th November, 1883; also the "Project of a Contract", as proposed by the Department of the Treasury, "For a settlement of the Debt contracted in London" and an extract from the Letter of the Committee to "The Times" published 12 December 1883* (London,1884).

313. Ibid.

314. CFB *Report* (1885), p. 83.

315. There is a copy in *The Times*, 19 September 1884.

316. W.J. Reader, *A House in the City*, p. 105.

317. Reports of the meeting in *The Times*, 25 September 1884; *The Bullionist*, 27 September 1884; *Herepath's Journal*, 27 September 1884.

318. See reports in *The Morning Post*, 22 November 1884; *The Daily News*, 24 November 1884; *Statist*, 13 December 1884.

319. *United States of Mexico. Law for the Consolidation and Conversion of the National Debt. 22nd June, 1885* (London, 1885).

320. *The Times*, 20, 27 August, 1 September 1885.

321. Ibid., 8 September 1885; *The Standard*, 8 September 1885.

322. W.H. Bishop to Editor, *The Times*, 11 September 1885.

323. *The Times*, 10 September 1885.

324. *The Daily News*, 10 September 1885; *The Bullionist*, 12 September 1885; *The Money Market Review*, 12 September 1885.

325. CFB *Report* (1886), p. 104.

326. He finally presented his credentials to Queen Victoria on 13 May 1887; D. Hidalgo, ed., *Representantes de México en Gran Bretaña (1822–1980)* (Mexico, 1981), p. 64.

327. Letter addressed to Emilio Velasco, AGN, Galería 6, Deuda Exterior, vol. 9, fols. 81–97.

328. Amsterdam Stock Exchange Archive, 40/109.

329. CSAB *Report* (1839), p. 52.

330. See the report in *The Morning Chronicle*, 29 June 1836.

331. CSAB *Report* (1839), p. 51.

332. CMB *Report* (February 1850), pp. 3–4.

333. CMB *Report* (December 1850), Appendix 1.

334. Ibid., p. 6.

335. *Resolutions. At a General Meeting of Mexican Bondholders at the London Tavern, on the 15th May, 1854* (London, 1854), no. III; *Report of Proceedings at a General Meeting of Mexican Bondholders, held at the London Tavern, on the 16th October, 1855* (no printer, place, or date), p. 2.

336. Details from CMB *Report* (1852), appendices 3 and 4.

337. The accounts are in Barings Archive, AC 28.

338. CMB *Report* (1869), p. 21.

339. Amsterdam Stock Exchange Archive, 40/37a.

340. CMB *Report* (1876), p. 7.

341. CMB *Report* (1876), p. 7.

342. Ibid., p. 21.

343. CMB Minute Book, meeting of 22 March 1876.

344. Ibid., meeting of 29 March 1876.

345. Ibid., meeting of 28 July 1876.

346. Stock Exchange Quotations, Ms. 18000, 13B 240.

Chapter 5

The Investors

That long suffering and patient tribe, the holders of Mexican bonds.[1]

Why did British investors put their money into Mexican bonds? Were they all rich, affluent people who could well afford to take a risk with their capital or were they from low- and middle-income groups with some small savings, perhaps accumulated over a career in the armed services or the Church? What other social and economic groups were represented? Were there many landowners and aristocrats or were they largely drawn from mercantile, banking, and commercial circles? To what extent were they metropolitan-based, reflecting a concentration of wealth, information, and expertise in the city of London? Or did the spread of bondholders extend to the regions and towns across the whole of Britain? How many were speculators, skilled at playing the market in search of quick profits? Were there many small investors, looking for and even dependent on a secure, long-term income? Did many European investors buy Mexican bonds in the London market? In short, who were the bondholders?

It is with these and related questions that we are concerned in this chapter. Identifying individual bondholders and their private investments, however, poses a number of problems. In the first place, as indicated previously, all of Mexico's securities were in the form of Bearer bonds, similar to a banknote, payable to the Bearer, rather than to a named owner. There are, therefore, no lists of owners maintained, for example, by the Stock Exchange, and although the Corporation of Foreign Bondholders apparently hoped to compile a Register, the invitation to bondholders to enter their names and holdings was met with almost no response.[2] Similarly, the bonds, certificates, dividend coupons, and all the diverse documents issued by the Mexican government over the course of the nineteenth century were negotiable securities, which could be, and were, bought and sold in the market at any time. Hence, to some extent their owners were transient, although it was also the case that some retained their bonds for thirty years or more, always hoping that Mexico would honor its promises to them. Finally, over the sixty-two years between the first bond sale of 1824 and the Dublán conversion of 1886, the bondholders obviously changed as one generation followed another. No definite example has been found of a bondholder acquiring his bonds in 1824 and still retaining them in 1886, and it seems unlikely that any did so, although in at least one instance, Admiral Wallis, the possibility exists. Again, however, some qualification is needed in that in some cases, for example, Reverend Carnegie of Cranborne, bonds were inherited, thus remaining in the same family over a long period. Another difficulty is that, although in many cases the value of the holdings of individual bondholders has been ascertained, in others it has not proved possible to find the information. A selection of bondholders' wills has been perused in search of it, but it was not the practice in England to include itemized lists of effects. Hence, in those wills proved in the English courts, reference was certainly made to the testator's "foreign stocks" but no details were given. In contrast, in Scotland, a detailed inventory was attached to the will with the result that we can discover, for example, exactly how many foreign bonds David Robertson bequeathed to his heirs. Finally, except in rare cases where the bondholder reveals it, there is no practical way of knowing how much he paid for his bonds.[3]

Notwithstanding such problems, it has proved possible to identify a large number of bondholders. Various sources have enabled this to be done. The Committee of Mexican Bondholders provides the names of more than eighty of the foremost bondholders who served on it during the period from 1830 to 1886. The Committee's printed *Reports* reveal the names of others who contributed to its activities. The many public meetings, invariably reported at length in the newspapers, are equally informative because the press accounts usually give the names of the speakers who participated in the debates. Similarly, the newspapers, especially at times of debt conversions or negotiations, attracted many letters from often irate bondholders. Usually, these carry only a pseudonym such as "Disillusioned Mexican Bondholder," but in some instances, the author included his name. One notable example was Henry Guedalla, who always signed his dozens of letters to the daily newspapers and to *The Jewish Chronicle* either with his full name or simply HG, leaving no doubt as to the author. Another good source is the archive of Mexico's London Legation. Bondholders, anxious for information, or to express their anger at the failure to pay them their dividends, wrote to Mexico's diplomatic representatatives. Some of their letters have survived. Similarly, the British Foreign Office records contain letters from individual bondholders pressing their case for support. There are also several petitions or memorials signed by bondholders. In one case, there are over 100 signatures of men and women who held in excess of £1,000,000 worth of bonds between them. In another, the holders, or their representatives, of the 1837 Lizardi Deferred are named. These diverse sources have enabled a reasonably broad gallery of bondholders to be assembled, but before turning to them, some of the reasons why they chose to put their money into Mexican bonds may be considered.

The 1851 Census records that there were in Britain 144,254 "annuitants," of whom 23,032 were women and 121,222 were men. Included in such statistics were those people who were wholly or partly dependent for their incomes on the "Funds." These consisted of a variety of British government securities, the most famous of which were the Three per Cent Consolidated Bank Annuities originally formed in 1751. Nicely described as "the majestic 'Consols' of Victorian England, they provided an exceptionally safe home for the long-term investor throughout the nineteenth century, paying a regular and secure annual return.[4] There were some large individual and institutional investors in all the annuities, but analysis of the dividends payable on the Consols reveals that they were the favored choice of those of "slender means who had to be careful where they put their money."[5] The figures are clear: 81% of the dividends payable on the Consols in 1852 were for sums of up to £50 and almost 50% were for up to £10.[6] There seems no doubt that many of the investors were the widows, retired officers, country parsons, and what Martineau describes as "the aged ladies and retired servants" of the nation who put their small savings in what they correctly saw as a secure investment.[7]

The "Funds," therefore, provided the principal investment for the middle and upper classes of Britain, but in the first quarter of the nineteenth century, economic and fiscal circumstances changed. Following the end of decades of war with the conclusion of the Napoleonic era at Waterloo in 1815, the borrowing requirement of the British government was reduced. As a result, dividend rates on its securities began to fall. In 1822, for example, the "Navy Five per Cents" were reduced to 4%. The great majority of the estimated 200,000 holders of these "Navy Fives," as they were called, chose to accept the new "Four per Cents," but some preferred to take cash. The Bank of England's report on the operation reveals that £2,604,055 was returned to investors, at least some of whom must have begun to look around for a better return on their capital.[8] Two years later, the 1789 "Four per Cents" were exchanged for 3½% stock. Above all, while the nominal rate remained unchanged, the real yield on the Three per Cent Consols declined from 5% in 1816 to 3.3% in 1824.[9] Although the return improved marginally in future years, it never rose above 3.8% for the rest of the nineteenth century. The trend was clearly downwards, provoking the contemporary saying that "John Bull can stand many things but he cannot stand 2 per cent."[10]

In an age when £10 or £12 per annum was enough to pay the wages of a domestic servant, a cut in the rate of return from 5% to 3% on even relatively small investments of the sort evident in the Consols could mean the difference between middle-class comfort and genteel poverty. Small-scale investors with perhaps a few hundred pounds or even a couple of thousand to invest were almost obliged to look for alternatives to the "Funds." As the Member of Parliament for Lymington, Mr. William Manning, remarked in a parliamentary debate on the Bank of England's interest rate policy, "to lower the rate of interest was to force British capital into foreign funds."[11] Two main, and seemingly very attractive, options were available. The first was a relatively new type of government bond. At the same time that the British government's need for money declined, the demands of other nations increased and the age of foreign loans began. Governments the length and breadth of Europe required loans and they came to London to raise them. They did so because one consequence of the twenty and more years of war preceding Waterloo was the consolidation of London as Europe's financial capital. The French occupation of German cities, the invasion of Holland, and religious persecution in the Ottoman empire accelerated a trend already evident whereby European merchants and bankers migrated to London, bringing with them their capital and their expertise in the business of foreign loans. The celebrated examples of the Rothschilds and Barings are well known but there were numerous other similar instances of the arrival in London of what Professor Chapman describes as "the new wave of international trading families."[12]

Britain's own industrial development was also generating large capital sums surplus to the requirements of the domestic economy and as one newspaper put it, there was a "redundant accumulation of wealth."[13] There are two good individual instances of the phenomenon among the Mexican bondholders. John Marshall, the Committee of Mexican Bondholders' first chairman, having built his Leeds textile business into a highly profitable concern during the war years, found that he had more money than he could profitably reinvest in his mills. Beginning in 1813, he chose to place "his spare resources" in the "Funds" and with the success of those investments by timely buying and selling, he was soon looking at foreign bonds. By the early 1820s, his interest from securities brought him almost as much income as his textile business, and ten years later, "he earned nearly twice as much from funds."[14] (Details of his Mexican holdings are given below.) Richard Thornton (1776–1865) is another good example. Like Marshall, he was born in the north at Burton-in-Lonsdale, close to the Yorkshire-Lancashire border. He became one of the Victorian era's wealthiest men, leaving effects valued at almost £3,000,000, much of which, as *The Times* (28 June 1865) noted in its report of his demise, "comprises very large amounts of foreign stocks." He began his career, and made his first fortune, as a merchant in the Baltic trade, making secret and highly dangerous journeys to Russia during the French blockade to buy hemp for the Royal Navy. He acquired his own fleet of ships and as a member of Lloyd's since 1798, he became the largest underwriter of marine insurance in the world. After the end of the Napoleonic era, he also began to employ his "surplus money" in foreign loans. At one time, he was said to be the personal creditor of the Spanish liberal and constitutional governments for £2,000,000.[15] In the 1840s, he was one of the largest investors in Mexican bonds with holdings of a par value of £50,000. He also had substantial investments in Venezuelan bonds and he was chairman of the Committee of Spanish bondholders.

Britain, therefore, had the banking expertise and the availability of capital which attracted impecunious foreign governments. The many foreign issues offered in the London market in the 1820s and their highly decorative bonds, or the Scrip, could be bought for a 10% deposit with the balance payable in installments over several months. They promised dividends of 5% or even 6% and with the issue price carefully discounted by the contractor, the real yield was significantly higher. There was also, of course, the prospect of a capital gain once the bonds were redeemed at par at the end of the term. Demand was so strong that the Stock Exchange resolved in 1822 that a separate Foreign Exchange should be established for dealings in foreign securities. Public interest was also reflected by *The Times'* decision in December 1825 that its hitherto irregular City or Money Market column should become a daily feature. It was not just the London press that gave extensive publicity to the loans. Local newspapers also gave details of all the new issues, thus ensuring that their readers in the cities and counties across Britain were fully aware of investment opportunities. As will be discussed below, residents from the tiniest of hamlets in rural Somerset to the fashionable spas of Bath and Cheltenham were tempted into the bond market. The interest in foreign bond issues was given even greater stimulus by the emancipation of Spain's empire in America. British participation in the various movements for independence has been well documented. All that needs to be noted here is that there seems to have been sincere public enthusiasm in Britain for the heroic efforts of Bolívar and the other liberators to free their continent from colonial rule. It may also be noted that among many British volunteers who fought alongside Bolívar was Belford Wilson, son of the Committee of Mexican Bondholders' second chairman, Robert Wilson. Six of the new republics, together with Brazil, offered loans in the London market between 1822 and 1825.

Both the professional and the small investor seeking a higher return than that offered in the "Funds" had a wide variety of foreign securities on offer but they also had another alternative. The early 1820s witnessed what was recognized at the time as an extraordinary mania for speculation in companies the like of which had not been seen since the South Sea Bubble. During 1824 and the early months of 1825, no less than 624 company prospectuses were issued, inviting investment in their shares of a total capital of £372,000,000.[16] "Bubble schemes," to quote *The Times* again, "came out in shoals like herring from the Polar seas."[17] Projects ranged from the fantastic to the fraudulent but initial respectability was easily achieved by the use of guinea pig or decoy directors, including Members of Parliament, willing to lend their names in return for a handsome fee or heavily discounted shares. The Peruvian Mining and Trading Association, for example, was formed in March 1825 and among its ten directors were a Member of Parliament, a Lord, and an Admiral of the Royal Navy. No lesser personages than the Dukes of York and Wellington lent their names as patrons of the American Colonial Steam Navigation Company.[18] With such notables prominently displayed on the prospectuses, subscribers were even found for one company formed to drain the Red Sea to recover the treasure abandoned by the Egyptians after the crossing of the Jews.[19] There were similar fanciful schemes promoted in the Spanish American republics—the Poyais swindle, in which investors were persuaded by General Sir Gregor MacGregor to finance the colonization of his imaginary Central American country of Poyais, is perhaps the best-known example. Not all the prospective companies were, of course, intentionally fraudulent even though for many there was scant hope of commercial success. To give just a few examples, there was the Colombian Association for Agricultural and other purposes, with a capital of £1,300,000. Its directors included J.D. Powles, I.L. Goldsmid and Robert Wilson, all well-respected figures and future Mexican bondholders; the Honduras Company for the growth of indigo, with £1,000,000 capital fully subscribed; the South American Gem Company, at £10 a share. Even more popular were the mining companies formed to work what was assumed to be the almost unlimited deposits of silver and other precious metals across the entire Spanish American continent. The General South American Mining Association, capitalized at £2,000,000, noted in its prospectus that South America was known "to abound in valuable minerals and contains inexhaustible Resources in Gold, Silver, Quicksilver, Copper and other metals."[20] Similar mining companies or associations were formed for most of the Spanish American republics. Mexico attracted particular attention. Several companies were formed to work its legendary silver mines which for 300 years had financed Spain and her empire. Throughout 1824, *The Gentleman's Magazine* carried articles on the mines of Mexico. "Great public interest," it said, "has been excited of late by the formation of companies in London, whose object is to work the silver mines of Mexico, and who have raised large capitals for that purpose."[21] "The Directors," it added, "have been chosen from among gentlemen of great respectability and influence."

The speculative bubble burst in October 1825, and by the end of 1826, only 127 of the 624 companies that had been formed were still in existence.[22] Before the crash, however, some people had made fortunes. For example, those who bought shares in the company formed to work the famous Real del Monte mines in Mexico, if they sold at the right time, made vast profits. The shares, issued at £400 but payable in small installments, rose to £1,550, only to collapse later to £200. Dr. Philip Mackie, Britain's first informal envoy to Mexico, was one of those who benefited. He was said (in a private letter of 6 July 1825) to have become "so rich by the rise of South American securities of all kinds and particularly of the mine shares that he does not wish to trouble himself further about money matters."[23]

Speculation in the market was, of course, a very risky business and fortunes could be lost as quickly as made. Dr. Mackie, for example, was in the King's Bench Prison for debt in 1827 after losing his gains in further speculations.[24] Investors were warned repeatedly by the newspapers to be careful and not to trust the dealers and brokers who fixed prices. Reporting the first Mexican loan in January 1824, *The Bristol Mirror* (24 January 1824) advised its readers as follows:

It is, we believe, quite unnecessary at this time, to advise caution in dealing with these foreign loans. Those who have not learned circumspection from the fate of the Spanish and Poyais bondholders, will scarcely acquire it from mere verbal admonition.[25]

Faced with declining yields from the Funds and especially the Consols, therefore, existing investors and those seeking to place their perhaps limited capital had two choices if they wanted to improve the return on their money. They could buy shares in the new companies which offered the possibility of spectacular returns as well the risk of the total loss of the investment. Alternatively, they could buy foreign bonds whose nominal dividends were 5% or 6% but on which the real return was significantly higher, depending on the level of the discounted issue price. Given the clear dangers of the former, and despite the fact that "the spirit of the times is essentially a gambling spirit,"[26] we can assume that the more cautious investor opted for the bond market. As we have seen, however, a wide choice was available, not least among the Spanish American republics. Why, therefore, choose Mexican bonds?

Various factors determined the undoubted popularity of the Mexican loans, both of which initially fetched a premium and were heavily oversubscribed. In the first place, Mexico enjoyed the reputation of having the greatest economic potential. It is worth noting that in 1821, the year of its emancipation from colonial status, its population was similar to that of the United States, at about 7 million people, and each country had approximately the same amount of territory. *The Gentleman's Magazine* proclaimed, "No region of the globe has in a higher degree the constituent elements of national greatness than the Mexican states."[27] Long known as the jewel in the Spanish Crown, Britain's commercial and financial community had for years aspired to get access to what was assumed to be Mexico's virtually unlimited natural resources. More than anything else, it was assumed that its minerals, especially silver, had inexhaustible reserves which the benefits of British capital, expertise, and steam power would soon turn into immense wealth. Potential investors were reminded that between 1690 and 1823, the mines had yielded the almost incomprensible sum of £1,940,493,784 6s. 4½d.[28] In addition to its natural resources, the country's strategic location midway between the two great oceans of the world was said to offer it an unrivalled opportunity to benefit from the growth in trade which was certain to follow the liberation of the American continent.

The newspapers of the early 1820s were filled with such predictions of economic progress but the potential investor did not have to rely on the press or on the exaggerated claims of company promoters and loan contractors. The highly respected works of the German scientist Alexander von Humboldt, with their vast compendium of data, were published in London and were discussed in essays in *The Quarterly Review* between 1815 and 1821.[29] In March 1824, just as the Scrip for the first Mexican issue was being circulated, a third edition of his book *Political Essay on the Kingdom of New Spain* was advertised by Longman.[30] Furthermore, almost as soon as the liberator, Agustín de Iturbide, had entered the city of Mexico on 27 September 1821, British entrepreneurs, merchants, and others travelled to the new nation in search of opportunities for trade and investment. Colombia, it was said by one correspondent in 1825, "is greatly thrown in the shade because of interest in Mexico owing to the greater facility of reaching the Capital as well as the greater population and richness of the Country." "We are," he went on, "much better informed as to Mexico than as to Colombia."[31] One of the early travellers was William Bullock, owner of the Egyptian Hall or, as he called it at one point, the London Museum of Natural History. He put on various exhibitions, including one of Napoleon's carriages used at Waterloo, and always in search of new ideas, he spent six months in Mexico from March to August 1823. On his return, he published a book describing his experiences and emphasizing the many commercial opportunities. He also mounted two exhibitions of Mexican artifacts and curiosities in his museum which were well received by the public. *The Times'* reporter, however, was not impressed by the use of an Indian "all alive" whom Bullock had brought with him from Mexico. He was made to stand in a corner of one of the exhibition rooms and the reporter asked, "Is he to be a fixture, like the stuffed birds and fishes [sic]?"[32] Another influential factor was the decision of Barings in 1826 to accept the role of Mexico's Financial Agent in Europe, following the collapse of the two loan contractors, Goldsmidt & Co. and the Barclay partnership. *The Times* (17 September 1827) commented that many people had put their money into Mexican stocks because of "the character which Messrs. Baring gave to it by undertaking the agency." Finally, there was the well-received, two-volume work by Henry George Ward, Britain's Chargé d'Affaires in Mexico who returned to London in 1827, following his successful negotiation of treaties of recognition and commerce. Although his book, *Mexico in 1827*, appeared in 1828, after the first dividend default, his enthusiastic endorsement of the country's potential was still influential. Years later, he was accused of misleading investors with his overoptimistic projections of profits, especially from the mining industry.[33]

There was, therefore, no shortage of very encouraging and positive information about Mexico's prospects. Even the early political difficulties whereby the empire established by Iturbide was overthrown after just ten months did not deter investors. Indeed, again just as the bonds were being marketed, the exiled ex-emperor arrived in Britain where he spent time in Bath, Taunton, and elsewhere. His subsequent return to Mexico, and his execution, were widely reported in both the London and provincial press, but again without any permanent impact on the sale or price of Mexican bonds. The adoption of the republican and federal form of government was welcomed in the British press and it was publicly known that British recognition of Mexico's independence was certain and that trade treaties were being negotiated. Again, it was not just the London or even southern residents who were kept informed. Readers of *The Leeds Mercury*, for example, were told, on 20 March 1824, that the British diplomats who had recently arrived in Mexico were being hailed in every town and village as "the harbingers of liberty and civilization." There was, they were assured, "an enthusiastic feeling in favour of England."[34] As the United States had already extended diplomatic recognition and President Monroe had issued his message warning European powers against any ideas of conquest in that hemisphere, nobody took seriously Spain's threat to reconquer its American empire.

Many of these factors were present when the first Mexican Five per Cents were offered for sale in January 1824. Compared to the yield from the "Funds," they must have been a tempting prospect for small investors. The "utmost harmony" prevailed in Mexico[35]; the contractors were well regarded in the city; all the legal formalities had been observed; specific revenues were promised to cover dividends; a Sinking Fund ensured redemption. Finally, a £100 bond was offered for £58, payable in installments, and thus promising a return of 8.62%. The following year, the Six per Cents entered the market and although the issue price was much higher at £89 15s., the annual return was still at almost 7% or double that on offer from the Consols. Welcomed by the press as sound investments, it was no surprise that both issues were fully subscribed and soon attracting a premium.

Hundreds, if not thousands, of cautious investors were thus persuaded to put their money into Mexican bonds in 1824 and 1825, but before turning to their identity, we must also ask why, after the default in October 1827, and for years thereafter, people still bought Mexican bonds. The reasons are in many respects the same as those which tempted the first wave of investors. Despite all the evidence to the contrary, the belief in Mexico's economic potential never subsided. In a House of Commons debate in 1846, for example, Disraeli spoke of Mexico as "a country, without any exception, of the richest resources in the world."[36] In 1847, *The Times* (9 February) still referred to Mexican mines as "those seemingly exhaustless deposits of treasure." Although dividend remittances were at times few and far between, newspaper readers would have noted that the monthly packets continued to bring cargoes of gold, silver, and other precious commodities. To quote just one example, in July 1844, the steamer *Thames* brought 1,419,203 dollars; 883 ounces of gold dust; 2,228 ounces of silver dust; 2,404 ounces of plata brita; pearls valued at 20,000 dollars; and large quantities of cochineal, vanilla, and indigo.[37] A decade later, David Robertson, by then with thirty years' experience of the Mexican bond market (a fact of which he liked to remind the Foreign Office), wrote of "Mexico, the richest of all the S. American States" and of "her unbounded treasure and ample means."[38] Even Henry Guedalla, after the break in diplomatic relations and Mexico's unilateral rejection of all its previous contracts with the bondholders, still insisted at a public meeting on 27 March 1868 that "the country is extremely rich, especially in minerals. There are no less than eighteen silver mines, and there are also gold and quicksilver mines. There is no country in the world like it."[39]

Rather like many Mexicans of the time, investors seem to have believed that the failure to develop its resources, and to exploit its potential, were the result of the chronic political instability which afflicted the country more or less continuously for the first fifty years after independence. "If it were not for the absence of a stable Government," one newspaper argued in 1877, "it would be one of the richest countries in the world."[40] The general welcome given in 1876 and subsequently to Porfirio Díaz, who was seen by the British press as an exceptionally strong and capable leader, reflected the widely held opinion that he would bring political peace and that economic progress was bound to follow. Just as in the 1820s it was assumed that British capital and expertise would enable the mining industry to flourish, it was believed in the 1870s that British money and knowledge would build the railway system necessary for economic development. Once that took place, Mexico's revenues would increase substantially and all its debts would be paid.

Finally, there were the conversions or reschedulings of the debt. These were invariably the subject of what appeared to be binding contracts, often vetted by the leading British, and sometimes, Mexican barristers of the day. As we have seen, to reassure potential buyers, the text of such agreements was usually inserted on the new bonds. Again, always included were specific assignments of revenues to service the debt and solemn assurances by the Mexican authorities that they would faithfully meet their obligations. When potential investors read letters in *The Times* (21 April 1854) from President Santa Anna, for example, in which he stated that "I certainly consider your claim to have the overdue dividends paid perfectly just" and "your just expectations shall not be disappointed," it is not surprising that some chose to risk a few pounds in Mexican bonds. Santa Anna's word, of course, as many Mexicans found to their cost, was entirely unreliable and within months he had seized dividend money awaiting shipment at Veracruz. Most other Mexican leaders were similarly unable or unwilling to keep their promises to the bondholders. Perhaps surprisingly, however, with one exception, they never seem to have lost their belief that Mexico would pay its debts to them. Over and over again, the Committee of Mexican Bondholders, in its published reports, carefully avoided open criticism of the nation or its politicians. Rather, they accepted that more often than not circumstances such as external aggression, internal dissension, and corruption at the local level, especially at the ports, were to blame for the lack of dividends. Only in the years between 1854 and 1862 was the bondholders' tolerance overstretched. Mexico's failure to pay dividends on the 1851 Three per Cents after 1854; its seizure of monies assigned to servicing the debt; and more than anything, the Legation theft of 1860 were too much for David Robertson and his colleagues. Their language changed in their references to Mexico and Mexicans. Now it was a matter of "the atrocious and bad conduct of Mexico"; "its flagrant and disgraceful" behavior; "forebearance has its limits."[41] The only solution, they argued, was direct military intervention.

There were also, of course, other factors which persuaded investors to buy Mexican bonds. As their price declined, the return increased. On 17 August 1846, for example, shortly after the agreed rescheduling of the debt, one enterprising dealer, Messrs. Jones & Co., placed this advertisement in *The Times*:

Mexican Bonds, Five per Cent Stock, the interest of which has been hitherto regularly paid, and which, at the present low prices, yield about 20 per cent, are at this moment the cheapest stock, either for temporary or permanent investment.

Stretching the truth, as this dealer did by claiming that interest had been regularly paid, does not seem to have deterred investors. A few years later, after the next conversion, the 1851 Three per Cents could be bought at about 25% of their par value, thus offering a return of around 12%. This level of yields, again compared to that of the 3% Consols, was always attractive. Although investors had been warned twenty years earlier by Alexander Baring at the first public meeting of bondholders that the greater the return the higher the risk, others clearly preferred the stock market dictum quoted earlier, "Always buy rubbish." In short, stocks at "shipwreck" prices, to use another contemporary phrase, were always worth a risk.[42]

These, then, are at least some of the reasons why investors put their savings into Mexican bonds. Now we must turn to the bondholders themselves. Given the large number of those who have been identified, and the changes which took place over the period, it is convenient to divide them into categories. The first comprises those who were members of the Committee of Mexican Bondholders. Brief biographical details of most of the men who served on that body have already been given. Analysis of their origins and occupational background provides several clear groups, especially if we include those who also served on the umbrella organizations with which the Mexican Committee was affiliated—the Committee of Spanish American Bondholders and the Corporation of Foreign Bondholders.

The first notable group is formed by the fifteen Committee members who were also Members of Parliament, either incumbent or retired. They included both Liberals like David Robertson and Henry Sheridan, and Conservatives such as George Robinson and William Thompson. There seems to have been no significance in their party affiliation as far as their Mexican interests were concerned. Five people, all of whom were serving Members of Parliament simultaneously—Marshall, Wilson, Robinson, D. Robertson, and Sheridan—chaired the Committee. Their professional backgrounds, apart from their political careers, include lawyers (Sheridan); merchants (Robinson); stockbrokers (Capel, John); manufacturers (Marshall); army officers (Wilson and Davies); and diverse bankers, company directors, aristocrats, and one former Lord Mayor of London (Thompson). Regrettably, in some cases it has not been possible to find out how much they had invested in Mexican bonds nor when they bought them. The wills of Bouverie and Wilson, for example, mention foreign bonds but give no details. There are three cases, however, in which some information is available.

The first is John Marshall, the Leeds mill owner and linen manufacturer. Fortunately, apart from being a very astute and successful businessman, he also kept a detailed private ledger in which he recorded his rapidly increasing personal assets and his investments. The ledger has survived and it reveals that he was a substantial investor in North and South American bonds in general, and Mexican in particular.[43] He seems to have begun his Mexican purchases in February or March 1825 when he bought £30,000 worth of the 1825 Six per Cents. We do not know exactly how much he paid but the issue price was £89¾ per £100 bond and he probably paid at least that amount. Hence, we can assume that he paid approximately £27,000 for his bonds, which was clearly a very substantial investment, from which he could expect an annual dividend of £1,800, or 6%, on the nominal value of £30,000. At first, all went well and he carefully records in his ledger each of the quarterly dividend payments of £450 which he received. The last entry is for July 1827 because Mexico defaulted on the next payment due in October 1827.

As we have seen in Part I of this study, early in 1830, Mexico initiated discussions with leading bondholders regarding the consolidation of the dividend arrears which had accumulated since the default of October 1827. The bondholders set up their first Committee of Mexican Bondholders in May 1830 and the first chairman was Marshall. Sometime in 1830, he chose to invest even more heavily in Mexican stock, buying another £10,000 nominal which he bought, as he records, at 35½. In other words, he paid another £3,600 approximately, including broker's commissions. Whether he bought the extra bonds before or after he became the Committee chairman is unclear. Similarly, we do not know if his decision to reenter the market was a straightforward speculation on his part or whether it reflected insider information arising from his discussions with the Mexican authorities. The charge against Committee members of using privileged information for their own benefit may have had some justification. At any rate, his total investment was now £40,000 and he received three more of the partial dividends paid in 1831 and 1832, amounting to one payment of £300 and two of £600. Also, he received another allocation of bonds. Again, to recall briefly the 1831 agreement, there were fifteen unpaid coupons from October 1827 to April 1831. It was agreed that these would be consolidated into new bonds on which interest was deferred until April 1836. Each £75 of interest arrears attracted one of these new Deferred £100 bonds. Marshall had £40,000 of bonds. At 6%, annual interest was £2,400 or £600 a quarter. His fifteen arrear coupons, therefore, had a face value of £9,000. That sum, coverted into the new bonds at 75%, gave him, as he again records in his ledger, £12,000 of "Mexican Deferred Bonds."

In total, therefore, Marshall had £52,000 worth of Mexican bonds. Unfortunately, we do not know how or when he disposed of them. In his ledger, he added the following note: "1833. All my Foreign Stocks are now entered in a separate small ledger and the dividends posted to Prime Ward and King's account in the same ledger, except those received by Glyn & Co." This foreign stock ledger has not been located. On the other hand, each year Marshall recorded the value of his effects and included an annual entry of "Funds as per Book," referring to his separate small ledger. These show in 1834 the sum of £323,972 rising yearly to £393,751 in 1840, which is the last entry. This suggests that he did not sell his foreign stocks. He records giving several of his holdings to his children and it seems entirely possible that his Mexican bonds were transferred to his son, William, who joined the Committee of Mexican Bondholders in 1850.

Marshall, therefore, was one of the original and largest holders, and he clearly suffered a considerable loss on his investment. Another even bigger holder was David Robertson. He affirmed on many occasions that he acquired his bonds in the mid-1820s at a time when he was the senior partner in the stockbrokers Marjoribanks, Capel & Co. He retained them through the conversions of 1831, 1837, 1846, and 1851, and at a meeting in 1858, he revealed that he was one of the two largest individual holders (the other was McGarel) with more than £270,000 worth of bonds between them.[44] He presumably kept them during his chairmanship until 1862, but after he left the Committee he seems to have disposed of them. This is deduced from the fact that in his will and all the codicils written between 1864 and 1873, he made very specific and detailed bequests of his holdings in Buenos Aires, Chilean, Paraguayan, and other Spanish American stocks but there is no mention of any Mexican. Similarly, in the itemized inventory of his estate, there is no reference to Mexican bonds. There is in the inventory, however, an intriguing item which is not entirely explicable. This is as follows: "Mexican Committee Certificates. Certificates representing a nominal value of £101,150 are in the possession of Messrs. Coutts & Co. for behoof [sic] of the deceased. These are considered to be altogether worthless but for confirmation are valued at £1."[45] What were these certificates? The fact that they were written off as worthless must mean that they were neither 1851 nor 1864 Three per Cent bonds, since these could have been sold in the market at 14 or 7 per cent, respectively, in 1873, thus realizing several thousand pounds. The only alternative seems to be that they were 1851 certificates of the sort illustrated earlier. It may be recalled that they were issued by Facio in exchange for arrear coupons but also bear the signature of the chairman of the Committee of Mexican Bondholders. We know that the certificates had circulated in the market, some being bought by Dutch investors, but after the failure to persuade Maximilian's government to pay them off, they were considered worthless until the Dublán conversion of the 1880s. Robertson may have acquired them in the market as a speculative investment—they were said to have been available at a shilling each[46]—or he may simply have retained them when he gave up the chairmanship of the Mexican Committee. Unfortunately, there is no record of them in Coutt's archive.

We have more details of the investments of George Robinson, chairman of the Committee of Spanish American Bondholders from 1836 to 1850. As indicated earlier, among many things, he was a merchant, Member of Parliament, chairman of Lloyd's, and father of four "natural" children. The dispute over his will meant that many documents were submitted to the Court and these have survived. Among them there is a "declaration instead of inventory" which provides an itemized list of all his effects, with their market value.[47] This reveals that he owned farms in Kent, several properties in Poole, and land and property in St. John's, Newfoundland. He also had a substantial portfolio of stocks and shares in a range of businesses, including insurance and railway companies. In addition, he had investments in a variety of foreign bonds. His Spanish American holdings comprised Chilean Six and Three per Cents, valued at £12,570; Brazilian (£3,680); Peruvian (£1,155); New Granadan (£327); Venezuelan (£377); and two types of Mexican. His main Mexican holdings were given a market value of £1,381 10s. These were presumably 1846 Five per Cents which at the time the valuation was made (January 1851) were around 32–35 in the market, giving a par value of approximately £4,100. His other "Mexicans" are simply described as "Deferred," value £230 5s. Again, we can assume that these were 1837 Deferred Five per Cents and they may have been part of the Lizardi excess issue. They were no longer quoted on the Stock Exchange's official price lists but there was an unofficial market in them. Hence, Robinson had Spanish American bonds worth a total of approximately £20,000 at market values in January 1851. As he had first come to prominence at bondholders' meetings in 1828, he was probably among the early buyers of the various issues.

Another group of the Mexican Committee members comprised those with aristocratic titles. There were twelve of these, none of whom it appears were merely "decoy" names used to give respectability. Again, little information is available as to their individual holdings of Mexican stocks. Admiral Wallis' will (he left effects valued at approximately £80,000) does not mention specifically his foreign bonds, but given that he stayed on the Committee for almost forty years, we can take it that he had significant investments. In the case of the multimillionaire Isaac Lyon Goldsmid, although we do not know the total, we do know that he had at least £10,000 in Mexican bonds since that was the required mininum sum for Committee members in 1853.

Several of the titled members also had military backgrounds. In all, there were four admirals, two generals, two colonels, and a captain on the Committee, but the largest professional groups, as might be expected, were stockbrokers (18) and merchants/bankers (12). With most of the stockbrokers, we do not know if they personally had investments in Mexican bonds or if they were simply acting for their clients. In some cases, however, for example, George Rougemont & Co., it stated that it was involved for itself and for clients.[48] Similarly, James Capel revealed at a public meeting in 1843 that while he represented clients with over £500,000 in Mexican stock, he also had personal holdings. He was another Committee member elected in 1853 on the understanding that he had at least £10,000 of bonds on his own account. James Corbett Irving, who was on the Committee for almost twenty years from 1868 to 1886, also had personal investments while also representing clients with £550,000 of the stock.

Perhaps the best illustration of the range and diversity of the bondholders who served on the Committee is provided by a summary of the chairmen. First, there was the Leeds mill owner, John Marshall, who gave away several hundred thousand pounds to his family during his lifetime and still left effects valued at £170,000 at the time of his death in 1846.[49] He was followed by General Sir Robert Wilson, whose assets and investments are unknown but who without doubt was a wealthy man. Then there was the Newfoundland merchant, George Robinson, whose estate was valued at £157,000. His successor was the Scottish merchant, William Parish Robertson, whose exact wealth is unknown.[50] Next was the millionaire bullion dealer and foreign loan contractor, Isaac Lyon Goldsmid, whose effects were estimated at more than £1,000,000. He was succeeded by James Capel, leading stockbroker for many years and prominent member of several bondholders' committees; he left £140,000. The Irish sugar merchant, Charles McGarel, chairman from 1854 to 1856, left over £600,000. David Robertson, retired stockbroker and Scottish landowner, with large investments in many Spanish American stocks, left £250,000. Finally, there was the longest-serving chairman, Henry Sheridan, poet, parliamentarian, and barrister, but of whom we have no details of investments or final estate.

In sum, those who served on the Committee of Mexican Bondholders included Members of Parliament, admirals, generals, merchants, bankers, lawyers, and stockbrokers, and as far as can be ascertained, almost without exception, they were drawn from the wealthy elite of Victorian Britain. There were many other bondholders from similar backgrounds who were never on the Committee but who attended and spoke at meetings or wrote to the newspapers. Again, the largest group was probably stockbrokers and merchants. In 1849, for example, a letter with 34 signatures of "bondholders and agents for bondholders" was sent to the Committee of Spanish American Bondholders supporting the deduction of 6d. in the pound from the next dividend payment to pay for Parish Robertson's mission to Mexico.[51] Most of those who signed were stockbrokers such as W. Goldsmid, John H. Golding, William Hartridge, William and John Smallbone, James Henry Tyre, Theodosius Uzielli, William West, William Hammond, Lewis and Albert Levy, Lewis Cohen, and "Jas. Capel, Norbury, Trotter & Co. (for selves and friends)." Sir David Salomons, a Lord Mayor of London and one of the founders of the London and Westminster Bank, was a notable financier who did not serve on the Committee but who regularly attended and spoke at bondholders' meetings.[52] Joseph Tasker is another example. In its announcement of his demise, he was described by *The Times* (11 April 1861) as "a well-known and esteemed member of the Committee of Spanish American Bondholders." Among many other commercial interests which gave him assets worth over £500,000, he was a director of the United Mexican Mining Assocation.[53]

Several of these names, and especially of those who served on the Committee, appear again in the next category of bondholders which comprises those individuals, rather than companies, who had holdings of more than £10,000. By their own admission, the largest individual holders, as noted above, were David Robertson and Charles McGarel with £270,000 between them; John Marshall with £52,000; and Richard Thornton, the notable merchant and speculator, with £50,000. In 1868, one of the first acts of the newly constituted Sheridan Committee was to organize a memorial for submission to the Foreign Office.[54] Bondholders were asked to sign it, or to authorize their London representatives to sign on their behalf, and to include the nominal value of their bonds. This memorial, addressed to the Foreign Secretary, Lord Stanley, was left at the Foreign Office on 6 May 1868. It reveals several other large holders. For example, George Henky of Chichester, with £45,000; Captain Charles James Barnett, a deputy lieutenant of Gloucestershire who lived at 5 Bays Hill lawn, Cheltenham, with £42,000; Henry Lindus, 4 Albert Road, Peckham, £30,000; Robert Finnegan, 3 New Road, Hornsey Avenue, £20,000; F. Delmar and Thomas Burke, both London residents, each with £15,000, while Robert Gray who lived at Temple Hill, Black Bush, Dublin, and Mathew Holbecke, a solicitor at Rugby, had, respectively £14,700 and £14,500. Herbert Jeffreys, described in the 1871 Census as a retired Australian landowner, living at Culmhead House, Pitminster, near Taunton, had £11,000. There were two holders with £10,000. One was John Forster, of Waverley, near Newbury. The other was B.P. Wilson who did not give his address. There are also several illegible signatures of persons with holdings of between £12,000 and £20,000. There would certainly have been others with more than £10,000 but some of those who signed the petition chose not to disclose the information. These included, for example, Sheridan, Guedalla, Gerstenberg, Admiral Wallis, and the Dorsetshire landowner, Henry Francis Brouncker. Also in the £10,000 or more group were Richmond, Ross, and Staniforth, who were all elected to the Committee in 1853. Finally, there are several names with between £3,000 and £10,000, for example, Susan Townsend, London, with £3,700; George Stone, Regent's Park (£7,000); Nathaniel Ames, Spitalfields (£8,000); Robert Boult, a barrister at Lincoln's Inn (£8,950); and W. Gibbs, Bexley Heath, Herts., who listed £2,000 "old" and £6,000 "new."

One impression that the Mexican Committee was always anxious to dispell, however, was that most bondholders were in this rich category of investors who could well afford to do without their dividends. David Robertson and his colleagues insisted over and over again that the archetypal bondholder was, in fact, the small investor who had risked his life savings and who had suffered real hardship, if not destitution, from Mexico's failure to pay dividends. Robertson told Lord Russell in 1860 that "fathers, husbands, and brothers embarked their all in these funds in 1825."[55] On more than one occasion, *The Times* noted that "hundreds of families have been impoverished by these improvident investments." Among them, it said, were many naval and army officers for whom "the misery produced by those ill-advised South American loans has spread very widely."[56] Reporting to a public meeting of bondholders in 1846, George Robinson noted that while there were certainly some rich holders, "there were many poorer creditors whose regular receipt of the dividends was a matter of vast importance to them."[57] Finally, William Parish Robertson told Lord Palmerston in 1848 that "thousands of families, it may be safely affirmed, are interested in the payment of Mexican dividends; and in a multitude of cases, their daily wants are affected by the greater or lesser punctuality of the Mexican Government."[58]

On the basis of those bondholders who have been identified, it appears that there was much truth in such claims. The 115 names in the 1868 Memorial, for example, include many who held only small amounts: Robert Johnson, 358 Wakefield Road, Bradford (£600); John Collins, 23 Union Street, Hereford (£800); George Briggs, 71 Lower Sloane Street, Chelsea (£950); Mary Catchpole (£200), Mary Legrey (£200), George Hall (£600), F. Wilmott (£600), and M. Petit (£300), all of 4 Clarges Street, Piccadilly; J. Webber, Manningtree, Essex (£400); Charles Smith, Lincoln's Inn Fields (£500); Mary Robertson, 1 Albion Villas, Folkestone (£800); Thomas Holdsworth, John Hudson, Thomas Humble Walker, Amelia Boult, Thomas Baily, James McDonald, and John Lipscombe were among many London residents with between £1,000 and £3,000; Frederick Smith, South Vicarage Park, Plumstead (£2,500); Richard Jenkins, 4 Morgan Street, Tredegar (£1,400); Richard Cowan, Bathwick Priory, Bath (£1,500). Finally, confirming the claim that there were retired officers among the bondholders are James St.Clair Doyle, late captain in the 51st Regiment (£700), and Commander Charles Mallard, retired Royal Navy officer, 5 Woodland Road, Bristol (£1,100). Mallard had joined the Navy in January 1821. At the time of his death in 1875, his estate, which was valued at "under £25,000," included Britsh and foreign stocks, a farm in Gloucestershire, and various properties in Bristol including one which he named Dundonald House, perhaps, if we may speculate, because he had served with Admiral Thomas Cochrane, Earl of Dundonald, in his Spanish American campaigns.[59]

Were families reduced to poverty or destitution as a result of their purchases of Mexican bonds? Was the Reverend Carnegie, vicar of Cranborne, justified in stating in 1861 that many people throughout the British Isles "have suffered and are suffering the greatest privations in consequence of the non-payment of the Mexican dividends"?[60] Clearly, evidence to answer the question is now difficult to find, but some examples, both real and fictitious, can be cited. In 1839, for example, Thomas Walker Hartley, of Loddon, near Norwich, wrote to the Mexican Legation requesting details of the recent rescheduling of the debt. He hoped, he said, that after waiting "ten long years" for his dividends, the Mexican government was finally going "to make good its obligations and permanently relieve the bond-holders from the distress and misery which so many of them have felt from the withholding of the interest for so long a period." "There are many," he added, "whose all has been embarked in the concern and whose circum-stances, in consequence of your nation having neglected to fulfil her en-gagements, have been straitened to the greatest degree."[61] William Morgan is another example. He wrote to Lord Clarendon on 20 August 1856. He was, he said, a Mexican bondholder and he had agreed to the reduction of interest on his bonds from 5% to 3% as stipulated in the 1851 conver-sion. But the dividends were still not being paid and "I cannot pay my debts because the Mexican Government forcibly retains my property—many bondholders are unfortunately in the same position."[62] Reverend Richard Holmes, Minister at the parish of Marsham, near Norwich, wrote to the Mexican Legation in 1839. He had seen, he said, repeated statements concerning "the speedy settlement of the affairs of Mexican Bonds and the payment of dividends thereon." He was anxious to know when the divi-dends would be resumed but his letter to Messrs. Lizardi & Co. had not been answered. The non-payment for such a long time had caused him "great distress."[63] Reverend Thomas Hare, of 5 Chatham Place, Hackney, sounded even more desperate. He wrote to Lord Malmesbury, Clarendon's successor as Foreign Secretary, on 5 March 1858. His dividends were five years in arrears and three years had passed since even a half dividend had been paid. "All my property," he went on, "is invested in the Mexican security and my income (as a Clergyman) is precarious and small—and wholly insufficient to maintain myself and family exclusively of the divi-dends. There is no escape by selling out now. The iniquity of the Republic is so patent—the Security has sunk so low—the act would be suicidal."[64]

Such cases of indigence brought about by investments in Mexican stocks are also well represented in the fictional Allnutt family who form the prin-cipal characters of a three-volume novel published in 1837.[65] The family live in a leased cottage, "in a remote part of one of the western counties of England" where they enjoy the secure, uneventful life of minor country gentry. Their combined income of £500 per annum is derived from inher-ited capital safely invested in the Three per Cents. Then, at the urging of the eldest son, John, who at the start of the story is about to leave for Mexico to make what he expects to be a quick fortune in the mining in-dustry, they are persuaded "to sell your stock out of the Three per Cents and to buy in Mexican stock." "By that single operation," he told them, "you will get at least another two hundred a year to yourselves." There was no risk because Mexico was "a whole continent full of gold and sil-ver." Despite their brother's enthusiasm, the family decides to seek the advice of a wealthy, retired stockbroker, Mr. Woodby, who lives nearby. For his own reasons, and to benefit his private speculations in Mexican stocks, he assures them also that there is no risk. "Mexico," said Woodby, "is an astonishingly rich country. We are told that every domestic article there is made of silver, down to their wash-hand basins, pewter pots etc."[66] The Allnutts are convinced and their London banker is instructed to put all their capital into Mexican bonds. The rest of the plot is largely predictable. Dividends fail to arrive, the family is impoverished and they are forced to move to London to seek some means of earning a living. The head of the household, Abel, cannot pay the rent and is confined to a debtors' prison. Eventually, all ends well when the beautiful niece marries into money and rescues her relatives from the poverty which their Mexican investments have brought them.

Whatever its merits as a novel—it received a mixed review in *The Athenaeum*[67]—*Abel Allnutt*'s characters and themes seem to have reflected the reality of "this time that England began to run mad upon the subject of the emancipation of the Spanish colonies from the mother country, upon loans to the new republics, and particularly upon mines and mining companies."[68] Its depiction of the misery brought upon those who put their money into Mexican bonds was no doubt welcome publicity for the bondholders' Committee in its attempts to persuade the Foreign Office to help. The author, James Justinian Morier, was himself a diplomat with personal knowledge and experience of Mexico. He had spent several months in the country between 1824 and 1826 as one of the British commissioners sent by Canning to negotiate a commercial treaty. It is not known if he had invested any of his own money in Mexican stocks, although it seems unlikely since in March 1827, that is, before the default on dividends, he advised his brother not to do so. "I should be loath," he said, "to risk any think [*sic*] of such magnitude among them as to endanger my fortunes and independence."[69]

Morier's decision to place the central characters of his story in the depths of rural England probably reflected another often-stated assertion that far from being confined to London, the Mexican bondholders were spread across the length and breadth of the British Isles. Again, many individual examples may be cited. On the basis of those addresses that can be read and by no means all are legible, the 1868 memorial has bondholders from twenty-two places, excluding London. These include England, Scotland, Ireland, and Wales, and range from small hamlets like North Barrow in Somerset to such towns and cities as Bath, Bristol, and Cheltenham.[70] In the north, there is Bradford and Manchester. In the south, and to cite only a sample, there is Brighton, Chichester, Folkestone, Hereford, Newbury, and Sherborne. The Mexican Legation archive has letters from many other places. In 1843, for example, Samuel Sparkes, Huish House, Langport Eastover, Somerset, listed as "Gentry" in a local directory, wrote to protest at the "low and ruinous price" of his Mexican stock.[71] He condemned the "obnoxious decrees" recently promulgated in Mexico which imposed "exorbitant duty" on foreign imports and were certain to reduce customs revenues "and most probably prevent the regular payment of Dividends."[72] Other letters are from Portchester, Guisborough (Yorkshire), and elsewhere.

Another petition confirms the profile of bondholders drawn from the gentry and professional classes of provincial England. Addressed to Lord Palmerston, it was presented to the Foreign Office on 9 August 1836 by Henry Aglionby, Member of Parliament for Cockermouth.[73] It bears the signatures of seventeen "residents of Kendal and its vicinity in the County of Westmoreland." In brief, the petitioners told Palmerston that they were "severally creditors of the Republican Governments recently established in South America." The total debt of those nations to British subjects was £25,000,000. The failure to pay dividends or interest for many years had caused "great injury and inconvenience" to numerous British people in various parts of the United Kingdom. Even allowing for the "convulsions and changes" liable to occur in newly established countries, it was their firm conviction that all the debtor republics had shown a "want of probity" and that all of them could have done more toward meeting their obligations. Bondholders' representations had been met with "unjust pretences and flimsy excuses" and in some instances, money allocated to the foreign debt had been used instead for internal or domestic debts. It was clear that the demands of bondholders would not be met in any negotiation "without the direct interference and support of the British Government on their behalf." The petitioners, therefore, called on Lord Palmerston to adopt the measures he deemed necessary in the circumstances of the case "as may lead to their obtaining speedy and ample justice."

The petition is signed by the following: B. Batty; W.W. Butcher; W.D. Crewdson; Susanna Harrison; Edward Holme; Robert (or Roger) Moser; Thomas Proudfoot; Thomas Reveley; John Richards; Alicia Ann Thomson; Elizabeth Thomson; Sarah Thomson; W. Thomson; Jacob Wakefield; Thomas Watters; Isaac Wilson; William Wilson.

Somewhat unusually, several of the above added their profession and further research has provided some details of the background of others. This reveals three doctors (Batty, Holme, Proudfoot); two bankers (Crewdson, Wakefield); two solicitors (Moser, Reveley); two manufacturers (Isaac and William Wilson); one naval officer (Butcher); and two listed in the various directories of the day as gentry—Richards and Watters. The three Thomsons were almost certainly sisters, ranging in age from 47 to 56, and in a curious parallel to the fictional Allnutt sisters, they were perhaps also spinsters dependent on their investment income. Harrison was certainly in a similar situation. She is described in the 1851 Census as a 70-year-old spinster and annuitant. Finally, there is the fourth Thomson, William. He may have been related to the sisters and he was probably the bank clerk, described in the 1851 Census as aged 63 and retired. Coincidentally, they shared the same name, although different spelling, as another Kendalian investor in Mexican bonds whom we have already encountered. This was Alderman William Thompson, wealthy iron-master of Grayrigg, near Kendal, Member of Parliament, Lord Mayor of London, and various other high offices, including the Committee of Mexican Bondholders.

Most were very prominent members of Kendal society. Richards, for example, had been elected Mayor on 1 January 1836. Watters and Isaac Wilson were Aldermen of the town and several of the others had been candidates in municipal elections. Reveley was clerk to the commissioners of taxes and to several local bridge and turnpike road companies. Dr. Proudfoot played a leading role in several local cultural societies, for example, the Kendal Natural History and Scientific Society of which he was a founder member and later president. Five people—Proudfoot, Moser, Reveley, I. Wilson, Crewdson—had signed an anti-slavery petition in 1830. Finally, Wakefield and Crewdson were both members of local banking families. Their banks were amalgamated in 1840 to form the Kendal Bank, later absorbed by Barclays.

In short, the Kendal residents who signed the petition offer an excellent gallery of the sort of persons who risked their money in Spanish American bonds. Regrettably, little information about their individual wealth or investments is available and it is not possible to state with certainty that they all owned Mexican rather than other Spanish American bonds. Some details, however, are available. Dr. Holme, for example, who practiced medicine in Manchester for most of his career but who returned each year to his home town of Kendal, left more than £50,000, all amassed, apparently, from his professional activities.[74] Even more useful is the case of Dr. Proudfoot. He had begun his career as an army medical officer serving under the Duke of Wellington. After various travels in Sicily, Spain, France, and North America, he retired from the army in 1818. He practiced medicine in Kendal from around 1820 and in 1858, the year before his death, he made a list of his assets.[75] This shows that he held the following Spanish American stocks:

Mexican Stock, new 3% consolidated (21,000 at £22%)	£4,620
New Granada bonds (500)	77 10s.
More New Granada bonds	960
Buenos Aires bonds	2,558
Peruvian loan	1,365
Venezuelan bonds	1,500

He also had shares in railway and canal companies and his total assets added up to £15,515 9s. 8d. His Spanish American stocks, therefore, amounting to £11,080, were about two-thirds of his entire wealth. As they produced at best only intermittent dividends, his investment income must have varied from erratic to non-existent. His Mexican bonds were 1851 Three per Cents with the substantial nominal value of £21,000. We do not know exactly when he first began to invest in Mexican bonds but in his personal bank book, which has survived, there is an entry for 1829 indicating that he had bought £1,000 of the 1824 Five per Cents. Also among his financial records are various accounts listing the numbers of the bonds he held. For example, one undated list shows that he held £20,000 of the 1846 Five per Cents, including twelve bonds of the £100 series; seventeen of the £150; twenty-seven of the £250; and nineteen of the £500. He had presumably accepted the conversions of 1837 and 1846 and eventually, that of 1851 which provided him with the Three per Cents he listed in 1858. It is also evident from his financial records that he was active in buying and selling in the market. In another of his notebooks in which he listed his bonds held at his bank and "in my possession," he notes his purchase in February 1851 of £2,000 Mexican at 33¼. Further purchases and sales were made in 1852 and a letter from his London broker of 17 April of that year confirms the sale of some of his Peruvian stocks and the purchase of £1,000 of Mexican at 29¼. Finally, when his executors realized his estate, all of his bonds were sold. The Mexican Three per Cents, totalling £21,000, were sold in four batches between July and August 1861 at around 22⅜ per cent, yielding £4,643 plus £123 in dividend arrears. Unfortunately for his heirs, the market price, responding to the Tripartite Intervention, rose substantially over the next few months, reaching 33 by January 1862. Bankers rejected complaints that they should have anticipated the rise, insisting that "no blame can attach to us."[76]

Dr. Proudfoot's local bank manager was William Dilworth Crewdson, Jr. He was the third generation of the Crewdson family in the bank founded by his grandfather, Thomas, in 1788 as the Maude, Wilson and Crewdson bank. In 1840, the bank was merged with the Wakefield family bank to form what became known as the Kendal Bank, which was later absorbed by Barclays Bank. The Crewdson family papers are in the Kendal Record Office and those of the Kendal Bank are held in the group archives of Barclays.[77] They reveal that William Dilworth II (his father had the same names) was an active investor in South American and Mexican stocks. The bank's ledgers indicate that he first bought Colombian bonds in 1823, and subsequently he invested in those of Chile, Venezuela, New Granada, and other countries, including Spain.[78] It is not entirely clear when he began to buy Mexican stocks but he had become a regular investor by the early 1840s. The ledger records various purchases, beginning on 2 November 1843.[79] On that date, £5,000 worth of Mexican Five per Cents were bought at 31, at a cost of £1,550, plus £3 2s. brokerage fees, and £5,000 of the 1837 Deferred Five per Cents at 9½, costing £475, plus brokerage. Similar purchases were made, always for £5,000 par value, in 1844, 1846, and

1853. By 1864, a note in the ledger states that "the amount of the Bonds, held for many years, has been nominally, £26,000." In that year, the Maximilian government agreed to capitalize the dividend arrears which in the case of Crewdson's bonds amounted to £7,410. These were converted by offering a new £100 Three per Cent bond for £60 of the arrear coupons. Thus, Crewdson received £12,350 of the new 1864 Three per Cents. His total holdings now amounted to £38,350 but, as the ledger puts it, "being desirous of holding an even sum," he instructed his London brokers, Foster & Braithwaite, to buy enough additional bonds to raise the total to £40,000.[80]

Crewdson kept a meticulous, itemized record of his personal income and expenditure in his annual pocket diary.[81] The minute handwriting and figures in these diaries mean that some of the entries are not legible but those that can be deciphered show the dividends he received from his Mexican stocks. Under income for the third week of January 1849, for example, he wrote "¾ of a div. on 21,000 Mexican Stock—£393 15. 0." Thereafter, each year, usually in January, he recorded the dividends he received. The January 1852 entry is "Mexican div. 3 p Cents on 21,000 converted stock £305 16.3." Over the next few years, dividends were rarely distributed but he noted a partial payment in 1858 and with the resumption of payments by the Maximilian regime, he recorded in 1864 "Mexican div 1 year on the original bonds £749 8.2." Further entries were made in following years but the last one he recorded in his diary was the partial dividend paid by Barings in 1867, recorded as "Mex.div due 1 July 66, part "255 13.4." The dividends were also entered in the ledger. This gives more details and includes, for example, the sums he received from the distribution of the United States indemnity payment in 1852, together with the various amounts paid on the 1851 certificates. Allowing for errors of transcription—the numbers are not all easy to read—the dividends paid from 1843 to 1869, the last recorded entry in the ledger, amounted to £7,930.

Given that his Mexican bonds were bought over several years and that brokerage and other costs as well as income tax payments on dividends would have to be included in the calculations, it is difficult to assess Crewdson's investment and whether he would have done better to put his money into, for example, Consols. The fact that he retained his bonds for twenty-six years, however, suggests that he was not entirely dissatisfied with the return. The ledger shows that he paid £8,199 for them and that he received a total of £7,930 in dividends. Unfortunately, we do not know when he sold them but if he did so in 1869 after the last entry in the ledger, at around the average market price, he would have received approximately £3,900 for his £26,000 worth of 1851 Three per Cents, and £980 for his £14,000 of 1864 Three per Cents or £4,880 in total. Hence, for an outlay of £8,199, his return over twenty-six years was approximately £12,810, including all the dividends and the final sale value of the bonds. On a very rough calculation, £8,199 of Three per Cent Consols would have brought him about £15,000 over the same period, including dividends and the final sale of the stocks.

In his book on Mexico's foreign debt, Professor Bazant suggests that most of those who bought their bonds in the initial wave of enthusiasm of the early 1820s would have sold them once prices began to fall. "Normally," he states, "the investor takes fright at the first fall in the market and sells his bonds to the speculator."[82] While that may have been the case to some extent, it is also true, as David Robertson and his colleagues were always anxious to affirm, that many of the original buyers retained their bonds for many years. This seems to have been particularly the case in what may be called the first generation of bondholders, that is, those who bought in the 1820s and accepted the conversions through to that of 1851. Parish Robertson told the Mexican Finance Minister in 1849 that it was a "notorious fact that many of the largest bondholders now are those who originally subscribed to the Loans or made purchases of it [sic] at 80 to 90 per cent."[83] A few years later, David Robertson made the same point in a memorandum to the British Foreign Office. Referring to the debt, he wrote, "the greater part of it is still in the hands of the original Bondholders or their direct representatives."[84] Finally, the Committee's secretary, Nilsen, reminded Lord Russell in 1861 that the great majority of the bonds "are held as a permanent investment by the original subscribers, their descendants and heirs, and other British subjects."[85]

Such claims can also be supported by individual examples. Reverend Carnegie, whose letter to the Foreign Office of 1861 has already been cited above, inherited his bonds from his father. Samuel Herbert, also quoted earlier, told the Mexican Legation secretary in 1850 that his bonds had been in his family "from the very time they were first issued."[86] In 1842, Henry Vance wrote to the Mexican Legation to complain that nothing was being paid on his Debentures which "have fallen to 13!! 50% lower than the price they bore at their issue six months since." "After having been a holder of the Bonds for a great many years," he said, "I was induced to dispose of them and invest the proceeds in Debentures on the faith of the conditions attached to them."[87] John Walter Wilkinson who, among other things, was the Spanish Vice-Consul for Portsmouth, also wrote to the Mexican Legation in April 1849. "In the year 1825," he said,

I became possessed of £2,200 Mexican Six per Cent stock, and which, confiding in the honour of the Mexican Republic, I purchased at 93½ per cent. From that time to the present day I have held the said stock without any deviation or change whatever on my part, accepting always and conforming to the terms and dispositions which the Republic has been pleased to adopt on all former occasions.

In 1843, a bondholder wrote to *The Morning Herald* (24 April). Signing himself "A Holder of Mexican Stock to the amount of Several Thousands and a stranger to the mysteries of Stock Dealing," he began his letter by emphasizing that he was "an unfortunate holder of Mexican stock, purchased at a high price, and now held, probably stupidly enough, for a long series of years."

Such examples, and others could be cited, confirm that the first holders, especially in the provinces, retained their bonds in the hope that dividends would be resumed and that principal values would recover. Furthermore, after the break in diplomatic relations in 1867 and Mexico's rejection of all prior agreements concerning the bonds, prices collapsed and it seems unlikely that many owners would have sold even if they could find buyers. The daily quotations on the Exchange indicate that very few bargains were made, especially in the mid-1870s when the 1851 Three per Cents had fallen to around 7 and the 1864 Three per Cents to as low as 2. On the other hand, as Professor Bazant also points out, it was the case that in some periods there was widespread speculation in all Mexican securities. At the time of the first issues in 1824 and 1825, it is clear that there was considerable speculation by buyers who entered the market on a strictly short-term basis, often using borrowed money, in the hope that prices would rise and some capital gain be achieved. Of course, it is difficult now to identify them, but one who was to achieve fame and fortune in later years was Benjamin Disraeli. In 1824 and 1825, he played the market in both mining company shares and bonds. In particular, he invested frequently in Mexican bonds, buying and selling at times almost on a daily basis, but rarely making a profit. His speculations in Buenos Aires, Chilean, and Colombian bonds were also unprofitable but he seems to have retained his belief that "the prosperity of this country depends upon our patronage of America."[88] It was also generally recognized that the loan contractors were among those who played the market. They retained bonds for themselves and their friends, acquired at the issue price, and only sold when the price had risen. Among those who almost certainly benefited was the Mexican agent, Borja Migoni—his personal estate at the time of his death in 1831 was £120,000. He was by no means the only Mexican speculator. The accounts of the Martínez del Río firm of merchants show frequent speculation in the London bond market between 1840 and 1843.[89] Manning and Mackintosh, agents of the bondholders in Mexico for many years, also were regular investors. In 1846, while in London to discuss the conversion of that year, the businessman, Manuel Escandón, took the opportunity to profit from the rising price of the time.[90] Manuel Payno, who was instrumental in arranging the 1851 conversion, took advantage of a visit to London "to procure a rise in the Mexican Bonds for his own purposes and those of his friends."[91]

The minutes of the Foreign Exchange Committee's meetings have various references to disputes between dealers and to failures among brokers who had speculated unsuccessfully in the Mexican market.[92] The newspapers also reported some very large purchases, for example, one of £80,000 reported in *The Morning Chronicle* on 18 August 1826. A few weeks earlier, *The Times* (2 May 1826) had noted the sale of £30,000 of the 1824 Five per Cents. They had been sold at 50, the owner, who had paid 75, taking a loss of £12,500. Even after the dividend default of October 1827, there were those who were willing to take a risk. Large purchases were reported in March, May, and June 1828 when "there was a struggle between two parties of speculators, one endeavouring to depress, the other to raise the stock."[93] The extant ledgers of brokers such as Foster and Janson (later Foster & Braithwaite) show that buyers were still plentiful. Their Day Journal showing business done between 27 February and 1 March 1828, for example, has two entries for Mexican stocks. In one, 5,000 Mexican Five per Cents were bought for a Mr. Bainbridge at 26¼. A few days later, 2,000 were bought at 27 for Stephen Nicolson.[94]

All manner of tactics were used to influence the market. False rumors of the imminent arrival of dividend remittances were common. On one occasion, a notice was posted in the Stock Exchange announcing that £700,000 was about to be shipped from Mexico. "The communication was so ignorantly and obscurely worded" that it was quickly realized that the report was a crude hoax and an attempt to raise prices.[95] Another attempt to influence the market was a rumor that Iturbide was alive and in hiding. One enterprising but anonymous character opened "policies" offering, in return for a five-guinea bet, to pay £100 if the story turned out to be true.[96] Good or bad news from Mexico, often inaccurate reports of rebellions or internal disorder, rumors of new offers to convert the stocks or that dividends were to be resumed, all maintained the atmosphere of uncertainty in which "the affirmative and the negative have been maintained, with almost equal pertinacity, by two distinct classes of speculators."[97] At times, "so many artifices are daily resorted to by the speculators in Mexican stock to mislead the public that it has become extremely difficult to distinguish truth from falsehood" and there was always "the suspicion of unfair play."[98]

Following the early, often frenzied, speculation of the 1820s, the market for the bonds was much calmer. Prices fluctuated according to the circumstances of the day, the conversions, the likelihood of dividends being paid, and in the 1850s, the possibility of British intervention. Professional speculators were, of course, always present. They included several nationalities, in addition to the Mexicans already noted. On 9 June 1830, John Marshall, in his first letter as chairman of the newly formed Committee of Mexican Bondholders, wrote that "there are no less than forty thousand of these bonds in circulation, dispersed all over England, Scotland and Ireland—in France, Holland and Germany—and some of the holders are even resident in the East Indies."[99] The Dutch, in particular, always seem to have been active buyers. In 1830, the London merchant, Herman Sillem, acted on behalf of Dutch holders of £800,000 worth of the bonds. Years later, as noted above, the Dutch acquired many of the 1851 certificates. A significant proportion of the 1851 and the 1864 Three per Cents found their way into the hands of Amsterdam stockbrokers for themselves and for their clients. The Amsterdam Stock Exchange archive has many lists of the holders and their claims were always a significant factor in the negotiations which eventually led to the Dublán conversion.[100] French, Swiss, Prussian, and Spanish investors were said to be among other European holders although few details are available.[101] United States buyers were prominent in the 1870s and early 1880s, apparently hoping to use their bonds in negotiations with the Mexican government over railway concessions or to acquire public lands.[102] German buyers entered the market very strongly for the 1888 Six per Cents.

Exact details of the extent to which Mexico's foreign debt was owed to non-British bondholders are not known but there were some estimates. Isaac Goldsmid told Lord Malmesbury in 1852 that about one-quarter of the debt was in the hands of French, Dutch, and United States citizens. He suggested that the British Foreign Office should seek the help of the governments of those countries to put joint pressure on Mexico.[103] A few years later, in 1861, the situation appears to have changed. The Foreign Office was told that there were only two or three bondholders in Germany, Switzerland, and Mexico but that there was "a traffic" in the bonds between London and Amsterdam with "at times up to two million of Mexican bonds oscillating between England and Holland."[104] Finally, perhaps it is appropriate to leave the last word on the matter of foreign holders to David Robertson. He told the British ambassador to Mexico, Sir Charles Wyke, in a letter written from Ladykirk on 26 November 1861, that "it is well known that nine-tenths, if not nineteen twentieths, of them (bondholders) are so at this moment, and ever have been Englishmen, and a very respectable body."[105]

There remains one other group of bondholders. They were the so-called Deferred bondholders. It may be briefly recalled that in 1837, it was agreed that the debt represented by the 1824, 1825, and 1831 bonds should be consolidated into new Five per Cents, half of which were to be Active, paying interest immediately, and half to be inactive or with interest deferred for ten years. The Financial Agent, Lizardi & Co., had issued and sold a substantial number of these 1837 Deferred bonds in excess of the authorized number. As a result, when the debt was again refunded in 1846, there were more Deferred bonds in the market than there were new bonds to exchange for them. The new Financial Agent, Schneider & Co., had accepted Deferred bonds to the value stipulated in the 1846 agreement and then had closed its books. Some holders of Deferred bonds, who were slow in presenting them, thus found themselves excluded from the conversion. They were left holding bonds for which there was no official market and hence few, if any, buyers. They were, as they loudly proclaimed, innocent victims of the fraudulent conduct of Lizardi. As explained in earlier pages, they campaigned from the mid-1840s to the mid-1880s to have their bonds recognized and paid off, a campaign which was finally successful in the Dublán conversion. Who, then, were the Deferred bondholders?

Three lists of Deferred holders have been found. The first, comprising in fact several small lists, is in the reports which Schneider sent to Mexico in 1849, giving details of the progress of the 1846 conversion.[106] The second was sent to the British Foreign Office in 1851 by one of the bondholders.[107] The third, dated September 1855, was compiled by Mexico's Financial Agent in London, Colonel Facio, in which he listed the claims made to him by Deferred bondholders.[108] These sources provide us with the names of the individuals concerned and the value of their Deferred bonds. They do not, however, give addresses or any other information and hence, in most cases, it is not possible to trace biographical information. It is also the case that after the mid-1860s, although the Committee of Deferred Bondholders continued to exist, there are no records of those who by then held the unconverted Deferred bonds. Although we know that many holders were represented in the 1880s by the solicitors, Foss and Ledsam, again there are no details of individuals.[109]

The available lists, from 1849 to 1855, appear to confirm those characteristics evident in the "ordinary" bondholders already identified. For example, it is clear that there were some very large individual holders. George Hamer and George Warner, for example, both had £20,450 of the bonds. At the same time, there was also a large number of small investors with £1,000 or less. Among their names are E. Daniels, E.S. Morgan, S. Poole, each with £100; Charles Moss (£150); Andrew Sharpe (£165); S. Dacre and Edward Fisher, each with £300; George Dyer (£350); and a further ten names with up to £1,000. Included in this group is the stockbroker, Isidor Gerstenberg, with £950. As we have seen earlier, he became the driving force behind the establishment of the Committee of Deferred Bondholders and, later, the first chairman of the Corporation of Foreign Bondholders.

Gerstenberg, of course, was not the only stockbroker. There are others who were probably representing their own investments, as well as those of their clients. Some of them registered more than one claim and it is not clear if the amounts they quoted were cumulative totals or separate entries. For example, they include firms such as Hichens & Harrison, which had three amounts of £150, £650, and £1,850; Gosling & Sharpe, £700 and £20,200; Mullen, Marshall & Co., £300 and £7,600; Doxat & Co., five ranging from £700 to £5,700; Albert Levy, £10,479 and £20,200. On a smaller scale were Ellis & Co. with £500 and £900, and Foster & Braithwaite, with £150.

Although we have no information on the geographical origins of the Deferred holders, another feature of the lists suggests that they were spread around the United Kingdom and overseas. This is the presence of a large number of banks among the claimants which we can assume were representing clients from a wide area, given the amount of the bonds they held. For example, the merchant bankers, Glyn, Mills, Currie & Co. had £82,000; Raphael & Sons had several smaller amounts, from £100 to £1,600; the Commercial Bank of London (£22,500); L. Cohen, with at least twelve accounts from £100 to £900; and among others were Schroeder & Co. and Smith, Payne & Co. The largest individual holder seems to have been the estate of E.H. Adams with £60,600. This was represented by Barings who told Schneider that it had accepted the bonds from Lizardi in 1837 in exchange for the original bonds belonging to its client. They had been in the bank's possession ever since (the bank acting as agents for the owner). Barings registered its claim with Schneider in 1849 and did not explain why it had waited until then before presenting them for conversion into the 1846 Five per Cents. Whatever the reason, it was too late and the Adams estate was left as the largest single holder of the 1837 Deferred. It also appears that Barings had other clients with holdings of almost £50,000. It is perhaps because it was involved to such an extent that some of the original bonds have survived and remain in the company's archive.

What seems to have been a substantial number of foreign holders also registered their claims with banks and brokers in London. Schroeder & Co. acted for a Hamburg holder with £100; L. Cohen represented two holders in Leenwarde with £150 each and several other unspecified foreigners. The most prominent foreigners were certainly the Dutch, particularly from Amsterdam. Raphael & Sons had four Amsterdam clients with £1,900; Schroeder & Co. had another with £100, and the London office of Hope & Co., the Dutch bankers, had two accounts of £20,000 and £30,000. Above all, there was Sillem & Co. which had represented Dutch investors since at least 1830. According to the 1851 list, it had clients with £101,000, although for reasons which are not clear, the 1855 list records only £53,000.

For the most part, therefore, the names and amounts held by, or on behalf of, the Deferred bondholders can be established. The 1851 list names sixty-two holders with a total of £251,700 and the 1855 list has forty-one with £517,554. For the majority of these names, however, especially the individuals, little information is available, but there are two exceptions. The first is Mr. S.P. Knowles. He had £1,300 worth of the bonds which he had tried to convert but had been turned away by Schneider. He protested to the Mexican Legation in May 1850, demanding that "the necessary steps may be taken to put me in possession of my property."[110] Then, in June 1851, writing from his address at 6 New Bridge Street, Blackfriars, he made his first direct appeal for support to the Foreign Secretary, Lord Palmerston. He asked him to help the Deferred bondholders in their campaign for a fair and just share of the 2,500,000 dollars to be paid by Mexico from the United States indemnity. The Committee of Mexican

Bondholders was unwilling to include them in the distribution and because they always had a majority at public meetings, the Deferred holders were powerless. "I feel satisfied Your Lordship," he continued, "will not allow the weak, with right and justice on their side, to be overpowered by the strong."[111]

Notwithstanding this appeal, the Deferred holders were excluded from any share in the indemnity money and a decade later, in February 1862, Knowles renewed his letters to the Foreign Office. Now writing from Newton Abbot in Devon where he seems to have retired, he reminded Lord Russell of his and his fellow bondholders' plight. Years of continuous negotiations with Mexican agents, he said, as well as with the Mexican government, had not brought them any justice. He wished to remind the British government of their situation in the hope that they would not be forgotten in any settlement which the Allied Intervention in Mexico might bring.[112]

Knowles' letters to the Foreign Office were always acknowledged and brought the usual promises of whatever assistance was appropriate. He was by no means the only Deferred holder who appealed to the British government. The most persistent was John William Dover, a merchant, of Fenchurch Street, and later Stanley Street, London. Over a period of twenty-five years from 1840 to 1865, he maintained a regular correspondence with successive Foreign Secretaries. At first, his complaints were related to the non-payment of dividends by Portugal, Chile, and Mexico. He wrote in November 1840 that he was the trustee for three minors whose circumstances had changed from "comparative affluence to indigence" as a result of the defaults. In a later letter, he spoke of "the hard case of minors awaiting the Dividends of what constituted nearly their sole dependence." He was also very critical of the Committee of Spanish American Bondholders, describing its members as "Directors, Agents, and Committee men, pretending to work for the public, yet all the while it being but a cloak for their own exclusive advantage."

By 1851, Dover's campaign had changed. In several letters to the Foreign Office, he stressed that he had held his Mexican bonds since the mid-1820s. Following the 1837 conversion, he had placed his Active and Deferred bonds in the London Joint Stock Bank. It had sent them to Schneider to be exchanged for the 1846 bonds but they were received too late to be included. Dover, therefore, became one of the Deferred bondholders unable to realize any money from his £2,550 worth of Mexican stocks. More letters to Lord Palmerston followed and in July 1851, he included the list of names of the sixty-two Deferred holders from which we have quoted above. How he managed to compile the list is not clear. He wrote again in 1856 and 1857, asking, "How much longer is the State of Mexico to be permitted thus to procrastinate and to thwart its creditors? I have been one for more than thirty years." Like Knowles, he also kept up the pressure during the Allied Intervention. His final letters came in August and September 1865, still pressing his case.[113] Dover's efforts were, of course, in vain and the Deferred bondholders remained for another twenty years, to use the words of *The Money Market Review* (28 May 1864), "the worst used class of Mexican creditors."

In sum, the picture which emerges from this bondholders' gallery conforms to the claims made at the time. For example, although not referring specifically to Mexican bondholders, a House of Commons Select Committee found in 1875 that the buyers of foreign stocks included wealthy capitalists and "country clergymen, widows, poor professional men and tradesmen who have got a little money to invest."[114] Our individual examples confirm this picture, demonstrating that those affected by Mexico's default ranged from rich, millionaire bankers and businessmen to country parsons, doctors, solicitors, and diverse other members of the British gentry. While there was a concentration in the London metropolitan area, both of large and small holders, many others were scattered across most regions of the United Kingdom, including Scotland, Ireland, and Wales. Small towns like Kendal in the north and Sherborne in the south had their investors who had been persuaded either by their country bankers or by their own reading of the newspapers, both London and locally based, to risk their money in foreign bonds, perhaps switching their investments from solid but low-interest Consols to the more risky but potentially much more profitable Mexican stocks. Some certainly suffered much hardship, if not penury, as a result of the default in 1827 and the subsequent erratic payment of dividends. Many may well have given up and sold out at a loss but there is also much evidence that others retained their bonds, even passing them from one generation to another, in the hope that the efforts of their Committee of Mexican Bondholders to achieve the return of their capital, if not their accumulated dividend arrears, might have some success. Foreigners—mainly Dutch but also French, German, Mexican, and North American—are also prominent but it seems likely that their holdings never exceeded, as contemporary estimates calculated, more than about one-quarter of the bonds. Most were certainly held by British investors, large and small, and they included those who may be termed professional speculators who continually played the market in all Spanish American and, of course, other stocks.

Who held the bonds in the 1880s when they were finally paid off under the Dublán conversion is largely unknown except for those who were members of the Committee of Mexican Bondholders or who attended and spoke at the various public meetings. One exception, of course, is the Colliers, merchants of New Broad Street, London, who still had their original 1824, 1825, and 1831 bonds as late as 1888. In their letters to the Stock Exchange Committee at that time, they mention the 1846 conversion, implying that they had held the bonds for more than forty years. Other names like Gillig, Robotham, Hamilton, and Thorne, all of whom attended a bondholders' meeting in 1886, could be cited but nothing is known of them nor when they acquired their bonds.[115] Further research into testamentary bequests or stockbrokers' archives may reveal more information. For the time being, we are left with the Reverend John Carnegie of Cranborne, or Dr. Thomas Proudfoot of Kendal, or retired Royal Navy Commander Charles Mallard, as the typical Mexican bondholder. All three, and many others like them, expected that the British government would come to their aid in persuading the Mexican government to honor its promises to them. It is to the reasons why it failed to do so for many years that we now turn.

NOTES

1. *The Daily Telegraph*, 28 July 1883.

2. The Register is in the CFB Archive in the Guildhall Library.

3. In theory, the prices paid by at least some bondholders might be gleaned from stockbrokers' ledgers which have survived.

4. Reader, *A House in the City*, p. 13.

5. Ibid., p. 15.

6. Figures from ibid., pp. 13–15. In 1830, individual holders of Consols were thought to number nearly 275,000, of which 250,000 received dividends of less than £200 per annum; E.V. Morgan and W.A. Thomas, *The Stock Exchange: Its History and Functions* (London, 1962), p. 123.

7. H. Martineau, *A History of England during the Thirty Years' Peace, 1815–1845* (London, 1848, reprinted 1971), p. 2.

8. The Bank of England report is in *The Times*, 2 April 1822. See also Dawson, *The First Latin American Debt Crisis*, pp. 20–21.

9. There are various calculations of the yield on Consols: I have used B.R. Mitchell, *British Historical Statistics* (Cambridge, 1988), p. 678. There is also a useful retrospective view on the changes in *The Times*, 19 April 1844.

10. A. Andréades, *History of the Bank of England* (2nd ed., London, 1924), p. 249.

11. House of Commons session of 1 April 1822, reported in *The Times*, 2 April 1822.

12. Chapman, *The Rise of Merchant Banking*, p. 4.

13. *The Bristol Mirror*, 17 April 1824; R.W. Hidy, *The House of Baring in American Trade and Finance, 1763–1861* (Cambridge, Mass., 1949), pp. 55.

14. Rimmer, *Marshalls of Leeds*, pp. 95–96.

15. W.G. Hoskins, "Richard Thornton: A Victorian Millionaire," *History Today* (1962), pp. 574–579.

16. Morgan and Thomas, *The Stock Exchange*, p. 83.

17. *The Times*' quotation is cited in C.B. Hunt, "The Joint-Stock Company in England, 1800–1825," *Journal of Political Economy* 43 (1935), p. 17.

18. Dawson, *The First Latin American Debt Crisis*, pp. 100, 103.

19. Andréades, *History of the Bank of England*, p. 250.

20. Dawson, *The First Latin American Debt Crisis*, p. 100.

21. *The Gentleman's Magazine*, March 1824, p. 260.

22. Hunt, "The Joint-Stock Company," p. 24.

23. English Papers, Suffolk Record Office, HA 157/3/118.

24. H. McKenzie Johnston, *Missions to Mexico. A Tale of British Diplomacy in the 1820s* (London, 1992), p. 37.

25. Ferdinand VII, restored to absolute power in Spain in 1823, had repudiated the loans raised by the preceding liberal governments.

26. *The Bristol Mirror*, 24 April 1824.

27. Issue of June 1826, p. 540.

28. *The Bristol Gazette*, 10 March 1825.

29. Dawson, *The First Latin American Debt Crisis*, p. 11.

30. Advertisement in *The Bristol Mirror*, 13 March 1824.

31. English Papers, Suffolk Record Office, HA 157/3/118.

32. J. King, "William Bullock: Showman," in *Viajeros Europeos del siglo XIX en México* (Mexico, 1996), pp. 117–125; *The Times*, 8 April 1824: W. Bullock, *Six Months' Residence and Travel in Mexico* (London, 1824).

33. *The Times*, 11 September 1838.

34. *The Leeds Mercury*, 20 March, 3 April 1824.

35. *The Bristol Mirror*, 9 February 1824.

36. Debate reported in *The Times*, 25 August 1846.

37. *The Times*, 8 July 1844.

38. Letters of 4 November 1857 and 29 April 1858, in CMB *Report* (1861), pp. 129, 140–141.

39. *Report of the Proceedings of a Public Meeting of Mexican Bondholders held at the London Tavern, 27th March, 1868* (London, 1868), p. 12.

40. *The Financier*, 30 May 1877.

41. Robertson correspondence in CMB *Report* (1861), pp. 17–129.

42. *The Financier*, 30 May 1877.

43. The Marshall papers are in the Brotherton Library, University of Leeds, Ms. 200. The ledger is listed as item 1, Book 1, John Marshall's private ledger, 1791–1840. Marshall had very substantial investments in various United States bonds and £36,000 in Colombian and £19,000 in Chilean. The details of his Mexican holdings are on fol. 82 of the ledger.

44. Report of the meeting of 28 May 1858 in *The Morning Chronicle*, 29 May 1858. The figures given for the holdings of individual bondholders are at par or nominal rather than market values.

45. Scottish Record Office, SC60/41/25, fol. 148.

46. *The Financial News*, 14 March 1887.

47. The "inventory" was made by Charles Middleton and is dated 24 January 1851. It is in PRO, Prob. 37/1618.

48. Rougement Brothers to M. Garro, 13 April 1839, SRE, 3.11.4711, fols. 50–53.

49. Rimmer, *Marshalls of Leeds*, p. 118.

50. Although W.P. Robertson's career is fairly well established in the historiography, very little is known about his final years. The National Probate Calendar records the value of the effects of two William Parish Robertsons who died around the same time. One died in London in 1864, leaving less than £20, later revised to under £200. The other died at Valparaiso in 1861, leaving £3,000. It is not clear which was the Mexican bondholder, although it was probably the former.

51. Robertson, *The Foreign Debt*, p. 63.

52. Salomon was one of the main speakers at the meeting held on 6 October 1843. See *The Times*, 7 October 1843.

53. Rubinstein, *Men of Property*, p. 174, n. 25.

54. The memorial is in PRO, F.O. 97/282, fol. 27.

55. CMB *Report* (1861), p. 183.

56. *The Times*, 3 August 1846 and 7 September 1836.

57. Report in *The Morning Herald*, 19 May 1846.

58. W.P. Robertson to Ld. Palmerston, 13 November 1848, PRO, F.O. 50/225, fols. 258–264.

59. *The Navy List* (London, 1822), p. 89. Mallard's will was proved at Bristol on 6 August 1875.

60. CMB *Report* (1861), pp. 191–193.

61. SRE, 40.11.7.

62. PRO, F.O. 97/274, fols. 331–333.

63. SRE, 40.11.7.

64. PRO, F.O. 97/275, fols. 206–209.

65. J.J. Morier, *Abel Allnutt. A Novel* (3 vols., London, 1837).

66. Quotations from the novel are from vol. 1, pp. 1, 34, 35, 69.

67. *The Athenaeum*, 18 February 1837, pp. 116–117.

68. Ibid., p. 11

69. Morier's career has been studied in two books by H. McKenzie Johnston, *Missions to Mexico* (London, 1992) and *Ottoman and Persian Odysseys. James Morier, Creator of Hajji Baba of Ispahan, and His Brothers* (London, 1998). The quotation is from a letter Morier wrote to his brother David on 1 March 1827. It is in the Morier Family Papers housed in the library of Balliol College, Oxford, reference D2.7. It is also quoted in *Missions to Mexico*, p. 292, n. 24. I am grateful to Mr. McKenzie Johnston for drawing my attention to *Abel Allnutt*.

70. The bondholder at North Barrow was Bartholomew Wake, a retired doctor.

71. *A General Directory for the County of Somerset* (Taunton, 1840), p. 215.

72. SRE, 40.11.7.

73. The petition is in PRO, F.O. 50/103, fol. 169.

74. G. Atkinson, *The Worthies of Westmoreland*, vol. 2 (London, 1850), pp. 217–224.

75. This information on Proudfoot is from B. Tyson, "James Towers, a Kendal Surgeon (1785–1846) and Some of His Medical Colleagues," in B.C. Jones and W.G. Wiseman, eds., *Transactions of the Cumberland and Westmoreland Antiquarian and Archaeological Society*, vol. 93 (Stroud, 1993), pp. 206–213.

76. The Proudfoot Papers are in Kendal Record Office, WD/MM/175. They have not been indexed.

77. Kendal Record Office, WD/CR. The Barclays Bank archives are at Wythenshawe, Manchester. I am grateful to Mrs. J. Campbell, Senior Archivist, and to her colleagues for help in using the archive.

78. Barclays Group Archives, Acc. 25/325, fol. 38.

79. Details of the Mexican bonds are in ibid., fols. 94, 217.

80. The Crewdson and Braithwaite families were related. Both were Quakers.

81. Most of the the pocket diaries are in Kendal Record Office, WD/CR, 6/3–8. There are a few in Barclays Archive.

82. Bazant, *Historia de la deuda exterior*, p. 131.

83. W.P. Robertson to Finance Minister, 11 June 1849, in CSAB, *Proceedings*, p. 58.

84. PRO, F.O. 97/274, fols. 376–378.

85. Ibid., 95/289, fols. 256–257.

86. SRE, 40.11.7

87. Ibid.

88. The records of Disraeli's stockmarket dealings are in the Hughenden Papers, Bodleian Library, Oxford, Box 301/2. The quotation is from a letter Disraeli wrote to John Murray on 1 April 1825. See J.A.W. Gunn et al., eds., *Benjamin Disraeli. Letters, 1815–1834*, vol. 1, no. 20 (Toronto, 1982).

89. Walker, *Kinship, Business and Politics*, p. 42.

90. Escandón invited Percy Doyle, Britain's Chargé d'Affaires in Mexico, to join in the speculation, an invitation that was refused. See the documentation in PRO, F.O. 50/259, fols. 181–193.

91. P. Doyle to Lord Palmerston, 5 October 1851, ibid., 50/246, fol. 63.

92. Foreign Exchange Committee Minute Book, 1823–1828, Guildhall Library, Ms. 14617.

93. *The Times*, 7 June 1828.

94. Reader, *A House in the City*, illustration number 2.

95. *The Morning Chronicle*, 25 August 1826.

96. *The Times*, 16 November 1824.

97. Ibid., 3 January 1828.

98. Ibid., 27 August, 1 September 1826.

99. CMB *Report* (1830), p. 24.

100. The lists of names are in vol. 40. There is also an account in Barings Archive, AC 28, which shows that Dutch investors held £64,450 of the 1837 Deferred and £3,455 of the 1842 Debentures.

101. CMB *Report* (1853), pp. 20–23. The 1868 Memorial (PRO, F.O. 97/282, fols. 27–29) has the names of two Paris-based holders: F. Rawes with £4,000 worth of bonds and Oppenheim, Alberte et Cie, no amount given.

102. CMB Minute Book, Guildhall Library, Ms. 15.795, meeting of 4 May 1881.

103. CMB memorial, signed I.L.Goldsmid, 9 August 1852, PRO, F.O. 50/256, fols. 170–177.

104. CMB to Lord Russell, 30 November 1861, ibid., 95/280, fols. 256–257.

105. CMB *Report* (1862), p. 187.

106. Schneider's reports are in SRE, 3.11.4721.

107. PRO, F.O. 50/249, fol. 135.

108. This document carried the heading "Reclamos presentados a la Agencia a resultas de las propuestas que indebidamente y sin ninguna autorización hizo el Sr. D. Benito Gómez Farías en nombre del Gobierno a los tenedores de bonos diferidos." It is in AGN, Deuda Pública, vol. 16, fol. 260.

109. See *The Times*, 25, 28 June 1886; *The Financial News*, 1 July 1886; *The Bullionist*, 3 July 1886.

110. S.P. Knowles to J.M.L. Mora, 28 May 1850, SRE, 40.11.7.

111. Correspondence in PRO, F.O. 97/273, fol. 227.

112. Ibid., 97/280, fols. 308–309.

113. Dover's letters, in chronological order, are in PRO, F.O. 50/156, fols. 283–286; 50/249, fols. 90–91, 133, 154–155; 92/274, fols. 350–352; 97/280, fol. 316; 97/281, fols. 115, 119.

114. Cited in Marichal, *A Century of Debt Crises in Latin America*, p. 113.

115. Reported in *The Financial News*, 1 July 1886.

Chapter 6

The Bondholders and the British Government, 1824–1886

On 3 June 1830, John Marshall, chairman of the newly formed Committee of Mexican Bondholders, wrote to the British Foreign Secretary, Lord Aberdeen. He asked if the Committee "may be permitted to avail itself of the assistance of His Majesty's Minister in Mexico, and of the British Vice-Consuls at the ports of Vera Cruz, and Tampico." Help from the Minister would, he hoped, be in the form of "friendly support" to whatever representations the bondholders might make. As for the Vice-Consuls, it was requested that they be authorized to receive monies assigned to the bondholders by the Mexican government and transmit them to Britain. A few days later, the Under Secretary at the Foreign Office, John Backhouse, replied to say that Lord Aberdeen was "glad to have the power to comply with your request." Appropriate instructions had been sent to the Chargé d'Affaires in Mexico City and the Vice-Consuls had been authorized to receive dividend monies.

The next day, 9 June 1830, Marshall wrote to the Mexican Minister in London, Gorostiza, to tell him of these developments. We want, he said, two agents at each port to receive the customs dues assigned to the dividend fund. One of the agents could be nominated by Mexico but the other should be a Vice-Consul and the Foreign Office had given its assent "for the British Vice-Consuls at the respective ports to undertake the proposed agency." The commission payable to the agents must be on the Mexican account.[1]

This letter to Gorostiza was released to the press for the benefit of bondholders at large. It provoked, however, an angry response from the Foreign Office. It seems to have interpreted phrases used by Marshall as an underhanded but obvious means of establishing an official involvement of the

British government in the bondholders' affairs. Backhouse wrote to Marshall on 29 June to say that while the Vice-Consuls may receive money, they were not allowed to act as "agents of the bondholders in the more general and extended significance of that term." Moreover, the Vice-Consuls could refuse to act as receivers of money if they wished and that if they did accept, "they will undertake the business entirely on their own responsibility." Any commission paid to them must certainly not be from the Mexican government because such payments from a foreign source would be "quite incompatible with the character of a British Vice-Consul." In short, any participation by British diplomats in the bondholders' affairs implied no official sanction or support by the British government.[2]

Relations between the Committee of Mexican Bondholders and the British government, therefore, started badly and they never fully recovered. Both parties maintained a position from which, although there was some movement in practice, there was little, if any, change in principle. In short, the bondholders, arguing that they had a constitutional right to it, demanded the assistance of the British government in their efforts to persuade Mexico to pay its debts to them. The Foreign Office response was consistently negative and it refused to accept that it was under any obligation to provide the help demanded. Both sides built their case on a variety of points, combining principle and pragmatism. A compromise, or middle way between the two polarized positions, however, was to some extent represented by the statements and actions of the Foreign Office between 1848 and the Allied Intervention of 1862. Assistance at governmental level was given during those years, including diplomatic and military, but without conceding the principle that as far as the British government was concerned, the bondholders' problems were entirely a private matter between themselves and the Mexican authorities. The three positions—bondholders, British government, and compromise—are the subject of this chapter.

Bondholders who wrote to the British Foreign Office or to the newspapers, almost without exception, made the same point. They had bought their bonds in the 1820s, they said, because they had been encouraged to do so by the British government in general, and by Foreign Secretary George Canning, in particular. While there may have been no official public sanction of the loans, nobody had been in any doubt at the time that they were at least tacitly approved of by the British government. It had made it clear that the liberation of the Spanish American republics was in Britain's strategic and commercial interest. Also, money from the loans was spent, or substantial amounts of it, on ships and other armaments supplied by British manufacturers. Those weapons were needed by Mexico and the other new nations to defend themselves against external aggression and especially against the threatened reconquest by the reactionary Spanish king, Ferdinand VII. By putting their money into Mexican bonds, therefore, the bondholders argued, they had supported British foreign policy and its manufacturing and shipping industry. Above all, they had enabled the new republics to consolidate their independence. As *The Times* (27 August 1825) put it, the Spanish and Portuguese monarchies had been conquered by "Change-alley," and Spanish America owed its independence to British money.

This belief that the British government had wanted its citizens to buy the bonds and that the money raised had consolidated Spanish American independence persisted for many years. Even Lord Palmerston apparently shared it and certainly, it was asserted by the Committee of Mexican Bondholders on many occasions.[3] The Kendal petition of 1836 noted that it was the British who had provided the Spanish Americans with money "by way of loans in the achievement of their Independence." Forty years later, in 1876, in a letter to the press, "A Mexican Bondholder" recalled that "The British Government encouraged the original loans to Mexico."[4] Another correspondent in the same year, signing himself as "1851," insisted that the British government was obligated to help "considering the encouragement given to the Bondholders by Mr. Canning's Acts and Speeches."[5]

No British government ever acknowledged any responsibility for the loans, but as far as the bondholders were concerned, believing themselves to have been officially encouraged to invest their money in them, they were entitled to governmental support when they tried to recover their money. In his letter to Lord Clarendon of 20 August 1856, William Morgan forcefully expressed this view: "I call on your Lordship, as the organ of the British Government, to obtain me redress." When the citizens of other countries are wronged, he insisted, for example, Americans, French, or "even Spanish citizens," their governments "not only claim but enforce redress." "British subjects alone are pillaged with impunity," he said, "but my Lord, this must no longer be—for the interests of England, it must no longer be. The last war with Russia arose because our forbearance had grown proverbial and because it was thought that England either could not, or would not, enforce her rights."[6]

Morgan's views were widely shared and none more so than his final demand. "It is," he said, "the bounden duty of the British Government to protect the property of British subjects." The bondholders maintained that their investments and their dividend monies were entitled to the same protection as would be afforded to the property and possessions of any British subject, either within the kingdom or overseas. Any distinction between goods and money, it was argued at the inaugural meeting of the Committee of Spanish American Bondholders in June 1836, was "outrageous."[7] Both were entitled to the same protection, especially, as the chairman, George Robinson emphasized, since the British government had encouraged the loans, knowing that without them Spanish America would not have won its independence. The assembled bondholders passed the following resolution:

That this Meeting confidently rely [*sic*] on the active support of His Majesty's Government in this object, to which they humbly consider themselves entitled on every principle of justice and protection; it being manifest, that whether a foreign nation unlawfully detains the property of British subjects, or unjustly withholds from them the performance of engagements into which it has voluntarily entered, the wrong and injury are alike, and the claims for redress equal.[8]

Ten years later in 1846, in a letter to Palmerston, George Robinson put the point very clearly. He was concerned with the problem of customs dues assigned to the dividend fund being seized by the Mexican authorities:

those monies from the moment they are set apart for transmission to England are bona fide the property of the bondholders, and the Government can have no control over them any more than they would have over the property of a British merchant residing in that country. It is in fact, in spirit, if not in letter, a complete violation of the treaty between Great Britain and Mexico by which the property of British subjects is protected in that country

He wanted "such instructions" as were necessary to obtain justice for the bondholders sent to British diplomatic representatives in Mexico and elsewhere.[9]

A decade later, Charles McGarel was still making the same demand, arguing that monies assigned to the dividends "became virtually the private property and revenue of British subjects."[10] Not for the first time, the bondholders had sought counsel's opinion to justify their case. The leading advocate, Dr. Robert Phillimore, obliged with an opinion that the British government was fully entitled under international law to use force to recover the seized monies or property of its subjects.[11] In 1869, the Sheridan Committee, in a memorial to the Foreign Office, cited several precedents.[12] One was Lord Castlereagh who, in 1814, had successfully claimed from France the repayment of money invested by British citizens in French funds. Another was Lord Russell, who had stated in the House of Commons with reference to British interests in China that "We are prepared to protect British interests and property wherever they exist." The Mexican bondholders demanded "active steps" to compel Mexico to satisfy their claims. Their demand for the protection of the British government was not "a questionable right." On the contrary,

the claim is founded upon the most elementary principle of that social compact on which our whole civil policy is built up, viz., upon the reciprocal duties of sovereign and subject, as laid down in the British Constitution, by which the inalienable fealty and allegiance of the latter both in person and property is exacted or demanded in exchange for the equally inalienable protection of both person and property to be exercised by the former.[13]

Expediency, it was added, cannot supercede or relieve either party from these obligations.

The rather legalistic tone and language in this 1869 memorial almost certainly reflect the influence of the Brighton barrister and Mexican Committee member, Richard Garde. He had already published, in the form of a letter to Earl Russell, a forty-three page opinion "on the absolute right of the Mexican Bondholders who are subjects of Her Most Gracious Majesty." Here is not the place to present the detailed and at times dense legal arguments of his text, but suffice to say that he maintained that the bondholders had an absolute right under the British constitution and fundamental laws of the nation to "the protection of their persons and properties in foreign countries as well as in England." He asked that the British government should act "according to the immutable rules of justice, and obtain for the Queen's subjects from Mexico that redress to which, by the laws and constitution of these realms, they are entitled, even though unfortunately the creditors of that Republic."[14]

The same points were made repeatedly in the 1870s by the Committee of Mexican Bondholders' chairman, Henry Sheridan. Diplomatic relations with Mexico were, of course, suspended at that time but Sheridan raised the bondholders' case in the House of Commons nine times between 1869 and 1884.[15] In 1871, and again in 1873, for example, he pressed for the renewal of relations and asked if the government was prepared to take measures to protect the property of Mexico's English creditors. The answer he received was negative.[16] He also announced, however, his intention to move for a Select Committee to investigate the whole question of foreign loans and in this respect, allied with the Corporation of Foreign Bondholders, he was more successful. In March 1875, the Select Committee on Foreign Loans began to hear evidence. While the hearings produced much useful information on the mechanics of the loan business, the Committee chose to restrict its enquiry to the bond issues of only four nations—Costa Rica, Honduras, Paraguay, and Santo Domingo.[17]

Nothing came out of the Select Committee of any immediate help to the Mexican bondholders but Sheridan kept up the pressure. He led more deputations to the Foreign Office to urge the renewal of relations with Mexico, always insisting that the British government's duty was to "protect not only the lives of the citizens, but also their property."[18] In a meeting with Foreign Secretary Lord Derby on 9 March 1876, he added other points to his case. One concerned an offer made by the United States in 1861. Anxious to dissuade the British government from participating in the Tripartite Alliance and invasion of Mexico, the United States government had intimated its willingness to assume responsibility for the interest payments on Mexico's London debt. Although the exact nature of the offer is obscure, it was refused by the Foreign Office "for Imperial reasons," but according to Sheridan, "the British Government from that moment assumed the position of trustees for the Bondholders." If the government was unwilling to meet this obligation, would it allow the bondholders to collect their own debts and "should they not be permitted to take every possible means to protect themselves as they would do in barbarous countries."[19] The bondholders' implied threat of privately sponsored military action to recover their debts was ignored, but Lord Derby gave a generally sympathetic hearing, offering to consider any substantive proposal "which could be reasonably adopted."

Like all his predecessors who had led the Mexican Committee before him, Sheridan failed to persuade the British government that the bondholders were entitled to its protection and, if needed, military support. He chose, therefore, to adopt another tactic which had also to some extent been tried before. This was to concentrate on the loss of trade and commercial opportunities caused by the disruption in diplomatic relations between the two countries. In 1876, he wrote to the British Association of Chambers of Commerce, urging it "to bring pressure to bear upon H.M. Government to have a resumption of such relations brought about."[20] A few months later the Association, listing fifty-one members, obliged with a petition to the Foreign Office, emphasizing the difficulties of trading without diplomatic protection. British merchants trading with Mexico, the Association insisted, deserved the traditional consular and diplomatic support given by Her Majesty's government to similar interests throughout the world.[21] In 1877 and later years he participated in or headed delegations of mercantile interests to the Foreign Office, pleading the case for a renewal of relations. British trade with Mexico was being lost, he argued, to France, Germany, Spain, and other countries which had diplomatic representatives in Mexico. Opportunities for investment were being missed as long as the debt issue remained unresolved and Mexican business was excluded from the Stock Exchange. British residents in Mexico were also left unprotected. The topic was regularly raised in Parliament and on each occasion, the official response was sympathetic, but no more, with the British position consistently being that it was up to Mexico to initiate any move for the resumption of relations. In the early 1880s, when unofficial talks with Mexican representatives began, Sheridan reminded the Foreign Office once again of the bondholders' case. In letters to Sir Charles Dilke in July and August 1882, for example, he pointed out that the debt totalled £18,127,720. It was in everyone's interest, he said, that Mexico should prosper but the bondholders must not be forgotten. Moreover, he reiterated the point that the British government had in effect adopted the bondholders' claims when, at the time of the Tripartite Intervention, Lord Russell had rejected the United States' offer to pay dividends on the debt.[22] Dilke's reply was again reassuring but little more. "The Mexican Government," he wrote, "declares that they have no intention whatever of repudiating their pecuniary obligations." They had been told privately to reach an agreement on the debt with the bondholders and that if they did so, a new treaty of commerce could be negotiated. No reply, however, had yet been received. Subsequent talks between the two goverments finally led to the resumption of relations in 1884.[23] The debt issue was not raised, at least officially, but the settlement opened the way for the Dublán conversion of 1885–1886.

Sheridan had not been the first bondholder to introduce the loss of trade argument. In 1838, the French had invaded and occupied Veracruz to collect the debts allegedly owed to their citizens. The subsequent so-called Pastry War reduced trade and brought a reduction in customs dues assigned to the dividend fund. Merchant groups from many parts of Britain hastened to the Foreign Office to press for protection of their interests. The Mexican bondholder, J.D.Powles, for example, led a delegation of representatives from Glasgow, Liverpool, Manchester, and Belfast.[24] A formal petition from the bondholders was delivered to Palmerston on 30 June 1838. It declared that the French blockade was prejudicial to their interests and that Britain ought to intervene to reopen the Mexican ports to international trade.[25] Mexico's interim Chargé d'Affaires in London reported in July that the bondholders had been to see him to say that they were trying to persuade the British government to offer to mediate the dispute.[26] In August, the House of Lords debated the situation and although the Duke of Wellington and Viscount Strangford, among others, expressed their indignation at French conduct, they favored the use of British diplomacy and "moral influence" rather than the direct intervention urged by the bondholders.[27] The Committee of Spanish American Bondholders told the Foreign Secretary that Mexican dividends of about £250,000 a year were at stake. They also emphasized that while the interests of merchants and shipping companies were important, so were those of the bondholders.[28] Although Palmerston's reply to this concerted pressure was described by *The Times* (8 September 1838) as "laconic," it finally brought the decision to dispatch a British squadron to Veracruz, where it arrived at the end of December 1838. One of the passengers was the British diplomat, Richard Pakenham, and his offer to mediate the dispute brought about a cessation of hostilities and eventual settlement. Under its terms, Mexico agreed to pay 600,000 pesos to French claimants. As far as the bondholders were concerned, that conclusion was clear evidence that the use of force against the Mexicans paid off and they were to cite the episode as a precedent on many occasions.

The United States–Mexican War of 1846–1848 engendered much the same sort of demands on the Foreign Office from both merchant associations and bondholders. The merchants sent delegations and submitted memorials asking for protection of their trading interests and the bondholders demanded protection and assistance. In the House of Commons, which debated the situation in August 1846, both Lord George Bentinck and Benjamin Disraeli supported the demands of the merchants and bondholders for British intervention, at least in the form of mediation. Disraeli, in particular, reaffirmed the bondholders' often-stated point that they had a mort-gage on California and other Mexican territories threatened by United States expansionism. He urged that some form of protectorate in Mexico should be imposed by European powers for a period of two years. Others advocated mediation which Palmerston confirmed had been offered.[29] The following year (1847), "on the motion of Mr. Disraeli," the House of Commons asked the Executive to lay before it all the correspondence relating to the loans with Spain, Portugal, Greece, Mexico, and other Spanish American States.[30] This was followed by a Select Committee, chaired by John Roebuck. It began hearing evidence in the summer of 1849 and among the witnesses was J.D. Powles. In his view, "This enquiry is a very important one and I am anxious to see what measure Mr. Roebuck thinks of founding upon it. The enquiry will not be allowed to remain a dead letter."[31] The bondholders' chairman, George Robinson, also believed that "there is little doubt that some movement will be forthcoming from it."[32] In fact, although Disraeli was a member of it, the Roebuck Committee met only four times and failed to produce a report on the grounds of lack of time in the parliamentary session. Notwithstanding its recommendation that it should continue its enquiry in the following session, it does not appear to have reassembled.[33]

More than anything, as we have seen in an earlier section, the bond-holders were anxious to have at least some of the American indemnity payment assigned to their claims. More delegations led by George Robinson and others were received in the Foreign Office and Palmerston was told that the bondholders "naturally expect" to have their dividends paid out of the indemnity money.[34] When the Mexican Minister in London, Mora, publicly rejected the claims, appeals for support again poured into the Foreign Office. British representatives in Mexico, notably the Chargé d'Affaires, Percy Doyle, applied what pressure they could. The bondhold-ers' agent in Mexico City, Ewen Mackintosh, who was a British Consul, also pressed the claim very strongly. In fact, according to Tenenbaum, Brit-ish military action was threatened if Mexico failed to allocate indemnity funds to the bondholders.[35] Such threats may have been made but they were certainly not part of official Foreign Office policy. Again, as indicated in an earlier section, Mexico failed to respond to such threats, waiting until the 1851 conversion had been agreed upon before allocating 2,500,000 dollars of the final indemnity installment to the payment of interest arrears on the foreign debt.

The most persistent campaign by the bondholders for British government support came in the 1850s, coinciding with the rise to prominence on the Mexican Committee of Charles McGarel and David Roberston. Robertson, in particular, pressed the Foreign Office very hard with increasingly strident demands for the help to which he argued the bondholders were entitled. He began with letters to Lord Clarendon in May and June 1856 in which he argued the case for military intervention in the form of frigates to occupy the Customs Houses at Veracruz and Tampico, where British personnel would collect the bondholders' share of the customs dues. Within days, he was invited to the Foreign Office in person to hear why such a policy would not be adopted. Several reasons were advanced. The dispatch of frigates would be tantamout to a declaration of war on Mexico. British and all international trade would be disrupted and seizure of customs dues would be a measure "of a bucaneering character." The tariff to be used would have to be decided by the British occupiers. Merchants would have no guarantee that at a later stage when the Mexicans were back in control, they would not be required to pay again. How, Robertson was asked, could a United States vessel be forced to pay if it refused to acknowledge the British right to collect them? Finally, Mexico might well declare war and seek the aid of the United States.[36]

According to the Foreign Office record of the meeting, Robertson accepted the force of these arguments, but he was told that if he and his colleagues could present a plan of action that was practical, it would receive full consideration. Over the next few weeks, Robertson consulted with his colleagues on the Mexican Committee and also with J.D. Powles and the former agent, Falconnet. In July 1856, he sent to the Foreign Office a plan whereby interventors or receivers would be placed in Mexican Customs Houses to collect the share of customs dues assigned to the dividend fund. This was not a new idea and, as he pointed out, under the terms of the October 1850 law which had brought about the 1851 conversion, the bondholders had been authorized to appoint agents in Mexican ports. Several had been appointed but subsequently Mexico had withdrawn its recognition of them, and even where they still existed they were ignored by the customs officials. What Robertson now proposed was that such agents be given "a more efficient protection" by means of a full Diplomatic Convention with the force of an international treaty.

Robertson made several points in support of his case. For example, he was able to quote Whitehead, the bondholders' agent in Mexico, who had reported in June 1856 that "the only mode which lies open to the Bondholders to get their interests respected is to use their interest with Her Majesty's Government to obtain for their agreement the sanction of a diplomatic Convention." Without it, he went on, "my mission here is superfluous."[37] Without a Convention, and the Mexicans had said this on several occasions, Robertson noted, they did not have to recognize the bondholders' agents. Nor would they be able, as again they had done, to tell British diplomats who raised the debt question that it was none of their concern. Above all, he insisted that the bondholders had a right to expect parity of treatment with those other British creditors of Mexico whose interests had already been protected under the Doyle Convention of 1851. He reminded the Foreign Office, as he had done several times previously, that "our claims arise out of a much earlier Debt and are of a more ancient date as well as of a more sacred character."[38] Finally, anticipating an obvious objection, he argued that there could be no "inconvenient precedent" whereby bondholders of other debtor nations might demand similar treatment because only the Mexican bondholders had the right to place agents in Mexican ports enshrined in a Mexican law. That was a right conceded to no other bondholders. "The question," he concluded, "is narrowed to the mere point of getting this particular right confirmed and the exercise of it defined by treaty."[39] Only "an absolute Convention" would work; anything less would be "utterly nugatory and delusive."[40]

None of these campaigns and pressure exercised by the bondholders and their Committees was noticeably effective in changing British policy. In some respects, this is surprising. First, as we have seen in the analysis of the bondholders, they included in their ranks many members of the British elite: Members of Parliament, generals, admirals, financiers, and other prominent figures in political, commercial, and social circles. They had easy and ready access to the corridors of power and their case was always promised serious consideration by successive Foreign Secretaries. There is also some suggestion that the bondholders tried to use their influence to extract concessions at election times. In 1857, for example, the Mexican Minister in London reported to his government that he had been summoned to the Foreign Office to discuss the continued failure to pay dividends to either the bondholders or the Convention creditors. He added, "now that the Government needs to win the elections for the next Parliament, some of the bondholders, who are also electors, would be demanding something be done to force Mexico to pay."[41] David Robertson implied the same point in a letter to the British Chargé d'Affaires in Mexico City. Referring to his talks at the Foreign Office, he noted: "such men as Lord Palmerston, Lord Clarendon and Lord Malmesbury, know well that nothing makes them so popular as justly taking the part of ill-used Englishmen against foreign governments."[42]

Second, apparently without regard to the political complexion of the administration in office, the press in general, and *The Times* in particular, consistently gave their backing to the bondholders' case for governmental assistance. In 1833, for example, *The Times* (27 December) remarked that the whole question of the Spanish American debt was "a matter well worthy of the attention of the government." Three years later (21 January 1836), it proclaimed that the debt was "of national importance," meriting the "energetic interference" of the British government. Even military action might be necessary and justified: "On the part of England, were the interference to take an offensive shape, after other expedients have been tried in vain, it would be difficult for the countries against which it was directed to offer any valid plea or remonstrance against it." Welcoming the formation of the Committee of Spanish American Bondholders in 1836, it remarked that "to make some effort for the recovery of this enormous debt is a duty absolutely incumbent on the government," adding that the United States "would not allow its subjects to be robbed with impunity" (12 July, 9 August, 1836).

This kind of press support continued into the 1850s, becoming increasingly critical of the failure of all goverments to take active steps to assist the bondholders. On 6 October 1857, *The Times* included the following acerbic comments in its City Column:

> The manner in which the leading governments of the world continue to hold terms with such states as Mexico, Venezuela etc. is a blot upon the age. If a private individual were to negotiate with blacklegs, he would at once be disgraced but it seems not to be thought unbecoming either for the Sovereign of England or France or the President of the United States to admit to their receptions the representatives of nations for whose infamy and meanness it would be hard to find a parallel among the lowest cheats of the turf or the gambling table.

At their public meeting on 4 July 1861, the bondholders acknowledged this support by passing a resolution of thanks to "the press of England generally, and especially to the Editor of the City Article of the *Times* for their consistent and able advocacy of the outraged rights of the Mexican Bondholders."[43]

Nothwithstanding their political status, therefore, their easy access to Downing Street and elsewhere and the long-standing support of the press, the bondholders failed to persuade the British government to give them the support they demanded. In his analysis of "H.M. Government and the Bondholders," Professor Platt has demonstrated that Foreign Office policy toward holders of all foreign bonds was throughout the nineteenth century a mixture of principle and expediency.[44] Its response to the Mexican bondholders was much the same as to the bondholders of the other Spanish American republics and to those of European nations such as Spain and Portugal. The essence of the policy was unequivocally set out in 1829. It may be recalled that following the first open public meeting of Spanish American bondholders in London in May 1828, a delegation had gone to the Foreign Office to ask for support. Unfortunately, we have no details of the discussions, but official British policy was stated soon afterwards in a reply to one of the bondholders, a Mr. Ewing. He had written of the "hardships to which the holders of South American and Mexican bonds are subjected by the non-payment of the dividends due thereon." He urged "the necessity of the interference" of the British government with the defaulting nations to persuade them to meet their obligations. The reply was succinct and to the point. "The grievances," Mr. Ewing was told, "of which you complain arise out of speculations of a purely private nature." The British government could not in such circumstances, "as a matter of right, claim to exercise any authoritative interference with foreign States." On the other hand, the government could not be indifferent to the interests of the numerous individuals involved, and it was willing to support, "by their countenance and good offices," any representations which the bondholders themselves might make to the countries concerned. Instructions to that effect would be sent to "His Majesty's Chargé d'Affaires and Consuls in the several States."[45]

As far as the British government was concerned, therefore, the loans and dividends on them, the conversions, defaults, and all subsequent dealings, were strictly private transactions between individuals and foreign governments in which there had been no official involvement. Although in later years the bondholders' collective memory certainly recalled their being encouraged to invest their money, especially by Canning, in fact he had set out his policy very clearly in 1823 and 1824. He had refused diplomatic intervention in the Colombian default of 1823 on the grounds that the loan had been entered into on the clear understanding that the government was neither involved nor responsible in any way. A few months later, in reply to a request for intervention in Spain, he reiterated that it was no part of "the duty of the Government to interfere in any way to procure the repayment of loans made by British subjects to Foreign Powers, States, or individuals."[46] He had further demonstrated the government's determination to distance itself from the loans in the case of the envoy to Mexico, Lionel Hervey. In 1824, Hervey was reprimanded and ordered to return from Mexico because he had involved himself in loan negotiations and had assured the parties involved that the British government would guarantee payment. He was told that he should have known that "money dealing is of all forms of commercial adventure that in which it is most unfit that a publick [sic] officer, to whom all trade is interdicted, should engage."[47]

This policy of no official intervention was maintained for the whole of the nineteenth century and countless appeals and protests by the Mexican Committee between 1830 and 1886 were invariably met with the same response. Nothing could or would be done on any official intergovernmental level. George Robinson, for example, was told in October 1843 that the Chargé d'Affaires in Mexico City would be instructed "to use his good offices, as far as may be proper, on behalf of the Mexican Bondholders." The letter actually sent to Doyle from the Foreign Office was more direct: "I do not desire you to interfere authoritatively with the Government of Mexico on behalf of the Bondholders."[48] Charles Bankhead, British Minister Plenipotenciary in Mexico, was told a couple of years later to do what he could to support the bondholders' case but always "short of official and authoritative interference."[49] In 1871, Edmund Hammond, by then Permanent Secretary at the Foreign Office, replied to Hyde Clarke, secretary of the recently formed Corporation of Foreign Bondholders, that there was no change in policy nor likely to be. The British government, he wrote, was not a party in any way to private loan transactions with foreign states. They were "speculative enterprises" entered into by capitalists in the hope of large profits. Hence, the government's aid "will continue to be limited to unofficial support and friendly remonstrance with such foreign states as from time to time fail to meet their obligations."[50] Finally, in 1892, in response to a claim that the government was to intervene in Argentina on behalf of creditors, Foreign Office officials advised that "our general line is to confine ourselves entirely to giving the representatives of the Bondholders such unofficial assistance as seems judicious."[51]

What, then, was "unofficial support and friendly remonstrance"? Professor Platt provides a good summary. Letters of introduction and personal introductions were provided to bondholders' agents, for example, William Parish Roberston, who was formally presented to the Mexican Finance Minister by the Chargé d'Affaires, Doyle.[52] British diplomats were often used as channels of communication whereby the bondholders' Committee was able to have protests, memorials, and general correspondence delivered directly to Mexican officials. The initial refusal to allow Consuls to engage in commercial or monetary transactions was relaxed in later years and several acted as agents of the bondholders on a commission basis. The example of Ewen Mackintosh has been referred to several times. He was British Consul in Mexico City from 1839 to 1853 during which time he was also the Mexican bondholders' agent, as well as a prominent entrepreneur and financier. When diplomats delivered correspondence or presented agents, the distinction between official and unofficial support was perhaps at times blurred, but Foreign Office instructions were always that the nature and extent of the support should be clear.

British government policy toward the bondholders, therefore, was firmly based on the principle of non-intervention or interference in what it considered were the private affairs of investors. Other reasons of expediency or pragmatism were also sometimes used. For example, a range of points was put to David Robertson to explain the Foreign Office refusal to make the Mexican debt the subject of a diplomatic Convention. In June and July 1856, officials and the Foreign Secretary, Lord Clarendon, considered their reply. In his opinion on the subject, Hammond pointed out that the bondholders were not a chartered or permanent organization. Hence, if a Convention were arranged, there was no way of ensuring that a future Committee of Mexican Bondholders might not reject it on the grounds that it was not bound by the actions of its predecessors. It might be possible, he thought, to take up the case "in general adjustment of grievances" but Robertson should probably be told that "HMG do not clearly see their way of advocating the interests of the Bondholders without compromising the general interests of the country."

Clarendon wanted a stronger reply. Could we compel Mexico, he asked, to enter into a Convention if it was unwilling to do so? Was Britain prepared to go to war with Mexico if a future government of the country defaulted on the terms of a Convention? Was the British government willing to press for Conventions with all the other debtor republics in Spanish America? Mexico, he added, in his opinion was a bankrupt country and no Treaty or Convention would alter that fact. What was the point, therefore, of demanding commitments which could not be met? Furthermore, people with Spanish blood in their veins like the Mexicans did not willingly pay their debts or see money exported to foreigners.

The note eventually sent to Robertson on 20 August 1856 included all these points, together with two others suggested by the Law Officers to the Crown who had also been consulted. These were briefly that a Convention of the sort proposed by Robertson covering the relatively narrow issue of agents or interventors in the ports might be adverse to the bondholders' interests. It would restrict the government's ability in the future to demand payment of the whole debt. Second, contrary to the argument put by Roberston, the Convention would certainly create a precedent which other creditors of foreign nations would use. Finally, "such a Convention would almost force this country to go to war with Mexico each time its government failed to abide by it."[53]

Such reasons of principle or expediency largely determined the Foreign Office attitude to the bondholders but there were also three other factors which need to be taken into account. The first concerns the so-called English Convention debt and its bondholders. It may be recalled that this was based on formal agreements between the governments of Britain and Mexico incorporated into the Doyle Convention of 1851. Mexico had recognized certain British claims and had assigned customs dues to meet them. It had failed to keep up the payments and as Robertson had put it in 1858, "the British Convention creditors are in the same boat" as the Mexican bondholders. What Robertson hoped to achieve was to "make common cause with them" in putting pressure on the British government to take active steps to persuade Mexico to pay. Unfortunately for him, the Convention creditors had their own priorities and had no wish to see their own pleas to the Foreign Office confused or diluted by those of the Mexican bondholders. Hence, Robertson was told by Loftus Otway, Britain's Chargé d'Affaires, that "I do not think the Convention Bondholders will ever consent to make common cause with you—they are in a better position and they know of it and are of opinion in this instance that *l'union ne fait pas la force.*"[54]

The Convention creditors were not the only lobby competing with the bondholders for Foreign Office support. The second factor which officials had to take into account involved the attitude and demands of at least some of the merchants trading with Mexico. Although the volume and value of British trade with Mexico was not especially significant in the nineteenth century (compared, for example, with Argentina), those merchants engaged in the commerce were always anxious that nothing should be done to disturb relations between the two countries. Similarly, there were substantial British investments in the Mexican mining industry and the companies involved wanted nothing done to risk their capital or jeopardize their daily activities. Many of these commercial and industrial interests were members of an organization known as the South American and Mexican Assocation. It represented merchants and others from Liverpool, Manchester, Glasgow, and elsewhere and it acted as an energetic lobby on their behalf. When their trading activities were threatened, for example, by the French blockade of Veracruz and Tampico in 1838, or by the United States invasion of 1846 and the war which followed, deputations and representations were promptly submitted to the Foreign Office asking for action to protect their interests.

One member of the Association was Robert McCalmont. He was a partner in the trading company of McCalmont, Brothers & Co., which had interests in Mexico, Brazil, and other Spanish American countries. In October 1861, a bitter polemic, waged largely in public by both sides, was conducted between McCalmont and David Robertson on behalf of the Mexican bondholders. Its origins lay in a letter sent to Lord Palmerston by McCalmont in July 1848. At that time, the bondholders were pressing the British government very strongly for assistance in persuading Mexico to pay the dividends on its debt and to allocate any indemnity money to the coupon arrears. McCalmont wrote to oppose any such help which, he argued, was not deserved. "The Bondholders in question," he alleged, "consist of Dutchmen, Germans, Frenchmen, Spaniards, some Englishmen, and some Mexicans, and others—a collection of speculators not identified with this country." The Committee of Mexican Bondholders, he added, had recently stated that it was a matter of indifference to the bondholders where the money for their dividends came from. But to the merchant community, the source of such funds was of grave importance because, if the bondholders' demands were met, it would mean "the imposition of increased duties on British merchandize, and exactions from British merchants." He urged the Foreign Secretary, therefore, not to be "the instrument of stimulating the Governments of Mexico and of South America to increase their exorbitant exactions on us and on our goods."

We do not know if the Committee of Mexican Bondholders was aware of this letter at the time it was sent in 1848, and nothing more was heard about it until thirteen years later when the Tripartite Alliance for the occupation of Mexican ports was being discussed. In October 1861, McCalmont sent another letter to the Foreign Secretary of the day, Lord Russell. He again appealed to the British government not to intervene in Mexico on behalf of the bondholders, repeating the claim that most of the latter were not British subjects. Any use of force to collect customs dues, he insisted, "is calculated to postpone the satisfaction of *bona fide* British claims, and to prejudice British interests." What the government should do was to take steps to protect British property in Mexico but any hope of that being done successfully "would be greatly prejudiced by British claims and Bondholders' claims being treated in the same category."[55]

McCalmont chose to send these letters for publication to the London newspapers where they attracted the attention, and irate reponse, of Robertson, Garde, and other bondholders, as well as of editors of papers which had long supported the bondholders' case. Robertson replied on behalf of the Mexican Committee in the form of a letter to McCalmont, also sent to the press. He accused him of inaccurate facts and of "deductions from false data." His allegation that the bondholders were largely foreign speculators was completely wrong and "a more utterly inaccurate statement never was made by man, or house of business." It was a "cruel injustice" inflicted on "your fellow countrymen" intended to advance personal interests at their expense. While some bonds had been acquired by Dutch and German investors, "and very properly too, according to Free Trade principles," the great majority were held by the original buyers, "excellent people with families, and many poor widows and children." "We now know," he continued, "who have been our secret enemies at home and in Mexico."

The newspapers were equally critical of McCalmont. *The Money Market Review* (26 October 1861), for example, accused him of "bad taste and injustice"; "surely some strange selfishness at the bottom of this bold procedure"; and factual inaccuracy, especially regarding the allegation of foreign bondholders. It was to be hoped, it concluded, "that Messrs. M'Calmont [*sic*] & Co. stand alone amongst British merchants in deprecating the grant of help by our Government to the defrauded and despoiled Bondholders." *The Daily News* was also hostile and the controversy provoked letters of protest from several bondholders. Richard Garde chose to write directly to Lord Russell and his words sum up the anger which he and his colleagues felt:

> On the part of the Committee and the Mexican Bondholders, allow me to assure your Lordship that with the exception of a few of the subjects of the King of the Netherlands, the Bondholders are the liege subjects of Her Majesty and not speculators either in public securities or merchandize. Many of them are men eminent in the Church, the Navy and the Army, the Law and Medicine—gentlemen who regard the term speculator as synonymous with thief.

Finally, the third factor influencing Foreign Office policy toward the bondholders was Edmund Hammond. If David Robertson is to be believed, one of the main causes of the British government's refusal to help the bondholders was the attitude of the Permanent Secretary. Hammond, educated at Eton and Oxford (3rd in Classics), entered the Foreign Office as a junior clerk in 1824. He rose through the ranks, eventually becoming Permanent

Secretary in 1854, a position he held until his retirement in 1873. His career, therefore, paralleled the years from the first Mexican loans in 1824 through and past the break in diplomatic relations in 1867. Those who have studied the Foreign Office and diplomatic service describe Hammond as a man of "energy and ability," with "thrusting and forceful ways."[56] He was also, however, "a very conservative bureaucrat who had opposed most of the reforms that had been carried out in the Foreign Office in the previous ten years" (1850–1860).[57] As far as Charles McGarel and David Robertson were concerned, it was this conservatism and resistance to change which were at the root of Foreign Office reluctance to help them. Praising one of the more helpful officials, Robertson wrote,

I only wish that his department included also that of Mexico, as Mr. Hammond, whose province it usually is, though a personal friend of mine, and civiler to me than to most people, is notoriously in the office a man of the old school, who will do nothing out of the jog trot, and really would never succeed in anything, or let other people succeed, and will not move one step for English bondholders if he can help it, or for anyone else, as was the practice when he was young there, twenty or thirty years ago.[58]

Hammond, Roberston wrote in other letters, "seems always disposed to do as little as possible for bondholders or anyone else."[59]

The origin of these hostile opinions about the Permanent Secretary seems to have been in McGarel's and Robertson's attempts to get Foreign Office support in the 1850s. They both had several interviews with Hammond in which he dismissed out of hand their various suggestions. For example, as noted earlier, Robertson was very hopeful at one point that the United States would annex Mexico and thus assume responsibility for the debt. "You told me," Robertson wrote in a letter to Hammond in February 1857, that "you were opposed in principle to any or all such annexations."[60] The next year, Robertson accused him of deliberately sabotaging the bondholders' efforts to get official backing by misleading and misinforming the Foreign Secretary. Lord Malmesbury, he said, was very angry with Hammond "for not more correctly informing him, and throwing cold water upon our undoubted just requests to the Foreign Office."[61] Palmerston, Clarendon, and Malmesbury, he thought, had always been sympathetic to the bondholders but Hammond was the problem because "he hates bondholders in his heart."[62] Months later the situation had not changed: "Mr. Hammond adheres to the most decided hostility to the right and just claims of all bondholders, and has thwarted the good intentions of Lord Malmesbury towards the Mexican bondholders."[63] Finally, the episode of the Legation theft in Mexico City brought angry confrontations with McGarel and Robertson. Hammond told them that they were responsible for the loss of the money because they should have had it sent to

England long before the Mexicans had the opportunity to seize it. He accused them of "a desire to go to war." Robertson complained to Lord Wodehouse at the Foreign Office of Hammond's "choleric treatment"of McGarel, "an excellent man." In a later letter, he wrote that Hammond was unhelpful and rude: "I am disgusted with every interview I have ever had with him."[64]

Of course, we cannot know to what extent Hammond influenced official policy toward the bondholders during his long career. True to the traditions of the Civil Service, he defended himself by insisting that it was the Secretary of State who took decisions and wrote the letters. He had nothing like the influence, he insisted, that Robertson and McGarel thought he had.[65] That may have been the case but there seems little doubt that his conservatism and, in Robertson's words, his cavalier dismissal of the bondholders' appeals, did not help. Perhaps surprisingly, however, as he seems to have been resolutely against intervention, Hammond was unable to stop British participation in the Tripartite Alliance. In several respects, the Foreign Office's decision to join with France and Spain in the military occupation of Mexican ports had its origins in a circular issued by Palmerston in 1848. Under strong pressure from the Committee of Spanish American Bondholders, and from the creditors of several European countries and North American states in default on their loans, Palmerston had refined the policy of no official interference hitherto followed. He warned the defaulters that the British government claimed the right to take up the loan questions, if it chose to do so, and that the fact that it had so far opted not to do so was merely a matter of discretion and domestic considerations rather than of international right. While to date successive governments had thought it undesirable that British subjects should invest their money in loans to foreign governments rather than in "profitable undertakings at home," and had therefore not taken up the complaints made against foreign governments, that situation could change because,

> it might happen that the loss occasioned to British subjects by the non-payment of interest upon Loans made by them to Foreign Governments might become so great that it would be too high a price for the nation to pay . . . and in such a state of things it might become the duty of the British Government to make these matters the subject of diplomatic negotiation.[66]

The threat in Palmerston's circular was obvious and it seems to have encouraged British diplomats in Mexico, and presumably elsewhere, to adopt a firmer line and stronger language in notes to their Mexican counterparts. In the 1850s, especially following the Doyle Convention, the threats of military retaliation became increasingly direct. In 1855, for example, Santa Anna suspended payments to both the bondholders and the Convention creditors and ordered the seizure of money set aside for the dividend fund at Mazatlán. The British Chargé d'Affaires, Lettsom, was instructed to protest and to warn that unless the money was returned, "HMG will be under the necessity of resorting to measures of coercion."[67] The following year, Lettsom was told to inform the Mexican Foreign Minister that "if faith is not kept with the British Bondholders and they require the aid of this Government, it will be afforded them, for such is the usage among civilized nations."[68] Finally, when Lettsom reported that the Mexican government "cavilled at the right of the British Government to interfere on behalf of the British Bondholders," he again was told to assert "its right to interfere on behalf of its oppressed subjects."

The civil war and virtual collapse of law and order in several regions of Mexico between 1855 and 1860, especially in the mining districts where silver was produced and at the ports where customs dues were paid, brought various incidents in which British-owned money or property was seized. Strong diplomatic protests always followed, accompanied by more threats of military action. Then, in 1858, the decision was taken to send a naval force "for the protection of British interests."[69] The warships arrived at Veracruz where their commander, Captain Hugh Dunlop, promptly demanded "the punctual payment to the British Convention claimants, as well as to the British Bondholders."[70] Left with no choice, the Mexican authorities then in control of Veracruz accepted the demands, signing an agreement to resume payments to both the "English Convention" holders and "to holders of Mexican bonds in London."[71]

Neither the terms of the Dunlop Convention nor the amendments obtained a few months later by Captain Cornwallis Aldham were observed by the Mexican government. More seizures of British property followed, culminating as we have seen in the Legation theft in November 1860. "This outrage," thundered *The Times* (21 December 1860), "passes the limits of all forbearance." Dr. Phillimore, whose opinion was again sought by the bondholders, advised that "if subjects abroad have ever a right to call for the protection of their government, surely it must be in such an instance as this."[72] Negotiations with the Juárez regime followed and promises were made but not kept. The bondholders renewed their campaign for a firm response by the British government and for an International Convention covering the debt owed to them. Questions were asked in Parliament and the newspapers demanded action. Lord Russell's policy was derided as "feeble and inconsistent" and one correspondent to *The Times* (6 March 1861) asked, "Is England's flag to be insulted with impunity." Then, on 29 May and 17 July 1861, President Juárez decreed the suspension of payments on all debts for a period of two years. Threats, protests, and the suspension of diplomatic relations by Britain and France followed.

Details of the negotiations and events of the Tripartite Intervention are readily available elsewhere and need not concern us here. From the Mexican bondholders' viewpoint, the decision to intervene militarily in Mexico, even if only at the ports, was a clear justification of the campaign which they had waged for many years. As far as they were concerned, military action was entirely justified as there was no other way in which Mexico could be obliged to pay its debts to them.[73] With British officers in control of the Mexican ports, they were entirely confident that henceforth they would receive their dividends regularly and that eventually their bonds would be fully redeemed from a Sinking Fund. Their Committee was redundant and as we have seen, it was dissolved in January 1862, much to the relief apparently of Britain's Minister Plenipotenciary to Mexico, Sir Charles Wyke. He was reported to be "very glad that the Committee is dissolved, and that he will be relieved from a very voluminous corrrespondence."[74] From the British government's viewpoint, Mexico had infringed international agreements between the two countries. Whereas in the early years, the Foreign Office position had always been that the bondholders' affairs were strictly private matters and did not merit official interference, that situation had changed materially with the Dunlop and Aldham agreements. In his instructions, Wyke was told that the bondholders'claims "to the extent provided for in these arrangements, have acquired the character of an international obligation, and you should accordingly insist upon the punctual fulfilment of the obligations thus contracted."[75] It appeared that at last the bondholders' case had been accepted, but in fact as we have seen, it was to be many more years before, to use David Robertson's words, "a most respectable and large body of ill-used Englishmen" were finally to get their money.[76]

NOTES

1. This correspondence is in CMB *Report* (1830).

2. Correspondence in BFSP, vol. 28, p. 972.

3. C.K. Webster, ed., *Britain and the Independence of Latin America, 1812–1830*, vol. 1 (Oxford, 1938), p. 78.

4. Letter in *The Financier*, 14 February 1876.

5. Letter in *The Money Market Review*, 21 July 1876.

6. PRO, F.O. 97/274, fols. 331–333.

7. Report of the meeting in *The Morning Chronicle*, 29 June 1836, speech of Mr. Young.

8. CSAB, *Statement of Proceedings* (1850), p. 107.

9. PRO, F.O. 50/206, fols. 200–202.

10. Report of CMB meeting of 6 August 1856 in *The Morning Herald*, 7 August 1856.

11. PRO, F.O. 97/280, fols. 195–196.

12. The text of the memorial is in CMB *Report* (1869), pp. 47–57.

13. CMB *Report* (1869), p. 16.

14. Garde, *A Letter to the Right Honourable Earl Russell*, pp. 42–43.

15. V.C. Dahl, "Business Influence in the Anglo-Mexican Reconciliation of 1884," *Inter-American Economic Affairs* 15 (1961–1962), p. 39.

16. There is a detailed report of Sheridan's speech in the Commons on 18 August 1871 and a subsequent letter to *The Times* (24 August 1871) arguing his case, in CMB *Report* (1876), pp. 29–30. His speech and the official replies in the Commons on 5 August 1873 are given on pp. 40–41.

17. Marichal, *A Century of Debt Crises in Latin America*, pp. 112–113.

18. *Investor's Guardian*, 8 April 1876. Sheridan led a deputation to see Lord Derby on 9 March 1876. Reports of the proceedings are in *The Echo*, 10 March 1876; *The Times*, 13 March 1876.

19. CMB *Report* (1876), pp. 46–47.

20. CMB Minute Book, Guildhall Library, Ms. 15.795, meeting of 28 July 1876.

21. Dahl, "Business Influence," p. 41.

22. The text of Sheridan's letters is in the CMB Minute Book, meetings of 11 August, 13 September 1882.

23. Dahl inexplicably concludes that Sheridan's persistence "contributed to prolonging Britain's estrangement with Mexico"; "Business Influence," p. 40.

24. PRO, F.O. 50/121b. This file has many letters from mercantile associations asking for protection.

25. Turlington, *Mexico and Her Foreign Creditors*, p. 73.

26. J.N. Almonte to Minister of Relations, 11 July 1838, SRE, 3.11. 4710.

27. House of Lords debate of Tuesday, 14 August, reported in *The Times*, 15 August 1838.

28. PRO, F.O. 50/121a, fols. 167–168.

29. The debate was fully reported in *The Times*, 25 August 1846.

30. See Correspondence between Great Britain and Foreign Powers, and Communications from the British Government to Claimants, relative to Loans made by British Subjects, 1823–1847, *Parliamentary Papers*, vol. 69 (1847).

31. J.D. Powles to W.P. Robertson, 29 June 1849 in Robertson, *The Foreign Debt*, p. 38.

32. G.R. Robinson to W.P. Robertson, 30 June 1849, ibid., p. 37.

33. See *Parliamentary Papers*, "Report from the Select Committee on Debts from Foreign Governments," (London, 1849).

34. G. Robinson to Lord Palmerston, 22 July 1848, PRO, F.O. 50/225, fols. 156–158.

35. B. Tenenbaum, "Merchants, Money and Mischief: The British in Mexico, 1821–1860," *The Americas* 35 (1979), pp. 323–324.

36. Correspondence and other documents in PRO, F.O. 97/274, fols. 228–238.

37. Ibid., fols. 233–234.

38. Ibid., fols. 171–172.

39. Robertson submitted a long memorandum on the subject, together with a draft Convention, already discussed with Mexican representatives. They are in ibid., fols. 265–280.

40. D. Robertson to Foreign Office, 8 August 1856, ibid., fols. 290–291.

41. J.N. Almonte to Minister of Relations, 20 May 1857, SRE, L.E. 1234, fol. 103.

42. CMB *Report* (1861), p. 137.

43. The resolutions approved at the meeting were printed separately as *Resolutions passed at a General Meeting of Mexican Bondholders, held at the London*

Tavern on Thursday, 4th July, 1861. David Robertson, Esq., M.P., in the Chair (no publisher or date given).

44. D.C.M. Platt, *Finance, Trade, and Politics in British Foreign Policy, 1815–1914* (Oxford, 1968), pp. 34–53.

45. BFSP, vol. 28, p. 970.

46. Cited in Platt, *Finance, Trade and Politics*, p. 35.

47. Webster, ed., *Britain and the Independence of Latin America*, pp. 455–456.

48. Correspondence in *The Times*, 20 October 1843 and PRO, F.O. 50/160, fol. 163.

49. PRO, F.O. 50, 183, fols. 5–6.

50. The full text of Hammond's letter is in Platt, *Finance, Trade and Politics*, pp. 400–401.

51. Quoted in H.S. Ferns, *Britain and Argentina in the Nineteenth Century* (Oxford, 1960), p. 476.

52. PRO, F.O. 50/227, fols. 205–206.

53. The various documents on the Convention issue are in PRO, F.O. 97/274, fols. 327–340.

54. L.C. Otway to D. Robertson, 5 November 1858, Barings Archive, 204326.

55. The various letters relating to the McCalmont affair were published as a separate pamphlet: *The "Mexican Bondholders." Letters of Messrs. M'Calmont, Brothers, & Co., and reply thereto, by David Robertson, Esq., M.P., Honorary Chairman* (London, 1861. The pamphlet is included as an appendix in the CMB *Report* (1861). The original of McCalmont's 1848 letter is in PRO, F.O. 50/225, fols. 133–134.

56. R.A. Jones, *The Nineteenth Century Foreign Office. An Administrative History* (London, 1971), p. 66.

57. R.A. Jones, *The British Diplomatic Service, 1815–1914* (London, 1983), p. 95.

58. Correspondence in CMB *Report* (1861), p. 157.

59. Ibid., p. 137.

60. Ibid., pp. 163–164.

61. Ibid., p. 158.

62. Ibid., p. 142.

63. Ibid., p. 173.

64. Correspondence in Kimberley F.O. Correspondence, Bodleian Library, fols. 15–16, 23–24.

65. Ibid., fols. 60–61.

66. The text of Palmerston's circular is readily available in several sources. I have used the copy given in Platt, *Finance, Trade and Politics*, pp. 398–399.

67. Draft to Mr. Lettsom, 30 June 1855, PRO, F.O. 50/275, fols. 104–108.

68. Ibid., 28 May 1856, PRO, F.O. 97/274, fol. 220.

69. Ibid., 97/275, fols. 231–233.

70. H. Dunlop to Manuel Gutiérrez Zamora, 31 December 1858, ibid., fols. 341–346.

71. The text of the Dunlop Convention and related documents are in ibid., 97/274, fols. 195–198.

72. CMB *Report* (1861), pp. 10–11.

73. P.J. Sheridan, "The Committee of Mexican Bondholders and European Intervention in 1861," *Mid-America* 42 (1960), pp. 18–29.

74. Reported in G. White to Barings, 3 March 1862, Barings Archive, HC4.5.31–33, no. 40.

75. PRO, F.O. 97/281, fols. 18–20.

76. D. Robertson to Lord Russell, 5 January 1860, CMB *Report* (1861), p. 176.

Epilogue

In Part I of this study, we examined the main aspects of the financial history of Mexico's nineteenth-century London debt. In 1824 and 1825, Mexico borrowed £6,400,000 in the London market by means of the sale of interest-bearing bonds. It contracted to pay dividends to the holders of those bonds four times a year for thirty years, at the end of which term it would redeem them at par. The interest rates of 5% and 6% per year were attractive and there was no problem in marketing the bonds initially at a premium over the agreed issue price. Within two years, however, or in October 1827, Mexico defaulted on its commitments and failed to provide the funds required for the dividends. Thereafter, for the next sixty years, there were all the various reschedulings of the debt, by which both Mexico as the debtor, and the bondholders as creditors, attempted to find a means whereby the terms of the contract between them could be honored. Each of these so-called conversions produced what at least appeared to be legally binding commitments in the form of agreed payment schedules. Specific revenues, largely from Mexican customs dues, were assigned for the regular payment of dividends and to the Sinking Fund with which it was intended to amortize the debt. To reassure the creditors, who needed written confirmation of their claims, new bonds, dividend coupons, certificates, or debentures, clearly stating the basic terms of the agreed conversion, were printed and distributed.

None of these promises were fully honored by Mexico. The reasons are myriad. Internal strife, political and military conflict, and foreign aggression were all contributory factors. Similarly, the new republic failed to find a form of government which enabled the central authorities to impose order and obedience to the law in distant peripheral regions where local chieftains helped themselves to whatever revenues became available, including those at the ports assigned to the dividend account. Above all, while economic historians argue over the rate of change, there was certainly little sign of growth in either the industrial or agrarian economy. International trade and the export of mineral and agricultural products, while not stagnant, did not achieve anything like the growth that was initially expected when independence from the restrictive practices of imperial Spain was finally won in 1821. The result was that predictions of government revenues were invariably wrong, and every Mexican Treasury Minister faced a fiscal deficit which imposed spending priorities that were in effect impossible to change. It is a commonplace of Mexican history in this period that the army absorbed well over half of national revenues and that all attempts to reduce that unsustainable level of expenditure were met with revolution by dissident generals. When the choice was between sending money to London to pay a dividend or to an army barracks to forestall a rebellion, there was only one decision. Dividends, therefore, except on a few occasions, were not paid because in the circumstances of the day, there was no money to pay them.

This failure to improve national wealth was a major disappointment to Mexicans. I have noted elsewhere that, like those investors who bought their bonds, Mexicans themselves believed in the legendary natural wealth of their country. They firmly believed that almost inevitably it was destined to become one of the most advanced and prosperous nations on earth. In the 1820s, borrowing a relatively small amount of money from Europe had seemed to all concerned to be a natural step to take, without risk to borrower or lender, given the natural resources, especially silver, simply awaiting exploitation. Of course, the loans did not produce the expected benefits. In the first place, of the £6,400,000, only a relatively small proportion reached the Mexican Treasury. Substantial amounts were taken by the contractors in what, it must be acknowledged, were agreed and normal rates of commission; the 1824 loan was sold to the contractor at 50% of par; large amounts were lost in the failure of both the contractors, Goldsmidt & Co. and the Barclay partnership; one-quarter of the second loan was spent on redeeming the Five per Cent bonds; other sums disappeared into the pockets of speculators, including Mexicans; £63,000 was loaned to Colombia; and finally, some of the money was spent on buying ships and armaments considered necessary for national defense, especially against the real threats of Spanish reconquest. In short, while the calculations vary and there is no exact figure, it is likely that Mexico received only about one-half of the £6,400,000 it committed itself to repay. Meanwhile, as dividend arrears accumulated, the principal debt rose inexorably from, in round figures, £5,000,000 in 1831, £9,000,000 in 1837, and £10,000,000 in 1851 to £15,000,000 in 1886. As Cumberland puts it, the loans "kept the new nation strapped and scrambling for funds for the next fifty years."[1] Mexican credit in the capital markets of Europe was destroyed for much of the nineteenth century.

Independent Mexico's first experience of international finance, therefore, was unfortunate, and most historians have tended to describe the situation from its point of view. But, as we have shown in the second part of this work, there was another viewpoint, that of the creditors. They were not banks in the modern sense, nor large institutions with substantial amounts of investment capital at their disposal. On the contrary, they were individual investors who had put their money into Mexican stocks in the 1820s in good faith. Some may, or may not, have been concerned with the strategic issues of British imperialism and commerce but all were looking to raise their income, to make a profit from their investments. Like the Mexicans, they believed in the economic potential of the New World and although, as Alexander Baring told them in 1828, the higher the return, the greater the risk, they seem to have had little doubt about the security of their investments. After all, they were guaranteed by legally binding contracts and they had the tangible reassurance of their bonds which could always be sold in the market. Hence, Mexico's loans were oversubscribed and initally fetched a healthy premium. As we have seen in the chapter on the bondholders, those who were persuaded to buy the bonds ranged from aristocrats, Members of Parliament, generals, admirals, millionaire financiers, and manufacturers to country clergymen, solicitors, widows, and retired annuitants who derived their income from more traditional stocks such as Consols. Although many lived in the London metropolitan area, others resided in all parts of England from Guisborough in the north to Portsmouth in the south. The Scots, Welsh, and Irish were also represented and there was a largely undetermined number of foreign, especially Dutch, investors. Some were wealthy individuals—stockbrokers, landowners, manufacturers, merchants—and others were professional speculators skilled at playing the market. Many, however, were of modest means with no more than a few hundred pounds to invest. For some, it was money they could ill afford to lose and we have illustrated individual cases which seem to justify the claims of the time that numerous families were badly hit by Mexico's failure to honor its commitments. Those like the fictional Allnutt family, or the real Reverend Hare, who put all their money into "Mexicans," may well have been unwise not to spread the risk. But, others like Dr. Proudfoot of Kendal, for example, maintained a broad portfolio including Mexican, Colombian, Peruvian, and Venezuelan. He fared no better as all the Spanish American republics defaulted.

Perhaps surprisingly in the circumstances, at least until the 1850s when the War of the Reform destroyed any hope of the regular dividends agreed upon in the 1850 conversion, most bondholders expressed some sympathy with Mexico's political and economic difficulties. In public meetings, speakers often emphasized the futility of condemnation and in its reports, the

Committee of Mexican Bondholders always favored negotiation rather than confrontation. But the failure to adhere to the terms of the 1850 agreement, allied to the confiscation of bondholders' funds and, above all, the Legation theft in 1860, brought about a marked change in attitude. In reports, letters to the press, and pleas to the British Foreign Office, the bondholders constantly emphasized the sacrifices they had made in their attempts to respond to the reality of the situation in Mexico. It is worth summarizing briefly the history of the debt from their point of view. In 1830–1831, they had agreed to capitalize almost four years' unpaid dividends into bonds on which no interest would be paid for five years. Also, they accepted the Mexican proposal to pay only half the interest due on the existing debt for the next five years. In 1837, they agreed to accept the deferral of dividends on half the total debt for the next ten years. Half the unpaid dividends in following years were written off and the other half replaced by non-interest-bearing Debentures. In 1846, in return for pledges of payments to the dividend fund from export taxes on silver, tobacco revenues, and other sources, they agreed to a reduction of 10% in the value of their Active stocks and 40% of the Deferred and Debentures, giving, in effect, a gift of more than £2,000,000 worth of bonds to the Mexican Exchequer. In 1850, they agreed to a 40% reduction in the interest on their bonds, from 5% to 3%. Finally, a substantial number of bondholders were deprived of all their dividends as well as the capital value of their stocks by the fraudulent conduct of Mexico's official Financial Agent, Lizardi & Co.

There is no doubt that the bondholders "sacrificed," to use their verb, millions of pounds to which their contracts with Mexico entitled them. To cite just one example, in presenting the 1850 conversion proposals to the bondholders, their Committee noted that "To accept this offer in satisfaction for all arrears will, therefore, inflict a loss of nearly 6,000,000 dollars on the Bondholders, in addition to sacrifices amounting to 17,000,000 dollars, to which they have on former occasions submitted."[2] In short, there was a loss of between £4,000,000 and £5,000,000. Further substantial losses followed in the 1850s and 1860s when Juárez repudiated the capitalization of dividend arrears represented by the 1864 Three per Cents and suspended all dividend payments. Between 1867 and 1886, the bondholders received nothing.

A major part of this work has been devoted to the Committee of Mexican Bondholders. We have seen how, for almost sixty years, either independently or under the umbrella of the Committee of Spanish American Bondholders and later the Corporation of Foreign Bondholders, members of the Committee, especially chairmen like George Robinson, David Robertson, and Henry Sheridan, worked vigorously to promote the interests of the bondholders at large. More than eighty men served on the Committee, many of whom were prominent in London's financial, commercial, and social élite. It was the Committee that conducted the negotiations with Mexico for reschedulings of the debt, that financed agents and commissioners, and that pressed the British government constantly for help which, with the exception of the Tripartite Intervention, was not forthcoming. Its published *Reports*—twenty-three in total—plus all the miscellaneous documents it sponsored, provide an unparalleled wealth of statistical and other data on the debt. It waged continuous campaigns in an effort to find alternative means of extracting funds from Mexico, ranging from its successful demands for some of the United States indemnity money to its unsuccessful offer to have the deeds of Church property in Mexico assigned to bondholders. Under the leadership of Henry Sheridan between 1867 and 1887, it kept the problem of Mexico's unpaid debt in both the public and the parliamentary mind and it was able to ensure that new Mexican loans for both public and private investment were excluded from all the European Bourses.

The Dublán conversion of 1886–1890 finally brought about the redemption of all the outstanding Mexican stocks related directly to the original loans of 1824 and 1825. The success of the whole operation had immediate effects. Mexico's international credit was restored in the financial markets and among entrepreneurs and industrialists anxious to seize the business opportunities which they now saw open to them. Foreign investment from Britain and elsewhere flowed in increasing amounts into railways, ports, mining, petroleum, and all manner of industrial and agrarian projects. As in the 1820s, although not on the same scale, speculative companies were formed. The Adventurers of Mexico Limited provides a good example. It was created in 1890 with a capital of £50,000 divided into shares of £1,000 each, for which there was no shortage of subscribers. Its Articles of Association reveal that the objects for which the company was established were to exploit any opportunity in mining, agriculture, manufacturing, banking, public works, property development, livestock, and any other activity where profit might be made.[3]

Over the next twenty years, Mexicans also took advantage of the situation. Several new loans were floated by federal, state, and city governments. Some were for railways, for example, the Tehuantepec Railway Loan (1889); others were for port development and public infrastructure works; and soon there were issues designed once again to consolidate outstanding stocks. There were major government issues, for example, in 1899 with the 5% External Consolidated Gold Loan for £22,700,000, and again in 1904, 1910, and 1913. While there were occasional difficulties, by and large the economic progress seen during the regime of Porfirio Díaz, and the huge increase in federal government revenues in the 1890s and early 1900s, enabled the country to service these borrowings without much difficulty and thus retain its high credit rating in the international financial markets. Then, in 1910, the Madero Revolution and the collapse of the

Díaz dictatorship occurred. Bondholders began to panic and when, in January 1914, the Huerta administration suspended all payments on both the internal and foreign debts, protests were long and loud. As half a century before, when Juárez had done the same, threats of seizure of Customs Houses, or more extensive military intervention, soon appeared in the press and in demands to the British Foreign Office. Finally, in 1917, the Corporation of Foreign Bondholders decided that it was once again necessary to have a separate Committee of Holders of Mexican Bonds. Like its direct predecessors of the nineteenth century, it was to remain in existence for many more years. The work of that generation of bondholders, however, awaits investigation.

NOTES

1. C.C. Cumberland, *Mexico: The Struggle for Modernity* (New York, 1968), p. 144.
2. CMB *Report* (December 1850), p. 13.
3. Barclays Group Archives (Manchester) kindly provided me with a copy of the Articles of Association.

Appendix

The following document was sent to the British Foreign Office on 21 June 1857 by David Robertson. In a letter of the previous day to Edmund Hammond, he wrote, "Tomorrow I will send you authenticated copies of the original Mexican Bond and of all the others that have grown out of the conversions including the last of 1850." The copies he sent included these bonds: 1824 Five per Cent; 1837 Five per Cent Deferred; 1846 Five per Cent; 1851 Three per Cent. In respect of the latter three bonds, he also included a copy of what appears "On the back of the Bond." These reverse sides contain the text of relevant decrees and other documents. In the case of the 1824 bond, although he does not specifically state, as with the others, "On the back of the Bond," it is followed by an English translation of the law of 1 May 1823. It can be assumed, therefore, that the law was printed on the back of the 1824 Five per Cent. All these copies are in PRO, F.O. 97/275, fols. 119–152. I have kept the spelling and punctuation of the original.

"Mexican Loan   Letter A No
£3,200,000   £100 Sterling

  Loan of Three millions Two hundred Thousand pounds sterling.
  For the service of the State of Mexico. Divided into 24,000 Certificates, or special engagements, and secured by a General Mortgage Bond of which the following is a copy.

(Original Bond on a
£25 stamp)

To all to whom these presents shall come, Don Francisco de Borja Migoni, Agent of the Mexican Government residing in London sends greeting. **Whereas** the Sovereign Congress of the State of Mexico did on the first of May One thousand eight hundred and twenty three, Decree that a Loan to procure for the service of the State, eight millions of hard dollars should be raised, and charged the Supreme Executive power of Mexico with the execution of the said Decree **And whereas** their Highnesses, Don Jose Mariano de Michelena, Don Miguel Dominguez, and Don Pedro Celestino Negrete who composed the said Executive power did under date of the fourteenth day of the said month of May, grant to me the above mentioned Francisco de Borja Migoni, full, ample and special power to negociate and raise the said Loan and to mortgage and pledge the whole of the revenues of the State as a security for the same, the said Supreme Executive power thereby engaging religiously to fulfil, recognize, and ratify the Contract or Contracts which I might make for the said Loan: **And whereas** in pursuance of such powers, I the said Francisco de Borja Migoni have negotiated a Loan of Three millions two hundred thousand pounds sterling for the service and on behalf of the said State of Mexico, the amount whereof has been placed at the disposal of the said Government of Mexico in the manner and form agreed upon: *Now Know all Men* by these presents, that I the said Francisco de Borja Migoni, by virtue of the above mentioned full, ample, and special powers to me granted, do hereby, on behalf and in the name of the said State of Mexico, declare and agree, to and with the holders of every and any part, share or interest of or in the said Loan of Three millions two hundred thousand pounds sterling that the same has been made and raised under the stipulations and conditions following: that is to say,

Article 1.   The said Loan has been raised on security of this present Instrument or General Mortgage Bond, which shall be divided into Certificates as follows, viz—

Letter A	8000 of £100 each, making		£800,000
B	16000	£150	£2,400,000
	24,000 amounting altogether to		£3,200,000

to be hereafter issued payable to Bearer with Interest at the rate of five pounds per centum per annum, which interest shall commence from the first day of October, one thousand eight hundred and twenty three, and shall be paid quarterly in London without any deduction, the two first payments to be made on the first of April One thousand eight hundred and twenty four; and the succeeding payments on each first day of July, first day of October, first day of January and first day of April next following and so continue in each succeeding year

Article II   All the revenues of the state of Mexico are hereby declared to be mortgaged and pledged by this General Mortgage Bond for the payment in the manner herein mentioned both of the principal and Interest of the said Loan of Three millions two hundred thousand pounds sterling independently of the Tax which according to the fifth article of the said decree of the Sovereign Congress of the 1st day of May, is to be imposed and to be specially charged and pledged with and for the payment of the interest of the said Loan and the redemption of the same in the manner hereinafter mentioned

Article III   In order to give an unequivocal proof of the good faith of the Government of Mexico and a satisfactory security to the Creditors for the punctual payment of the Interest of the said Loan, and for the redemption of the capital, The Treasurer General of Mexico shall be authorized and bound by a formal and irrevocable Decree of the Sovereign Congress and of the Executive Power to collect and keep separate the amount of the Tax which according to the fifth article of the said Decree of the first day of May 1823 is to be specifically pledged for the purposes of this loan in order that the amount of the same may not be applied to any of the ordinary or extraordinary expenses of the State until the sum which is to be remitted to London for the payment of the quarterly interest and for the redemption shall be completed and ready for transmission and if from any cause it should occur that the amount of these revenues is not sufficient for the payment of the quarterly interest and redemption the said Treasurer general are bound to make good such deficiency out of the general revenues of the State, and that no part of such general Revenues of the State shall be applied to any other purposes until the said payments required for this Loan shall have taken place; and in order to provide for the redemption of the principal sum of the said Loan the sum of Sixty four thousand pounds sterling shall be appropriated in the first year dated from the first day of October last past, and the sum of Thirty two thousand pounds shall be remitted to England in every succeeding year in equal half yearly payments, to be applied as a Sinking fund for the redemption of that part of the Loan unredeemed at or under par, the first of which payments, amounting to Thirty two thousand pounds sterling, to be so applied as a sinking fund shall be made on the first day of April next ensuing. The Treasurer general for the time being shall be especially charged with the execution of this Article in all its parts, and with the remittance under the direction, at the expense and for the account and risk of the Government of Mexico to the Agents in London, of the necessary funds for the payment of the quarterly interest and provision for the sinking fund as aforesaid which said remittance shall respectively at all times be forwarded from Mexico at least two months before the said payments shall severally fall due and become payable in London.

Article IV   The redemption of this loan shall be made as follows, viz—

The amount engaged to be provided for the sinking fund shall in the first instance to the extent of such provision, be employed in the purchase of certificates; and all future half yearly payments for the same purpose hereinbefore provided for shall be added to the amount of interest arising from the total amount redeemed to that period the whole of which sum shall then be applied to the further redemptions of the Loan within the period of the half year next following that in which the said remittance shall, according to the conditions of this Agreement have been made and in which the said two quarters interest shall have accrued. If at any time the said Loan shall be above par, exclusive of the dividend then due, then in order that the sinking fund may continue in due operation, the Agents in London, together with the Envoy for the time being or some other person duly authorized by him, or by the Government of the said State of Mexico, shall in such manner and form as they think proper, cause it to be determined by lot which of the then outstanding Certificates shall be paid off at par; but those thus determined to be paid off shall not exceed the amount of the then unapplied produce of the sinking fund for that half year. The numbers of such Certificates as may then be determined to be paid off shall be advertised in the London Gazette and shall be paid at par on presentation, with interest for the quarter current at the time of such advertisement, and all further interest on the same shall thenceforth cease. All Certificates redeemed or paid off shall be cancelled, and deposited in the Bank of England, in the presence of a Notary Public, of the said B.A. Goldsmidt & Co and of the Envoy from Mexico for the time being or of some person duly authorized for that purpose by him or by the Government of the said State of Mexico. The numbers so paid off or redeemed and cancelled in each half year shall be advertised in the London Gazette and the same shall remain deposited in the Bank of England until the whole Loan is paid off when the said Certificates together with this Mortgage Bond shall be delivered up and be at the disposal of the said Government of Mexico. Nevertheless if at the expiration of thirty years from the first of October last past, any part of the said Loan should remain unredeemed then and in that case the Government of the State of Mexico shall pay off the same at par.

Article V   The present instrument or general Mortgage Bond together with the original special power granted by the Executive power of the State of Mexico to me the said Francisco de Borja Migoni shall be deposited in the Bank of England in my presence, and in the presence of the said B.A. Goldsmidt & Co and of a Notary Public of the City of London and the same shall be given up and cancelled only when the whole Loan shall have been redeemed or repaid, as hereinbefore mentioned.

Article VI   I the said Francisco de Borja Migoni, in the name and on behalf of the said Government of Mexico, do hereby engage that the payment of the interest of this loan, and the redemption thereof shall be effected in time of war as well as in time of peace, without distinction whether the holder of any of the Certificates belongs to a friendly or hostile nation. That if a foreigner be holder of any such Certificates and die intestate, the same shall pass to his representatives in the order of succession established by the laws of the Country of which he was a subject, and that such Certificates shall be and are exempt from sequestration, both for claims of the State and those of Individuals.

Now therefore be it known to all Men, that I the said Francisco de Borja Migoni, do hereby as Agent of the State of Mexico and in virtue of the powers vested in me, bind the State of Mexico and all the public Authorities thereof which now exist or which may hereafter exist, to perform faithfully and truly all the foregoing engagements and conditions, and for no reason and on no pretence at any time or under any circumstance to refuse, evade or delay or attempt to evade or delay the full and ample performance of the said engagements and conditions or any of them. **In Witness** whereof I the said Francisco de Borja Migoni have signed the present General Mortgage Bond, and have affixed thereto my seal this seventh day of February one thousand eight hundred and twenty four.

Signed, sealed and delivered by
the said Francisco de Borja Migoni
in the presence of   (signed by Francisco de Borja Migoni)
E.M. Sauer
John Newton
    Notary Public"

The first version of the 1824 bond found in AGN, Deuda Externa, vol. 12, fols. 60–61, which had to be amended to avoid the Stamp tax, has the following additional section. It is not clear why Robertson's copyist did not include it. We may assume that the words "special Bond" were replaced with "Certificate," and "half yearly" with "quarterly," as was done in all the other sections.

"The above named Francisco de Borja Migoni do hereby certify that the Bearer hereof is intitled to   Sterling part of the Loan of Three millions two hundred thousand pounds Sterling and the interest thereon secured by the General Mortgage Bond deposited in the Bank of England of which the foregoing is a copy and I hereby declare this to be a special Bond for   Sterling granted by me in conformity to the Engagement contained in the said General Mortgage Bond bearing an Interest of Five pounds per centum per annum payable half yearly on sixty dividend warrants hereunto annexed—London seventh February one thousand eight hundred and twenty four—

We hereby Certify that the above is the signature of Don Francisco de Borja Migoni."

Sources and Works Cited

MANUSCRIPT AND PRIMARY SOURCES

Full details of the archival references for the manuscript sources are given in the notes. The following archives and collections were used.

Great Britain

Balliol College Library, Oxford; Morier Papers

Bank of England Archive/Museum; Deposit Books

Barclays Bank Group Archives, Manchester; Wakefield, Crewdson & Co. Papers

Bodleian Library, Oxford; Kimberley F.O. Correspondence

Guildhall Library, London. Several of the Guildhall Library's outstanding collection of business records were consulted but those found to be most useful were:

Corporation of Foreign Bondholders' archive

Foster & Braithwaite archive

Gibbs & Co. archive

James Capel & Co. archive

Stock Exchange archive

ING Barings Archive

Leeds University Library, Marshall Papers

Public Record Office: F.O. 50; 97; BT 40/27; B6/178–183, 201; TS25/180; Prob.37/1618; 11/1793

Record Offices. County and local Record Offices were mostly used to find biographical information on the bondholders. National Census returns for the nineteenth century and many published local directories were also consulted. Among the latter, the most common are Kelly's *Directories* published throughout the nineteenth century.

The following Record Offices were visited (others supplied information by post): Bath; Bristol; Cumbria (Kendal)—Crewdson Papers, Wakefield Papers, Milne Moser Papers, Proudfoot Papers, Wilson Papers; Dorset (Dorchester); Gloucester; Leeds; Shropshire—Marrington Papers.

Europe

Amsterdam Stock Exchange Archive, vols. 40–43.

Mexico

Archivo General de la Nación

Archivo de Hacienda, in particular, various bound volumes of manuscripts entitled "Deuda Externa" or "Deuda contraída en Londres."

Aduanas

Archivo Histórico "Genaro Estrada," Secretaría de Relaciones Exteriores

Archivo del Banco Nacional de México

United States

Bancroft Library, University of California; Baring Papers (copies of manuscripts in National Public Archives, Ottawa, Canada).

N.L. Benson Latin American Collection, University of Texas: Manning and Mackintosh Papers.

Many other archives and libraries provided information, photocopies of documents, and so on, by post. These included in the U.K.: Companies House (Cardiff); the Cumbria Record Office; East and West Sussex Record Offices; Larne Record Office (Co. Antrim); National Register of Archives; Probate Registry (York); Scottish Record Office; Suffolk Record Office (Ipswich); in the United States: Duke University Library; Louisiana State University Library (Baton Rouge); Princeton University Library; Yale University Library; in Canada: the National Public Archives of Canada, Ottawa, loaned microfilm copies of its Baring Papers.

Publications of the Committee of Mexican Bondholders; Committee of Spanish American Bondholders; Corporation of Foreign Bondholders

1830   *Proceedings of the Committee of the Holders of Mexican Bonds, appointed at the General Meeting of Bondholders, held at the City of London Tavern, the 26th of May, 1830. Published for the information of the Bondholders, by order of the Committee*. London, Effingham Wilson, Royal Exchange, 1830, Price Two Shillings. 37 pp.

1831 *Second Report of the Proceedings of the Committee of the Holders of Mexican Bonds*. London, Printed by R. Clay, Bread-Street-Hill. 1831. 19 pp.

1839 *Report of the Committee of Spanish American Bondholders, presented at A General Meeting of the Bondholders, held at the London Tavern, May 8, 1839*. London: Richard Clay, Printer, Bread-Street-Hill. 1839. 52 pp.

1846 *Mexican Debt. Copy of the Proceedings at the meeting of Mexican Bondholders, held at the London Tavern on the 4th June, 1846. Report of the Committee*. Printer not given; no date. 4 pp.

1850 *The Report of the Committee of Mexican Bondholders, 14 February 1850*. London: Published by Letts, Son, and Steer, 8 Royal Exchange. 1850. Price Threepence. 23 pp.

The Second Report of the Committee of Mexican Bondholders. London: Published by Letts, Son, and Steer, 8 Royal Exchange. 1850. Price Sixpence. 32 pp.

Statement of Proceedings in relation to the Mexican Debt. Published by the Committee of Spanish American Bondholders. London: Published by Baily Brothers, 3 Exchange Buildings. 1850. Price Sixpence. 122 pp.

Report of the Committee of Mexican Bondholders. 11 June, 1850. London: Published by Letts, Son, and Steer, 8 Royal Exchange. 1850. Price Sixpence. 32 pp.

Report of the Committee of Mexican Bondholders. 17 December 1850. London: Published by Letts, Son, and Steer, 8 Royal Exchange. 1850. Price Sixpence. 20 pp.

1852 *Report of the Committee of Mexican Bondholders. 10 March, 1852*. London: Published by Letts, Son, and Steer, 8 Royal Exchange. 1852. Price Sixpence. 14 pp.

Report of the Committee of Mexican Bondholders. 23 April, 1852. London: Published by Letts, Son, and Steer, 8 Royal Exchange. 1852. Price Sixpence. 12 pp.

1853 *Report of the Committee of Mexican Bondholders. 24 January, 1853*. London: Published by Letts, Son, and Steer, 8 Royal Exchange. 1853. Price Sixpence. 36 pp.

At a General Meeting of Mexican Bondholders, held at the London Tavern, Bishopsgate Street, on Wednesday, the 26th JANUARY, at 1 o'clock. JAMES CAPEL, Esq., in the Chair. The following resolutions were passed: London: Letts, Son, and Steer, Printers, 8 Royal Exchange and Old Swan Lane. 1853. 4 pp.

1854 *Report of the Committee of Mexican Bondholders, presented to the General Meeting of Bondholders at the London Tavern, 15 May, 1854*. London: Published by Letts, Son, and Steer, 8 Royal Exchange. 1854. Price Sixpence. 40 pp.

Resolutions. At a General Meeting of Mexican Bondholders at the London Tavern, on the 15th May, 1854 (London, 1854). 7 pp.

1855   *Report of the Committee of Mexican Bondholders, presented to the General Meeting of Bondholders at the London Tavern, 26 February, 1855.* London: Published by Letts, Son, and Steer, 8 Royal Exchange. 1855. Price Sixpence. 27 pp.

Report of Proceedings at a General Meeting of Mexican Bondholders, held at the London Tavern, on the 16th October, 1855. CHARLES McGAREL, Esq. in the Chair. No Printer etc. 4 pp.

1856   *Report of the Committee of Mexican Bondholders, presented to the General Meeting of Bondholders at the London Tavern, 6th August, 1856.* London: Published by Letts, Son, & Co., 8 Royal Exchange. 1856. Price Sixpence. 18 pp.

Report of Proceedings at a General Meeting of Mexican Bondholders, held at the London Tavern, on Wednesday, 6th August, 1856. CHARLES McGAREL, Esq. in the Chair. No Printer etc. 3 pp.

1858   *At a PUBLIC MEETING of MEXICAN ENGLISH BONDHOLDERS, held in London on the 28th of May, 1858, to consider the state of their affairs, DAVID ROBERTSON, Esq., Chairman.* No Printer etc. 2 pp.

1860   *Mexican National Debt, contracted in London. Decrees and regulations since the adjustment of October 14th/December 23rd 1850.* London: Printed by Letts, Son & Co., 8 Royal Exchange, E.C. 1860. 27 pp.

1861   *Report of the Committee of Mexican Bondholders, April 29, 1861.* Printed and Published by Letts, Son & Co., 8 Royal Exchange, E.C. 1861. Price Sixpence. 223 pp.

Resolutions passed at a General Meeting of MEXICAN BONDHOLDERS, held at the London Tavern, on Thursday, 4th July, 1861. DAVID ROBERTSON, Esq., M.P., in the Chair. No Printer etc. 8 pp.

The "MEXICAN BONDHOLDERS." LETTERS of Messrs M'Calmont, Brothers, & Co., and REPLY thereto, by DAVID ROBERTSON, Esq., M.P., Honorary Chairman. Printed and Published by Letts, Son & Co., 8 Royal Exchange, E.C. 1861. 18 pp.

A LETTER to the RIGHT HONOURABLE EARL RUSSELL, on the absolute right of the MEXICAN BONDHOLDERS, who are subjects of HER MOST GRACIOUS MAJESTY, by RICHARD GARDE, Esq., A.M., Trin.Col.Dub., Barrister-at-Law of the Middle Temple. Printed and Published by Letts, Son & Co., 8 Royal Exchange, E.C. 1861. 43 pp.

1862   *Report of THE COMMITTEE of MEXICAN BONDHOLDERS, January 23rd, 1862.* Printed and Published by Letts, Son & Co., 8 Royal Exchange, E.C. 1862. Price Sixpence. 192 pp.

Report of THE COMMITTEE OF MEXICAN BONDHOLDERS, February 25th, 1862. Printed and Published by Letts, Son & Co., 8 Royal Exchange, E.C. 1862. Price Sixpence. 179 pp.

LETTERS protesting on behalf of the MEXICAN BONDHOLDERS against the alienation of the public lands of Mexico. By RICHARD

GARDE, Esq., A.M., Trin.Col.Dub., Barrister-at-Law of the Middle Temple. Letts, Son & Co., Printers, 8 Royal Exchange. 1862. 4 pp.

A LETTER to the Right Honourable Lord VISCOUNT PALMERSTON, K.G. G.C.B., L.L.D., M.P., F.R.S., on the rights of NATURAL-BORN SUBJECTS and NATURALIZED SUBJECTS. By RICHARD GARDE, Esq., A.M., Trin.Col.Dub., Barrister-at-Law of the Middle Temple. Printed and Published by Letts, Son & Co., 8 Royal Exchange, E.C. 1862. 12 pp.

1868   *Report of the Provisional Committee of Mexican Bondholders, March 27th, 1868.* Published by Francis Fisher, at the office of the "Money Market Review," 2 Castle Court, Birchin Lane, E.C. 1868. Price Sixpence. 26 pp.

Report of the Proceedings of a Public Meeting of Mexican Bondholders, held at the London Tavern, 27th March, 1868. Published by Francis Fisher, at the office of the "Money Market Review," 2, Castle Court, Birchin Lane, E.C. 1868. Price Sixpence. 16 pp.

1869   *Report of the Mexican Bondholders' Committee, May 6th, 1869.* Published by Francis Fisher at the office of the "Money Market Review," 2, Castle Court, Birchin Lane, E.C. 1869. Price Sixpence. 57 pp.

Memorial of Mexican Bondholders. Published by Francis Fisher, at the office of the "Money Market Review," 2, Castle Court, Birchin Lane, E.C. 1869. 11 pp.

1870   *Report of the Mexican Bondholders' Committee, 7th July, 1870.* Published by Francis Fisher, at the office of the "Money Market Review," 2, Castle Court, Birchin Lane, E.C. 1870. Price Threepence. 47 pp.

1876   *Report of the Mexican Bondholders' Committee. March 31st, 1876. To be submitted to a General Meeting of Bondholders to be held at No.10, Moorgate Street, on Tuesday, 4th April, 1876.* London: Councilhouse, No. 10, Moorgate Street. 1876. 47 pp.

1879   *Letter of the Chairman of the Committee of Holders of Mexican Bonds to the Bondholders.* The Council of Foreign Bondholders. London: No. 17, Moorgate Street. 29th July, 1879. 8 pp.

1883   *Report of the Mexican Bondholders' Committee.* London: No. 17, Moorgate Street. May, 1883. 15 pp.

Report of the Committee of Mexican Bondholders on the state of the negotiations with the Special Envoy of the President of the Republic of Mexico, for carrying out the Agreement made with him, and approved by the Bondholders, on the 12th May, 1883. Councilhouse, No. 17, Moorgate Street. 22 November, 1883. London. Printed by Wertheimer, Lea & Co., Circus Place, London Wall. 24 pp.

1884   *Mexican Bondholders' Committee. Reprint of an article in the Mexican "Diario Oficial," of the 29th November, 1883; also the "Project of a Contract", as proposed by the Department of the Treasury, "For a settlement of the Debt contracted in London" and an extract from the Letter of the Committee to "The Times" published 12 December 1883.* London.

1885   *United States of Mexico. Law for the Consolidation and Conversion of the National Debt. 22nd June, 1885.* London. Council of Foreign Bondholders, No. 17, Moorgate Street, E.C. 1885.

1886   *Arrangement agreed upon between the undersigned . . . as representatives of the Holders of Mexican Bonds, to fix the mode of payment of the unpaid interest of the Mexican debt of 1851. . . .* London.

Corporation of Foreign Bondholders

First Report of the Council of the Corporation of Foreign Bondholders. London: Councilhouse, No. 10, Moorgate Street, 17 February, 1874. 64 pp.
Annual *Reports*, 1874–1900, 1938, 1946.

NEWSPAPERS AND PERIODICAL PUBLICATIONS

I have consulted a large number of nineteenth-century newspapers. For issues before the late 1860s, originals or microfilm copies were used, but for those after that time, except for *The Times*, I have relied on the outstanding collection of newspaper cuttings assembled by the Corporation of Foreign Bondholders. These contain virtually every item relating to Mexican bonds printed in all British newspapers after 1869. The original volumes containing the cuttings are in the Guildhall Library. The following are the main newspapers cited in the text. The dates are for issues I have used rather than the complete run of the publication.

The Bullionist (1869, 1876, 1882–1887)

The Daily Chronicle (1886)

The Bristol Mirror (1824)

The Bristol Gazette (1825)

Daily News (1853, 1884–1885)

(The) Daily Telegraph (1865, 1874, 1876, 1879, 1883, 1886)

The Echo (1883)

Financial News (1886–1887)

The Financier (1874, 1876–1882)

The Financial Times (1888, 1892)

The Gentleman's Magazine (1824–1825)

Herepath Railway Journal (1884)

Investors' Guardian (1876)

The Jewish Chronicle (1904)

The Leeds Mercury (1824)

Mexican Financier (1889–1895)

Money (1883)

The Money Market Review (1864, 1874, 1876, 1881–1885)

The Morning Chronicle (1826, 1828, 1836, 1840, 1843, 1846, 1855)

The Morning Herald (1828, 1846, 1855–1856)

The Morning Post (1853, 1870)

The Standard (1876, 1881–1885)

The Statist (1880–1884)

The Times (1824–1890)

BOOKS AND ARTICLES

The following list contains those works cited in the text together with a few others which have pertinent information.

Acts of the Mexican Congress relating to the conversion of the foreign debt, 1837–1839. London. 1839.

Adamson, A.H. *Sugar without Slaves: The Political Economy of British Guiana, 1838–1904*. New Haven, Conn., 1972.

Alamán, L. "Liquidación general de la deuda esterior de la República Mexicana hasta fin de Diciembre de 1841." In *Obras: Documentos Diversos*, vol. 9. Mexico, 1945–1947, pp. 323–472.

Allibone, S.A. *A Critical Dictionary of English Literature and British and American Authors*. 3 vols. London, 1859–1871.

Anderson, W. *The Scottish Nation. Biographical History of the People of Scotland*. 3 vols. Edinburgh, n.d.

Andréades, A. *History of the Bank of England*. 2nd ed. London, 1924.

Arrangoiz, Francisco de. *Piezas justificativas del arreglo de la deuda externa de México que se celebró en 6 de julio de 1849 entre el Exmo. Sr. Ministro de Hacienda Don Francisco de Arrangoiz y Don Guillermo Parish Robertson, comisionado especial de los tenedores de bonos mexicanos en Londres*. Mexico, 1849.

Atkinson, G. *The Worthies of Westmoreland*. London, 1850.

Bank, D. and MacDonald, T., eds. *British Biographical Index*. 2nd ed. Munich, 1998.

Barclay, H.F. and Fox, A.W. *A History of the Barclay Family*. London, 1924.

Bateman, J. *The Great Landowners of Great Britain and Ireland*. London, 1971.

Bazant, J. *Historia de la deuda exterior de México (1823–1946)*. Mexico, 1968.

Bermant, C. *The Cousinhood*. London, 1970.

Brett-James, A., ed. *General Wilson's Journal, 1812–1814*. London, 1964.

Brown, P.A.H. *London Publishers and Printers, c. 1800–1870*. London, 1982.

Bullock, W. *Six Months' Residence and Travel in Mexico*. London, 1824.

Burch, R.M. *Colour Printing and Colour Printers*. Edinburgh, 1983.

Burk, K. *Morgan Grenfell, 1838–1988*. Oxford, 1989.

Bruce, C.R. *Standard Catalog of Mexican Coins, Paper Money, Stocks, Bonds, and Medals*. Iola, Wisc., 1981.

Calendar of the Grants of Probate and Letters of Administration Made in the Probate Registers. London, various years between 1858 and 1900.

Casasús, J.D. *Historia de la deuda contraída en Londres, con un apéndice sobre el estado actual de la Hacienda Pública.* Mexico, 1885.

Chapman, S. *The Rise of Merchant Banking.* London, 1984.

Collinge, J.M. *Foreign Office Officials, 1782–1870.* London, 1979.

Conversion of Mexican Bonds. Report of the Committee of the Stock Exchange. London, 1842.

Cope, S.R. "The Goldsmids and the Development of the London Money Market." *Economica,* 9 (1942).

Costeloe, M.P. *Response to Revolution. Imperial Spain and the Spanish American Revolutions, 1810–1840.* Cambridge, 1986.

———. "The Extraordinary Case of Mr. Falconnet and 2,500,000 Silver Dollars: London and Mexico, 1850–1853." *Mexican Studies* 15 (1999), pp. 261–289.

Dahl, V.C. "Business influence in the Anglo-Mexican Reconciliation of 1884." *Inter-American Economic Affairs* 15 (1961–1962), pp. 33–51.

Dawson, F.G. *The First Latin American Debt Crisis. The City of London and the 1822–25 Loan Bubble.* New Haven, Conn. and London, 1990.

Dictionary of National Biography. London, 1885–1903.

La Diplomacia Mexicana. 3 vols. Mexico, 1910–1913.

Dublán, M. *Informe que presenta al Congreso sobre el convenio celebrado con los tenedores de bonos de la deuda contraída en Londres.* Mexico, 1886.

———. *Informe que el Ministro de Hacienda, Manuel Dublán presenta al Congreso sobre el empréstito contratado en Europa de £10,500,000.* Mexico, 1888.

Dublán, M. and Lozano, J.M., eds. *Legislación mexicana.* Mexico, 1876.

Duguid, C. *A History of the Stock Exchange.* London, 1902.

English, H. *A Complete View of the Joint Stock Companies Formed During 1824 and 1825.* London, 1827.

Expediente de la Secretaría de Hacienda sobre reclamaciones de los tenedores de bonos mexicanos en Londres. Mexico, 1870.

Falconnet, F. de P. *Manifestación dirigida a la honorable Cámara de Diputados por el agente de los tenedores de bonos mexicanos.* Mexico, 1852.

Fenn, C. *A Compendium of the English and Foreign Funds and the Principal Joint Stock Funds.* London, 1837.

Ferns, H.S. *Britain and Argentina in the Nineteenth Century.* Oxford, 1960.

Foster, J. *Men at the Bar: A Biographical Handlist of the Members of the Various Inns of Court, Including Her Majesty's Judges.* London, 1885.

Fulford, R. *Glyn's, 1753–1953. Six Generations in Lombard Street.* London, 1953.

A General Directory for the County of Somerset. Taunton, 1840.

Gibbs, D.E.W. *Lloyd's of London.* London, 1957.

Grajales, G. *Guía de documentos para la historia de México en archivos ingleses (siglo XIX).* Mexico, 1969.

Green, T. *Precious heritage. Three Hundred Years of Mocatta and Goldsmid.* London, 1984.

Gunn, J.A.W. et al. *Benjamin Disraeli Letters, 1815–1834,* vol. 1, no. 20. Toronto, 1982.

Hennessey, E. *Stockbrokers for 150 Years. A History of Sheppards and Chase, 1827–1977.* London, 1978.

Hidalgo, D., ed. *Representantes de México en Gran Bretaña (1822–1980)*. Mexico, 1981.

Hidy, R.W. *The House of Baring in American Trade and Finance, 1763–1861*. Cambridge, Mass., 1949.

Hogg, E. M. *Quintin Hogg. A Biography*. London, 1904.

Hoskins, W.G. "Richard Thornton: A Victorian Millionaire." *History Today* (1962), pp. 574–579.

Hunt, C.B. "The Joint-Stock Company in England, 1800–1825." *Journal of Political Economy*, 63 (1935), pp. 1–33.

Hutchins, J. *The History and Antiquities of the County of Dorset* (1868). 3rd ed. Reprint, Wakefield, W. Yorkshire, 1973.

Ibarra Bellón, A. *El Comercio y el Poder en México, 1821–1864*. Mexico, 1998.

Jenks, L.H. *The Migration of British Capital to 1875*. London and New York, 1927.

Jones, C. *Antony Gibbs & Sons Ltd. A Record of 150 Years of Merchant Banking, 1808–1958*. London, 1958.

Jones, O.L. *Santa Anna*. New York, 1968.

Jones, R.A. *The British Diplomatic Service, 1815–1914*. London, 1983.

———. *The Nineteenth Century Foreign Office. An Administrative History*. London, 1971.

Judd, G.P., ed. *Members of Parliament, 1734–1832*. New Haven, Conn., 1955.

Kaufmann, William W. *British Policy and the Independence of Latin America, 1804–1828*. Hamden, Conn., 1967.

Kindleberger, C. *Manias, Panics and Crashes. A History of Financial Crises*. 3rd ed. London, 1996.

King, J. "William Bullock: Showman." In *Viajeros Europeos del Siglo XIX en México*. Mexico, 1996, pp. 117–125.

Kozhevar, E. *Report on the Republic of Mexico to the Council of Foreign Bondholders*. London, 1886.

Liehr, R., ed. *La deuda pública en América Latina en perspectiva histórica*. Vervuert, Germany, 1995.

———. "La deuda exterior de México y los "merchant bankers' británicos, 1821–1860." *Ibero-Amerikanisches Archiv* 9 (1983), pp. 415–439.

Lill, T. *National Debt of Mexico: History and Present Status*. New York, 1919.

Ludlow, L. and Marichal, C., eds. *Un Siglo de Deuda Pública en México*. Mexico, 1998.

Marichal, C. *A Century of Debt Crises in Latin America from Independence to the Great Depression, 1820–1930*. Princeton, N.J. 1989.

Martineau, H. *A History of England during the Thirty Years' Peace, 1815–1845*. London, 1848 (reprint 1971).

Mathias, P. *The Brewing Industry in England, 1700–1830*. Cambridge, 1959.

———. *The First Industrial Nation*. London, 1969.

Matthews, P.W. *History of Barclays Bank Ltd*. London, 1926.

Mayo, J. "Consuls and Silver Contraband on Mexico's West Coast in the Era of Santa Anna." *Journal of Latin American Studies* 19 (1987), pp. 389–411.

McCaleb, W.F. *The Public Finances of Mexico*. New York, 1921.

McKenzie Johnston, H. *Missions to Mexico. A Tale of British Diplomacy in the 1820s*. London, 1992.

———. *Ottoman and Persian Odysseys. James Morier, Creator of Hajji Baba of Ispahan, and His Brothers*. London, 1998.

McKillop, F. *History of Larne and East Antrim*. Belfast, 2000.

Mitchell, B.R. *British Historical Statistics*. Cambridge, 1988.

Mora, J.M.L. *Obras sueltas de José María Luis Mora, ciudadano mexicano*. 2nd ed. Mexico, 1963.

Morier Evans, D. *The Commercial Crisis, 1847–1848* (1849). Reprint, Devon, n.d.

Morgan, E.V. and Thomas, W.A. *The Stock Exchange: Its History and Functions*. London, 1962.

Morier, J.J. *Abel Allnutt. A Novel*. 3 vols. London, 1837.

Mosse, R.B. *The Parliamentary Guide: A Concise History of the Members of Both Houses of Parliament to March 26, 1836*. London, 1836.

Murphy, T. *Documentos oficiales relativos a la conversión de la deuda Mexicana exterior verificada en 1846*. London, 1846.

———. *Memoria sobre la deuda exterior de la República Mexicana desde su creación hasta fines de 1847*. Paris, 1848.

Orbell, J. *Baring Brothers & Co., Ltd. A History to 1939*. London, 1985.

———. *A Guide to Tracing the History of a Business*. Aldershot, 1987.

Ortiz de Montellano, M. *Apuntes para la liquidación de la deuda contraída en Londres*. Mexico, 1886.

Palmerston, Viscount. *Circular addressed by Viscount Palmerston to Her Majesty's Representatives in foreign states respecting the debts due by foreign states to British subjects*. London, 1849.

Parliamentary Papers, vol. XII (1849), pp. 275–278. "Report from the Select Committee on Debts from Foreign Governments," vol. LXIX. "Correspondence between Gt. Britain and Foreign Powers and Communications to Claimants relative to loans made by British subjects, 1823–1847," pp. 75–117, 522–571.

Pasado y presente de la deuda externa de México. Mexico, 1988.

Payno, M. *Memoria en que Manuel Payno da cuenta al público de su manejo en el desempeño del Ministerio de Hacienda*. Mexico, 1852.

———. *Mexico and Her Financial Questions with England, Spain and France*. Mexico, 1862.

Perry, E.J. *Petición que hace el representante de los tenedores de bonos mexicanos en Londres al Congreso de la Unión*. Mexico, 1869.

———. *Petición que eleva al octavo congreso de la Unión el señor Eduardo J. Perry, como apoderado del Comité de los tenedores de bonos mexicanos en Londres*. Mexico, 1876.

Platt, D.C.M. *Finance, Trade and Politics in British Foreign Policy, 1815–1914*. Oxford, 1968.

———. "British Bondholders in Nineteenth Century Latin America: Injury and Remedy." In M.D. Bernstein, ed., *Foreign Investment in Latin America. Cases and Attitudes*. New York, 1966, pp. 81–102.

———. "Finanzas británicas en México, 1821–1867." *Historia Mexicana*, 32 (1982), pp. 226–261.

Pressnell, L.S. and Orbell, J. *A Guide to the Historical Records of British Banking*. Aldershot, 1985.

Prieto, G. *Informe que presenta el Secretario de Hacienda sobre el estado que guarda la deuda extranjera pidiendo se cubra el deficiente extraordinario de 1,500,000 pesos para el pago de dos dividendos que se adeudan.* Mexico, 1852.

Reader, W.J. *A House in the City. A Study of the City and of the Stock Exchange Based on the Records of Foster & Braithwaite, 1825–1975.* London, 1979.

Reed, M.C. *A History of James Capel & Co.* Bristol, 1975.

Report of the Committee of Public Credit of the Mexican Chamber of Deputies on the Adjustment of the English Debt. Mexico, 1850.

Report on the Effect of the Depreciation of Silver on Mexico. F.O. 1893. Misc. Series, no. 302. London, 1893.

Richardson, C. *Mr. John Diston Powles, or the Antecedents as a Promoter and Director of Foreign Mining Companies, or as an Administrative Reformer.* London, 1855.

Rimmer, W.G. *Marshalls of Leeds. Flax-spinners, 1788–1886.* Cambridge, 1960.

Rippy, J.F. *The United States and Mexico.* New York, 1926.

———. *British Investments in Latin America, 1822–1949* (1959). Reprint, Hamden, Conn., 1966.

Robertson, W.P. *The foreign debt of Mexico, being the report of a special mission to that State undertaken on behalf of the Bondholders by W. Parish Robertson.* London, 1850.

———. *A Visit to Mexico, by the West India Islands, Yucatan and United States, with Observations and Adventures on the Way.* 2 vols. London, 1853.

Robinson, H. *Carrying British Mails Overseas.* London, 1864.

Robson's London Commercial Directory. London, 1830.

Rodríguez O., J. "Mexico's First Foreign Loans." In J. Rodríguez O., ed., *The Independence of Mexico and the Creation of the New Nation.* Los Angeles, 1989, pp. 215–235.

Rubinstein, W.D. *Men of Property: The Very Wealthy in Britain Since the Industrial Revolution.* London, 1981.

———. "British Millionaires, 1809–1949." *Bulletin of the Institute of Historical Research* 47 (1974), pp. 202–223.

Sheridan, P.J. "The Committee of Mexican Bondholders and European Intervention in 1861." *Mid-America* 42 (1960), pp. 18–29.

Smith, I. "Security Printing." *International Bond and Share Society Journal* (November 1997), p. 36.

Stanton, M., ed. *Who's Who of British Members of Parliament: A Biographical Dictionary,* vol. 1 (1832–1885). Sussex, 1976.

Stern, F. *Gold and Iron. Bismarck, Bleichroeder and the Building of the German Empire.* London, 1977.

Tenenbaum, B. *The Politics of Penury. Debts and Taxes in Mexico, 1821–1856.* Albuquerque, 1986.

———. "Merchants, Money and Mischief: The British in Mexico, 1821–1860." *The Americas* 35 (1979), pp. 317–339.

———. "Neither a Borrower nor a Lender Be": Financial Constraints and the Treaty of Guadalupe Hidalgo." In J. Rodríguez O., ed., *The Mexican and the Mexican American Experience in the Nineteenth Century.* Tempe, Ariz., 1989, pp. 68–84.

————. "La deuda externa mexicana y el Tratado de Guadalupe Hidalgo." In *Pasado y Presente de la Deuda Externa de México*. Mexico, 1988, pp. 43–55.

————. "Streetwise History. The Paseo de la Reforma and the Porfirian State, 1876–1910." In W. Beezley et al., eds., *Rituals of Rule, Rituals of Resistance. Public Celebrations and Popular Culture in Mexico*. Wilmington, Del., 1994, pp. 127–150.

Tischendorf, A. *Great Britain and Mexico in the Era of Porfirio Díaz*. Durham, N.C. 1961.

————. "The Loss of British Commercial Preeminence in Mexico, 1876–1911." *Inter-American Economic Affairs*, 11 (1957), pp. 87–102.

————. "The British Foreign Office and the Renewal of Anglo-Mexican Diplomatic Relations, 1867–1884." *Inter-American Economic Affairs* 11 (1957).

————. "The Anglo-Mexican Claims Commission, 1884–1885." *Hispanic American Historical Review* 37 (1957), pp. 471–479.

True, C. Allen. "British Loans to the Mexican Government, 1822–1832 (A Decade of Nineteenth Century Financial Imperialism)." *The Southwestern Social Science Quarterly* 17 (1967), pp. 353–362.

Turlington, E. *Mexico and Her Foreign Creditors*. New York, 1930.

Tyson, B. "James Towers, a Kendal Surgeon (1785–1846) and Some of His Medical Colleagues." In B.C. Jones and W.G. Wiseman, eds., *Transactions of the Cumberland and Westmoreland Antiquarian and Archaeological Society*, vol. 93. Stroud, 1993, pp. 197–213.

Walker, D.W. *Kinship, Business and Politics. The Martínez del Río Family in Mexico, 1823–1867*. Austin, Tex., 1986.

Walne, P., ed. *A Guide to the Manuscript Sources for the History of Latin America and the Caribbean in the British Isles*. London, 1973.

Webster, C.K., ed. *Britain and the Independence of Latin America, 1812–1830*. Oxford, 1938.

Wetenhall, J. *Course of the Exchange*. London, 1825–1908.

Williams, J.B. *British Commercial Policy and Trade Expansion*. Oxford, 1972.

Wyllie, R.C. *To G.R. Robinson, Esq., Chairman of the Committee of Spanish American Bondholders, on the present state and prospects of the Spanish American loans*. London, 1840.

Zaragoza, J. *Historia de la deuda externa de México, 1823–1861*. Mexico, 1996.

Index

A. Schwareschild & Co., 131
Aberdeen, Lord, 10–11, 53, 167, 169, 301
Acapulco, 116
Ackermann, Rudolph, 6
Adams, E.H., 68, 292
Admiralty (British), 120, 123
Adventurers of Mexico Ltd., 120, 123
Agents at Mexican ports, 117–18
Aglionby, Henry, 283
Aguirre, Bengoa & Sons, 67
Alamán, Lucas, xiv, 27–28, 46, 166–67, 169
Aldham, Cornwallis, 319
Aldham Arrangement, 102, 319–20. See also Aldham, Cornwallis; Convention debt creditors; Convention debts; Diplomatic conventions
Almonte, Juan Nepomuceno, 219
American Bank Note Co., 6, 91–92
American Colonial Steam Navigation Co., 268
Amsterdam, xiii, 94, 140, 290. See also Holland; Stock Exchange (Amsterdam)
Anglo-Mexican Mint Co., 59
Annexation by United States, 205, 208–9. See also United States

Antony Gibbs & Sons, 96–97, 128
Archivo General de la Nación (Mexico), xvi, 13, 46
Argentina, 153, 191, 313–14
Arrangoiz, Francisco de, 74, 181
Arrangoiz/Robertson Convention, 74, 181, 187, 189

B.A. Goldsmidt & Co., xviii, 11–20, 22, 146, 271, 326
Backhouse, John, 301–2
Bailey, Mr., 176
Baily, Sir Henry, 211
Baily, Thomas, 280
Bainbridge, Mr., 289
Bankhead, Charles, 312
Barclay, David, 18–22. See also Barclay, Herring, Richardson & Co.
Barclay, Herring, Richardson & Co., xix, 18–22, 128, 146, 271, 326
Barclay, Robert, 19
Barclay loan, 18–22
Barclays Bank, 284–85
Baring, Alexander, 157, 162–64, 166–67, 171, 274, 327
Baring, Thomas, 212, 215
Baring Brothers: Baring Committee, 215; bond distribution, 31, 34, 62,

85–87; bondholders' representative, 68, 84–85, 126–27, 201, 211–17, 219–20, 249, 292; debt negotiations, 27–31; financial agent, xvi, 8, 10, 22, 27–31, 34–35, 164, 175, 201, 212, 270–71; loan contractors, xiii, xviii, 72, 75; petition to, 234; resignation, 34, 175, 219–20. *See also* Barings Certificates

Barings Certificates, 132–35
Barnett, Charles James, 279
Barron, Forbes & Co., 103–4
Barron, William, 228–29
Barrow, Richard Bridgeman, 217, 219, 221
Bath, 267, 271, 280, 282
Batty, B., 283
Belfast, 307
Belgium, 94
Bell, Charles, 230
Bennoch, Francis, 231, 235, 238, 241
Bentinck, George Cavendish, 71, 230–32, 307
Bentinck, Lord Frederick, 232
Berlin, 96
Beverley, 188
Bexley Heath, 279
Birmingham, 237
Bishop, W.H., 239, 242, 244
Bismarck, O. von, 95, 97
Bleichroeder, Gerson, 95–96
Bolívar, Simón, 267
Bonar, Lionel, 231–33
Bondholders' meetings, xx–xxi, 28, 32, 154–55, 165, 169, 215, 230 passim. *See also* Committee of Spanish American Bondholders
Bonds: cancellation, xvi, 8, 16–23, 44, 50, 65, 79–80, 95–99, 145–47; description of, xv–xvi; forgeries, 8; lottery bonds, 18; marketing, xv–xvi, 4, 16, 20, 273; numbers of, xv, 12, 19, 22–23, 29–31, 39–40, 44, 51–54, 63, 66–67, 76–78, 80–81, 85, 91, 96, 145–47 passim; prices, xvi, 20, 24, 32, 64–65, 165–66, 171, 173–75, 241, 271–72, 285–88 (*see also* tables of prices, 25–99 passim); prin-

ters, 6, 31, 54, 76, 85, 91–92, 162; types, xvi, 4–6, 14–15, 18, 263–64. *See also* Certificates; Convention bonds; Deferred bonds; Fractional certificates

Borja Migoni, Francisco de, 11–13, 35, 146, 288
Boughton & Grinstead, 10
Boult, Amelia, 280
Boult, Robert, 279
Bouverie, Edward Pleydell, 231–32, 235, 244–47, 274
Bradford, 280, 282
Bravo, Nicolás, 161
Brazil, xiv, 267, 315
Bribery, 193, 235
Briggs, George, 280
Brighton, 282, 305
Bristol, 280, 282
British government policies, xix, 71–72, 81, 118, 163, 175–77, 209, 220, 302–20 passim. *See also* Diplomatic Conventions
British government securities, 265
British Guiana, 188
Brouncker, Henry Francis, 217–18, 221–22, 279
Brussels, 140
Buchanan, James, 208
Buenos Aires, xiv, 161, 176, 180
Buisson, Charles, 168
Buisson & Morlet, 168
Bullock, William, 270
Bulman, Mr., 239
Burke, Thomas, 279
Bustamante, Anastasio, 27, 165–66
Butcher, W.W., 283

California, 36, 57, 72
Camacho, Luis, 96
Campbell, Sir Robert, 177
Campeche, 116, 180
Canning, George, 282, 302, 312
Cannon, Stephen, 56
Capel, James, 53, 84–85, 136, 153–54, 177, 182, 184, 187–193, 213–14, 277–78; Capel Committee, 194–98
Capel, John, 157, 162–63, 177, 274

Capel & Co. 211, 234, 278. *See also* Capel, James

Capital markets, 197, 225–26, 228, 237–38, 329

Capper, Charles, 221

Carlisle, 188

Carnegie, John Hemery, 115, 211, 219, 264, 280, 287, 294

Castello, D., 231

Castlereagh, Lord, 304

Catchpole, Mary, 280

Cazenove & Co., 234

Certificates, 131–41, 210, 276. *See also* Barings Certificates; Fractional Certificates

Cervantes, José de Jesús, 228, 235–36, 238, 251

Chait et Cie., 6

Chambers of Commerce, 306

Chapman, Stanley, 266

Cheltenham, 267, 279, 282

Chichester, 279, 282

Chihuahua, 36, 209

Chile, xiv, 59, 161, 176–78, 212, 293

Church property (Mexican), 174, 202–3, 206–7

Clarendon, Lord, 208, 219, 281, 303, 308–10, 313, 317

Clarke, Hyde, 225, 227, 230, 251, 312

Clay, R., 159

Coape, Henry, 177

Cochrane, Admiral Sir Thomas, 177, 280

Cockermouth, 283

Cohen, Albert, 215

Cohen, L., 219, 234, 278, 292

Collier, F.H. & A., 23–24, 31, 294

Collins, John, 280

Colombia, xiv, 161, 176, 245, 326

Colombian Association for Agricultural and Other Purposes, 268

Commercial Bank of London, 292

Committee of Spanish American Bondholders, xx, 34, 46, 51, 72, 154, 159, 175–89 passim, 216, 229, 293, 303–4, 307, 311; formation, 176–77

Committee of Spanish Bondholders, 154, 194, 267

Comonfort, Ignacio, 202–3

Company formation, 268–69

Consols, 71, 265–66, 269, 271, 274, 286–87, 294, 327

Contraband, 116–19

Convention bonds, 99–104, 224, 243

Convention debt creditors, 99–104, 211, 314, 318

Convention debts, xx, 99–104, 224, 314. *See also* Diplomatic Conventions; Spanish Convention

Cordier, Charles, 93

Corporation of Foreign Bondholders, xx, 92, 99, 135, 145, 151, 156, 160, 215–16, 221, 227, 243; foundation of, 229–30; relations with Mexican Committee, 230–31, 244, 250–51, 330

Corro, José Justo, 36

Corwin, Thomas, 209

Costa Rica, 305

Cotton licenses, 181–82

Coupon Agency Ltd., 94, 131, 140

Coutts & Co., 155, 276

Cowan, Richard, 280

Cranborne, 115, 219

Crawford, Joseph, 117

Crewdson, William Dilworth, 283–87

Crews, Mr., 238

Crowder & Maynard, 192

Cuba, 161

Cumming, Lieutenant-General Sir H., 177

Customs certificates, 36–37, 44–47

Customs dues, 19, 21, 28, 44, 73, 116–19, 219, 225, 243, 309

Dacre, S., 291

Damant, W.C., 177

Daniels, E., 291

Davidson, Nathaniel, 228

Davies, Thomas Henry, 162–63, 177, 274

Davis, Mr., 163

Dawson, Frank Griffith, xiv, xvii, 18, 161

Debentures, 47–50, 54, 58–59, 61, 67, 287, 328

Debt negotiations, 28–31, 34–39, 46–
   47, 59–61, 70, 73–75, 78, 84–85,
   171–74, 228–29, 234–36, 238–41,
   245–46; Mexican debt repudiation,
   118, 222–23
Deferred bondholders, 57, 60–61, 65–
   71, 85, 93–94, 206, 214–17, 265,
   285, 290–95, 328; identity of, 290–
   95. *See also* Lizardi & Co.
Deferred bonds, 38, 40, 51–54, 57–59,
   61, 65–71, 79, 159, 179, 200, 210,
   214–17, 224, 243, 275, 277, 290–
   95. *See also* Lizardi & Co.
Delmar, F., 279
Denholm, George, 205
Derby, Lord, 213, 305
Díaz, Porfirio, xviii, 78, 116, 235–36,
   241–43, 272, 329
Dilke, Sir Charles, 306
Diplomatic Conventions, xix, 100–
   104, 309–10, 313–14, 319. *See also*
   Aldham Arrangement; Doyle Convention; Dunlop Arrangement; Otway Convention; Pakenham
   Convention
Diplomatic relations, 78, 87, 104, 220–
   21, 237, 242, 306
Disraeli, Benjamin, 4, 71, 272, 288,
   307–8
Dividend certificates, xvi, 6, 93, 94,
   95, 131
Dividends: advertisements, 128;
   amounts of, 79, 91, 115–41 passim,
   273–74; capitalization, 27–28, 36–
   37, 46–47, 58, 74, 79–80, 84–87,
   115–41 passim, 164; coupons, 13,
   29–30, 40–41, 56, 75–76, 115–41
   passim; fund, 61, 74, 115–41
   passim, 181, 185–86, 192, 197, 212–
   13, 219, 248; levies on, 115–41 passim, 248–50, 278; number of, 115–
   41 passim, 202; payment of, 19, 22,
   27, 33–34, 63, 71, 78–99, 115–41
   passim, 171, 191, 196, 202, 209,
   214–17, 219, 265–95 passim, 328
Dodgson, W.O., 234
Dodson, John, 63, 73
Dover, John William, 293–94

Doxat & Co., 291
Doyle, James St. Clair, 280
Doyle, Percy, 53, 100, 181, 194, 308,
   312–13
Doyle Convention, 100, 309, 314, 318
Dublán, Manuel, 145–46, 242
Dublán conversion, 57, 65, 70, 78–81,
   90–99, 116, 135, 139, 232, 243–47,
   290, 329
Dublin, 237, 279
Dudley, 156
Dudley, Earl of, 164
Dunlop, Hugh, 319
Dunlop Arrangement, 102, 319–20
Dyer, George, 291

E Bonds, 66–71
East India Company, 154
Easthope, John, 162–63, 177
Ecuador, 174, 178, 180, 182, 230
Ecuador Land Company, 215
Edinburgh Life Assurance Co., 194
Effingham Wilson, 159
Ellis, Samuel Herbert, 198
Ellis & Co., 198, 291
English and Australian Copper Co., 59
Escandón, Manuel, 59, 181–82, 189,
   288
Ewing, Mr., 311
Exchange rates, xiii, 125–28
Export taxes, 61, 96, 116
Eykyn, Roger, 231

Facio, Francisco, 74–78, 127, 136–38,
   181–86, 191–92, 197, 200, 212,
   248–49, 276, 291
Falconnet, Francis de Palezieux, 117,
   127, 191–94, 196–97, 213, 249,
   309
Falk, Philip, 245
Falmouth, 122–23
Ferdinand VII (Spain), 14, 34, 161,
   174, 302
Fernández, Ramón, 104
Field, John, 177
Financial agents. *See* Baring Brothers;
   Facio, Francisco; John Schneider &
   Co.; Lizardi & Co.; Schneider,

Henry William; Schneider, John
  Henry Powell
Finnegan, Robert, 279
Fisher, Edward, 291
Fitzgerald, Seymour, 213
Folkestone, 282
Forey, General, 81
Forster, John, 279
Forsythe, John, 208
Foss & Ledsam, 57–58, 70, 94
Foster & Braithwaite, 234, 288, 291
Foster & Janson, 288
Fractional certificates, 40, 87, 94, 210
Franco/Egyptian Bank, 237
Frankfurt, 228
Fretwell, W.C., 242

Gadsen, James, 196–97
Gadsen purchase, 196–97, 200
Garde, Richard, 103, 188–89, 211–14,
  222, 305, 315
George Rougement & Co., 277
Germany, 11, 97, 166, 168, 289–90,
  306
Germiny, Count of, 85, 216
Gerstenberg, Isidor, 215–16, 221, 230,
  279, 291
Gibbs, Herbert, 96
Gibbs, W., 279
Gillig, Mr., 294
Glasgow, 180, 237, 307, 315
Globe Insurance Co., 154
Glyn, George, 215
Glyn, Mills, Currie & Co., 35, 79, 84–
  85, 184, 245, 275, 292
Godfrey, Alfred, 185
Golding, John H., 278
Goldsmid, Isaac Lyon, 127, 138, 168,
  177, 184, 268, 277–78, 290; bio-
  graphical details, 153–54; Goldsmid
  Committee, 187–94
Goldsmid, W., 278
Goldsmidt, I.A., 5, 22
Goldsmidt loan, 11–18. *See also* B.A.
  Goldsmidt & Co.
Gómez Farías, Benito, 62–63, 74, 80,
  93, 147
Gómez Farías, Valentín, 62, 74

Gómez Pedraza, Manuel, 165
González, Manuel, 104, 236, 238, 241
Gordon, Alexander, 35
Gorostiza, Manuel Eduardo, 28–33,
  166–173, 301
Goschen, G.J., 230
Gosling & Sharpe, 291
Gower, R.F., 211
Graham, William, xviii, 168
Gray, James, 227
Gray, Robert, 279
Greene, Mr., 225
Gros, Alexandre de, 196
Guadalajara, 125
Guadalupe Hidalgo, Treaty of, 72
Guanajuato, 203
Guatemala, xiv, 161
Guaymas, 56, 116, 119, 122
Guedalla, Haim, 183–84, 187, 194,
  217, 220–25, 229–46 passim, 264,
  272, 279
Guerrero, Vicente, 165
Guildhall Library (London), xvi, 156
Guisborough, 158, 283, 327

Halifax (Nova Scotia), 198
Hall, George, 280
Hall, McGarel & Co., 188
Hamburg, 74, 292
Hamer, George, 291
Hamilton, Mr., 294
Hammond, Edmund, 220, 312–13,
  316–18
Hammond, Thomas, 177
Hammond, William, 163, 177, 278
Hare, Thomas, 281, 327
Harrison, Susanna, 283
Hart & Robinson, 151
Hartley, Thomas Walker, 280–81
Hartridge, William, 278
Haydson, Daniel Kerkman, 71
Heath, R.A., 84
Henderson, J. Pinkney, 38
Henderson, James, 177
Henky, George, 279
Herbert, Samuel, 23, 287
Hereford, 280, 282

Herman Sillem, Son & Co., 168. *See also* Sillem, Herman
Hermenegildo Viya & Co., 102–3
Hermosillo, 125
Herring, Charles, xviii, 18–19, 168, 177, 188–91
Herring, George, 242
Hervey, Lionel, 312
Heygate, Sir William, 177
Hichens & Harrison, 291
Hodgson, R., 224
Holbecke, Mathew, 279
Holdsworth, Thomas, 280
Holland, 11, 166, 168, 266, 289–90. *See also* Amsterdam; Stock Exchange (Amsterdam)
Holme, Edward, 283–84
Holmes, Richard, 281
Holmes, William, 221, 229, 231, 233, 238–40, 244, 250–51
Honduras, 268; Honduras Co., 268
Hope & Co., 234, 292
Houston, Sam, 209
Hudson, John, 225, 280
Hullett Brothers & Co., xix
Humboldt, Alexander von, 270

Ibarrondo, Ignacio, 216
Imperial Brazilian Mining Association, 154
Import taxes, 27–29, 33, 56, 60–61, 96, 116, 178
Indemnity payment. *See* United States
Insider trading, 157, 224, 275
Insurance rates, 123, 125, 127
Interventors, 200, 309
Irving, James Corbett, 217, 221, 231, 246, 277
Irving & Slade, 219, 221
Iturbide, Agustín de (diplomat), 34, 38, 40, 51
Iturbide, Agustín de (ex-emperor), 16, 270–71, 289

J.P. Penny & Co., 100
Jacobson, G., 234
Jaffrey, Richard, 19

Capel James & Co., 234. *See also* Capel, James
Jeffreys, Herbert, 279
Jenkins, Richard, 280
John Perring, Shaw, Barber & Co., 168
John Schneider & Co., 59–71, 74, 127, 146, 179, 185–86, 191–92, 248, 290–92. *See also* Schneider, Henry William; Schneider, John Henry Powell
Johnson, Robert, 280
Jones, Mr., 242
Jones & Co., 273
Jonson, Frederick, 180
Juárez, Benito, 69, 78, 81, 103, 118, 203, 221, 319, 328

Kemple, Mr., 163
Kendal, 283–84, 294
Kendal Bank, 284–85
Kendal Record Office, 159
Knowles, S.P., 292–93
Kunhardt & Ewart, 117

L. Messel & Co., 234
Ladykirk, 155, 205, 290
Land colonization/sales, 136–38, 196–97, 209–10
Land grants, 36–38, 72, 210
Land warrants, 36–38, 72, 210
Langport Eastover, 282
Larne, 188
Lebrún, Jorge, 117
Leenwarde, 292
Legation theft, 121–22, 203–5, 212, 273, 328
Legrey, Mary, 280
Leominster, 188
Lerdo de Tejada, Miguel, 202, 206–7
Lerdo de Tejada, Sebastián, 226
Letts, Son & Steer, 6, 76
Lettsom, William, 319
Levy, Albert, 53, 215, 278, 291
Levy, Lewis, 182, 278
Lindus, Henry, 279
Lippman, Rosenthal & Co., 96
Lipscombe, John, 280

Liverpool, 35, 180, 237, 245, 307, 315
Lizardi, F. de, 225
Lizardi, Francisco de Paula, 35
Lizardi, Helena de Cubas, 35
Lizardi, John Javier, 35
Lizardi, Manuel Julián, 35, 63, 69–70
Lizardi & Co., 8, 10–11, 22, 36–56
  passim, 59, 66–70, 102, 123, 132,
  146, 178–79, 214, 281, 290–92,
  328; company history, 34–35. *See
  also* Deferred bonds; Deferred bond-
  holders
Loan contractors, xiii–xx, 3–5, 288
Loan contracts, xviii–xix, 3–4, 12–21
  passim
Loddon, 280
London and County Joint Stock Bank,
  184, 189, 214, 293
London and Westminster Bank, 278
London Bank of Mexico and South
  America, 103, 235
London Dock Co., 154
London Tavern, 20, 28, 37, 52, 60,
  85, 162, 182, 221, 224
López de Santa Anna, Antonio de. *See*
  Santa Anna, Antonio López de
Lory, William, 123
Lower California, 209
Lowther, R.P., 176

MacGregor, Gregor, 268
Mackie, Philip, 269
Mackintosh, Ewen, 59, 181, 308, 313.
  See also Manning & Mackintosh
Mackintosh, Mrs. E., 196
Mallard, Charles, 280, 295
Malmesbury, Lord, 193, 209, 281,
  290, 310, 317
Manchester, 237, 282, 284, 307, 315
Manning, Markoe & Co., 117
Manning, Robert, 18, 59
Manning, William, 266
Manning & Mackintosh, 59–60, 62,
  72, 100, 117, 180–82, 185, 193,
  196, 200, 288
Manning & Marshall, 47, 59, 117,
  123, 171. *See also* Manning &
  Mackintosh

Manzanillo, 116
Mariquita and New Granada Mining
  Co., 169
Marjoribanks, Capel & Co., 154, 276.
  See also Robertson, David
Marjoribanks, Sir John, 154, 206
Markoe, Price & Co., 180–81
Marryat, Samuel, 14–15
Marshall, John, 167–70, 188, 266,
  274–75; investments, 274–76, 278–
  79, 288, 301–2; Mexican Committee
  chairman, 169–70
Marshall, William S., 18, 177, 186–88,
  276
Marsham, 281
Martínez del Río Hermanos, 100, 102,
  288
Martínez del Rio, Pablo, 200
Masson & Co., 57–58, 67–68
Matamoros, 116
Mathew, George, 121
Maude, Wilson and Crewdson bank,
  285
Maximilian (Empire), 69, 78, 103,
  118, 132, 139, 298; debt arrange-
  ments, 81–87, 214–17
Mazatlán, 56, 117, 119, 122, 319
McCalmont, Robert, 315–16
McCalmont Brothers & Co., 315
McDonald, James, 280
McFarland, Wallace, 235
McGarel, Charles, 157, 189, 192, 194,
  205, 208, 211–14, 221, 225, 276,
  278–79, 303, 308, 317–18; bio-
  graphical details, 188; McGarel
  Committee, 198–203
McLagan, Peter, 231
McLane-Ocampo treaty, 209
Memorials, 193, 220–21, 234, 250,
  265, 279, 283, 303
Mena, Francisco Z., 57, 79, 145,
  245
Mena agreement (1886), 57, 79–81,
  90, 94, 135, 139, 245–46. *See also*
  Mena, Francisco Z.
Mendoza, José María, 44, 50, 62–63
Merchant lobby, 307, 314–15
Mexía, Carlos, 245

Mexican and South American Co., 59
Mexican debt legislation, 74–75, 135, 164, 237, 239; 1885 Law, 78–79, 90–99, 243–44
Mexican dollars (pesos): exchange rates, xiii, 125–26; forged, 125; price of, 125–26; silver content, 125–26
Mexican Financial Agency, 58, 69–70, 80–81, 94–95, 99, 128, 136, 139–41, 145–47, 243, 245
Mexican Financial Commission, 85, 216
Mexican independence, recognition of, 174–75, 178, 267, 271
Mexican Railway Co., 225–29, 237, 250
Mexico: internal affairs, 27–28, 62, 78, 118, 138–39, 161, 165–66, 171–72, 201–3, 236, 242, 272; wealth of, 236, 270–72, 281–82, 326
Michelena, José Mariano, 19–21
Milbank, Mr., 163
Millans, General, 221
Mills, Francis, 184–85, 187
Minerva Life Assurance Co., 184
Miramón, Miguel, 121
Mocatta & Goldsmid, 127, 154, 186
Mora, José María Luis, 56–57, 62, 67, 71–76 passim, 179, 185, 202–3, 206, 308
Morelos, José María, 131
Morgan, E.S., 291
Morgan, William, 20, 184, 281, 303
Moriarty, Edward, 186–88, 191–92
Morier, James Justinian, 282
Morrison, Thomas, 235
Moser, Robert or Roger, 283–84
Moss, Charles, 291
Moxon, John, 167–68, 177, 205
Moxon, Thomas, 168, 205, 215, 230
Mullen, Marshall & Co., 291
Munroe, James, 271
Murphy, Tomás, xiv, 8–11, 23, 31–32, 45–47, 52–53, 56, 59–63, 67, 158
Murrieta & Co., 197, 239

Napoleon III, 83–84
National Bank of Ireland, 184

National Bank of Mexico, 79, 223, 235, 237–38, 241, 243
New Granada, 174, 178
New Mexico, 36, 72
New Orleans, 35, 67
New York, 75, 182, 226, 235
Newbury, 279, 282
Newgass, Benjamin, 231
Newton, John, 13, 15
Newton Abbot, 293
Nicolson, Stephen, 289
Nilsen, Nils Andreas, 192, 205–6, 213–14, 287
Noetzlin, Edward. *See* Noetzlin negotiation
Noetzlin negotiation, 139, 237, 241–4, 251
Norbury, John, 211
North and South American Coffee House, 167, 171, 183, 247
North Barrow, 282
Norwich, 280–81
Nuñez Ortega, Angel, 132, 219

O'Brien, William, 60, 63
Olano, Román de, 146–47
Olarte, Sr., 181
O'Leary, Mr., 245
Otway, Loftus C., 212, 314
Otway Convention, 102

Paisley, 180
Pakenham, Richard, 100, 173, 178, 307
Pakenham Convention, 100
Palmerston, Lord, 71–73, 119–20, 174–75, 177, 185, 211, 213, 280, 283, 292, 303–17 passim
Paraguay, 180, 305
Paris, 35, 63, 76, 85, 197, 216, 228, 237, 239
Pastry War, 10, 38–39, 44, 116, 198, 307, 315
Patteson, Henry, 167–68
Pavy, Captain, 239
Payno, Manuel, xiv, 65, 76, 288
Pelly, Raymond, 23
Peña, Tomas de la, 5, 93
Perkins & Bacon, 31

Perry, Edward Joseph, 94, 160, 221–33 passim, 250–51, 285
Perry, Francis, 94, 160, 251
Peru, xiv, 161, 176, 178, 212
Peruvian Mining and Trading Assocation, 268
Petit, M., 280
Philip Antrobus & Co., 154
Phillimore, Robert, 63, 73, 138, 303, 319
Pinna, A. de, 54
Plumptre, E.H., 19
Plumstead, 280
Plymouth, 16
Pollock, Fred, 14
Poole, S., 291
Portchester, 283
Portsmouth, 287, 327
Portugal, xiii, xx, 293, 308, 311
Potter, John, 19
Poulson, B., 217, 219
Powles, John Diston, xviii, 168, 177–78, 181–82, 186, 268, 307–9; biographical details, 168–69
Poyais, 268
Prevost, J.L., 188
Prim, General, 221
Protectorate. *See* United States
Proudfoot, Thomas, 283–86, 294, 327

Quintana, Pedro de la, 35

Railways, 196–97, 225–27, 236–38, 272
Raphael & Sons, 100, 292
Real del Monte Co., 269
Reform(a), La, 78, 102–3, 118, 125, 178, 203, 208, 327
Reveley, Thomas, 283–84
Rhodes, James, 184, 187–88
Richards, John, 283–84
Richardson, Christopher, 18
Richardson, Thomas, 22
Richmond, A.B., 194, 279
Rickards, John L., 197
Rivas, Carlos, 238–41, 251
Rivas negotiation, 139, 238–41. *See also* Rivas, Carlos
Robertson, David, 15, 102, 154–57,
177, 187–202 passim, 264, 272–74, 287, 290, 308–9, 313, 320; biographical details, 154–55; investments, 154, 276; Robertson Committee, 203–14
Robertson, John Parish, 180
Robertson, Mary, 280
Robertson, William Parish, 180–82, 188–91, 213, 248, 278, 280, 287, 313; mission to Mexico, 73–74; W.P. Robertson Committee, 183–87
Robins, George, 175
Robinson, George Richard, 34, 37–38, 46, 51–52, 162–63, 167, 185, 210, 274, 280, 303–4, 308, 311, 328; biographical details, 153; investments, 276–78; Spanish-American Committee chairman, 175–83
Robinson, John A., 117
Robotham, Mr., 294
Rocafuerte, Vicente, 164
Roebuck, John, 308
Romero, Matías, 87, 222–23
Ronald, Rowan, 184, 187
Rosecrans, General W.S., 223
Ross, Thomas, 184, 187–88, 191–92, 194, 279
Rothschild & Co., xviii, 72, 95, 197, 266
Rougement, George, 177
Rougement Brothers, 21, 277
Rowlands, Christopher, 228–29, 232
Ruding, John Clement, 188, 192
Rugby, 279
Russell, Lord, 84, 115, 211, 213, 279, 287, 304–6, 315, 319
Russia, xiii, 11, 267

Sadleir, John, 188–89
Salomons, David, 53, 163, 186, 278
San Blas, 56, 116, 119, 122
Santa Anna, Antonio López de, 54, 69, 173, 196–97, 201, 208, 273, 318
Santa María, Miguel, 34–35, 178
Sarmiento, José, 117
Sartorius, Admiral Sir George, 187–89, 198
Schneider, Henry William, 59. *See also* John Schneider & Co.

Schneider, John Henry Powell, 59. *See also* John Schneider & Co.
Schroeder & Co., 292
Schwabacher & Salmon, 219
Scrip certificates, 6–8, 12, 16, 21, 97, 267
Searle, J., 215
Select Committee, 294, 305, 308
Sharpe, Andrew, 291
Shaw, Gabriel, 168
Sheppard & Son, 56, 67
Sherborne, 281, 294
Sheridan, Dudley, 233, 239–41, 244, 251
Sheridan, Henry Brinsley, 217, 220–26, 230, 274, 278–79, 305–7, 328–29; biographical details, 156; Sheridan Committee, 231–52 passim
Sillem, Herman, 168, 177, 289, 292. *See also* Herman Sillem, Son & Co.
Silver: demand for, 119; production, 118–19; shipments, 118–20, 122–23, 272; taxes, 60–61, 116, 118–19, 186–87; value, 125–26, 272
Sinaloa, 209
Sisal, 116
Skipper & East, 97
Small, J., 158
Smallbone, John, 278
Smallbone, William, 278
Smith, Charles, 280
Smith, Frederick, 280
Smith, Payne & Co., 292
Smythe, William, 50
Sonora, 36, 209
South American and Mexican Association, 315
South American Gem Co., 268
Southampton, 76, 122–23, 126, 180
Souza, Custodio, 117
Spain, xiii, xx, 27, 34, 81, 100, 191, 245 passim
Spanish Convention bonds, 100–102
Sparkes, Samuel, 282–83
Speculators, 4, 229, 240, 268–69, 288–89
St. John's (Newfoundland), 277

Staniforth, Charles, 194, 205, 212–14, 279
Stanley, Frederick, 226
Stanley, Lord, 221, 279
Stern, David, 219
Stern, Herman, 219
Stern Brothers, 235
Stewart L. Jolly & Co., 117
Stock Exchange (Amsterdam), xiii, xvi, 5, 94, 96, 139–40, 197, 216–17, 226–27, 237, 245, 250, 290
Stock Exchange (London), xiii–xiv, 5, 50–54, 197; archive, xvi, 95, 136, 169; Foreign Exchange, 5, 12, 22, 166, 267, 288; General Purposes Committee, 8, 40, 51–54, 56–57, 66, 80, 87, 94–95, 140–41, 160, 226–28, 237–38
Stoker, Mr., 242
Stokes, Mr., 20
Stone, George, 279
Sutton, John, 125
Switzerland, 290

Tampico, 13, 28, 34, 36, 44, 56, 60–61, 116, 121–23, 174 passim
Tasker, Joseph, 187, 278
Taunton, 271, 279
Taylor, Mr., 225
Tebbutt, John, 10–11, 22
Tehuantepec, Isthmus of, 223–25; railway loan, 329
Texas, 34, 36–38, 57, 72, 174–75
Thomas Kinder & Co., xix
Thompson, William, 162–63, 167, 274, 283
Thomson, Alicia Ann, 283
Thomson, Elizabeth, 283
Thomson, Sarah, 283
Thomson, W., 283
Thorne, Mr., 294
Thornton, Richard, 184, 266–67, 279
Thornton, Thomas, 184, 187
Tobacco, 72–73; monopoly, 60–61; revenues, 50–61, 73, 116
Tolucca Mining Co., 250
Townsend, Susan, 279
Tredegar, 280

Tripartite Intervention, xix, 78, 81, 118, 125, 138, 205, 305–6, 315, 318–19
Tulancingo revolt, 161–62
Tyre, James Henry, 278

United Mexican Mining Association, 162, 278
United States: indemnity payment, 57, 72–76, 126–27, 179–80, 191–94, 308; protectorate, 205, 208–9, 308. *See also* Annexation
United States–Mexican War, 57, 62, 72, 116, 208, 307–8
Uzielli, Theodosius, 278

Van Raalte, Mr., 239, 242
Van Sommer, James, 51
Vance, Henry, 287
Venezuela, 174, 178, 212, 230
Veracruz, 13, 16, 28, 34–39, 44–45, 56–57, 60–61, 78, 84, 97, 116–26, 173–74, 180, 198, 203, 226 passim

W.T.F.M. Ingall & Co., 94, 140
Wakefield, Jacob, 283–84
Waley, Mr., 186
Walke, John, 188
Walker, Thomas Humble, 280
Wallis, Admiral Sir Provo William Parry, 211–14, 221, 225, 230–31, 235, 246, 264, 277, 279; biographical details, 198–99
Ward, Henry George, 162, 271
Ward, William, 162–63, 167
Warner, George, 291
Warrington, J., 175
Waters, Mr., 193
Watters, Thomas, 283–84

Webber, J., 280
Webster, Richard, 58
Weetjen, L., 217
Welch, John, 117
Wertheimer, Lea & Co., 160
West, Mr., 131
West, William, 278
White, George, 84, 213–14
Whitehead, Charles, 197, 213, 309
Whiting, Charles, 6, 54, 132
Whiting, James, 6
Whiting & Branston, 6
Wilkinson, John Walter, 287
Wilmott, F., 280
Wilson, Belford, 267
Wilson, B.P., 279
Wilson, Edward Thomas, 219
Wilson, Isaac, 283–84
Wilson, Sir Robert, 152–53, 165, 167, 177–78, 200, 247, 267–68, 274, 278; biographical details, 152–53; Mexican Committee chairman, 171–75
Wilson, William, 282
Wodehouse, Lord, 155, 206–7, 213, 318
Wood, A.F., 211–14
Woodall & Co., 234
Worth, H.C., 120
Wright, Edward, 222, 225, 231
Wyke, Sir Charles, 290, 320
Wyllie, R.C., 46, 177

Young, James, 163, 176–77
Yucatán, 200–201

Zavala, Lorenzo de, 165
Zichy, Count of, 84
Zuloaga, Felix, 203

About the Author

MICHAEL P. COSTELOE is Professor Emeritus and Senior Research Fellow in Hispanic and Latin American Studies at the University of Bristol. He is a Fellow of both the British Royal Historical Society and Mexico's Academia de la Historia.